21 Gifts:

Your Inner Child's Guide to Activate the Law of Attraction for Happiness and Success

By Cary G. Weldy

Edited by Devi B. Dilliard-Wright

Los Angeles, California

21 Gifts:

**Your Inner Child's Guide to Activate
the Law of Attraction for Happiness and Success**

FIRST EDITION

Published by Cary G. Weldy
Golden Spiral Productions, LLC
Printed in the USA

Library of Congress Control Number:

ASIN   eBook
ISBN 979-8-48204-854-2   Paperback
ISBN 979-8-48205-208-2   Hardcover

Amanda —

May you be blessed
with vibrant health,
harmony, + joy.

Cory

Table of Contents

Foreword

Human civilization began in the great river valleys of the world: the Nile, the Tigris and Euphrates, the Jordan, and the Indus. It is little wonder that creation myths often revolve around a great flood, like those depicted in ancient texts such as the Book of Genesis, the Epic of Gilgamesh, and the Vishnu Purana. The flood has a two-fold symbolism: the flooded river valley carries new soil and moisture to crops and wildlife, representing sustenance and vitality. At the same time, when a river floods, it can bring devastation in its wake, carrying away homes, crops, livestock and families. Our ancestors realized that the successful navigation of life in society meant staying on the right side of the forces of nature, remaining in harmony with the world around them. Similarly, we must recognize and work with both the shadow side and light side of our existence.

Cary Weldy brings back this ancient wisdom in his book — *21 Gifts*. In our technologically advanced society, we find ourselves alienated from nature and disconnected from our communities. We have the diseases of affluence: anxiety, depression, boredom, and addiction. At the same time, we become numb to the suffering all around us and seek escape through the alluring technological addictions of cellphone apps, video games, and streaming media. We suffer the constant exposure of messages telling us to express ourselves and improve our lives through the consumption of consumer goods. We want all of the goodies, but none of the responsibility. We crave the euphoria without hard work. We flee from negative states of mind while simultaneously compounding them.

At the heart of our dysfunctional lifestyles lies a refusal to confront our true problems. We avoid looking at the psychic injuries from our own traumatic pasts that have led us to seek external validation. These abuses may have been inflicted on us in childhood by our parents or caretakers, our teachers or coaches, by schoolyard bullies and our own peers, and even cultural demands attempting to mold us. We tend to bury abusive and painful events within the recesses of our memories, where we often neglect to take care of hidden wounds. Without knowing it, we hinder our further development as human beings by failing to process our pasts. Often, we reach adulthood without knowing why we find it difficult to express our emotions or realize a creative vision. We tend to anesthetize ourselves, rather than undertaking the necessary task for healing and wholeness.

We know that something holds us back in life, but it can be difficult to understand what that something might be. In this book, Cary Weldy provides readers with a wonderful diagnostic tool that identifies the areas in life where they might have some underlying trauma that might need to be resolved. Weldy then gives readers specific activities and exercises that will help to heal that injury to our "Divine Child" — that inner part of ourselves that we tend to protect and even, on occasion, over-protect. As we practice cultivating these 21 traits, or gifts, we become more open and spontaneous. We express our thoughts and feelings more freely. We see those hidden obstacles that prevent us from entering into maturity.

Readers may come to this book for different reasons. It will appeal to artists and creative professionals looking to find a way back to the fountain of inspiration. It will be beneficial for those going through major changes in life, like going back to school, processing grief, or moving to a new home. Some readers may want to improve their income or make their physical space feel more inviting. Even companies and other organizations may discover the need to cultivate these 21 powerful traits within their culture.

Cary's message has 21 different aspects, or gifts, of our inner Divine Child — curiosity, creativity, joy, vulnerability, intuition, love of nature, and more. But at the core of it, the message is simple: To improve our lives and to feel better, we have to reconnect to the childlike part of ourselves that simply wants to play, create, and be free.

Life doesn't have to be drudgery. Being a grownup doesn't have to mean setting aside all of the things that make us feel more alive. We live in a world that will happily allow us to work ourselves to death. We can stop seeing overwork and stress as a badge of honor, and closely examine how we treat ourselves. Those of us reading this book most likely already have an intuition that healing should be about more than just popping pills at night before bed. We have received nudges and hunches which suggest that we should look for a lifestyle change instead. This book can be the kind of jumpstart that readers need to begin living in healthier and more fulfilling ways. Best of all, this journey towards wholeness can be fun!

The path to well-being does not require martyrdom or self-punishment. We already have enough guilt that we have inherited. Instead, we need to find a vision that drives us forward, a culture of "yes" instead of a largely negative culture of "no." We can make this life a grand fulfillment of our dreams, without waiting for an afterlife or winning the lottery! That's the message that Cary Weldy drives home in a number of different ways. For people who are fact-oriented, the studies and data are there. More intuitive and artistic types will find suggestions for creative projects that will allow your inner artist to shine. No matter what your personality type, this book will speak to you.

Another dimension of this work lies in its attention to the social and environmental problems of today. The tendency to control and manipulate others through a lack of attention to the Divine Child manifests itself in epidemics of drug abuse, domestic violence, and deaths of despair. Our heedless consumption leads to a plundering of the earth's resources and ecological devastation. Society finds it more useful to throw people and places away rather than heal them, to treat the world as a garbage disposal rather than a cherished home. When we undertake the work of healing, we do nothing less than mend our broken world. This healing potential lies in the heart of every being, and unlocking this restorative energy illuminates our shared spiritual quest.

I have found it a delight to read this book, and I will certainly return to it often. I know that the work of healing cannot be accomplished overnight. We all have ways that we tend to hold back from living fully. We all have unconscious methods for hiding our true selves for fear of rejection or failure. And we all have a Divine Child waiting to express itself. This Divine child waits beneath the surface, looking for an opening, for a chance to shine. Only our personalities have often formed in maladaptive ways, so that we hold it back in the shadows.

Think about taking your car for an oil change or a tune-up. This routine maintenance work doesn't cost much, and it can be a little inconvenient to take your car to the shop. It's easy to let it get overdue, sometimes resulting in bigger problems. Sometimes, we try to ignore the "maintenance required" light flashing on the dashboard. Our emotional lives work the same way. If we don't attend to our inner lives, our problems get bigger. We struggle with our relationships, addictions, mood problems, and a host of other difficulties. We need a simple repair manual for the spirit, and that's what Cary Weldy has given us. He guides us through a series of diagnostic tests to keep the soul firing on all 21 cylinders.

Try the suggestions in this book. Yes, you may feel awkward at times, like a wallflower at a junior high dance. But the readings and daily exercises will give you a big boost for just a little bit of your time and effort. It's worth a little bit of beginner's wobbliness to gain what could be a new lease on life. I firmly believe that we all have an inner Divine Child that seeks to gain expression. For many people, this book will be a welcome remedy. May we become a community of like-minded people looking for healing and wholeness. My wish for all of us is that we find the laughter and play that our hearts desire.

Devi B. Dilliard-Wright
Augusta, Georgia
April 2021

Introduction

Children are the keys to paradise.

Eric Hoffer

One of the things that brings me immense joy is watching small children at play. Near my home, fountains draw children to their dancing waters like powerful magnets. The moment when children see the joyful pools of water, their eyes light up as sparkling jewels. Then off the kids race to the fountains to explore and play in them.

Small children captivate the attention of us adults. Our eyes light up when we watch children at play. This seems to be especially true with groups of people, such as during family reunions when the adults are enchanted with the magic of small children in their midst. Their boundless energy, radiant curiosity, exploring nature, pure expressiveness, and refreshing authenticity instantly magnetizes us to them.

Small children spontaneously express specific qualities that are inherent at birth. From the moment of our physical incarnation, we engage the world using our innate energies that radiate from us. As small children, we are playful and expressive. We live fearlessly in the present moment, without a care about tomorrow or pondering what happened yesterday. Our thinking is magical, as we believe that all things are possible. We imagine that we can touch the stars.

As little children, our nature is completely authentic. We have no ego for pretense to impress or manipulate others around us. We speak honestly in an unfiltered manner. We express our creativity, building fortresses with blankets, making mud pies, and erecting elaborate palaces with boxes, scissors, and crayons. Our compassion for others is apparent, as we express concern and feel pain for those who are also hurting. As small children, we gravitate towards those things that brings us more joy.

This book is an exploration about how we can harness the powerful energies of our childlike nature to help us attract higher levels of achievement and realize our goals with ease. When we share these potent gifts with others, we activate the Law of Attraction.

The Secret to All Success is Within You

The greatest spiritual teachers and philosophers in the world have said that the key to success lies within you. The ancient Egyptians, Rumi, Carl Sagan, Eckhart Tolle, Peace Pilgrim, Marcus Aurelius, Rudolf Steiner, and Jesus have all emphasized that this power is within you. This is not a new philosophy, program, or doctrine outside of you to be learned. The journey of uncovering this precious secret is truly within you, waiting to be rediscovered and released.

The most prolific teacher who has influenced more of humanity than any other is Jesus. His words described the secrets to success when he said that the kingdom of heaven is here and now, it is within you — *and it is accessible when you come as a little child*. He promised that if you first seek this internal kingdom that is within you, then all of material success would be added to you. The words of Jesus and other great perennial philosophers said that this roadmap to high achievement, true happiness, and complete fulfillment is already yours.

These simple yet persuasive words inspired me to explore the secrets of our inner child — the pure, innocent, and powerful aspects of us that I affectionately refer to as our "Divine Child." It was a term that seemed fitting to the wholesome and untainted essential nature of our "inner child" that the late educator, philosopher, and best-selling author John Bradshaw described in his groundbreaking book, *Homecoming: Reclaiming and Championing Your Inner Child* written in 1992.

Swiss psychiatrist Carl Jung, who founded analytical psychology, wrote about the Divine Child in his 1969 book *Essays on the Science of Mythology: The Myth of the Divine Child and the Mysteries of Eleusis* with co-author Carl Kerényi. In their aim to elevate the study of myth to science, Jung wrote that the Divine Child is an archetype of living psychological realities that bring meaning to people's lives, while Kerényi treated the child-God symbology as a significant figure in Greek, Norse, Finnish, Etruscan, and Judeo-Christian mythology.

Later, spiritual mystic and best-selling author Caroline Myss outlined the various types of child paradigms in a series of books that include *Sacred Contracts* and *The Four Archetypes of Survival*. The archetypes she describes include the Orphan, Wounded Child, the Magical/Innocent Child, the Nature Child, the Divine Child, and Puer/Puella Eternis (Eternal Boy/Girl). Myss wrote, "Everyone has expressions of each one of these aspects of the Child within his psyche, although one aspect is usually so dominant that it eclipses the energy of the others."[1]

I believe that the Divine Child is the true spiritual blueprint of every single person born on this planet, rather than an archetype of some people. According to the numerous bodies of research and scientific studies cited throughout this book, the Divine Child is quite literal and real. Furthermore, these 21 traits are what unite humanity and allow for synchronicity to spontaneously occur, where "like attracts like" to produce incredible, transcendent experiences gained by sharing our sweet yet potent childlike gifts with others. Resonating with these energies and sharing them through expression is what brings the Law of Attraction to life.

> I can feel your heartbeat. It's the same as mine. I am part of you. You are part of me. Neither one alone, but together we can strengthen the pulse of the world.
>
> Kate McGahan

This book takes a different approach, exploring the 21 energy qualities and characteristics that are within each of us. It is a guidebook that can help reengage those energies within us adults that are already alive within babies and small children. While many of these energies were traumatized or wounded in childhood for nearly all of us, we can reactivate them through a healing process to the point where they are "firing on all 21 cylinders" again.

These Divine Child traits are quite real and are indeed the secret to our success, as Jesus and many other spiritual thought leaders have emphasized throughout history. When we share these 21 gifts with others, our lives become more magical and miraculous, attracting success on all levels.

The Gateway to Personal, Organizational, and Cultural Success

The Divine Child within each of us is expressed as the pure and powerful energies of our inner child. Several years ago, I began to list which energies and characteristics that babies seem to have from the moment of birth. As I continued to research these "Divine Child" traits, the list grew to 21 qualities that we appear to have in common.

These 21 gifts inside of each of us seem to connect us in perfect harmony — the curious, creative, playful, joyful, observing, present, intuitive, passionate, expressive, courageous, exploring, vulnerable, gentle, authentic, free, equal, empathetic, nature-loving, grounded, accepting, and hopeful energies that are ready to be shared with others.

The Divine Child is our energy code and blueprint that *magnetizes all success toward us*, as these 21 traits activate the "Law of Resonance" in nature that spontaneously attracts the resources needed to fulfill our dreams with far greater ease. When our Divine Child's gifts are expressed and shared with others, synchronous moments frequently erupt that some would label as miracles.

Perhaps this why we adults look a little forlorn and saddened as we gaze upon small children. Do they remind us of our magic inside that was crushed by early childhood trauma and may now be suppressed? What happened to our precious innocence, our courage that knew no fear, the spontaneous joy flowing from within, our eagerness to explore the world freely? What abuse or woundings occurred that caused our most treasured energies to become diminished?

Our tiny teachers are wonderful reminders that our journey as adults is to *heal* the original pain that squelched our ability to create and attract wonderful things. Learning about our unique healing journey that can restore these potent gifts is the path to inner and outer fulfillment. When we rediscover and reignite our most powerful qualities within us, we return back to the essential nature of our Divine Child inside and begin to attract those same energies around us.

For example, when we are expressing our natural joy, we will draw other joyful people and circumstances. And when we share our joy and attract even more joy, we ignite the world with this precious energy. As we continue sharing, those positive energies keep building. The added benefit of turning within to activate our Divine Child's 21 energies is that we not only transform ourselves in magnificent ways, we become spiritual catalysts that activate these energies in others when we share these marvelous gifts.

Expressing and sharing our Divine Child energies lights up the world.

What Happens When Our 21 Gifts Are Traumatized?

Success, whether in our relationships, career, or physical well-being, occurs when our Divine Child gifts are readily shared — including at the organizational and cultural levels. For example, prosperity for all naturally unfolds when equality is shared. Physical health is more abundant when our innate energies of joy, groundedness, and connection to nature are expressed. Relationships become more harmonious when we are open, vulnerable, and present.

But when any of our 21 gifts become damaged at an early age, those energies begin to shut down, much like an engine becomes sluggish when its oil turns grimy. For example, when small children are taught to "be seen and not heard," they begin to believe that they are not worthy of love or of being acknowledged. Consequently, their natural joy begins to suffer and diminish in potency and magnitude.

As I suggested in my first book, *Spiritual Values in the Workplace: The Soul of Success in the 21st Century*, these spiritual energies make our personal lives more exciting and fulfilling. They are also the secret to success for every organization and culture. To the extent that these childlike gifts of energy are shared determines the amount of success a person and organization can experience. Indeed, *love may be defined as the sharing of our 21 gifts with others*. To the extent we share our Divine Child's gifts determines how much we truly love ourselves and those around us.

When employees or members of a group are not allowed to speak their voices, they learn to shut down inside, and the organization suffers. When women are ordered to be silent and subject to men, as commanded by numerous religious teachings from the Bronze Age, everyone suffers — especially women. And if these spiritually abusive and false teachings become widespread, the energies of freedom and equality becomes severely damaged on personal, organizational, and cultural levels.

Consequently, spiritual pandemics, such as the trauma of our innate sense of equality, affect us on other levels of our personal and collective being, including the mental, emotional, and physical aspects of our lives. Even in the 21st century, we still tragically witness economic and wage disparity among women, who get paid roughly 28 percent less than males on average.

Spiritual abuse and trauma based on ancient, barbaric teachings that are unethical, immoral, and untrue for any period of time contaminate the spiritual DNA of our cultural soul. Everyone suffers. Healing these spiritual abuses on personal, organizational, and cultural levels is critical to restoring the Divine Child energies in our lives and to the thriving of any great society.

Breaking Down Barriers to Success: Healing Our Wounded Child

21 Gifts also guides the reader along a journey of discovery, revealing how each of these 21 magical traits becomes wounded. Research shows that early trauma to our inner child usually occurs before age ten. When our Divine Child becomes traumatized, we begin to shut down inside. When any of our 21 Divine

Child traits become suppressed or damaged, those wounds then become unconsciously expressed through both our actions and experiences we attract.

For example, joy can become squashed through false belief systems that say, "children should be seen and not heard," or "spare the rod, spoil the child" that has been used as Bronze-Age justification to beat children in order to "teach them a thing or two." When this happens, our joy can turn into dark states of negativity, such as anger, rage, violence, anxiety, fear, and depression. Is this why the rate of self-harm among teenage girls is as high as 31 percent, according to a massive study involving 64,671 public high school students ages 14 to 18 from 11 states?[2]

It is vital to understand where and how our personal wounding began in order for true healing to occur, including at cultural levels that leads to epidemics of spiritual wounding. This book reveals the numerous ways in which early trauma is inflicted, including through physical harm, emotional abuse, mental trauma, and most importantly, through spiritual abuse such as false belief systems or suppression of equality, for example. Trauma results from receiving messages that we don't deserve to express our true selves, that we have an innate wrongness or deficiency. As you read about how these early wounds occur, you may identify with them, seeing traces of abuse in your own history.

21 Gifts outlines the various tools we can use to heal the wounded aspects of our Divine Child. When we work on ourselves to heal past trauma, we win big — and everyone around us wins big, too. Otherwise, these wounded aspects chew up precious energy and feed a challenging cycle of negativity, just as how a depressed state of mind will keep one stuck, unhappy, and unfulfilled. The healing ointment for these spiritual values ultimately releases enormous energies that can be channeled to materialize our goals, dreams, and heartfelt wishes.

The Journey Back Home

The return to your Divine Child state will be the most magical experience of your life. All healing comes from discovery, even at the cellular level, and discovery comes from learning as a result of our Divine Child's innate curiosity that expands our consciousness.

With learning and discovery, real growth and progress can then occur, which we label in pop culture as "success." High levels of achievement begin with a profound, self-actualizing relationship with our Divine Child that is within each of us. As we heal and grow our connection to the Divine Child, we begin to see positive changes ripple through our personal and working relationships.

21 Gifts is about your journey back home to your precious inner child. By recognizing and healing the Divine Child, then the adult part of you — which I refer to as the "Divine Adult" — learns to accomplish your cherished desires with greater ease. The secret to our success, both individually and collectively, lies within, not in something outside of ourselves that we need to learn. Rather, rediscovering this precious, powerful part of us, which may have become largely lost or buried deep within ourselves, is the answer. Psychologist Peter A. Levine said, "Trauma is hell on earth. Trauma resolved is a gift from the gods."

It is all too easy to get caught up in the illusions with which we surround ourselves today. Certainly, life can be challenging at times to the point we want to numb the pain. We work long days, go home, pop open a bottle of beer or pour a glass of wine, plop on the sofa, and watch a rerun of the Golden Girls or latest show about the Kardashians. Entertainment and social media keep us distracted long enough from looking at ourselves for who we truly are. Then we go back to work the next day, continuing the hamster mill cycle, running frantically to achieve the dreams that often others want for us. We have buried our true selves with illusions and distractions to the point where it is difficult to find our power within.

But you can break this cycle. You can transcend the daily grind. You are unique. You are here to do greater things. This precious journey of awakening, higher achievement, and success begins with your Divine Child.

Cary

---

[1] https://www.myss.com/free-resources/sacred-contracts-and-your-archetypes/appendix-a-gallery-of-archtypes/

[2] https://www.ajc.com/news/health-med-fit-science/nearly-teen-girls-the-self-harm-massive-high-school-survey-finds/EQnLJy3REFX53HjbHGnukJ/

The Four Spiritual Laws of Success

> We're so engaged in doing things to achieve purposes of outer value that we forget the inner value, the rapture that is associated with being alive, is what it is all about.
>
> Joseph Campbell

The journey of discovering the magic of our Divine Child begins with taking a closer look at Jesus — the most influential person in history who has shaped the spiritual beliefs and behaviors of humankind. Today, approximately 30 percent of the world's population subscribe to the teachings of Jesus, who simplified the numerous laws that preceded him into a few basic codes for living. These guidelines for success according to Jesus can be found in the Bible, the most widely read book in the world that has sold more than 3.9 billion copies over the last 50 years.[1]

While the words of Jesus have been popular for many, some prominent theologians and critics have dismissed the majority of biblical scripture as the Bronze Age writings of uneducated, misogynistic men. Thomas Jefferson, a forefather of the United States and principal author of the Declaration of Independence, intently studied the life and words of Jesus. A noted theologian of his time, Jefferson regularly corresponded with John Adams, another forefather of America, after they met during the Revolutionary War. Their relationship as friends and pen pals lasted until 1800, when the election divided their friendship for twelve years. Historians regard their correspondence spanning half a century as an intellectual dialogue on the highest plane, embracing topics of politics, government, philosophy, religion, and the human experience of family living and aging.[2]

> Learn from yesterday, live for today, hope for tomorrow. The important thing is not to stop questioning.
>
> Albert Einstein

A champion of religious freedom, Thomas Jefferson was influenced by the principles of deism, a construct which envisioned a supreme being that created the beginnings of the world but did not intervene directly in daily life. At the same time, Jefferson was a product of the Age of Enlightenment, a period of science and reasoning that began in Europe and migrated to America in the late 17th and early 18th centuries. After the "dark" Middle Ages, intellectuals like Jefferson believed illumination was finally occurring,[3] which ushered in a deeper study of the mind and focus on science which started around the mid-1850s, when the Industrial Age began.

Jefferson was particularly enamored with the written words of Jesus, but disenchanted with most of the other writings in the Bible. With a pair of sharp scissors in hand, Jefferson literally cut out the majority of the Bible, eschewing anything that was "contrary to reason," such as the miraculous events described in numerous biblical texts. He tossed out the majority of scripture, retaining only parts of the four Gospels for his intense study that began even while he was president of the United States.

Like a number of other notable theologians, Jefferson considered the writers of the four Gospels to be untrustworthy, not only due to their variations, but because the authors of those four books wrote them 40 to 100 years after Jesus had died.[4] After careful examination of the Four Gospels, Jefferson referred to the King James version as "the corruption of schismatizing followers." In his 1820 letter to William Short, Jefferson wrote, "I find many passages of fine imagination, correct morality, and of the most lovely benevolence; and others again of so much ignorance, so much absurdity, so much untruth, charlatanism, and imposture, as to pronounce it impossible that such contradictions should have proceeded from the same being."[5]

In 1804, while Jefferson was president of the United States, he continued separating the "diamond from the dunghill," as he referred to the King James version of the Bible. For many years thereafter while at Monticello, Jefferson continued to pore over various editions of Latin, Greek, French, and the King James English, clipping out the passages he thought were the genuine teachings of Jesus and pasting them in the four respective languages, side by side onto blank pages. In 1820, Jefferson produced a leather-bound, 84-page volume entitled *The Life and Morals of Jesus of Nazareth, Extracted Textually from the Gospels in Greek, Latin, French & English*, just six years before his death at 83.[6]

> God is a metaphor for that which transcends all levels of intellectual thought. It's as simple as that.
>
> Joseph Campbell

The "Thomas Jefferson Bible," which is a tiny fraction of the 66 books of the King James version, focuses on the moral teachings of Jesus that are organized by topic. A secularist, Jefferson ended his gospel story with the execution and burial of Jesus, but omitting the resurrection, a proclaimed but inexplicable miracle that Jefferson also rejected. His monumental task was finally complete. In his 1813 letter to John Adams, Jefferson explains that the retained passages contain "the most sublime and benevolent code of morals which has ever been offered to man."[7]

In 1895, the Smithsonian Institution acquired the surviving bible that Jefferson created, purchasing it from Carolina Randolph, Jefferson's great-granddaughter. Regarded by many as a newly discovered national treasure, his version of biblical scripture was printed in 1904 by act of Congress. Each newly elected senator received a copy of the Jefferson bible on the day that legislator took oath of office until the 1950s, when the supply of 9,000 copies ran out. The original book can be seen at the National Museum of Natural History at the Smithsonian in Washington, D.C.,[8] and reproductions of the Jefferson bible can be ordered online.

While it is doubtful that scribes living 2,000 years ago could accurately record the exact words of Jesus, as most people were illiterate and lacked modern-day recording devices, there are four principal laws of success that are based on the words ascribed to him. The tenets of success are connected with the energies of the Divine Child and exemplified by the influential writings of Thomas Jefferson, who embedded many of these spiritual precepts into the Declaration of Independence, while his dear friend, John Madison, infused some of these traits, such as equality and freedom, into the document he authored that eventually formed the Constitution of the United States.[9]

These words of Jesus are usually applied to the individual level as a guide to living a better life. However, as Thomas Jefferson acknowledged, these precepts attributed to Jesus are also important for organizational prosperity and humanity itself. Spanning the personal and organizational levels of our lives, the four spiritual laws are the basis for the energy code of the Divine Child:

1. Do unto others as you would have them do unto you.

Written in Matthew 7:12 and Luke 6:31, this spiritual law is the Golden Rule in action. It is accompanied by a passage in Matthew 22:39: "Love thy neighbor as thyself." The energy of how we treat someone begins with us. We cannot treat others with love and kindness if we beat ourselves up, judge ourselves negatively, or diminish our own power. Loving others begins with first accepting and loving ourselves fully.

If we are self-critical and continually judging ourselves, we unconsciously are likely to treat others similarly. The angry person is first angry with himself, then projects that anger toward others. The unkind person who mistreats and abuses others is usually first unkind and abusive to himself.

A truly spiritual life of material abundance must begin within. When we repair our trauma and unhealed wounds from the past, we become more whole. What makes us powerful is accepting our internal light, as well as our dark shadows, because the dark shadows of our Wounded Child are the gateway to success when we heal and restore our Divine Child.

The subject of love is perhaps one of the most widely discussed topics by motivational speakers, therapists, poets, and spiritual books. But what does it mean to "love" yourself, let alone someone else? Is it a mushy gushy feeling we have inside for someone else, or does love resemble more of a verb, where we take some sort of action, such as sharing our 21 vibrant gifts with others?

The entire bible and every other spiritual text could largely be summarized into the principle of the Golden Rule: <u>Treat others as you would like to be treated</u>. This also points to the need to put that energy out proactively, rather than wait for others to treat you with love, kindness, respect, equality, and joy. When we initiate those gifts inside of ourselves rather than wait for them to come to us, we illuminate the world by operating from these simple eight words. Sharing our gifts is the creative process in full bloom that attracts success.

2. The kingdom of heaven is here and now...and is within you.

When I was raised in a Pentecostal church for 18 years, the teaching was that heaven was in the future, a place where I would someday walk on streets of gold somewhere "up there." This promise of ultimate salvation would happen at some point after the rapture, where I would suddenly be whisked away and be saved from the turmoil on earth. This teaching was based on Revelation, the final writings of the 66 books of the Bible[10] written by John the Divine,[11] whom the majority of Christian scholars believe authored the book, while he was allegedly in exile by the Romans on the Greek island of Patmos.[12]

> Animals never worry about Heaven or Hell. Neither do I. Maybe that's why we get along.
>
> Charles Bukowski
> *The Last Night of the Earth Poems*

But the words of Jesus reveal something very different about the future of heaven portrayed by John the Revelator, who even described physical dimensions of a future city. The heaven described by Jesus didn't include literal streets of gold, walls of jasper, sapphires, agate, emeralds, and all of the glittery treasures that kept us salivating in Sunday school. Instead, when the Pharisees asked Jesus when the kingdom of heaven would finally be seen, Jesus said not to follow those who proclaim that it exists outside of yourself.[13]

You, too, can ignore ancient teachings still taught that widely promote a future, literal heaven that is outside of you. Do not follow them, as Jesus said, because this kingdom is already within you. Your inner child will show you the way. The real treasure lies within you.

3. The key to entering the kingdom is to come as a little child.

The biblical teachings to which I was exposed also included complex requirements for my future salvation, including repenting, being baptized in the name of Jesus, speaking in other tongues, following the Ten Commandments, not having a television, attending church four times a week, paying ten percent of my pre-tax income to the church, praying for forgiveness every day, and keeping my hair cut above my ears. Pentecostal children, like many other conservative Christians, were told to avoid swearing, drinking, dancing, playing with dice, and having premarital sex. And of course, we were never to question the Bible or religious authority. That would be blasphemy.

That is the short version of a very long list of rules. The list was even longer for women. It was not only very confusing, it was exhausting.

> While we try to teach our children all about life, our children teach us what life is all about.
>
> Angela Schwindt

None of these rules are familiar to your Divine Child. Instead, your inner truth resonates with spiritual qualities, such as joy, creativity, equality, intuition, freedom, empathy, and other natural characteristics found naturally at birth — rather than beliefs engrained into our mental bodies.

The kingdom of riches is accessible here and now, and *the key to the kingdom is our own inner child* — the Divine Child that connects us to each other. It is the incredible secret to infinite joy, achieving inner happiness, enjoying passionate relationships, and attracting material abundance and prosperity.

The kingdom of untold riches — the realm of your true inner potential, success, and real joy — can be yours now.

4. If you first seek the kingdom of God, all material prosperity will be yours.

The promise for unlimited prosperity is apparent in the words of Jesus. In John 17:10, Jesus said, "All I have is yours." The parable of the Prodigal Son in

Luke 15:31 also promised, "Everything I have is yours." John 10:10 teaches, "I came that they may have life, and have it abundantly."

But there is a catch. The key is to first focus on your inner child — the Divine Child that most of us have largely abandoned years ago when we were forced to "grow up" and become an adult. However, when we come as our little child in the inner kingdom, the gates of the material kingdom are opened. In Matthew 6:25-32, Jesus refers to the worrisome quest for food, drink, and beautiful clothing, and then promises this and more in Matthew 6:33: "But seek ye first the kingdom of God, and his righteousness; and all these things shall be added unto you."

If Jesus indeed said these words, he believed that the qualities of the little child are the secret to achieving unparalleled success. In Matthew 18:4, he said, "Therefore, whoever humbles himself like this little child is the greatest in the kingdom of heaven." Jesus wanted the focus to be on ourselves and our own greatness found in our inner child. Ian Wallace, the author of popular children's books that include *Hansel and Gretel*, said, "Why are you trying so hard to fit in when you were born to stand out?"

In Matthew 19:14, Jesus reemphasized the power of children and their profound destiny: "Let the little children come to me, and do not hinder them! For the kingdom of heaven belongs to *such as these*." As babies, we enter this world with nothing. We are poor, without clothing or coin, but our Divine Child is enormously rich with treasures. Luke 6:20 teaches, "And he lifted up his eyes on his disciples and said: 'Blessed are you who are poor, for yours is the kingdom of God.'" Sometimes our outer world of materialism can cloud our vision from seeing the richness of our inner world, our inherited kingdom.

In John 3:5, Jesus said, "Truly, truly, I say to you, unless one is born of water and the Spirit, he cannot enter the kingdom of God." We receive physical birth from the waters of the womb, and we breathe spiritual energy. This breath of life is both the very real breaths that we take and the inspiration that we receive from our natural state of being.

The Real Law of Attracting Success

Most people want to learn how to be a success in some aspect of their lives. It is a natural desire to achieve and accomplish — a characteristic perhaps unique to the human species. We want to discover a magic formula for attaining what we want with far less effort. How do we attract our heartfelt goals, dreams, and wishes more easily, regardless of what they may be?

The Law of Attraction says that "all thoughts turn into things eventually."[14] The problem is the "eventually" might take a very...long...time. Meanwhile, our biological clocks tick onward. They stop for nothing, while we sit and wait with our thoughts will manifest in hopes they will somehow attract material riches or the other desires that we have, such fulfilling work or a life partner.

Despite what numerous motivational speakers, writers, and philosophers say, attracting success likely does not begin with our thoughts, and here's why: First, the mind is a very tricky and complex instrument. It is constantly evolving and changing. "The snake which cannot cast its skin has to die. As well the minds which are prevented from changing their opinions; they cease to be mind," Friedrich Nietzsche wrote, describing intellectual slavery.

Secondly, a number of researchers have said that our mind processes about 50,000 to 60,000 thoughts a day,[15] excluding the millions of unconscious thoughts that lie beneath the surface of our conscious mind. Monitoring all of them is virtually impossible.

Finally, many of our thoughts are in direct conflict with each other, as we are complex beings. Our individual history is quite varied with many different experiences that make us who we have become. Making sure our thoughts are aligned is an impossible task, due to the number of conscious and unconscious thoughts, as well as the embedded unresolved trauma in the body that is doing its own thing, too.

If we start "force-feeding" our consciousness with new thoughts, we are not allowing the mind to serve as a valuable mirror of self-reflection. The risk of planting new thoughts is that they are often contrary to existing rooted thoughts which keep popping up in the garden of our minds. It just creates even more stress if we haven't taken care of those unwanted older weeds by fully removing them. Herein lies the dilemma.

Suppose your goal is to lose 30 pounds. You could spend half of your day repetitively torturing yourself with a number of force-fed thoughts that resemble positive affirmations: "My ideal weight is 165 pounds. I am attractive and thin. I am beautiful. I am my ideal weight." But also, you will be unconsciously tormented by other automatic thoughts that creep in, such as, "This gym thing is really hard! I miss eating bread, chocolate, cookies, and cheese. I am hungry." Because your physical body has been programmed to crave sugar and fat, it isn't really that interested in running at the gym on a spinning hamster mill.

If your "authentic" thoughts that are deeply embedded into your physical, emotional, mental, and spiritual bodies are in conflict with your "goal" thoughts, success may be improbable. It requires addressing the embedded programs and cycles that have entrapped us.

If thoughts aren't the secret sauce to magically attracting our desires, then what is? The words of Jesus reveal the secret to attracting unlimited success with far less effort and greater ease. The powerful secret that these master achievers have used is one that is rarely discussed but is how everything in nature magically transpires.

That energy phenomenon is the Law of Resonance.

The Law of Resonance

Simply put, resonance is the mysterious energetic phenomenon that attracts something to itself. "Like attracts like" is what draws every significant relationship together, including deep friendships and your intimate partner. Resonance determines how you spend your time, energy, and resources. It is why people choose their jobs, or their jobs choose them. Resonance is the magical rocket with an endless supply of fuel that propels you to your greatest dreams, enabling you to become a high achiever with significantly less effort.

Encoded within the hieroglyphs of the ancient Egyptian temples, the canvasses of da Vinci's masterpieces, and the alleged words of Jesus are the keys to how to create profound resonance in your life. It is far more than words. The great Sufi poet and mystic Kahlil Gibran said, "All our words are but crumbs that fall down from the feast of the mind." We must learn to get into contact with a deeper and more intuitive aspect of ourselves to access powerful resonance with the positive energies that bring true change.

There are numerous scientific examples that illustrate the Law of Resonance. Color, for instance, dramatically affects our emotions and behaviors when we instantly and unconsciously go into resonance with it. Certain shades of pink, for example, have an immediate calming effect on the mind and body.

When researchers discovered that some shades of pink reduce anger and aggression, prison authorities in the United States, Germany, Switzerland, Poland, Austria, and the UK began painting the walls of prisons pink and saw positive results. In Switzerland, twenty percent of police stations and prisons have at least one pink cell, using the color blancmange pink or "Baker-Miller pink" that was named after two U.S. Naval officers first studied its effects that pink prison walls had on its occupants.[16]

This shade of pink is widely used in the holding cells for prisoners to reduce violent and aggressive behavior, with some reports of reduced muscle strength in under five seconds after exposure to this potent color.[17] Ancient Feng Shui practitioners, however, have known for centuries the energy secret of what happens we go into resonance with shades of pink. Consequently, some advocates have long recommended using light pink on the walls to activate the calming abilities of the Heart Chakra.

Today, many U.S. prisons and detention centers, such as the co-ed residential facility for delinquents in San Bernardino, California and the Santa Clara County Jail in San Jose, have reported rapid results in the lowering of aggressive behavior. Dr. Paul Boccumini, Director of Clinical Services for the San Bernardino County Probation Department, said, "In fact, it has worked so well that staff must limit their [delinquents'] exposure because the youngsters become too weak."[18]

Clint Low, the sheriff of Mason County in Texas, said to the Associated Press that pink walls were intended to calm tempers at the cramped prison. Built in 1894, the tiny jail is a historical site and does not need to conform to the guidelines of state prisons. The sheriff also reported that the reoffending rate dropped by 70 percent after introducing the color pink in the prison, and no fights occurred among inmates since the walls were painted pink.[19] Energy fields around us can invisibly yet profoundly shift our lives when we go into resonance with them — even without having any knowledge of their presence or effect.

The Law of Resonance transcends conscious thought, as this phenomenon silently works by exchanging energy and information dynamically. This law of nature is what you can use in your life to make the most amazing transformations and create the highest level of achievement with the least effort. Jesus pointed to your inner child as the secret to achieving greater things.

Your Divine Child is your real law of attraction. The spiritual gold you have inside will spontaneously attract the same energy qualities that are core to everything you wish to achieve and receive. From weight loss to attracting your ideal partner to experiencing the fullness of joy that life is ready to give you, all of that can be yours.

The passport to success and high levels of achievement is to energize your child within. The esoteric meaning of Mark 12:30-31, which expresses that the greatest commandment of Jesus is to love God with all your heart and love your neighbor as yourself, can be realized by allowing the Divine Child to express itself. Love is the expression of these 21 gifts by sharing them with others — the spiritual qualities that some may label as "God." When you share these powerful qualities with others, you will magnetize everything around you that is similar.

The magic of resonance attracts pure synchronicity, the revitalizing ingredient that exponentially increases energy within any system. All can be yours. The journey of magic begins within you.

All stories and myths become powerful only when they reveal something about ourselves that is useful. When those stories unlock the portal to our Divine Child, we gain access to our kingdom of inner and outer riches. It is the secret to fulfillment in life, applicable to both the individual human experience and to any organization or culture.

Astrophysicist Neil deGrasse Tyson said, "We spend the first year of a child's life teaching it to walk and talk, and the rest of its life to shut up and sit down. There's something wrong there." Rediscovering your inner child and healing any trauma is the way to establishing an intimate relationship with your Divine Child.

When your adult part grabs your little child by the hand and says, "I've got you now," you reconnect and engage the two potent forces within you that are the embodiment of your Divine Child and Divine Adult. Your salvation and success lie in freeing the Divine Child's potential to create more powerfully.

Now go for it. Begin your journey with a curious and open mind.

---

[1] https://www.businessinsider.com/the-top-10-most-read-books-in-the-world-infographic-2012-12

[2] https://www.smithsonianmag.com/arts-culture/how-thomas-jefferson-created-his-own-bible-5659505/

[3] https://www.livescience.com/55327-the-enlightenment.html

[4] https://www.pbs.org/wgbh/pages/frontline/shows/religion/story/mmfour.html

[5] http://www.openculture.com/2013/09/thomas-jeffersons-cut-and-paste-bible.html

[6] IBID

[7] IBID

[8] https://www.smithsonianmag.com/arts-culture/how-thomas-jefferson-created-his-own-bible-5659505/

[9] https://www.constitutionfacts.com/us-founding-fathers/

[10] Stephen L Harris, *Understanding the Bible*, (Palo Alto: Mayfield, 1985), p. 355; SOURCE: Ehrman, Bart D. (2004).

[11] *The New Testament: A Historical Introduction to the Early Christian Writings*. New York: Oxford. p. 468.

[12] Souvay, Charles. "Patmos." *The Catholic Encyclopedia*. Vol. 11. New York: Robert Appleton Company, 1911. Jan. 12, 2009.

[13] Luke 17:20-23 — King James Version

[14] http://www.thelawofattraction.com/what-is-the-law-of-attraction/

[15] https://www.psychologytoday.com/us/articles/200107/depression-doing-the-thinking

[16] http://www.bbc.com/future/story/20150402-do-colours-really-change-our-mood

[17] http://www.ncbi.nlm.nih.gov/pmc/articles/PMC1297510/#b22

[18] http://citeseerx.ist.psu.edu/viewdoc/download?doi=10.1.1.631.8721&rep=rep1&type=pdf

[19] https://www.theguardian.com/world/2006/oct/11/usa.danglaister

Curious

Curiosity will conquer fear even more than bravery will.

James Stephens
Irish novelist, poet, and broadcaster

Small children are naturally curious. As babies, we are born with approximately 100 billion brain neurons, nearly double the amount that adults have. In the first 90 days after birth, our brains double in size, consuming the majority of our energy intake. This helps us navigate the period of engaged learning.[1]

Maria Montessori, the Italian physician who studied special education in the early 20th century, noted that curiosity is a key characteristic in children and is an essential component of learning. Her work that involved experimenting with various teaching methods led to her opening the first Montessori school in Rome in 1907. Today, there are over 22,000 Montessori schools in 110 countries that are based on her methods, with the underlying principle that children are naturally absorbent and curious to learn.[2] Montessori wrote, "The child has a mind able to absorb knowledge. He has the power to teach himself."

The thirst for learning is the innate soul ingredient that facilitates growth and evolution. Discovery is the portal for growth. Without our thirst for creating something new in our lives, we lose our real power and begin to die inside. But with curiosity, we live in a state of learning and therefore prosperity.

> We keep moving forward, opening new doors, and doing new things, because we're curious, and curiosity keeps leading us down new paths.
>
> Walt Disney

Even at the cellular level, learning occurs continuously. Cells are conscious, scanning for new or uninvited guests. If the cell thinks that the visitor is harmful, the body sends out an army of soldier antibodies to defend the cell from the foreign entity. Macrophages often surround the strange visitor, essentially gobbling it up to protect the rest of the cell from harm.[3] Curiosity reigns throughout our being, from the most complex mental processes to the ordinary functioning of our cells.

The Power of Your Curiosity

The gateway to curiosity that leads to all discovery, learning, and ultimate success is in the Crown Chakra, the source of energy that connects us to the Universe. By remaining curious, we spontaneously engage with deep interest in the world around us, as well as the profound Universe *within* us.

Neuroimaging reveals that the brain learns better when curiosity gets piqued, according to a 2014 study from the University of California, Davis. Neuroscientist Charan Ranganath and his fellow researchers discovered that the more curious someone is, the better memory he or she has. Ranganath and his team believe that their findings may help explain memory and learning deficits in people who suffer from disorders such as Parkinson's and Alzheimer's disease[4] that involve low dopamine levels.[5] Dwindling curiosity partly explains why memory-related issues emerge later in life, if we no longer seek out new challenges to stimulate our learning faculties in the brain.

> The important thing is not to stop questioning. Curiosity has its own reason for existing.
>
> Albert Einstein

In 1899, philosopher and psychologist William James called curiosity the "impulse towards better cognition." He noted that the hunger for learning drives children toward objects of novel, sensational qualities that are "bright, vivid, and startling." James also suggested that curiosity gives way to a "higher, more intellectual form" that leads to more complete scientific and philosophical knowledge. In 1903, the pioneering work of psychologist-educators G. Stanley Hall and Theodate L. Smith showed that babies as early as the second week of life exhibit curiosity with "passive staring," progressing through four developmental stages that culminate in "curiosity proper" at around the fifth month.[6]

In a meta-analysis of data from 200 different studies encompassing 50,000 students, Sophie von Strumm and her team of researchers learned that curiosity and conscientiousness had big positive effects on academic performance, and they were the two primary predictors for achievement. Published in the *Perspectives on Psychological Science* in October 2011,[7] the research suggests that conscientiousness is a marker of effort and intellectual curiosity is the primary influencer for intelligence, shaping career paths and individual life trajectories. Von Strumm wrote, "I'm a strong believer in the importance of a hungry mind for achievement, so I was just glad to finally have a good piece of evidence. Teachers have a great opportunity to inspire curiosity in their students, to make them engaged and independent learners. That is very important."[8]

Curiosity Transcends the Survival Instinct

With the 2017 discovery of human fossils from *Homo sapiens* at an archaeological site in Morocco called Jebel Irhoud, we have learned that modern humans have been around for at least 300,000 years.[9] For these early humans, curiosity became a necessary survival skill for finding food and understanding threats. Curiosity could make the difference between going hungry or finding a meal, between securing shelter or remaining exposed.

Even today, we go to school to learn a different kind of survival. We attend primary and secondary school to cultivate communication with one another, learn math and biology, and grow in our understanding of the physical world. In technical school and college, we build even greater curiosity and understanding, as we hone specific skills to help us earn a living.

In the last century, the human experience has dramatically shifted. For most of us, we do not face daily physical battles on the field to defend our huts or hunt for animals. We have evolved from the physical level of survival to higher levels of cultural maturity. Today, most of us engage in learning about our emotions, mental states, thoughts, and spiritual qualities, rather than mere physical survival.

> I think, at a child's birth, if a mother could ask a fairy godmother to endow it with the most useful gift, that gift should be curiosity.
>
> Eleanor Roosevelt

In modern culture, curiosity is not just used to protect and defend ourselves from others, but to connect with others and create ideas together that we turn into businesses, for example. As we learn more about our physical world, we focus on the finer energy planes of our individual and collective beings. Certainly, curiosity can be used proactively to co-create art, music, food, and more, rather than using this powerful quality for self-preservation and safekeeping. As Swiss physicist and Nobel Prize winner Heinrich Rohrer said, "Science means constantly walking a tightrope between blind faith and curiosity; between expertise and creativity; between bias and openness; between experience and epiphany; between ambition and passion; and between arrogance and conviction — in short, between an old today and a new tomorrow."

Curiosity: The Natural Habit of Success

Our happiness increases as we expand our curiosity. In a recent study with college students that was published in *Motivation and Emotion*, researchers discovered that more curious people report frequent growth-oriented behaviors and greater life satisfaction.[10] The people with higher amounts of curiosity also exhibited an appreciable presence of meaning and search for meaning.

Associate Professor Dr. Maria Kangas of Macquarie University's Department of Psychology studies curiosity and its impact on our lives. "It probably won't surprise you to learn there's no one universally accepted definition," explains Kangas, "but, broadly speaking, we think of curiosity as an openness to exploring one's environment, being broad-minded and being open to new experiences and learning opportunities."[11]

She continues, "At the basic level, of course, curiosity promotes an openness to unfamiliar experiences and information. Curious people ask questions, they read more and, in doing so, significantly broaden their horizons." In her research, Kangas has learned that curious people connect with others, including strangers, on a deeper level. This provides social benefits with enormous potential for interpersonal bonding experiences with others.

> Standardized testing is at cross purposes with many of the most important purposes of public education. It doesn't measure big-picture learning, critical thinking, perseverance, problem solving, creativity or curiosity, yet those are the qualities great teaching brings out in a student.
>
> Randi Weingarten
> Former president of the United Federation of Teachers

By exercising our curiosity, we gain emotional benefits as well, such as compassion and empathy. This illustrates how deeply interconnected each of the 21 Divine Child traits are. Kangas says, "[Curious people] ask questions, then actively listen and absorb the information instead of just waiting for their turn to speak. The result is they become more empathetic and better able to understand and accept different viewpoints, experiences and lives to their own, which has particular importance when we're attempting to bridge cross-cultural divides."

Her team discovered that the brain releases dopamine when it makes new discoveries, which is the "feel good" hormone that results in lower anxiety, heightened satisfaction, and higher levels of positive emotions. This innate thirst for learning also fosters better self-awareness, allowing us to question our individual motivations and value systems. The desire to learn is indicative of the self-actualized person.

Dr. Kangas says that everyone can increase their own levels of curiosity, regardless of age. If you are stuck in a cycle or feel stagnant, she suggests the following tips:

- Engage with activities you have let lapse.
- Start new activities you've always wanted to try.
- Talk to new people outside of your normal circle.
- Listen to others.
- Be present.

Children naturally express curiosity, but, as adults, we need to make a conscious effort to connect with our sense of wonder about the world. When our Adult parts create and foster the right conditions, we allow the Divine Child to shine.

The Genius of Curiosity

Albert Einstein said, "I have no special talents. I am only passionately curious." With his innate thirst to learn, the German-born physicist made important advances in science, including his development of the theory of relativity, a pillar in modern physics. Generally considered to be the most influential physicist of the 20th century, Einstein won the Nobel Prize in physics in 1921 for his explanation of the photoelectric effect.[12]

Genius arises when the childlike quality of curiosity is powerfully unleashed. Neil Blumenthal wrote, "Creativity flows when curiosity is stoked." We are reading with light pouring from glowing filaments in glass bulbs, thanks to Thomas Edison, whose innate inquisitiveness led him to try thousands of times before eventually creating one of the most significant inventions of the 20th century. When a reporter asked Edison, "How did it feel to fail 10,000 times?" Edison replied, "I have not failed 10,000 times. I have not failed once. I have succeeded in proving that those 10,000 ways will not work. When I have eliminated the ways that will not work, I will find the way that will work."[13]

With curiosity, innovation is born. Curiosity should not be dismissed as idle, as it can be incredibly proactive, engaging, and productive, as Edison showed. We owe our most important inventions that propel science and engineering forward to curiosity's awe-inspiring power.

The Negative Expressions of Curiosity

The end of curiosity is the beginning of spiritual death. The moment we stop discovering, a big part inside of us suffocates. If we become damaged in childhood because of our natural exploration, it is easy to incorrectly assume that curiosity and discovery are unsafe. Consequently, we shrink from learning, forgetting that curiosity is a critical factor to all progress and success.

Sometimes that inadvertent shutting down begins with widespread colloquialisms, such as "curiosity killed the cat," a proverb that originated as "care killed the cat" from English playwright Ben Jonson's play *Every Man in His Humour*, 1598: "Helter skelter, hang sorrow, care'll kill a Cat, up-tails all, and a Louse for the Hangman."[14] When sayings, however true or false, become distributed in the consciousness of millions of people, it has a lasting cultural impact that runs deep. It is imperative that we shed cultural baggage in order to advance to the next stages of our personal and collective development.

The negative, traumatized expressions of the curious mind are indifference, disinterest, and apathy. Boredom is also a telltale sign that the innate sense of curiosity has become damaged and disengaged. Habits and routine overtake the curious mind, where the tendency to fill it with relatively useless information leads to the village of "Nowhere." This empty void leaves the soul hungry, where we become restless and unsure of how to deal with fidgeting energy or where to direct it.

Dr. Diane Hamilton, author of *Cracking the Curiosity Code*, says, "We are all born naturally curious. However, by the time we enter grade school, it starts to wane." She mentions four factors that negatively impact curiosity: fear, assumptions, technology, and the environment (FATE). "The good news is that we can improve curiosity once we realize what inhibits it," Hamilton says.[15]

> To me, having the courage to tell your own story goes hand in hand with having the curiosity and humility to listen to others' stories.
>
> Sarah Kay
> American poet

The tendency to shut down our curiosity happens not only early in childhood, but also at the organizational level as adults, Hamilton warns. "Many employees fear to have their ideas shut down and looking foolish. Organizations that want real cultural change must demonstrate that ideas and questions have merit. Sometimes it helps for leaders to ask or volunteer something that they usually would not do to show that they embrace the notion that 'no question is a dumb question.' Assumptions are the things that we tell ourselves things such as 'that sounds boring.' It is that little voice in our head that talks us out of doing the status quo," Hamilton says.[16] Leaders must make space for inquisitive thinking, which can be somewhat scary for an organization that desires structure and conformity.

A major recurring theme throughout this book suggests that technology produces more Masculine energy on the planet, which in turn generates more movement, faster vibrational energy, and subsequently more chaos and noise. Hamilton cites technology as an intimidating source of frustration that puts increasing pressure on employees. Concurring with Hamilton, business coach Roberta Matuson describes the environment within organizations as a potential source of wounding, where a number of her coaching clients relate situations at work where "people are immediately shut down whenever they ask a question. It doesn't take long for employees to realize that curiosity can quickly kill one's career."[17]

How to Reengage Curiosity

Igniting our power and unlimited potential begins with healing the original trauma that impaled our sense of curiosity. All healing comes from learning, even at the cellular level. To heal anything in our lives, curiosity and learning are required.

Your journey of healing, evolving, and growing begins with you, not with necessarily with first "fixing" the outer conditions and people in your life. Denis Waitley, the motivational speaker and writer said, "What you make of your life is up to you. You have all the tools and resources you need. Your answers lie inside of you."[18]

Change becomes difficult when we become stuck in fear, because we close up. We subconsciously erect barriers between ourselves and others. And there we remain, stuck in our trauma cycles. As someone once said, the definition of "shy" is being afraid of going after what you really want.

On the other hand, curiosity is filled with anticipation and enthusiasm. When we are open and enthusiastic, then we live from a place of joy and curiosity. Our anxieties and fears shrink, and discovery brings new adventures each day. "When you meet people, show real appreciation, then genuine curiosity," wrote Martha Beck.

Curiosity invites understanding something new, interesting, and useful. With learning, the foggy vapors of fear disappear. Our horizons expand with each new discovery, and the thrill of learning and understanding leads us to continue the search.

Curiosity is like a muscle: It grows with exercise and use. The more curious we are, the more we learn and discover. Over time, curiosity becomes a natural extension of who we are, as those burning embers that expand us in positive ways never extinguish.

Through curiosity, we discover that our true potential is limitless. Our capacity to succeed grows as we explore both our inner world and the universe around us. As we integrate and connect our inner and outer worlds, we become an unstoppable powerhouse.

To be successful as a human being requires that your sense of curiosity is alive and functioning at full speed, much like a small child. Building majestic sandcastles and drawing portraits with crayons translates to the Michelangelo within us painting legendary masterpieces. Making paper airplanes could mean soaring new heights like Amelia Earhart. The curious mind does not accept things on blind faith; rather, it questions everything and seeks out what is true.

The singer and songwriter Michael John Bobak said, "All progress takes place outside the comfort zone."[19] The successful one is the pioneer whose curiosity pulls him or her outside of the comfort zone. After all, isn't safety an illusion?

The *feeling* of safety is either born from curiosity, but can become damaged from early wounding. Learning about what can keep us safer helps us navigate while we are on our path of discovery. Through curiosity, we learn about the nature of things inside us and in our world.

> Curiosity about life in all of its aspects, I think, is still the secret of great creative people.
>
> Leo Burnett

The health of our relationships, our physical health, and our financial success is linked to our ability to be curious every day. When we enter the kingdom of our curiosity, good things happen. We not only become more productive using fewer resources, we transform ourselves as well. Maintaining our sense of discovery and learning at high levels is essential for high achievement and success.

The Polish-French physicist Marie Curie, who pioneered research on radioactivity, said, "If I see anything vital around me, it is precisely that spirit of adventure, which seems indestructible and is akin to curiosity." When our natural curiosity is sparked within, its close cousin shows up — creativity.

[1] https://www.theguardian.com/canon-bring-curiosity-to-life/2018/jun/08/the-curious-case-of-curiosity-and-its-intrinsic-link-to-a-happier-existence)

[2] https://brooklyneagle.com/articles/2018/12/17/montessori-schools-what-are-they-and-why-brooklyn-parents-should-consider-them/

[3] https://www.ncbi.nlm.nih.gov/pmc/articles/PMC2561478/

[4] https://www.healthline.com/health-news/low-dopamine-link-to-alzheimers-diagnosis

[5] https://www.scientificamerican.com/article/curiosity-prepares-the-brain-for-better-learning/

[6] https://www.ncbi.nlm.nih.gov/pmc/articles/PMC4635443/

[7] https://journals.sagepub.com/doi/abs/10.1177/1745691611421204

[8] https://www.wiley.com/network/societyleaders/research-impact/why-curiosity-and-wonder-are-critical-for-the-next-generation-of-scientists

[9] https://www.theguardian.com/science/2018/jan/25/oldest-known-human-fossil-outside-africa-discovered-in-israel

[10] https://www.businessinsider.com/whats-the-connection-between-curiosity-and-happiness-2011-9

[11] https://www.theguardian.com/canon-bring-curiosity-to-life/2018/jun/08/the-curious-case-of-curiosity-and-its-intrinsic-link-to-a-happier-existence

[12] https://www.britannica.com/biography/Albert-Einstein

[13] https://www.forbes.com/sites/nathanfurr/2011/06/09/how-failure-taught-edison-to-repeatedly-innovate/#7b6cee7465e9

[14] https://www.phrases.org.uk/meanings/curiosity-killed-the-cat.html

[15] https://www.forbes.com/sites/robertamatuson/2019/03/19/the-link-between-curiosity-and-human-performance/#67a59e6c2184

[16] IBID

[17] IBID

[18] *Rethink: The Way You Live* by Amanda Talbot. p. 77.

[19] https://www.inc.com/jayson-demers/51-quotes-to-inspire-success-in-your-life-and-business.html

Creative

Be brave enough to live life creatively. The creative place where no one else has ever been.

Alan Alda
Actor

Babies and toddlers learn through free expression, such as stacking blocks or building forts with blankets. Unhindered, children live and thrive by expressing themselves openly. The unique way that we each create gives us the feeling of being special and fulfilled.

Creative energy is expressed through purposeful but often chaotic action. It may not be easy to understand where this drive originates, as it is a continual, invisible flow of energy. "It's actually hard for creative people to know themselves because the creative self is more complex than the non-creative self," Scott Barry Kaufman, a psychologist researching creativity at New York University. "The things that stand out the most are the paradoxes of the creative self ... Imaginative people have messier minds."[1]

> The creative adult is the child who survived.
>
> Ursula K. Le Guin

According to Kaufman and psychologist Rebecca L. McMillan, who co-authored a paper entitled "Ode to Positive Constructive Daydreaming," the wandering mind helps in the process of "creative incubation." When ideas come out of the blue, it seems the best ones arise when our minds are seemingly disengaged but brewing beneath the surface.

Children naturally daydream. When we allow the power of our minds to unfold, it can lead to sudden insights and valuable connections. Removing ourselves from the "energetic noise" of life — our cell phones, the endless barrage of news, media, information bombardment, and the rumbling sea of other people's opinions — allows for the creative process to naturally unfold.

Daydreaming requires temporary, constructive solitude, which can be the key to producing our best work. As Kaufman said, "You need to get in touch with that inner monologue to be able to express it. It's hard to find that inner creative voice if you're not getting in touch with yourself and reflecting on yourself."

When we are alone in inner silence, the imaginative networks of our brains work better. The solitude generates a state called "constructive internal reflection," what neuroscientists describe as being crucial to creativity and the generation of new ideas. By tuning out the external world, our brains are better at making specific connections, processing information, and crystallizing memories. In his best-selling book *The Power of Now: A Guide to Spiritual Enlightenment*, author and philosopher Eckhart Tolle writes, "To know yourself as the Being underneath the thinker, the stillness underneath the mental noise, the love and joy underneath the pain, is freedom, salvation, enlightenment."

A relaxed mind is ironically highly productive. In their book *Wired to Create: Unraveling the Mysteries of the Creative Mind*, authors Scott Barry Kaufman and Carolyn Gregoire cite a 2014 study conducted by Kaufman, where he found that 72 percent of respondents around the world get their creative insights in the shower.[2] Is this the washing away of the old which can drag us down that allows the new to spontaneously emerge? Like pushing "restart" on a computer, taking a shower gives us the room for fresh thinking that otherwise might have been hampered.

Another study reveals that by allowing the frontal cortex of the brain that manages executive and organization skills to rest, the creativity centers in our brains light up, which explains how creative energy engages when we are resting or showering.[3] Psychology professor Lile Jia calls this "psychological distance." He and his colleagues at Indiana University Bloomington demonstrated that problems feel further away after rest, thereby stimulating creativity.[4] By taking a step back from our normal thought processes, we become less attached to the routine.

While the left brain's capabilities for analysis and critical thinking are important, giving it a temporary "time out" can be vital. Have you noticed how small children do not judge themselves or each other, never evaluating how someone failed? Instead, children learn from the experience, pick themselves up, and move forward to do something again, perhaps moving in a completely different direction.

Where Creativity Energy Resides in the Body

The spark of inspiration that initiates the creative process ignites in the Sixth Chakra, which is located around the center of the head. The Second Chakra — its polar opposite energy center situated in the Feminine, lower part of the body — is the birth of creative expression. The term "creative" itself was born around 1670 during the Second Chakra era, where the term comes from the Latin term *creo* that means "to create, make." The word "create" appeared in the 14th century writings of English poet writer Geoffrey Chaucer,[5] whose famed *Tales of Canterbury* written between 1387 and 1400 interestingly contain a number of scandalous sexual references and descriptions,[6] an energy that is also deeply connected with the Second Chakra, the seat of sexual expression.

Creativity involves *doing something*, while the Sixth Chakra is about imagining something. While imagination is the playground for creativity to express internally, true creativity involves motion in the external, material world. As Albert Einstein so beautifully said, "Nothing happens until something moves." Creativity only becomes real when it is tangibly expressed through some physical means of communication.

> The desire to create is one of the deepest yearnings of the human soul.
>
> Dieter F. Uchtdorf

Journalist Steven Kotler, Director of Research for the Flow Genome Project, wrote in *Forbes*, "There is a deep and meaningful connection between risk taking and creativity, and it's one that's often overlooked. Creativity is the act of making something from nothing. It requires making public those bets first placed by imagination. Taking risks is not a job for the timid. Time wasted, reputation tarnished, money not well spent — these are all by-products of creativity gone awry."[7] However, as the Second Chakra suggests, creativity is the energetic conversation that results from two fields of consciousness experiencing each other. At the point of convergence, something new emerges.

Kotler described Einstein as a creative lion who took risks. Einstein loved to sail but did not know how to swim. In the late 1930s, he summered in the Hamptons across the bay from New York, sailing his 15-foot dinghy "Tinef"

(Yiddish for "junk" or worthless") into troubled waters. Residents who knew Einstein would often rescue him during his sailing adventures, and he would occasionally get a thrill by sailing his friends, some of whom were also scientists, directly into storms for the sheer fun of it.[8] When we unleash the creative energy within, productivity soars. In his work, Kotler explains how the most brilliantly creative people like Einstein have the most output.

In another study, psychologist K. Andres Ericsson at Florida State University spent more than 30 years studying peak performance and expertise. He concluded that extremely talented people in various disciplines — sports, music, writing — *rarely practice more than four hours each day on average.* Many experts prefer to train early in the morning, when mental and physical energy is highest. Ericsson wrote, "Unless the daily levels of practice are restricted, such that subsequent rest and nighttime sleep allow the individuals to restore their equilibrium, individuals often encounter overtraining injuries and, eventually, incapacitating burnout."[9]

The Magic of Our Creative Power

Creativity unleashes ideas and energy from unexpected sources. Apple co-founder and CEO Steve Jobs said, "Creativity is just connecting things. When you ask creative people how they did something, they feel a little guilty because they didn't really do it, they just saw something. It seemed obvious to them after a while. That's because they were able to connect experiences they've had and synthesize new things."[10]

Synthesis is what enraptures the Divine Child's intuitive and creative power, while analysis is the Divine Adult's way of analyzing and examining things separately, engaging more of the Masculine energy and mental body. The past cannot be erased, but we can add new energy to what has occurred. By instituting the "Yes, and…" philosophy taught by comedian Charna Halpern, the artistic director who co-founded the famed ImprovOlympic theatre with Del Close in Chicago, we can keep creating more powerfully like small children at play, adding to what has happened rather than to fight it, a byproduct of the "No, but…" mindset. We have to retrain ourselves to live in the "Yes, and…" way of our inner child.

Analysis is a "violent" mental action where things are torn apart, while synthesis emerges naturally, peacefully, and without struggle. Coming together is far more creative and powerful than the separation of things that divides. But let's be clear: Analysis and judgment are necessary, valuable tools that keep our garden clean of toxic debris, while the creative power of synthesis grows our gardens to be lush and fruitful.

Why Children Lose Creativity as They Grow Older

The poet Maya Angelou, said, "You can't use up creativity. The more you use, the more you have." All positive qualities expand when we express and share them. In children, their natural inclination to create is apparent. Playing dress-up creates the movie star and explorer, while making their own fairy tales and stories ignites their imaginations. But as children grow older, why does much of their creative energy seem to taper off and stagnate?

Children practice spontaneous honesty, but adults often quash that spiritual quality by repeatedly tell them, in subtle or direct ways, that they should be quiet and compliant. With this policing behavior, adults unconsciously signal children that they do not matter. Being forced into groups that do not have natural synergies for the child or forcing a regimented lifestyle also stifles a child's creative energy.

Children are also naturally vulnerable, trying new ideas without the adult concept of "saving face" that cause kids to abnormally care about what others think about them. Kids naturally explore, asking questions without considering whether or not they feel stupid, and immediately moving on to the next idea that pops into their heads.

As they become older, however, children learn survival techniques to protect themselves from ridicule. Mistakes, which are often not tolerated by others, can subsequently have adverse consequences driven by societal norms, such as being punished emotionally, mentally, socially, or even financially. The loss of self-confidence that occurs through repeated criticism has rather damaging fallout that can last a lifetime. The innate spiritual values of spontaneity, tolerance, and equality become transformed into their negative expressions of passivity, disrespect, conformity, and manipulation.

Children are naturally authentic and expressive, without being bound by social norms. When we adults tell our children, "Do not touch that stove, because it is hot," the child naturally wants to touch the hot stove anyway, just see what that experience is like.

As fear of authority and retribution sets in, children learn to withhold their natural sense of self-expression. If children are unwittingly punished by others for creating and expressing their authenticity, fear begins to run the show. Ultimately, this type of self-censorship squelches natural creativity.

When our innate ability to generate new experiences gets stifled, we begin to die inside — spiritually, emotionally, mentally, and then physically. The Divine Child becomes caught between the natural sense to create and the learned need to please others. Given the choice, many children learn that creating to please others is the path, although unnatural. When the Divine Child is smothered, the game of contrived creation becomes assimilated. At that point, mimicry is born.

Negative Expressions of Creativity

Separation from others can occur as a negative consequence of inhibited creativity. When we isolate ourselves from others, or even worse, isolate from ourselves, we begin to die inside. We humans desire socialization to first understand ourselves and then learn about ourselves and our effective roles within the tribe. When children or adults learn the incorrect lesson that safety can only be found apart from others, harmful, maladaptive isolation results.

In his writings for *Harvard Business Review*, critically acclaimed novelist Eliot Peper points out that "seclusion is the enemy of creativity." Peper turns back the hands of time when he discusses the aging artist Jacopo da Pontormo, who scored a significant commission in 1545 from Cosimo I de'Medici, the Grand Duke of Tuscany, to paint the main chapel of Florence's church of San Lorenzo. To make the frescoes the crowning achievement of his career, Pontormo sealed off the entire chapel to prevent anyone from sneaking an early peek or stealing his ideas. Keeping human contact to a minimum, he spent eleven years holed up in the chapel, painting scenes of the Creation, Adam and Eve, Noah's ark, and Christ raising the dead on Judgment Day.[11]

New York Times bestselling author Robert Greene writes, "These frescoes were visual equivalents of the effects of isolation on the human mind: a loss of proportion, an obsession with detail combined with an inability to see the larger picture." Peper suggests that Pontoromo "let the consequences of self-imposed solitude undermine his legacy," and warned that leaders can likewise seclude themselves in similar destructive ways. [12]

If leaders erect metaphorical walls and push productivity while sacrificing creativity and play, those walls become a prison, inevitably closing in the human spirit. Splitting attention with work issues and talking to friends is symptomatic, as is exhausting energy by burning the candle on both ends. Peper says that executives tell themselves that ineffective multi-tasking is part of the job: "It's normal. Just power through it." However, lying awake at night with anxiety bombarding our thoughts is a result of disconnecting from ourselves and others, where it becomes difficult to ask for the help we need. Being tough is not so tough, and the body will quickly reveal pretenses and other imbalances.

Psychiatrist and educator Jacob L. Moreno believed that the opposite of creativity is anxiety. His theory suggested that lowering anxiety to a minimum is the way to increase the level of spontaneity, which allows one to unleash the full potential of creativity. The Yerkes-Dodson Law illustrates that peak performance can be achieved by increasing arousal up to a certain point,[13] but becomes impaired with strong anxiety as the state of arousal becomes too strong.[14] Indeed, creativity functions best in its natural center, nestled within the guardrails of too much and too little stimulation.

The right level of arousal is important for elite athletes to succeed. When performers become too aroused with the Masculine energy of motion and excitement that leads to sensory overload, they must learn to alter and shift their arousal to levels that are appropriate for achieving the task at hand.

However, many organizational leaders fall to prey to the overstimulation phase of the performance curve, thus becoming victims of burnout. At the extreme left of the performance curve is apathy and indifference, while the highest state of arousal also leads to stagnation and exhaustion, marked by high levels of anxiety and even panic.

Extreme levels may be indicative of self-sabotage, as destructive energy can defeat the creative process. At the same time, a certain amount of old energy that exists must be destroyed, transformed, or replaced to provide space for new creative energy fields to emerge. This is analogous to clearing the land to build a home, or when a child levels the sand and removes shells and rocks in order to build elaborate sandcastles and protective moats around them.

Awakening the Creative Force Within

Many powerful stories and songs have been inspired by our wrenching heartaches and pain as catalysts for healing. "Post-traumatic growth," an emerging field of psychology, is helping people use their early life traumas and challenges to reactivate their creative energies. Researchers have discovered that past adversity can help people grow five in five specific areas: personal strength, spirituality, an appreciation of life, interpersonal relationships, and seeing new possibilities — all essential ingredients for creativity.

"A lot of people are able to use that as the fuel they need to come up with a different perspective on reality," says psychologist Scott Barry Kaufman.[15] "What's happened is that their view of the world as a safe place, or as a certain type of place, has been shattered at some point in their life, causing them to go on the periphery and see things in a new, fresh light, and that's very conducive to creativity." The marginalization that occurs during traumatic experiences can become a catalyst for new ways of thinking, provided that the difficulty has been properly guided and directed into constructive outlets.

Some of the most eminent creators have overcome majority adversity. The secret was using their negative experiences to motivate their work and inspire others. Studies have shown that powerful creators have also had a high likelihood of harsh early life events, physical illness, and psychological disorders, especially among artists such as painter Paul Klee, who said, "I create — in order not to cry."[16]

Here are some simple techniques to reactive your innate creativity:

- Put yourself in new environments that foster creativity. When we surround ourselves with new people and ideas completely different from us, we grow and evolve, activating our creative power. Get outside of your comfort zone and be with creative people and new experiences, such as taking long walks in nature, attending theatrical performances, and visiting art museums. Best-selling author Jim Rohn said, "If you are not willing to risk the unusual, you will have to settle for the ordinary."

- Ask questions. Lots of them. Children do this naturally. Practice becoming immune to the opinions of others until the feedback of critics is no longer important or relevant.

- Practice creativity. You already have this powerful generative force within you. Do something creative every day, whether it is sketching something artful, decorating a table, cooking up a new recipe, or writing a poem to yourself or for a friend or partner.

- Move your body in playful ways. Dance. Sing. Walk. Run. Move your hips. Roll around in the grass. Play dress up games with your friends, family, and children. Put on a play in your living room. Tell stories theatrically using your body and face. Using your body as the expressive field of energy, these activate the creative process.

- Remove yourself from dream killers, naysayers, and other negative people. These energy vampires will unconsciously suck the life force out of you. You will become physically, emotionally, mentally, and spiritually contaminated. Becoming energetically deflated and spiritually polluted is what frequently causes physical illnesses and disorders on various levels. Eliminate these energy vampires completely from your life or dramatically reduce your time around them. Instead, find people who support your hopes, dreams, and best wishes, where your creativity can thrive in fertile ground. It is better to have a few positive cheerleaders in your life than to be surrounded by a dozen energy leeches, even if they are family members or supposed friends who chronically take the wind out of your sails.

> Out of silence comes the greatest creativity.
> Not when we are rushing and panicking.
>
> James Altucher

- Spend quiet time alone every day. Put your cell phone away and turn off the radio, computer, video games, and TV. When we surround ourselves by the noise of life, we not only stifle our creative power; we become more hyperactive, stressed, anxious, and subsequently drained. Then we burn out. Spend a certain amount of quiet time alone in nature each day. Take that energetic shower of pure silence to cleanse yourself, allowing the creative forces to bubble up.
- Start journaling each day. Record your dreams the moment you awaken from sleep. Journal throughout the day. The relationship you have with yourself is the most powerful and deepest relationship you will ever have. Achievers who journaled regularly include Mark Twain, Ludwig van Beethoven, Marie Curie, Albert Einstein, Frida Kahlo, Thomas Jefferson, Virginia Woolf, Charles Darwin, Benjamin Franklin, and Beatrix Potter. Journaling will activate your creative juices, make you a better leader and improve your organization. This practice will also clarify your priorities and values, help with decision-making, boost your attitude, and reinforce positivity.

When we rediscover our creative force within, we become alive. As Mr. Banks in the 2018 movie *Mary Poppins Returns* exclaimed, "I never thought I'd feel this much joy and wonder again." Mr. Banks found that he had become a rigid, uptight, anxiety-filled workaholic who was ultimately detached from his three children. By letting go and reengaging with his own Divine Child whom he abandoned long before that, Mr. Banks transformed himself into a playful, spontaneous, and creative being who became truly rich in life.

Albert Einstein once said, "To stimulate creativity, one must develop the childlike inclination for play." Learning how to play again is the third key to success.

---

1 https://www.huffpost.com/entry/creativity-habits_n_4859769

2 https://www.fastcompany.com/3063626/7-surprising-facts-about-creativity-according-to-science

3 IBID

4 https://www.scientificamerican.com/article/an-easy-way-to-increase-c/?utm_source=zapier.com&utm_medium=referral&utm_campaign=zapier

5 https://www.britannica.com/biography/Geoffrey-Chaucer

6 https://www.bustle.com/p/7-times-the-canterbury-tales-was-way-dirtier-than-50-shades-of-grey-66368

7 https://www.forbes.com/sites/stevenkotler/2012/10/11/einstein-at-the-beach-the-hidden-relationship-between-risk-and-creativity/#34c8b7f59f54

8 https://www.hamptons.com/Lifestyle/East-End-Heirlooms/12852/Sailor-And-Scientist-Albert-Einstein-Makes.html#.XCwUci2ZN0t

9 https://www.scientificamerican.com/article/mental-downtime/

10 https://www.wired.com/1996/02/jobs-2/

11 https://hbr.org/2018/09/why-seclusion-is-the-enemy-of-creativity

12 IBID

13 http://www.conqagroup.com/reaching-alpha-mitzi-hollander

14 https://www.bryan.edu/yerkes-dodson-productivity/

15 https://www.huffpost.com/entry/creativity-habits_n_4859769

16 https://blogs.scientificamerican.com/beautiful-minds/turning-adversity-into-creative-growth/

Playful

Life must be lived as play.

Plato

Maria Montessori, the physician who established schools in the early 1900s founded on unique learning methods for children, concluded that play is a child's work. Her approach was based on the belief that kids learn best through playing in an environment that is loosely structured in time but highly structured in space — the opposite methodology of traditional schools, noted Carol Anne Wien, a former Montessori teacher and professor emerita from the Faculty of Education at York University in Toronto.[1] Wien says, "If you know where children are in the room, you know what they're doing, but the time is free. In play-based childcare, teachers tend to swing between letting the children play and doing teaching activities."

While traditional schools focus on didactic learning where theoretical knowledge is taught, the playful strategy of Montessori schools seems to be paying off. In an October 2017 study published in *Frontiers in Psychology*, six researchers examined 140 students who attended two Montessori schools in Hartford, Connecticut that attracted both wealthy and lower income families, comparing them to non-Montessori preschools. Each group of 70 students started preschool at age three with similar achievement scores. Upon completing kindergarten after three years, the 70 Montessori preschoolers scored significantly higher in math and literacy tests. Softer skills, including executive function, creativity, and problem-solving, were statistically the same for both the Montessori and non-Montessori groups.[2]

Play is our brain's favorite way of learning.

Diane Ackerman
American writer

As Carl Jung wrote, "The creation of something new is not accomplished by the intellect, but by the play instinct." Play may indeed be the secret to creativity, growth, and evolution itself.

Nature's Instinct for Play

Animals play to facilitate learning and development, as research suggests. One study published in the journal *Primates* showed a close relationship between the amount of time that animals play and the size of their cortico-cerebellum system,[3] the largest part of the brain that is responsible for motor control and higher cognitive skills.[4]

Studies examining the habits of wild horses, brown bears, and squirrels have confirmed that the amount of time animals play when they were young has an important effect on their reproductive success and long-term survival in general.[5] While biologists aren't sure exactly why play is so beneficial, they have confirmed that "freely recreating" leads to bigger brains, lower stress, and learning development that increases success in life. Today, organizations who promote the principle of play in the workplace will win big.

Theories about why animal species play vary, including the idea that playing lowers stress. Some biologists have concluded that playing is a form of exercise that improves health and fitness. Other theories and studies suggest that playing increases learning and development, where animals conduct informal experiments by trying out behaviors, move around objects, and then observe the consequences to better understand cause-and-effect to help manage their relationships.

Our pets certainly spend a lot of time playing. If you take your dog for a walk in the park and meet other dogs, play spontaneously occurs. Dogs sniff each other, inspect, and engage in either fighting or play-fighting. Cats will wrestle, taking turns pinning each other down. Felines jump and toss around small objects, batting and poking at them, perhaps learning about how to deal with prey.

Domesticated dogs and cats aren't the only animals known to play. University of Vermont biologists Bernd Heinrich and Rachel Smoker discovered that ravens commonly snowboard. In Alaska and Northern Canada, ravens are known to repeatedly slide down steep, snowy roofs. After reaching the bottom, they will fly or walk back to the top, and slide down over and over again.[6] Herring gulls will drop clams from high places, allowing them to crack open and provide their juicy meal, but these shorebirds will also play catch, grabbing clams mid-air rather than letting them fall. Other types of gulls play this game of catch as well.

Animals do not only play for fun. It provides significant advantages in cooperation, intelligence, reproduction, and thriving. So, we humans must not discount play as unimportant or trivial. By learning to play more often, we refresh our lives and live more fully.

Play Makes Children and Adults Smarter

In his award-winning 2015 documentary *Where to Invade Next*, filmmaker Michael Moore visits a number of European and African countries to see how they deal with key global issues such as health care, education, work, equality, and prison reform. In the film, Moore sits down for lunch with French students from a poorer district to enjoy a four-course school meal. Later, Moore explores Slovenia's higher education system that is nearly free, attracting a number of American students to attend their universities.[7]

In the film, Krista Kiuru, Finland's Minister of Education, explains to Moore why Finnish children do not have homework. High school students and teachers also describe the emphasis on leisure and recreation, where kids make art, hike, bake, build things, sing, and engage in other playful activities. The school hours are shorter, having the "shortest school days and school year in the entire Western world."[8]

LynNell Hancock at *Smithsonian* writes about the Finnish school system: "There are no mandated standardized tests, apart from one exam at the end of the students' senior year in high school. There are no rankings, no comparisons or competition between students, schools, or regions. Yet, among millions of students worldwide, Finnish students have consistently ranked in the top ten countries in math, science, and reading." While Finland spends about 30 percent less per student on education than the United States does, 93 percent of Finns graduate from academic or vocational schools — 17.5 percentage points higher than the United States — and 66 percent of Finns advance to higher education, the highest rate in the European Union.[9]

In Western culture, we encumber our students with competition, as though comparison were valuable in its own right. I recall my college years, where lists posted outside of the classrooms ranked students and their grades. Competition is not only popular in sports and in education, but in many corporate cultures, where companies such as Accenture, Deloitte, and General Electric have traditionally used "stack ranking" and "rank-and-yank" in hopes of improving performance. This practice was popularized by Jack Welch during his tenure as CEO of GE, who used it to chop a third of its employees in the 1980s in an effort called "Work Out." I was there, and this practice quickly turned GE into a culture of fear and a downward trajectory, where the company became delisted from the Dow after 118 years.

In his book *Finite and Infinite Games: A Vision of Life as Play and Possibility*, James P. Carse, who was Director of Religious Studies at New York University for thirty years, describes the difference between competition and play: "A finite game is played for the purpose of winning, an infinite game for the purpose of continuing the play." We can learn from children and animals in nature to "play our way to success" in life in ways that the culture of competition and ranking cannot do for us. This presents an opportunity to reconsider our notions of achievement and redefine success as having a sense of fun and adventure, rather than conforming to a narrow metric like a standardized test score.

Where the Energy of Play Resides

The spontaneous energy of play flows from the Heart Chakra — the energy center connected to the present moment. We cannot freely play if we are anxious about the future or find ourselves stuck in our past of what happened ten years ago. Peak performance occurs when our attention is directed with what is happening now — the only moment that is real, exciting, and productive.

Children mesmerize adults with their ability to spontaneously and freely play. Children experience higher levels of achievement when they play, and that same energy allows adults to soar to new heights, too. The *joie de vivre* — the joy of living — can come from enjoying cheerful conversation, inventing delectable dishes, or playfully exploring outside. Playfulness and joy are intimately involved in a winning formula for achieving true wealth and success.

Living in our Heart center compels us to intuitively play. When we do not live in the present moment, we slip back into the past or project our past into the future. But small children remind us where the magic of life awaits us: in the beauty and power of free play. Even their imaginary careers link them to what brings them more joy, igniting all the chakras in the body like engaging the cylinders in a car engine, ready for another big adventure.

Why We Stop Playing

Competition, which is more about comparative sport and ranking, is not the only thing that stifles free play. According to a 2011 article in the *American Journal of Play*, true recreation is on the decline with both children and adults. The research also shows how the lack of play in adolescence can lead to behavioral issues later in life, such as anxiety and depression.

Peter Gray, the study's author and professor of psychology at Boston College, suggests adults are the cause.[10] "Since about 1955, children's free play has been in continuous decline, at least partly because adults have exerted ever-increasing control over children's activities," Gray wrote. "Over the same half century that play has declined, the mental health of children and adolescents has also declined," he added.

So, what exactly is play? Psychologist Kathryn Hirsh-Pasek, director of Temple University's Infant and Child Laboratory and author of *Why They Need to Play More and Memorize Less*, says there are three main characteristics that describe play:

1. It is voluntary, with no obligation to participate.
2. It is flexible and can be changed or manipulated.
3. It is enjoyable and fun.

For children and adults to freely and spontaneously enjoy play, these three characteristics must be cultivated and protected. In our work-obsessed world, we have lost our play time and the joy it brings, bustling between our jobs, raising our kids, listening to the 24-hour news cycle, and maintaining our homes.

Children do not comprehend the economic squeeze that their parents are experiencing. While parents deal with a work-obsessed adult world in a struggle to make a living, children see a playground of magic, where playing doesn't have consequences that their parents are experiencing.

Free play allows children to discover the world around them, presenting the opportunity to explore and experiment. Without someone looking over our shoulders, the freedom to explore facilities discovery and learning, resulting in real growth and transformation.

Yet play, ironically, has a stigma of childishness, while adulthood has the aura of seriousness and responsibility. Children are usually not taught how to balance work and play. When the sense of play becomes wounded early in childhood, the youngster carries that stifled energy into adulthood.

As children, we also stop playing when we learn that it has negative consequences. Daydreamers, for example, get punished with ridicule and criticism from peers and adults who urge them to focus and be serious. If children are too noisy while playing, parents or other adults may instruct them to settle down or be quiet. This subtle but significant trauma wounds the human spirit early in life.

> It is a happy talent to know how to play.
>
> Ralph Waldo Emerson

How do we begin the process to recover our lost child who seeks to play? The popular solutions for "how to have fun" in thousands of videos, websites, and articles promise to teach you how to play again but may not guide us on how to heal early wounds that likely suppressed our playful energy. Restoring our innate sense of play allows us to spontaneously create fun on our own, as the Montessori school philosophy suggests, rather than to be shown a solution outside of ourselves.

When play is free and spontaneous, it requires no teaching in *how* to have fun. As small children, we made up the games spontaneously in pure play. By defining the rules of how other people should play, then control, analysis, and judgment can smother much of the joy, passion, and spontaneity that true play brings.

With most sports, adults unconsciously program kids with the idea that playing is about competition, keeping score, and climbing to the top. There is a mixture of pleasure and anger that erupts for many sports fans and athletes playing a game, even gloating at the defeat of an opponent. When negative energies emerge from these artificial forms of childlike play, it is difficult for real joy and true happiness to thrive. "For every minute you are angry, you lose sixty seconds of happiness," Ralph Waldo Emerson wrote.

How many times have you heard the chant, "We're number 1! We're number 1!" at a game? Play becomes a battle in sports, rather than a spontaneous moment of shared genuine joy. We see this not only on the field, but in the stands, where violence among fans, often exploding at baseball, soccer, football, or hockey games.

According to the National Alliance for Youth Sports, about 70 percent of kids in the United States said they stopped playing organized sports by the age of 13 because "it was not fun anymore."[11] As a society, we fail our children when we take the joy out of activities meant to be fun forms of community-building, but that lack true play.

When we lose sight of what brings us true joy and aliveness, the playing stops. When the Divine Child is wounded, we begin to die inside. The great playwright George Bernard Shaw wrote, "We don't stop playing because we grow old; we grow old because we stop playing."

How Successful People Play

Play relieves stress, improves brain function, and helps bring us back into balance. By playing, we boost our creativity and improve our relationships with others. Researchers and psychologists have discovered that play is essential for development, and a lack of it is recognized as a genuine health problem for inner-city and poor children.[12]

A study by Michigan State University revealed the strong connection between professional success and having an artistic hobby. The researchers found that Nobel Prize winners who dedicated time to painting or drawing were seven times more likely to win a Nobel Prize. When they wrote creatively with stories and poems, their likelihood of winning increased by twelve times, and dancing increased their chances by 22 times.[13]

We are on the verge of a play revolution where we balance work and play as adults. Valuing experiences over materialism drives this evolutionary shift, versus the security sought by previous generations. The idea of a forty-year career with just one company has largely faded, as the lines between our work and play continue to blur, becoming the new standard for success.

> The playing adult steps sideward into another reality; the playing child advances forward to new stages of mastery.
>
> Erik H. Erikson
> American psychoanalyst

Some people may think that they are not playful, but that assumption doesn't seem to be true. All of these innate positive qualities are inside of us, and some amount of playfulness, however faint, is expressed even in the most serious person. The energy of play may have been dampened or even switched off temporarily, but this ever-present energy can be reactivated and burn brightly.

Here are some ways that you can reengage and exercise your playful child within and reap the golden rewards:

- Write down the ways that you truly play…then keep building your "play list." Find a new way to play every week or every month, and just do it! Grab a friend or two and make it even more fun. Playing video games and board games does not count, as this constitutes structured play and competition, rather than the free play that is spontaneous. If truly playing is a problem for you, then consider starting a "Play Journal" for yourself, where you can identify how you play, when you play, and what you are doing to freely play.

- Take play breaks every day. Schedule time to play throughout the day until you become naturally aware of when your body is telling you to take a break and go play. Give your Divine Child permission to romp for a while!

- Find work that is joyful, where it is your play. Your work should excite and energize you, not be a chore that depletes you. Do what truly engages and captivates your heart, soul, and childlike imagination.

- To engage the artist within you, buy some coloring books and crayons and start coloring. Reignite the magical child within you by painting, writing fantastical stories, or dancing in your living room or at work. Find coworkers, friends, and family members to join you on your playful adventures!

- Get outside and play like a small child. Nature is quite healing. Rolling around in the grass can energize the playful child within you. Go barefoot. Feel the sand at the beach between your toes and build sandcastles. Engage in play with kids, especially with small children who know how to be in the moment without trying to achieve anything. Make mud pies. Hug trees, animals, and strangers with their permission. Draw with your non-dominant hand. Scribble. Doodle. Paint your face for the fun of it.

Playful

The world needs you and your playful spirit, and you will feel delight in the freedom of letting go. When we live from the place of spontaneity, it expands the wonderful and boundless energy around us. It feeds the mind, body, and spirit of ourselves, intimate relationships, friends, and our workmates. When we engage in playful spirit with others, the energy is electrifying and contagious.

Ralph Waldo Emerson said, "The child amidst his baubles is learning the action of light, motion, gravity, muscular force..." Through free play, we become more knowledgeable, empowered, and more successful in all ways. That natural energy of spontaneous play goes hand and hand with another essential qualities of your Divine Child.

When play is present, you can be sure that joy is present, too.

[1] https://www.todaysparent.com/family/parenting/montessori-vs-traditional-preschool-how-to-choose/

[2] https://www.usnews.com/news/national-news/articles/2018-01-02/studies-shed-light-on-merits-of-montessori-education

[3] https://link.springer.com/article/10.1007/s10329-017-0615-x

[4] https://www.ncbi.nlm.nih.gov/pubmed/16791141

[5] https://theconversation.com/primates-at-play-show-why-monkeying-around-is-good-for-the-brain-79361

[6] http://www.bbc.com/future/story/20130109-why-do-animals-like-to-play

[7] http://blogs.edweek.org/edweek/education_and_the_media/2015/11/filmmaker_michael_moore_is_not.html

[8] http://www.openculture.com/2017/05/how-finland-created-one-of-the-best-educational-systems-in-the-world-by-doing-the-opposite-of-u-s.html

[9] https://www.smithsonianmag.com/innovation/why-are-finlands-schools-successful-49859555/

[10] http://www.journalofplay.org/sites/www.journalofplay.org/files/pdf-articles/3-4-article-gray-decline-of-play.pdf

[11] https://www.washingtonpost.com/news/parenting/wp/2016/06/01/why-70-percent-of-kids-quit-sports-by-age-13/?utm_term=.6429c7b77758

[12] https://psmag.com/social-justice/throw-out-your-computer-and-grab-some-legos

[13] https://www.thenational.ae/business/playtime-brings-creative-success-1.617067

Joyful

When you do things from your soul,
you feel a river moving in you, a joy.

Rumi

From the moment a baby takes its first breath, it begins expressing the qualities of the Divine Child. The curious baby begins its journey of discovery, learning what brings it joy, then seeking those activities that bring even more joy. Only in the necessary moments of pain or discomfort does the small child pause to be authentic, expressing its displeasure and need to satisfy temporary hunger or thirst, or to get its dirty diaper changed. The small child would never automatically say "I'm doing fine" when someone else asks how he or she is doing. Adults can learn valuable lessons from a child's openness and authenticity.

Of the 21 traits identified in the Divine Child model of evolution, the absence of joy reveals when we have veered off course. During the times we do not feel exhilarated, something within us needs attention. Any pain or discomfort that arises in our lives should be noticed and addressed, or it will fester. As much as we cherish our jubilation, sensations of pain or discomfort — the opposite side of the "joy coin" — are highly useful.

Pain and sadness occur in any normal life, but they should be balanced by corresponding feelings of joy and jubilation. As we address and resolve whatever brought us hardship, joy returns to say, "You are back in balance and harmony."

The memory of joy serves as a valuable indicator that can guide us back to our true selves. When we are off course, our joy will tell us. When we experience pain, our joy will notify us. When something is uncomfortable, our joy will alert us. When someone is abusive or controlling, our joy will speak to us. When we are not living our true purpose and fulfilling our heart's precious dreams, our joy will get our attention, too. When things become overwhelming, we can return to a joyful state, seeking that point of balance, stability, and true power.

Children are naturally joyful. When they aren't crying because of hunger, thirst, discomfort, or a painful experience, children spontaneously seek activities that feed them even more joy.

Joy is the barometer of the soul. It is the compelling force within that guides us, seeking activities that propel us forward to greater joy. True joy does not depend on materialism, as long as our basic needs are met. We create our own destiny, using our true sense of happiness as a guiding light.

The inspiring beauty of joy is that it gains tremendous value when shared. Joy profoundly expands when we share it with our family, friends, coworkers, and strangers. Walls that separate us crumble when we share our joy rather than our pain. For example, the power of our words can be increased substantially if "I miss you" is transformed into "I'm excited to see you again." As Charles Dickens wrote in his 1838 novel *Nicholas Nickleby*, "The pain of parting is nothing to the joy of meeting again."

In a recent survey of 53,000 children from 15 countries, children revealed that they tend to be happy regardless of the context of their lives.[1] In fact, the survey found that children tend to be more optimistic and happier than adults, regardless of their circumstances. From Norway to Ethiopia, researchers found no correlation between the lack of material goods and the satisfaction of the children. The survey from the Children's World project also found that "despite being generally happy, children in developed countries were relatively less satisfied with their body, appearance, and self-confidence."[2]

Where Joy Resides

Joy emerges from love and attention to the present moment, qualities which reside in the Heart Chakra, the spiritual center of the body. No one can express love without having some amount of jubilation. As expansive and positive energies, love and joy radiate their powerful spiritual qualities to everything and everyone nearby. Joy may be how we best demonstrate our love, as this potent energy enlivens all of the Divine Child's spiritual qualities, shining like a beacon in the world.

> Gratitude unlocks the fullness of life. It turns what we have into enough, and more. It turns denial into acceptance, chaos to order, confusion to clarity. It can turn a meal into a feast, a house into a home, a stranger into a friend.
>
> Melody Beattie

The expression of gratitude tells the Universe, "I love this experience, and I want more of it." Gratitude, love, and joy are wrapped together in a single bundle, and that energy radiating throughout the Universe will attract more of the same, engaging the natural phenomenon of resonance to work for you.

If we take care of someone or something without a shred of joy, that action emerges from devotion or duty, not necessarily an expression of joy or inner happiness. A programmed robot can take care of a dog, taking it for a walk, pouring water and food, and picking up dog poop. But a robot will never be able to express love or joy in the spiritual or energetic sense, because the robot does not possess these spiritual qualities as far as we know. Spontaneous joy, on the other hand, cascades naturally from our Heart centers in engaging ways.

How Our Joy Becomes Traumatized

Life can be exceedingly joyful and filled with fun. And life can also bring sadness, misery, and pain. Unhealed trauma results in chronic negativity. If we remain stuck in our trauma cycle filled with negative emotions without resolving them, that often turns into depression and bitterness. We must continue healing our past traumas until they release their psychic hold on our lives.

Other people in our lives, particularly authority figures, can suppress our natural joy. The damage usually begins at an early age and can occur in a number of subtle ways, such as when children are told to "settle down" when they become too excited for adults to handle. A parent, teacher, or babysitter can unintentionally traumatize a child's capacity for joy when they repeatedly take something away from the child, such as a favorite toy or stuffed animal that the young person treasures. Disconnecting children from the things that bring them joy forces them into emotional numbing, just as it does for adults.

Our parents and caretakers early in life can also traumatize our capacity for joy by not meeting our core needs, a concept Abraham Maslow discussed in his work. Consequently, we learn not to share, falling into a state of self-absorption. Remember the selfish seagulls in the movie *Finding Nemo* who continued chanting, "mine mine mine mine mine," when they saw the juicy crab as their next snack? Their self-absorbed reverie was finally interrupted by the instructive pelican, who reminded the flock of their mission to work together and find their missing friend Nemo.[3]

Sometimes it is easy to be so busy with our lives and fulfilling our own needs that we forget to be of service to others. If we aren't sharing like our tiny teachers tend to do, we lose out on the riches of life. The poet Tagore said, "I slept and dreamt that life was joy. I awoke and saw that life was service. I acted and behold, service was joy."

Losing touch with our inner child and natural joy happens when we buy into the dreams or delusions that others project upon us. That imposition could come from parents, as they want us to live a particular role or land a job that doesn't fulfill our innate purpose or ignite our passion. For example, employees may succumb to cultural or tribal pressures to take on a particular role, although unwanted.

We lose joy when we learn to seek love and approval from those who are unwilling or incapable of providing it. This can be described as a form of energetically prostituting the precious aspects of ourselves in exchange for something that is worth substantially less. For instance, we may take a job that is prestigious or high-paying but not satisfying, or when we marry someone whom our parents choose for us, rather than finding our partner with whom we naturally resonate on many levels.

Living the dreams that others want for us can quickly suffocate our natural sense of joy. The Divine Child becomes infected by the spiritual disease of inauthenticity, exchanging innate joy and passion for the bitterness of living another person's dream. In adults, this shows up as lethargy, boredom, apathy, or listlessness, where work does not inspire.

Grief and sadness are also negative expressions of joy, and these negative emotions primarily accumulate in the Heart Chakra as a "heavy heart." In my practice, many people with unresolved grief issues may end up having either heart or lung problems, because energy steps down from the fine to the dense levels of our reality, especially seen in the physical body.

It has been my observation that people who suffer heart attacks or lung issues usually have had their Heart Chakras traumatized on spiritual, mental, and emotional levels. If that trauma remains unhealed, then this vital energy center contracts and becomes congested like dirty engine oil. When the oil gets contaminated and not eliminated, the engine eventually seizes up and stops functioning properly. It is only a matter of time when our progress is halted.

When our emotional, mental, and spiritual centers and their corresponding energies have been traumatized, the energetic distortions often drop to the physical body level of our being, which is connected to the Root (First) Chakra. When someone experiences emotional trauma, that person also usually experiences some form of mental and spiritual trauma. Grief naturally emerges from the loss of someone we love or the passing of a cherished season of life, but grief must be handled carefully and processed, as it can become toxic when left unhealed.

The Pleasure Trap

While it has been demonized by religious orders for centuries, pleasure can be a wonderful thing that invigorates the body and elevates mood. Dr. Elisha Goldstein, an LA-based psychologist and author of books that include *Uncovering Happiness* and *The Now Effect*, created a coaching and mentorship program called "A Course of Mindful Living" that focuses on how to open up to joy in daily life.[4] On his website, he provides a list of 183 ways to pleasure yourself in healthy activities, such as knitting or crocheting, playing cards, or acting. The list is fun to read,[5] as you may discover which activities that resonate with you.

When our inner sense of true joy has been lost, however, we begin to seek momentary pleasure as its poor substitute, where it can become a trap. Conversations with friends and strangers on Facebook and other social media. Food. Caffeine. Cigarettes. Alcohol and other drugs. Roller coasters. Video games. Vacations. Sex, but not making love. Gambling. Feel-good group activities. All of these can be numbing devices that offer pleasure and a big momentary thrill, because they are commodities to be purchased. All of them come with a price.

But none of these bring true joy, because that precious energy is already within you awaiting to be expressed. Things that bring us pleasure can be beneficial, if it does not turn into an escape mechanism or addictive behavior.

The price of fleeting pleasure can be small or steep. Financial depletion. Poor health. Pain. Bloating. Anxiety. Hangovers. Fear. Isolation from loved ones. Feeling numb and empty. Addiction. Often, the pain and costs of momentary pleasure outweigh the short-term benefits that may have been gained.

For example, consider sexual abuse, a widespread tragedy that is strongly linked to pleasure but has aspects of power and control over others. Tragically, it is a very common and serious problem, and one that needs to be discussed more openly to facilitate healing and recovery. One in three women have been sexually abused, usually by a family member. One in four boys have been sexually abused. *These are known cases*, as an estimated 30 percent of sexual abuse is never reported.[6] This issue has become a global catastrophe and pandemic.

Sex trafficking turns this abuse to a sinister industry, where the horror is monetized by those who manipulate the victims. Many young women that are missing throughout the United States and around the world get caught in this $32 billion crime web, where young women are acquired by force, fraud, or deception with the intention of exploiting them for sex, slavery, servitude, forced labor, and even involuntary organ donation.

It is estimated that 200,000 women in America each year are forced into the sex trade, often lured with promises of exciting work with good pay to model, dance, or be a nanny for a wealthy family. Usually feeling lonely and isolated, these girls or women are seduced by a better life, then abducted and transported to a new area of the country. Their captors often administer drugs to the point of addiction and force the women into prostitution. Imprisoned in horrid living conditions, the captive women are frequently beaten and brainwashed.

This form of misogynistic inequality has had devastating consequences. Today, human trafficking ranks as the second largest criminal industry in the world, second to drugs and tied with arms dealing.[7]

When someone has been abused sexually, the Root and Second Chakras are corrupted and prematurely opened by the abuser. The state of fear grows in the victim, as the "flight-or-fight-or-freeze" response keeps the sufferer trapped in a vicious, unending cycle of nightmarish slavery.

The abuser usually does this out of the negative manifestation of control: manipulation. The energy of manipulation corrupts the Third Chakra — the energy center of personal power and self-control — which nearly destroys the will of the victim. Manipulation also corrupts the victim's Fourth Chakra, the seat of love, compassion, equality, and presence. The physical signs of sexual abuse include the following health and behavioral issues, where corresponding chakras have been corrupted:[8]

- Difficulty walking or sitting — First Chakra
- Bedwetting — Second Chakra
- Change in appetite — Third Chakra
- Pregnancy or contracting a sexually transmitted disease — First and Second Chakras
- Sudden refusal to participate in physical activities, like gym — First and Third Chakras
- Running away — First, Second, and Third Chakras
- Attaching very quickly to strangers or new adults — Third Chakra
- Reporting nightmares — First Chakra, due to excess fear
- "Bizarre, sophisticated, or unusual sexual knowledge or behavior" — First, Second, Third, and Fourth Chakras

Sometimes, signs of trauma can be mistaken for symptoms of attention deficit disorder (ADD) and attention deficit/hyperactivity disorder (ADHD), according to Taylor Laird, clinical director of the therapy program at the Exchange Club-Carl Perkins Center for the Prevention of Child Abuse.[9] Laird says, "Experiencing trauma can cause children to have difficulty regulating their emotions. Really, it's just that they have a lot in their mind that they're dealing with, like huge amounts of confusion and anger and trying to keep secrets." Laird said children who may have experienced trauma, including sexual abuse, may be seen as "acting out" or "out of control." Older children may display a lot of anger, become sexually promiscuous, or turn to drugs or alcohol as a form of self-medication.[10]

If you know of someone who exhibits these signs, please do something about it immediately. Seek out experts for the best way to proceed and report the problem. Otherwise, it perpetuates this ugly physical, emotional, mental, and spiritual disease, as both the victim and abuser continue to suffer in their unhealed states. By doing nothing, we become part of this pandemic.

A number of abused victims often become perpetrators. In a key study published in January 2018 in the *British Journal of Psychiatry*, 35 percent of 747 male perpetrators were early victims of sexual abuse.[11]

Sexual abuse is a very common reason why children stop playing. The symptoms of post-traumatic stress syndrome (PTSD) frequently appear. If the sexual abuse remains unhealed, depression is a common outcome. Researchers found that sex assault victims were *four times* more likely to have poor sleep, while another study found that 80 percent of teenage girls who experience sexual assault had mental health problems in the months following the abuse.[12]

Weight problems often ensue with sex abuse victims, as gaining weight may be a way of armoring in self-protection or holding on to deep pain. One study of 57,000 women revealed that those who experienced physical or sexual abuse as children were twice as likely to be addicted to food.[13] More than half of the women that Dr. Wendy Scinta, MD, works with at her medical weight loss practice in Manlius, NY, have experienced sexual abuse in their past.[14]

Any abuse can shut down inner joy. At the same time, know that when someone treats you terribly, it is also the abuser's cry for help, because the perpetrator committing the abuse is often doing it unconsciously. By acting out the destructive pattern over and over again, however, the abuser can then become consciously aware of his or her behavior.

The journey of healing awaits both the perpetrator and the abuser. With this understanding, we can be the light, compassion, and healing empathy that others need. We must recognize and actively call out traumatizing patterns, then stop them, while creating the space to heal ourselves and return to our joyful state.

The Plague of Depression

In his book *Lost Connections: Uncovering the Real Causes of Depression — and the Unexpected Solutions*, New York Times best-selling author and journalist Johann Hari describes the chemical imbalance myth surrounding depression, explaining that one in five U.S. adults is taking at least one drug for a psychiatric problem, and that antidepressant prescriptions have doubled in Britain in the past decade. Himself a previous sufferer of depression as a teen, and after swallowing antidepressants for 13 years, Hari inquired, "What has been causing depression and its twin, anxiety, to spiral in this way? I began to ask myself: Could it really be that in our separate heads, all of us had brain chemistries that were spontaneously malfunctioning at the same time?"[15] He was doubtful, and thus began a 40,000-mile trek around the world to interview hundreds of leading social scientists, psychologists, and psychiatrists to discover the cause.

Hari's impactful Ted Talk entitled "Everything You Think You Know About Addiction is Wrong" has been one of the most viewed of all time with more than 25 million views.[16] He says, "We have been telling ourselves this chemical story for 35 years, and every year, depression and gets worse." Hari points to statistics, where 65 to 80 percent of people on antidepressants fall into depression again within a year.[17]

"Drugs don't heal the underlying causes of depression," Hari says. He cites scientific evidence that shows depression is caused by key issues with how we live. Of the nine depression-causing factors, seven are rooted in disconnection. Journalist Azriel ReShel writes, "Disconnection from meaningful work, from other people, from meaningful values, and from childhood trauma. Disconnection from status and respect, from the natural world, and disconnection from a hopeful or secure future. Depression at its deepest roots, stems from a lack of connection. It is a disease of disconnection."

I further propose that depression arises from *being disconnected from ourselves*, especially from our Divine Child, which may have been suppressed, manipulated, or deceived, usually unconsciously by others. In other words, when our anger, rage, and fear caused by external trauma remains unhealed, that anger turns inward, unconsciously directed toward ourselves.

Hari says, "I found there is evidence that seven specific factors in the way we are living today are causing depression and anxiety to rise, alongside two real biological factors (such as your genes) that can combine with these forces to make it worse."[18] As our natural teachers, young children show us how to connect with others in ways that give our lives purpose and meaning.

In his book, Hari suggests seven reconnections to help heal depression and elevate mood. Reconnecting with other people, finding meaningful work, and subscribing to meaningful values are important. Reconnecting to sympathetic joy and "overcome the addiction we have to the self" are among other helpful ways to improve a depressed state. In his research, he discovered that doing something for others stopped the slide down into the dark recesses of depression, where reaching out to others and not trying to build ourselves up in solitary is critical. Finally, acknowledging and overcoming our childhood trauma is also necessary to restoring one's positive outlook and mood.

Trauma can cause us to stop playing and living joyfully, and usually it first happens when we are young children. The deep wounding can occur from a random incident, such as an accident, but more often than not, trauma starts with some sort of abuse that usually occurred in childhood. In my practice, I have found that abuse arises from the same unresolved trauma in past incarnations, and this trauma shows up in the energetic body as well.

These negative "samskaras," Sanskrit for "energetic imprints," then attract the same kind of abuse that was not healed in a past life, providing another opportunity for healing. In other words, being abused imprints the pattern of "needing" to be abused, which may be why victims unconsciously attract abusers with different faces until the original trauma cycle has been broken and healed. The cycle of abuse must be decisively halted by recognizing harm and inflicted trauma have taken place, then followed by loving and protecting our inner child. By engaging our Divine Child, we prepare the way for our Adult part to emerge and assist in our healing journey.

Healing must usually be done first at the finer levels of energy, including the emotional, mental, and spiritual levels of our being. When these levels are healed relative to the issue at hand, then the physical body can be healed, including the physical symptoms of depression or physical conditions.

Some energy and healing modalities are excellent for providing temporary relief but may not help with chronic issues. For example, massage therapy or acupuncture may address a physical issue temporarily and possibly even permanently, but if the cause of the condition is rooted in the other chakras and layers (i.e., emotional, mental, or spiritual levels), chronic conditions will often return.

I love both of these modalities and receive occasional treatments, but it has been my experience that healing any condition entails understanding the unique experience of the person. All healing involves learning about it. A "one-size-fits-all" approach — the magic bullet approach of traditional Western medicine — may not heal an individual condition and can even be risky if the origin of the wound has not been resolved.

Give yourself permission to be happy and joyful. Many of us have not had permission as little children from our parents and caretaker, where ourselves permission may be necessary. Surround yourself with people who smile and laugh, rather than those who are continually depressing. Life can be far more positive, hopeful, and joyful than miserable, painful, and tragic. The choice is up to you.

Your Artwork Drains or Increases Your Joy

Children smile as much as 400 times per day, according to research. But with adults, only 30 percent smile more than 20 times a day, and less than 14 percent of the population smiles less than five percent a day![19] This may explain why children often rebound more quickly from illness and accidents than adults.

I have worked with clients who have depression issues, only to discover that they have paintings or prints hanging on the walls that are not joyful. One of my clients fighting chronic sadness had a large portrait hanging above the fireplace in the living room, depicting the scene of a dead or dying animal who was about to be devoured by a vulture overhead. She had hardly chosen a picture of peace and happiness!

Vision boards have become popular over the past twenty years. Spiritual leaders, pop philosophers, and best-selling motivational books, such as *The Secret*, have encouraged people to create their own vision boards as a powerful tool to manifest their life's desires.[20] For some people, their vision board creations have helped their dreams come true. But for others, they remain disappointed, as their vision boards don't seem to magically materialize their goals.

The secret lies in their entire artwork, as my research over the past 25 years suggests. What is not always apparent is that our smaller vision boards conflict with our "larger vision board" — the art hanging on their walls at home, in their offices, on their body art via tattoos, or on their clothing. Sometimes words or popular colloquialisms posted in art can keep us trapped, such as the biblical scripture in 1 Timothy 4:8 that falsely promotes, "Bodily exercise profiteth little."

The art you wear, inscribe permanently into your skin, or hang on the walls of your home and workplace is your entire vision board, which collectively is creating your future. With some guidance, artwork can be used in powerful ways to attract an entirely new reality. It may be the reason why so many prolific inventors, innovators, and philosophers like Leonardo da Vinci and Michelangelo were also painters and sculptors. Change your art, and you can profoundly change your life experience.

How Art Can Extinguish Our Joy

The words and images we surround ourselves with — whether they be the art we have in our home, tattoos on our bodies, the clothing we wear, or the words we repeatedly read and believe — definitely impact our reality, as considerable research demonstrates. Art not only reflects our thoughts, emotions, and personal stories, it also creates the energies that pervade our lives, as I point out in my book entitled *The Power of Tattoos: Twelve Hidden Energy Secrets of Body Art Every Tattoo Enthusiast Should Know.*

Oscar Wilde wisely said, we become our art. For suffers of these types of negative conditions, I advocate removing any symbol, artwork, clothing, regular TV shows and radio programs, and reading materials from the home that are linked to sadness, grief, pain, torture, victimization, suffering, or death, especially key rooms like the living room, office, and bedroom where people spend the most time.

In my consulting practice working with numerous clients who suffer from chronic sadness, grief, or physical pain, I first examine their art around them to understand the quantity of nonverbal expressions and words linked to these conditions with which the client is resonating. Types of artwork in the "energy survey" I conduct with clients include wall art, permanent tattoos, clothing, TV and radio programs, books, magazines, and news sources they commonly read and digests. I have found an extraordinary correlation between these types of negative conditions and the symbolism, words, and images of artwork that the client absorbs and then assimilates.

Research confirms this connection as well. In a University of Pennsylvania study published in the December 2018 issue of *Journal of Social and Clinical Psychology*, researchers found that when students limited their use of Facebook, Snapchat, and Instagram to 30 minutes a day for three weeks, they experienced significant reductions in loneliness and depression.[21] The increased self-monitoring of time on social media had other beneficial impacts, including "significant decreases in anxiety and fear of missing out."

To experience joy at its fullest, steer clear of all forms of negative art in your home, body, and media. It is why all tattoos or art on our walls with images or words associated with death, disease, pain, misery, and other forms of negativity should be avoided. Repeatedly surrounding yourself with negative stories in movies, TV shows, video games, and books will have similar effects.

Depressing stories can have a deadly impact on your life — such as the biblical tale of mass genocide associated with the Noah and the ark, or the story of 42 children being torn apart limb by limb by two female bears "sent from god" because the kids made fun of the bald prophet Elisha.

In order to find joy, we need to undergo a detox from these toxic, negative influences. Just as a scrub our bodies and clean our kitchens on a daily basis, our art and words we surround ourselves with also need a good energetic cleansing.

Religious teachings that deny us of joy and advocate heavy suffering can be a modern form of spiritual martyrdom, which usually comes from implanted false messages early in life. "Suffering is good," "suffering is necessary to learn," "no pain, no gain," or "suffering will get me a high place in heaven" are common sayings that have become embedded in the collective unconscious of many.

Some passages of the Bible appear to make suffering a requirement for redemption. Psalms 34:19 says, "The righteous person may have many troubles, but the Lord delivers him from them all." While the first part of this passage may be true, this verse subtly expresses victimization, where one waits for a savior to send the rescue mission. James 1:12 teaches, "Blessed is the one who perseveres under trial because, having stood the test, that person will receive the crown of life that the Lord has promised to those who love him." Taking on extreme suffering is advised in numerous biblical passages, including Philippians 3:10: "I want to know Christ — yes, to know the power of his resurrection and participation in his sufferings, becoming like him in his death."

Widespread teachings like these can have a devastating effect on one's psyche and spirituality, as scapegoating is often used to guarantee restoration after "suffering a little while," as 1 Peter 5:10 advocates. These types of widespread teachings can quickly smother the energy of inner joy using the faulty tool of blind faith that overshadows the reasoning faculties, critical thinking, and analyzing abilities of our Divine Adult — a topic I will cover in future works.

False and negative teachings can victimize the sufferer who waits for an external rescue, as the negativity of burdens, suffering, guilt, and turmoil permeates one's consciousness. When these ideas are propagated at the tribal level in an organization or culture at large, the effects can be rather tragic and debilitating, producing extremism and fake news.

The energy of depression linked to religious beliefs was confirmed in a large study of more than 8,000 people from seven countries. Conducted in 2013 by a team of researchers led by Professor Michael King from University College London, the extensive study published in *Psychological Medicine* found that despite religious people having "good mental health habits and lifestyle," people of faith or "belief in some higher power or force than yourself that influences life" had significantly higher rates of depression than those with secular life views. In some countries such as the UK, the rate of depression was *three times higher* for believers than for the secular group.[22] Other prior studies examining the connection between mood and religious beliefs show mixed results, although likely all of those studies were conducted with substantially smaller populations.[23]

While each religion has some positive messages, it is essential to exercise our faculties of critical thinking, reasoning, and analysis to separate falsehoods from what is true. In his 1776 pamphlet *The American Crisis*, Thomas Paine wrote, "To argue with a man who has renounced the use and authority of reason, and whose philosophy consists in holding humanity in contempt is like administering medicine to the dead, or endeavoring to convert an atheist by scripture."

By leaving the violent, negative barbarism and incredible lies of our primordial ancestors, we can instead pass down a spiritual heritage of joy to our children that can only come from being rooted in truth and facts, rather than fantastical fiction. At the same time, it is essential to heal personal and cultural trauma that was inflicted upon our own Inner Child.

Smiling Can Increase Your Longevity

The imprint of a joyful smile can dramatically affect your emotions and even your life span, as recent studies suggest. In a surprising study in 2010 by Wayne State University, researchers examined the 1952 baseball cards of 230 Major League players, discovering that the smile of a baseball player could predict the span of his life. Players who did not smile in their photos lived an average of only 72.9 years, while those players who had beaming smiles lived an average of 79.9 years — nearly 10 percent longer.[24]

This demonstrates the phenomenon of how creating an imprint in a moment of time, such as a simple photograph that shows you smiling will make a positive impact on your future. Another interesting study by the University of Clermont-Ferrand in France showed that judgment was impaired when the smile was repressed.[25] A smile does not impact only the muscles of your face, it ripples throughout your entire mental outlook and elevates the soul.

How Joy and Financial Success Are Linked

Joy denotes both spiritual and financial success. Being naturally happy and joyful attracts many good things in life, as this energy radiates and draws similar energies to future experiences.

Studies show that happy people earn more money. Research published in the *Proceedings of the National Academy of Sciences* (PNAS) revealed that adolescents and young adults who report higher life satisfaction earn significantly higher levels of income later in life — as much as 73 percent more by age 29. A number of studies also found that richer people tend to be happier than average.[26]

Happy employees tend to earn more money because their optimism opens them up to opportunities and new experiences, says Lynda Spiegel, a human resources professional and founder of career coaching and the resume-writing service, Rising Star Resumes. She adds that happy employees view bad decisions as a learning opportunity rather than a personal failure. This sounds like how small children naturally operate.

> It is only when the mind is free from the old that it meets everything anew, and in that there is joy.
>
> Krishnamurti

Happy people record fewer sick days and are more productive. According to an empirical study published in Illinois Wesleyan University's *The Park Place Economist*, happy workers stay home 15 fewer days a year, on average, than unhappy employees — and live up to 10 years longer, as was the case with the baseball players who smiled in their baseball card photos.[27] Be sure to take more photos of you smiling, where distributed images of you smiling will have a profound energetic impact.

Researchers at the University of Warwick in Coventry, England, also found that happy people are more productive. Professors Andrew Oswald, Eugenio Proto, and Daniel Sgroi wrote in their paper "Happiness and Productivity" that randomly selected individuals who felt happier were up to twelve percent more productive than those who were not. Happy people invest in themselves, earning more because they are always improving themselves with exercising, learning more, and investing in their futures, said Elle Kaplan, CEO and founder of investment firm LexION Capital.[28]

How To Reignite Your Joy and Happiness

Joy is essential for all success in life. Joy is the spiritual lifeblood of our soul. Here are some tips that can help activate joy in every area of your life:

- <u>Heal your past</u>. The emotional and mental junk that has been inflicted upon you are roadblocks to your greater happiness and success. Of all of the healing modalities I've studied and trained in, EFT (Emotional Freedom Technique) has been the easiest and most powerful healing modality I have found that addresses all levels of our being — physical, emotional, mental, and spiritual. EFT Tapping is like knocking on the door of the chakras: "Knock, and the door shall be opened unto you," as the wise proverb goes. Anyone can tap, including small children. I recommend finding a good EFT practitioner and try it out for at least several sessions, as you cannot exercise once and see big results in your life. After five years of tapping, I continue to regularly tap via video conferencing with two of my favorite practitioners located in Illinois, and I tap on my own throughout the day, too, which helps balance my energy and clear out unwanted energetic clutter. EFT tapping can be especially helpful to alleviate anxiety and depression.

- <u>Be kind to yourself with words that empower the healing process and your future</u>. Horacio Jones, author of *I Am the Love of My Life: Unbroken*, wrote, "Instead of saying, 'I'm damaged, I'm broken, I have trust issues' — say 'I'm healing, I'm rediscovering myself, I'm starting over.'"

> Stay away from negative people. They have a problem for every solution.
>
> Albert Einstein

- <u>Be social</u>. Children are naturally social. As animals, we are meant to be social beings. Isolation stifles joyful companionship.

- <u>Practice looking at the optimistic side of life</u>. See everything as a learning, even when someone says something negative or critical about you. Ask yourself, "What can I learn from this, and how can I use this in a positive direction that moves me forward? What is true about this that can help me shift?"

- <u>Stop beating yourself up</u>. Many of us can be our own worst enemies. We often take over the roles of beating ourselves up after the abuse from others stops. Self-abuse comes from the false belief that "I am not worthy of love and acceptance." When you heal the part that is self-defeating, it opens up your joy, and you will begin to spontaneously compliment yourself more and treat yourself better.

Joy tells you when you are on track. While thrills feed you temporary excitement and pleasures that may or may not ultimately be good for you, authentic joy transcends momentary pleasure with long-term satisfactions.

This endless fountain of joy within enlivens us. Desmond Tutu said, "Discovering more joy does not save us from the inevitability of hardship and heartbreak. In fact, we may cry more easily, but we will laugh more easily too. Perhaps we are just more alive. Yet as we discover more joy, we can face suffering in a way that ennobles rather than embitters. We have hardship without becoming hard. We have heartbreaks without being broken."

Are you feeling exhausted or burned out, not really knowing your true purpose? Learning about what feeds your joy is the secret to finding your passion and purpose in life. Discovering adventures inside of yourself comes from playful curiosity and moving forward to even greater amounts of joy.

This thrilling adventure of your soul requires another essential ingredient that all small children naturally possess and use, but it is not so easy for adults who get caught in the rut of noise and excess movement. This magical quality within you is an essential ingredient for finding your passion and joy: observing.

---

[1] http://www.isciweb.org/_Uploads/dbsAttachedFiles/ChildrensWorlds2015-FullReport-Final.pdf

[2] https://qz.com/405960/most-children-are-happy-no-matter-what-but-materialism-catches-up-eventually/

[3] https://www.youtube.com/watch?v=p-3e0EkvIEM

[4] https://elishagoldstein.com/ecourses/basics-of-mindfulness-meditation/

[5] http://elishagoldstein.com/assets/183-pleasurable-activities-to-choose-from.pdf

[6] https://laurenskids.org/awareness/about-faqs/facts-and-stats/

[7] https://www.psychologytoday.com/us/blog/reading-between-the-headlines/201304/human-trafficking-in-america

[8] https://www.jacksonsun.com/story/news/local/2019/01/03/child-sexual-abuse-statutory-rape-west-tennessee-spotting-signs-reporting/2378297002/

[9] IBID

[10] IBID

[11] https://www.cambridge.org/core/journals/the-british-journal-of-psychiatry/article/cycle-of-child-sexual-abuse-links-between-being-a-victim-and-becoming-a-perpetrator/A98434C25DB8619FB8F1E8654B651A88

[12] https://www.theguardian.com/society/2018/jul/22/sexually-abused-teenage-girls-likely-suffer-mental-health-issues-months-later-study

[13] https://www.theatlantic.com/health/archive/2015/12/sexual-abuse-victims-obesity/420186/

[14] https://www.syracuse.com/news/index.ssf/2010/07/linking_sexual_abuse_to_obesit.html

[15] https://upliftconnect.com/transforming-depression-through-connection/

[16] https://2018.johannhari.com/index.php/biography/

[17] https://upliftconnect.com/transforming-depression-through-connection/

[18] https://upliftconnect.com/transforming-depression-through-connection/

[19] http://www.forbes.com/sites/ericsavitz/2011/03/22/the-untapped-power-of-smiling/

[20] https://www.huffpost.com/entry/the-scientific-reason-why_b_6392274

[21] https://www.health.harvard.edu/blog/is-a-steady-diet-of-social-media-unhealthy-2018122115600

[22] https://www.huffingtonpost.co.uk/dr-raj-persaud/religion-depression_b_3928675.html?utm_hp_ref=uk&guccounter=1

[23] https://www.ncbi.nlm.nih.gov/pmc/articles/PMC3426191/

[24] http://healthland.time.com/2010/03/25/grinning-for-a-longer-life/

[25] http://www.forbes.com/sites/ericsavitz/2011/03/22/the-untapped-power-of-smiling/

[26] https://www.pnas.org/content/109/49/19953

[27] https://digitalcommons.iwu.edu/cgi/viewcontent.cgi?referer=&httpsredir=1&article=1346&context=parkplace

[28] https://www.huffingtonpost.com/gobankingrates/why-happy-people-earn-mor_b_8038640.html

Observant

To acquire knowledge, one must study;
but to acquire wisdom, one must observe.

Marilyn vos Savant
American author, playwright

After my nephew Connor was born, the extended family grew concerned by how quiet he was. As a baby, Connor was not too vocal during his first year, spending most of his time simply staring at people without expressing himself or reacting to his surroundings.

For many, silence and observing can be uncomfortable. Connor was just being Connor, and it made other people uncomfortable. Some of us began to wonder, "Is he ok?" But Connor was using one of the most powerful energies that we all have within ourselves: the ability to simply observe.

By silently turning our full awareness to observe the world around us, we learn rapidly. Observation opens the portal to all learning and advancement. But we should not confuse observation with passivity. Observation can be an active and dynamic state that allows us to get "into the zone" and learn. With our senses attuned to a present state of receptivity and keen interest, we can discover more about the world around us and how we relate to it.

> Sometimes it is the quiet observer who sees the most.
>
> Kathryn L. Nelson
> *Pemberley Manor*

In a culture focused primarily on outer appearances, we have created external saviors for ourselves. The ubiquitous entertainment on screens, the magic bullet cures of medicine, the ever-changing styles of the fashion industry, the invention of numerous gods in religion — and now, the Internet and social media all captivate our attention in hopes for a better life. While useful, these pursuits also may serve as noise and distractions from our true power that awaits. After all, you are destined to do greater things, as Jesus and other spiritual leaders have said for millennia. Our true salvation comes by learning about the universe within, where we can understand what our real potential is. It begins with our observant Divine Child.

For a baby, observation happens in both worlds. The first level of growth and evolution, often connected to the Root (First) Chakra, relates to a focus on personal needs where we learn about our own identity and capabilities. The moment this energy center is activated while even in the womb, the advanced fetus sucks its thumb and wiggles around. The awareness of self has begun.

Babies are absorbing and learning about the external world around them. In a series of experiments with eleven-month-olds published in April 2015 in the journal *Science*, Johns Hopkins University researchers found that surprising information formed the seeds for learning. When the babies were given surprising or contradictory information, it helped them test and confirm their knowledge, causing them to learn faster than those who were given information that was not predictable.[1]

New and unexpected experiences accelerate our learning and growth, and observation makes us truly magical, pushing the boundaries of our potential. In order to grow and evolve, we must exit our comfort zones and embrace completely different ideas, interesting people, and new experiences.

Where the Observer Resides Within Us

The spiritual quality of observing lies in the upper chakras, predominantly with the Crown and Brow (Seventh and Sixth) Chakras. The Crown Chakra is the seat of infinite possibilities, the quantum soup of the Universe. Observation is connected to this powerful energy center, where it pulls from the infinite field of possibilities that helps us discover what is within reach. Using the five senses and this energy center, we can connect to the Universe and learn more about it.

As many masters and philosophers have said, "all things are possible." Children reside naturally in this consciousness of magical possibilities. They have not yet learned to doubt and be cynical, but look at reality from a standpoint of experimentation. The childlike mind exclaims, "Let's try this and see what happens!"

The Ajna — Sanskrit for "perceive", "command, or "beyond wisdom" — is the Sixth chakra located at the brow, the seat of awareness and intuition. Observation also connects us to this energetic center of perception. Often called the Third Eye, the Sixth chakra is the center for inspiration, triggering imagination and new ideas. This gets us moving forward in new directions. "People who possess a thirst for knowledge, are keen observers, and possess a compassionate heart, hold the requisite key for learning and sharing their knowledge with other people," wrote Kilroy J. Oldster.

Why We Stop Observing

Observation plays a big role in childhood, and it may well be both an innate and learned behavior. Former FBI counterintelligence agent, Joe Navarro, an expert on nonverbal communications and body language, said observation was crucial for human survival, as our ancestors lived in small groups where it was vital to observe others and the world around them.[2] He also argued that as the human species evolved over time while proximity drew us physically closer, it changed how we view, observe, and assess one another. The diminished need to be "on alert" for our own survival, we unfortunately have lost much of our observation skills that can help us in other areas of success, Navarro says.

Today, technology has provided numerous distractions such as cell phones, online games, texting, music and TV playing in restaurants, and social media, where the average teen spends 9 hours a day — a lifetime equivalent of spending 24 years online.[3] It seems our culture celebrates multitasking abilities more than valuing silence and observation, with the mistaken idea that "I will produce more if I do more."

We all have a tribal urge to "stay busy" and shine as a productive star, as impressing others may bring temporary rewards. We have been seduced to think we can manage a number of things simultaneously, but multitasking is an oxymoron. "The human brain doesn't really multitask," says Art Markman, cognitive psychologist and author of *Smart Thinking*. "What the human brain does is what I call time-sharing." While the brain can actively think about one task at a time, the shift is so rapid that it *feels* like we are multitasking. But in reality, it is actually time-sharing, much like one vacationer leaves a timeshare property with another one moving in immediately afterwards.[4]

It's no wonder why we are pressured to multitask. In the early 1980s, Buckminster Fuller unveiled his theory of his famous "Knowledge Doubling Curve" after he discovered that knowledge doubled in the world every century until 1900. During the Industrial Revolution driven by the sudden growth in scientific research and discovery, the growth of knowledge has accelerated exponentially. Recent research found that knowledge doubles approximately every 13 months. And now, we now generate the same amount of information *in just two days* that it took humanity over 300,000 years to generate previously. IBM now says that knowledge doubles every 12 hours, rather than every 12 months.[5]

Technology may be convenient in many ways, but it also overloads us with data, creating tremendous stress. The noise of information overpowers precious moments of silence, but our powers of observation provide us with magical opportunities for learning and growth.

In our data-oriented age, marketers and even governments carefully package information so that we receive a steady, curated diet meant to serve a particular agenda. These actors, who often remain hidden behind algorithms, tell us not *how* to think but *what* to think. Entertainment and news blur together when talking heads argue on air to feed our hungry appetites, much like a verbal wrestling match. We may fail to differentiate between news and entertainment due to the mental exhaustion of continual noise pollution bombarding us wherever we go.

As famed journalist Bill Moyers said, "When you mix fiction and news, you diminish the distinction between truth and fiction, and you wear down the audience's own discriminating power to judge." With news divisions of media giants largely reporting to the entertainment divisions, it is now difficult to get most people's attention without sensationalism.[6]

Today, we learn in shallower ways through the packaged delivery of bite-sized information, rather than through our own quiet observation or from sustained reflection, which can be gained by reading a book, for example. In 2014, Pew Research Center reported that 25 percent of American adults had not read a single book in a year, which is triple the rate of non-readers in 1978.[7]

During the past 20 years, attention spans have been trained by media and technology giants to be much shorter. In a multi-media presentation, such as a television news show, it is challenging to pull away for a minute or two and quietly contemplate the show when video streams, a multitude of sounds, and induced drama are designed to be compelling so that the consumer will stay glued to the program. True, we technically can read books on our smartphones, but a quick fix of "info-tainment" remains only a click away.

Constantly playing a TV or radio produces problems for the human psyche and health. Children from noisier homes suffer problems that include increased anxiety, delayed language skills, less cognitive growth, and impaired resilience, according to a study by Theodore Wachs, a Purdue University professor of psychological sciences.[8] Workplace noise, cars, and airplanes also have been found to have a significant negative impact on our well-being and health, including chronic stress, high blood pressure, and heart disease.[9] Imagine the "info stress" that a bartender or waiter absorbs while having multiple TVs burping all day and night in a bar or restaurant.

Quiet observation allows for better contemplation, with much of the external noise removed during the observing process. As the philosopher and literary critic George Steiner said, "There is something terribly wrong with a culture inebriated by noise and gregariousness."

The Value of Silent Observation

Observing increases our chances for success in every aspect of life. Maria Montessori used observation as the cornerstone for developing her methods for educating children. To her, we practice observation as an art, a skill to be developed. As she carefully watched children learn, she reflected on her observations of children to refine her teaching methods.

We spontaneously innovate when we engage in observation. Nature herself provides a wonderful and vast sanctuary to experience peace, while the higher mind engages in sweet silence. Radhanath Swami said, "Mother Nature speaks in a language understood within the peaceful mind of the sincere observer." Many inventors created new things while engaged in the observation and the playful exploration of nature.

When Swiss engineer George de Mestral took his dog on a hunting trip in the Alps in 1941, his pants and dog were covered in sticky burdock burs. Curious about the stickiness, de Mestral put a bur under the microscope to study them. When he saw the thousands of tiny hooks that efficiently bound themselves to nearly every type of fabric or dog hair, de Mestral realized he could create a synthetic form. Years after filing the patent for his invention called Velcro in 1955, it eventually became a success after hitting the market in the early 1960s.[10] In fact, Buzz Aldrin used Velcro to strap the Omega Speedmaster watch around his suit when he took America's first spacewalk in July 1969.[11]

Other great inventions have been created by observing nature. Termite mounds inspired an elaborate chimney cooling system for large office complexes, and NASA scientists developed a drag-reducing coating on boat hulls and ships after examining the microscopic scales on shark skin. The new coating for boats was so successful that competition authorities in the Americas'

Cup sailing race deemed it an unfair advantage to help the *Stars and Strips* boat win in 1987 and subsequently banned the nature-inspired technology. Later, it was reinstated.[12]

How Successful People Use Observation

In his article "Seven Behaviors That Really Successful People Have Mastered," Stuart Leung writes about one of the seven key factors that creates success, "You'll notice that highly successful people love to read and crave learning more. They are always absorbing more information they can apply to their lives and careers. This knowledge helps them constantly adapt and evolve."[13]

Psychologists and neuroscientists have been studying elite athletes, such as Serena Williams, to determine how they perform under extreme pressure to accomplish incredible wins. Williams succeeded in breathtaking comebacks, including at the 2003 and 2005 Australian Open, at Wimbledon in 2009, and at the China Open in 2014, where she snatched the win after her opponents served a match point.[14]

Scientists have now identified a phenomenon called the "quiet eye," marked by an enhanced visual perception that sharpens the athletes' concentration. The quiet eye appears to help at times of heightened stress, and researchers believe it may even lead to the "flow state" that has been described by psychologist Mihály Csíkszentmihályi in his 1990 book, *Finding Flow*.

In his groundbreaking work, Csíkszentmihályi outlines ten characteristics that are the secret to achieving the flow state, half of which are part of "silent observation." These associated factors include 1) concentration and focus, 2) losing feelings of self-consciousness, 3) timelessness; losing track of time passing, 4) lack of awareness of physical needs, and 5) complete focus on the activity itself.[15]

The flow state, a miraculous place of elation, brings immense joy. Kids don't need advice from athletes and experts on how to produce a flow state. Children know naturally how to be in it. Athletes and the rest of us need to relearn this from children — or simply recall or reactivate that state that may lie dormant inside ourselves. Children naturally do this, entering a sort of hypnotic state where they get absorbed in the present moment.

Activate Your Power of Observation

To succeed in nearly everything in life, you must increase your capacity to simply observe. As you watch silently for long periods of time, new discoveries occur that open the world to you. Star athletes, business leaders, and artistic visionaries, for example, must unlock and cultivate this critical skill in order to succeed.

Build on your success by modeling your life based on people who have already accomplished something that you want to achieve. By observing someone who has achieved weight loss and maintained an ideal weight, for example, we can discover the positive habits and behaviors of that person that led to their successful outcome. Asking questions and listening can be a part of the modeling process. We learn from our mentors by overcoming any bashfulness and simply requesting feedback in areas we need to excel.

Increase your ability to silently observe by trying these suggestions:

- Spend time each day quietly observing others. Best-selling author Eckhart Tolle created his most magnificent works, including *The Power of Now* and *A New Earth: Awakening to Your Life's Purpose*, after sitting quietly for two years on a park bench observing people while he was homeless.[16]
- Spend more time in nature observing it. The great lessons of life can be found in Mother Nature. Its healing energy will help bring balance and nurturing to you as well.
- Take a goal that you want to achieve, then model someone who has accomplished it. Interview that person to find out what exactly he or she did to achieve the outcome, then write down those keys to success and emulate them.

> Life is when we exist to observe and enjoy the beauties of nature, meditation is when we observe the beauties of the observer.
>
> Debasish Mridha, MD

- Meditate daily. Meditation has been found to reduce stress and anxiety, promote emotional health, increase attention span, reduce age-related memory loss, generate kindness, and improve decision-making. It is the power of being still in quiet observation.

- Practice observing your thoughts and emotions. In an externally focused world, many people are out of touch with themselves, especially with their emotions. We can grow tremendously through quiet contemplation and a daily meditation practice of 15 to 20 minutes consisting of complete silence, where watching our own thoughts and emotions is the only practice we do. We can calm the noise of the mind — which the Daoists affectionately refer to as the "monkey mind" — by simply observing the breath in silent meditation. The benefits of this practice are extraordinary.
- Slow down. The rate of new technology grows exponentially, and our speedy world is accelerating even faster. As chaos and the noise of the world increases, the need for slowing down to achieve balance will become increasingly critical.
- Ask lots of questions. The more questions we ask, the better answers we get. Small children spontaneously ask questions as a way of active observation. Asking makes us more open, wiser, happier, and improves the quality of our lives.

Observation facilitates the process of discovery, where we learn about our needs at each level, how important are those needs, and what we need to do individually to get them fulfilled. Through observation, we exercise this important quality that helps us eliminate anxiety and dissolve our fears.

Small children naturally use the tool of observation, which is why anxiety and fear are foreign to them. But for many adults, we have forgotten how to live in this state. Practicing silent observation will help restore our power through grounding. Our small spiritual teachers are our role models to teach us how to thrive in this related state of observation: being present.

---

[1] http://time.com/3769234/heres-a-new-trick-to-help-babies-learn-faster/

[2] https://www.psychologytoday.com/us/blog/spycatcher/201201/becoming-great-observer

[3] https://qz.com/1367506/pew-research-teens-worried-they-spend-too-much-time-on-phones/?fbclid=IwAR0IzcixY6QiYtbf_3jF9_nT6gsgCXHl24e2oQWI8k2x4WgwX_eTrDwCppl

4 https://www.entrepreneur.com/article/225865

5 https://tribune.com.pk/story/1855519/6-data-kings-new-crown/

6 http://www.medialit.org/reading-room/whatever-happened-news

7 https://www.theatlantic.com/business/archive/2014/01/the-decline-of-the-american-book-lover/283222/

8 https://www.newswise.com/articles/view/9111/.

9 https://www.verywellmind.com/stress-and-noise-pollution-how-you-may-be-at-risk-3145041

10 https://www.bloomberg.com/news/photo-essays/2015-02-23/14-smart-inventions-inspired-by-nature-biomimicry

11 http://www.thejewelleryeditor.com/watches/article/omega-speedmaster-moonwatch-history/

12 https://cosmosmagazine.com/technology/technologies-inspired-by-nature

13 https://www.salesforce.com/blog/2014/09/how-to-behave-successful.html

14 http://www.bbc.com/future/story/20180627-is-quiet-eye-the-secret-to-success-for-athletes

15 https://www.huffingtonpost.com/alayna-kennedy/flow-state-what-it-is-and_b_9607084.html

16 https://www.thesunmagazine.org/issues/319/beyond-happiness-and-unhappiness

Present

It's being here now that's important. There's no past and there's no future. Time is a very misleading thing. All there ever is the now. We can gain experience from the past, but we can't relive it; and we can hope for the future, but we don't know if there is one.

George Harrison

The only real moment we have is now. Tomorrow is a faint dream, and yesterday is a fleeting memory. "You must live in the present, launch yourself on every wave, find your eternity in each moment," wrote Henry David Thoreau.

Small children live in the consciousness of the present moment naturally and spontaneously. This ability to reconnect with this childlike trait can be magical for us as adults. Being present is what makes us alive and passionate. Living in the present fuels our dreams and allows us to to create powerfully with soul purpose.

As children, our purity and innocence allow us to live richer lives with greater ease by being present. Our natural state of presence connects us more fully with ourselves and the world around us. We express authenticity living in the present moment, the seat of truth. By removing the burden of being pulled back into the past or having anxiety about the future, we liberate ourselves.

Where Presence Is

Love, compassion, and truth reside in the Heart Chakra, the energetic center of the body that connects us to the present. The upper three chakras create the future, while the lower three chakras below the Heart center connect to the past, based on conditioned responses of the physical, emotional, and mental bodies.

"People don't realize that now is all there ever is; there is no past or future except as memory or anticipation in your mind," said Eckhart Tolle. As we grow into adulthood, we learn about important things like structure, planning, protection, and other key characteristics of the "Divine Adult." We can protect and support the Divine Child. But for some, over-planning can arise out of fear to protect ourselves rather than coming from a place of joy.

> Stop longing. You poison today's ease,
> reaching always for tomorrow.
>
> Robin Hobb
> *Fool's Errand*

I'm a big fan of the vast research done at the renowned HeartMath Institute, a global leader in research on heart-based living and global coherence. Their mission is to help people of all ages reduce stress, build energy and resilience, and help self-regulate emotions through the Institute's research and technology. Their work is largely centered on the heart area, where HeartMath scientists have discovered that we connect to others globally through this powerful energy center.[1]

Much of the work at HeartMath Institute focuses on being present.[2] When we are truly present, the connections with ourselves and others become heart-centered. This allows us to not only focus, but to open up our hearts to healing energy that connects us to others.

Love is one of those Hallmark greeting card terms that we use loosely but may be more difficult to grasp. Small children don't talk about love. They simply *embody* love, especially when they are sharing their gifts. We can think of love less as a mushy gushy feeling and more as a focused, open, and authentic connection to others in the present moment. *The expression of love is determined by the extent we share our 21 Divine Child gifts with others.*

Perhaps children instinctively know more about love than most of pop culture leaders who sell millions of books on the subject. Loving kindness naturally pours from us when we are in the present moment, focusing on what is before us with openness, authenticity, and empathy.

Why We Stop Being Present

From the time we take our first breaths, our thirsty minds and bodies crave learning. Babies fully live in each moment, discovering more about themselves and the world around them. Perhaps children have boundless energy because they live in the present moment. They concentrate on here and now, rather than waste energy on the past or future that is but a faint idea.

Children experience negative emotions, but they are not encumbered by them. They are able to pass through these states without being caught in their negative cycles. For us adults, however, negative emotions tax our bodies and stress our minds, causing us to feel tired. Negative emotions are generally rooted in the past, which is why they exhaust us.

Worry and anxiety affect nearly 40 million American adults, triggering the "fight-or-flight" response that puts the body on red alert. The sympathetic nervous system kicks into gear, releasing stress hormones such as cortisol. This can raise blood sugar levels and triglycerides, causing physical symptoms such as dizziness, elevated heartbeat, fatigue, dry mouth, headaches, inability to concentrate, muscle aches, nervousness, muscle tension, trembling and twitching, shortness of breath, and inflammation in the body.[3]

Worry and anxiety tax our physical, emotional, mental, and spiritual wellbeing. In a survey by the American Psychiatric Association released in May 2018, statistics show that Americans are more anxious than the previous year, with 39 percent of people reporting that they feel more anxious.[4] While Millennials are the most anxious generation, Baby Boomers had the greatest increase in anxiety at seven percent higher than the previous year.

The financial toll on our wallets is tremendous. Anxiety, the top mental health problem in America today, costs us more than $42 billion a year, nearly a third of the total $148 billion mental health bill for Americans.[5] People suffering from anxiety are three to five times more likely to visit the doctor and six times more likely to be hospitalized for psychiatric disorders than non-sufferers. Anxiety disorders plague more than 18 percent of U.S. adults, but curiously, babies and small children typically don't suffer from worry or anxiety.

In 2018, record numbers of college students sought help for anxiety and depression. In spring 2017, nearly 40 percent of college students said it was difficult for them to function because they felt so depressed, and 61 percent of students said they had felt "overwhelming anxiety" during the same time period in the prior year, according to an American College Health Association survey of more than 63,000 students attending 92 schools.[6]

Schools added mental health staff, such as Ohio State University who hired a dozen mental health clinicians during the 2016-2017 academic year. Additionally, OSU launched a counseling mobile app where students could make appointments, practice breathing exercises online, listen to cheerful playlists, and contact the clinic in case of emergency. Virginia Tech University also opened multiple satellite counseling clinics where students hang out, including above the Starbucks, in the graduate student center, and in the athletic department.[7]

We have built our entire society around attempts to escape from the present moment, which has produced an epidemic of worry and anxiety. We have pulled away from our inner child so much that we no longer know ourselves. Zen philosopher Alan Wilson Watts said:

> We must abandon completely the notion of blaming the past for any kind of situation we're in and reverse our thinking and see that the past always flows back form the present. That now is the creative point of life. So you see, it's like the idea of forgiving somebody, you change the meaning of the past by doing that...Also watch the flow of music. The melody as its expressed is changed by notes that come later. Just as the meaning of a sentence...you wait till later to find out what the sentence means...The present is always changing the past.

Sometimes we feel stuck, because we forget our point of power in the present, the power to not only change the future but also to change the meaning of the past. Our ability to create change in the present moment is often more potent than we usually believe.

Remaining grounded and connected to our Heart center is essential to living in the present moment. Recent research by the HeartMath Institute shows how the heart and brain are interconnected, continually sending each other energy and information. When we experience feelings of anxiety, anger, frustration, or insecurity, our heart rhythms become more erratic.[8] Those messages are then sent to the brain, which recognizes them as negative or stressful feelings. Chaotic heart rhythms also cloud our ability to think clearly.

Negative emotions serve a valuable purpose by informing us when something has become disharmonious or out of balance. But if we dwell on these negative emotions rather than resolve them, we become disconnected from the present, lost in the memory of what happened that frustrated or angered us, and even paralyzed by fear. When we believe that something terrible or unsafe that we experienced may occur again, the danger alarms go off, and the repetition of living that fearful past over and over in our heads creates a new unwanted friend that lives in a negative future — anxiety.

Engaging in the fear response and getting hooked into its ugly cycle is one of the ways we learn to chronically worry and feel anxious. Trauma causes stress, and if we keep reliving the same trauma over and over again, we risk shutting down. For people who have experienced a serious accident, rape, violent personal assault, or another traumatic event, post-traumatic stress syndrome (PTSD) can become the norm.

Coping may be difficult for the victim when flashbacks, nightmares, severe anxiety, and other symptoms show up, sometimes even years after the traumatic event has occurred.[9] The recurring pain is not meant to become a way of life full of suffering and difficulty. Instead, pain is a helpful signal that is calling for healing of the original wounding and experiencing complete restoration. Pain says, "It is time to shift."

Early childhood trauma pulls us away from our natural childlike way of being present and playful, sending us into a chaotic and repetitive fear patterns of anxiety, worry, and stress. When we do not address and heal early trauma, it quickly becomes a repetitive cycle that keeps us trapped.

Distractions are another major cause that disables our ability to be present. In the past century, disruptive technologies have brought us innovative and wonderful ways of living but have dramatically accelerated our detachment from our powerful childlike energies. The distractive nature of many of our recent breakthroughs is not only disastrous emotionally and mentally, but also problematic on spiritual and physical levels as well.

Today, the average American child owns a smartphone by age ten. By age twelve, 50 percent of children have social media accounts on primarily Facebook and Instagram.[10] About 51 percent of German children ages 6 to 13 reported having their own cell phones, according to a 2016 study by the Media Education Research Association Southwest's long-term KIM study in Germany.[11]

While many parents are pressured by their children to give them cell phones, some parents resist. In a recent interview, Microsoft magnate Bill Gates said he didn't allow his children to have cell phones until they entered high school, stating that age 14 is the safest age for children to have a smartphone.[12]

Parents and children alike are being distracted by their cell phones. In 2016, consumers spent five hours a day on their mobile devices, according to analytics firm Flurry.[13] This was *double* the time spent just three years earlier. Another study revealed that time spent on mobile apps increased 69 percent from 2014 to 2015, while time spent on social media apps increased a whopping 394 percent year over year.[14]

Today, many people could never imagine living without their cell phones. In a poll conducted by Leger, a large market research and polling firm in Canada, ten percent of respondents said that "they would rather lose their mother-in-law than their cell phones."[15]

The love affair with our cell phones has led to grave consequences. From 1999 to 2014, brain cancer replaced leukemia as the top cancer-causing death among U.S. children and adolescents aged 1 to 19 years, accounting for three out of ten cancer deaths in 2014,[16] and some researchers believe that the microwave frequencies operating on the cell phone and other wireless devices may be the cause. Worldwide, the incidence of brain cancer has increased 50 percent among children under 15 years from 1975 to 1995, according to data from the World Health Organization.[17] In a study published in May 2011, WHO researchers found that "heavy users" who operated their cell phone 30 minutes per day over a ten-year period up to the year 2004 showed a 40 percent increased risk of gliomas, a type of cancer that occurs in the brain and spinal cord which comprises about 80 percent of all malignant tumors.[18]

In the United Kingdom, more than 50 percent of seven-year-olds own a mobile phone, with that number reaching 75 percent by the age of ten. Experts there say that children who use cell phones could be up to five times more likely to develop a brain tumor than adults.[19] Dr. Justin Stebbing, a cancer specialist at Imperial College London, said, "Their cells are still growing, so they could be more sensitive to DNA damage."

Researchers say that the skulls of children are much thinner and less developed than those in adults, potentially allowing more radiation to affect the brain and nervous system. When a kid holds a mobile phone or Wi-Fi-based toy against her ear, she can absorb up to ten times more radio frequency (RF) energy than an adult can, according to a study review in the *Journal of Microscopy and Ultrastructure*.[20] The U.K. Department of Health urges that young children should only use their cell phones in case of emergency.

"Children may be more vulnerable because of their developing nervous system, the greater absorption of energy in the tissues of the head, and a longer lifetime of exposure," explains British biochemist Sir William Stewart after completing the UK government report, "Mobile Phones and Health."[21] Scientists in other countries are equally alarmed. After brain tumors became the leading cause of death in children under 15, Australian Senator Lyn Allison said, "Studies show there has been a 40 percent across-the-board increase in the number of brain tumors in the past twenty years. That twenty years has coincided with the use of mobile phone and many other radio frequencies."[22]

Dr. Anthony B. Miller, a Toronto physician and epidemiologist specializing in the causes of cancer, wrote a letter dated August 4, 2016, to the Petaluma City School district in California, where he expressed his deep "concern over the increasing exposure of children in schools to Radiofrequency Fields (e.g., from Wi-Fi, as required for cell phones and iPads, and emitted by cell towers) and the lack of concern expressed by many councils, governments and School Boards on this issue." An excerpt from his letter is as follows:

> In 2011, an IARC working group designated radiofrequency fields as a class 2B carcinogen, a possible human carcinogen. Since that review a number of additional studies have been reported. One of the most important was a large case-control study in France, which found a doubling of risk of glioma, the most malignant form of brain cancer, after two years of exposure to cell phones. After five years exposure the risk was five-fold. They also found that in those who lived in urban environments the risk was even higher. In my view, and that of many colleagues who have written papers on this issue, these studies provide evidence that radiofrequency fields are not just a possible human carcinogen but a *probable* human carcinogen, i.e., IARC category 2A. It would be impossible to ignore such an assessment in regulatory approaches.[23]

In his call for critical policy change and restriction of Wi-Fi, cellular phones, and other devices emitting electromagnetic fields (EMFs), Dr. Miller was joined by other physicians, cancer experts, and scientists, including neurologist Dr. Martha R. Herbert of Harvard Medical School and Drs. Lennart Hardell and Michael Carlberg of Örebro University Hospital in Sweden. In their urgent pleadings for further study, these group of scientists called for stricter standards and restricted use of these devices for people, especially children.

In her letter to the Petaluma School District, Dr. Herbert from Harvard Medical School stated, "Radiofrequency electromagnetic radiation from Wi-Fi and cell towers can exert a disorganizing effect on the ability to learn and remember, and can also be destabilizing to immune and metabolic function." She added a note dispelling the claim by Wi-Fi proponents that heat buildup, not cellular frequencies, was the problem: "Current technologies were designed and promulgated without taking account of biological impacts other than thermal impacts. We now know that there is a large array of impacts that have nothing to do with the heating of tissue. The claim from Wi-Fi proponents that the only concern is thermal impacts is now definitively outdated scientifically."[24] Dr. Herbert's letter ended with a stark warning to the school district:

> Powerful industrial entities have a vested interest in leading the public to believe that EMF/RFR, which we cannot see, taste or touch, is harmless, but this is not true. Please do the right and precautionary thing for our children.
>
> I urge you to opt for wired technologies in Petaluma City School District classrooms, particularly for those subpopulations that are most sensitive. It will be easier for you to make a healthier decision now than to undo misguided decisions later.

Despite these expressions of alarm from medical practitioners, many parents have not heard of the risks and have unwittingly exposed their children to harmful effects. The alarm bells are not just limited to a few fringe doctors.

The National Toxicology Program Cell Phone Radiation Study results showed a link between cell phone radiation and tumors that developed in rats. The American Academy of Pediatrics issued a lengthy response in 2016 for cell phone safety suggestions to reduce exposure to wireless radiation: "They're not toys. They have radiation that is emitted from them and the more we can keep it off the body and use (the phone) in other ways, it will be safer," said Jennifer A. Lowry, M.D., FAACT, FAAP, and chair of the AAP Council on Environmental Health Executive Committee.

The study exposed rats to radio frequency (RF) radiation for nine hours a day for two years beginning in utero and compared them to rats that were not exposed. Some of the male rats developed malignant tumors in their hearts and brains while the control group did not, according to the report, which included only partial findings. While Dr. Lowry, chief for the Section of Clinical Toxicology at Children's Mercy Hospital, said it is difficult to translate the results in rats to humans, the nine hours a day coincidentally reflects the current daily use of the average child (i.e., 9 hours of day) for social media alone on a smartphone or similar Wi-Fi device that emits these microwave frequencies.

> We are damaging the world more with our mobiles than our forefathers did with their musket.
>
> Amit Kalantri
> *Wealth of Words*

In *Pediatric Environmental Health, 3rd Edition,* the Academy recommends that "exposures can be reduced by encouraging children to use text messaging when possible, make only short and essential calls on cellular phones, use hands-free kits and wired headsets, and maintain the cellular phone an inch or more away from the head."

Other international groups are equally alarmed. After Dr. Gunnar Heuser of Agoura Hills showed neurological damage in California firefighters with cellular antennas on their stations that suggested RF radiation exposure, the International Association of Fire Fighters issued a statement opposing the use of fire stations as base stations for towers and/or antennas for the conduction of cell phone transmissions, until a study could be conducted proving they were not hazardous to the health of their members.[25] Ironically, numerous U.S. hospitals have cellular towers or antennas erected on their buildings, often with hidden or camouflaged methods.

Is Technology Pulling Us Back into the Past?

The tantalizing lure of an online world is not just damaging to the physical body but has other consequences as well. In an analysis of data, researchers discovered that the use of electronic devices by teens for at least five hours *more than doubled* from 2009 to 2015. That number reflecting daily usage is even higher today. These teens were 70 percent more likely to have suicidal thoughts or actions than those who reported only one hour of use.[26]

Study author Jean Twenge, a psychology professor at San Diego State University, said, "We need to stop thinking of smartphones as harmless. There's a tendency to say, 'Oh, teens are just communicating with their friends.' Monitoring kids' use of smartphones and social media is important, and so is setting reasonable limits." Dr. Victor Strasburger, a teen medicine specialist at the University of New Mexico, said that social media has the potential for causing real harm. The immediacy of checking social media to see what others are saying, coupled with anonymity, are cited as potential causes for the troubling trend that is rapidly growing for self-harm.[27] We may have all experienced the urge to see who has responded to our past Facebook or Instagram posts, which can easily pull us back into the past with a reactive mode that triggers us, rather than creating a more powerful future.

Online bullying is also a growing problem, according to studies. Nearly 43 percent of kids report being bullied online, and 25 percent said it happened more than once. But 70 percent of students report seeing frequent bullying online, and 68 percent of teens agree that cyber bullying is a serious problem.[28]

The Centers for Disease Control and Prevention (CDC) reports that from 1999 to 2017, suicide rates among boys increased 74 percent, while the rates for girls *more than tripled* during the same time period. Bullying is strongly linked to suicidal thoughts and attempts, says Sameer Hinduja, co-director of the Cyberbullying Research Center and professor of criminology at Florida Atlantic University.[29]

As a way of coping with their pain, 13 percent to 18 percent of distressed teens physically injure themselves via cutting, burning, or other forms of self-harm, according to research published in 2014 in the *British Medical Journal*.[30] Once the bullying starts, it doesn't just come from friends or anonymous sources. A new highly disturbing trend has identified another source that leads to even more anxiety and depression for the victim: self-bullying.

Clinical psychologists are sounding the alarms that some adolescents are engaging in a new form of self-aggression called "digital self-harm." Denver child psychologist Sheryl Gonzalez-Ziegler said the following about her self-cyberbullying client: "She set up ghost accounts on Instagram and posted mean comments about herself, saying things like, 'I think you're creepy and gay' and 'Don't sit next to me again.'"[31]

"We were alarmed to learn that six percent of the youth who participated in our study engaged in some form of digital self-harm," said Sameer Hinduja, co-author of the study and professor of criminology at Florida Atlantic University. Hinduja is also a co-director of the Cyberbullying Research Center. Another study in 2012 involving 617 high school freshmen found that nine percent of teens had bullied themselves online. Sadly, research shows that people who self-harm and are admitted to the hospital are up to 100 times more likely to kill themselves than the general population.[32]

Psychologists suggest that teens are anonymously cyberbullying themselves because they feel vulnerable and exposed. With the fear of being mocked by their peers, self-bullying beats the bullies to the punch. It also is a way to manage feelings of self-hatred and sadness, while gaining attention from friends. It is a cry for help.

The distraction of too much technology is also slowing the reading rates of children. As screens have taken over reading, child development experts say old-fashioned reading is more important than ever. Today, more than 67 percent of

12-year-olds have a cell phone, as well as 11 percent of eight-year-olds. Professor Donna Cross of Telethon Kids Institute said, "They're missing out on social experiences and perhaps if they're experiencing harm, it could be affecting their mental health as well."

The Telethon Kids Institute, a leading children's health research center in Australia, recommends no screen time for kids under two years old, and less than one hour of screen time for children ages two to five. For older children, TKI researchers recommend limiting screen time to less than two hours.[33] These limits are far lower than current usage of smartphone and other Wi-Fi devices such as toys, tablets, Wi-Fi-based watches, and baby monitoring devices, where children could be exposed to devices for many hours a day.

In a ten-year, ongoing study in the U.S. that has begun to examine 11,000 children ages nine and ten, scientists are learning more about the damaging effects of screen time on children. In the first wave of brain scan data of 4,500 participants, Dr. Gaya Dowling of the National Institutes of Health and her colleagues provided a glimpse of what they've learned so far: The MRI scans showed significant differences in the brains of some children who use Wi-Fi devices such as smart phones, video games, and tablets more than seven hours a day.[34]

Dowling noted that the cortex, the wrinkly outermost layer of the brain that processes information from the five senses, is thinning in heavy users of these devices. The data from the NIH study also revealed that kids who spent more than two hours a day on screens received lower language fluency and critical thinking test scores.

Dr. Dimitri Christakis at Seattle Children's Hospital was the lead author of the American Academy of Pediatrics' most recent guidelines for screen time for children. The AAP now recommends that "parents avoid using digital media, except for video chatting, in children younger than 18 to 24 months."[35] Christakis noted, "What we do know about babies playing with iPads is that they don't transfer what they learn from the iPad to the real world, which is to say that if you give a child an app where they play with virtual Legos, virtual blocks, and stack them, and then put real blocks in front of them, they start all over."

Dr. Christakis is one of the few scientists who have conducted experiments on the influence screens have on children under two years of age, a critical time period for human brain development. He said, "[Small children] don't transfer the knowledge from two dimensions to three." Christakis and his team of researchers also discovered that toddlers become more addicted to electronic gadgets that mimic toys than the actual physical toys. The electronic toys are more engaging and stimulating, as the toddlers were much less willing to hand back the iPads than they were with handing back the physical toys.[36]

The Pull Away from the Present World

Tristan Harris, a former Google manager who was one of the first technology developer insiders in Silicon Valley to admit that phones and apps are designed to capture and keep children's attention. Harris said, "This is about the war for attention, and where that's taking society, and where that is taking technology."[37]

Teens are also being affected by spending large amounts of time on their cell phones. Dr. Kara Bagot is an investigator with the $300 million National Institutes of Health (NIH) study who scans teenager's brains as they follow Instagram, the most popular social media app. Bagot revealed that part of the brain lights up when the subject feels good. She and other scientists believe that screen time stimulates the release of the chemical dopamine, which impacts desire and cravings. "So you're more likely to act impulsively and use social media compulsively instead of checking yourself," Bagot said, referring to how teens become addicted to the emotional ups and downs of the online roller coaster ride.

Dr. Jean Twenge, psychology professor at San Diego State University, spent five years analyzing national data of 11 million young people since the 1960s. She discovered that "I-gen" teens — those born after 1994 — exhibited sudden changes in mental health and behavior. "They're the first generation to spend their entire adolescence with smartphones, so a lot of them can't remember a time before smartphones existed," Twenge said. After smartphone usage became widespread among young people by 2012, teens reported having less sex and lower drinking rates, but the percentage of teens who said they were depressed or lonely spiked. Hospital visits for self-harm such as cutting also tripled among girls ages 10 to 14.[38]

The cell phone isn't the only distraction pulling us away from being present and mindful in the real world. When Nielsen began tracking TV viewing time in 1949, Americans watched about 4.5 hours of TV per day. That figure rose to 9 hours a day in 2010 and has fallen to around 8 hours as of May 2017.[39]

Despite the sudden rise of the new online dazzling technology services, such as Facebook, Netflix, YouTube, and Instagram, our new toys at our fingertips have only cut TV watching by one hour over the past eight years. Americans still largely watch TV, with an additional large chunk of their time on phones, computers, and social media and other apps. Increasingly, these new gadgets are stealing our physical time from being in the present with our loved ones and productive work.

Then there are video games, a new form of entertainment that struck America about forty years ago. About 67 percent of Americans play video games on their smartphones, tablets, or both, according to a 2018 study released by Electronic Entertainment Design and Research.[40] Gamers spend on average 12 hours per week playing video games. Another recent study reveals that American adults spend more time interacting with media than ever before. According to the 2018 survey by market research group Nielsen, Americans now spend more than 11 hours per day watching, reading, listening to, or interacting with media, up from 9.5 hours just four years ago.[41]

Are we distracted by our new toys? You bet.

How is our online world affecting us energetically? On the electromagnetic scale, the frequencies from Wi-Fi and cellular devices that emit electromagnetic fields (EMFs) overload the body, creating motion and chaos. This excess "noise" agitates especially the upper chakras in the body that are more sensitive to motion, pulling precious energy away from the lower chakras that ground us.

When the Masculine energy located in the upper part of the body is exacerbated, and the Feminine energy becomes depleted in the lower part of the body, the physical, emotional, mental, and spiritual bodies become chaotic and stressed. Hyperactivity, fidgeting, anxiety, and physical tension are often common symptoms of this imbalance. In my consulting practice, I also see headaches, insomnia, agitation, and nervousness in clients who are addicted to media. In my experience, excessive exposure to multi-media art and information is the primary cause for these types of chronic conditions.

A return to balance and harmony is critically needed when these symptoms alert us to take action. It requires removing the sources that cause trauma, while reengaging in activities that restore the energy that grounds and stabilizes.

Ways to Engage Mindful Presence in Your Life

Activating the power of being present in your life creates magic. Mindfulness in sweet stillness accesses incredible energy that refreshes your mind, body, and spirit. Being fully present is the one of the secrets of superstar athletes and successful business leaders who consciously bring more quiet and balance into their lives that energizes their work and lifts people around them.

All of us could probably benefit from being even more mindful and practicing being fully present each day. Using these tips, you will create more harmony and peace for yourself and others:

- Reduce complexity in your life. As Henry David Thoreau wrote in his book *Walden*, "Our life is frittered away by detail…simplify, simplify." Are you guilty of taking on too many projects or challenges in your life? It can lead to complexity and burn-out, with little accomplished.

- Stop trying to be perfect. As Jane Fonda once said, "Rather than try to be perfect, strive to be whole." We often set ourselves up for failure when we don't think we are good enough in the eyes of someone else. By trying to compensate and do something perfectly, we create more stress and less play for ourselves, setting ourselves up for failure.

- Get rid of your distractions. Find time each day to put away your cell phones, turn off your computer, and stop answering emails. Especially on dates. Especially with dinners with your family and loved ones. Are you bringing your work or conversations with others to the dinner table and sharing that with your loved ones? It may build quiet resentment by sending a big message: "You aren't that important to me right now." Instead, be fully present with whomever you are with at the moment. If you are in a meeting, be fully present with those at the meeting.

- Practice daily meditation. If you lack calm and groundedness in your life, this practice is essential. As the 17th century philosopher and mathematician Blaise Pascal noted, "All men's miseries derive from not being able to sit quietly in a room alone." A quiet and still mind is the answer to someone who suffers from many problems.

- Read something inspiring each day. I like to end my nights with inspirational readings from uplifting people who made significant advances on our planet. The moment just before drifting off to sleep is an important gateway to your Higher Self. Placing the seeds of positive thinking and higher consciousness during this time portal will elevate you to higher ground.

Albert Einstein said, "I think 99 times and find nothing. I stop thinking, swim in silence, and the truth comes to me." In our spiritual practice of being present, we not only find our truth inside, but we also find the magic that feeds and guides our life's purpose: our natural intuition.

1 https://www.heartmath.com/institute-of-heartmath/

2 https://www.heartmath.org/articles-of-the-heart/heartmath-tools-techniques/heart-hologramming-want/

3 https://www.webmd.com/balance/guide/how-worrying-affects-your-body#1

4 https://www.usnews.com/news/health-care-news/articles/2018-05-08/study-americans-are-more-anxious-today-than-a-year-ago

5 https://www.anxietycentre.com/anxiety-statistics-information.shtml

6 http://time.com/5190291/anxiety-depression-college-university-students/

7 IBID

8 https://www.today.com/health/does-your-heart-sense-your-emotional-state-2D80555354

9 https://www.mayoclinic.org/diseases-conditions/post-traumatic-stress-disorder/symptoms-causes/syc-20355967

10 http://influence-central.com/kids-tech-the-evolution-of-todays-digital-natives/

11 https://www.mpfs.de/studien/kim-studie/2016/

12 https://www.inc.com/melanie-curtin/bill-gates-says-this-is-the-safest-age-to-give-a-child-a-smartphone.html

13 https://flurrymobile.tumblr.com/post/157921590345/us-consumers-time-spent-on-mobile-crosses-5

14 https://techcrunch.com/2017/01/12/the-mobile-app-gold-rush-may-be-over/

15 http://studylib.net/doc/8254540/portable-phones

16 https://www.cdc.gov/nchs/products/databriefs/db257.htm

17 https://www.who.int/ceh/capacity/cancer.pdf

18 https://www.iarc.fr/wp-content/uploads/2018/07/pr208_E.pdf

19 https://www.express.co.uk/news/uk/226474/Tumour-risk-to-the-young-from-using-mobile-phones

20 https://www.parents.com/health/healthy-happy-kids/how-wireless-devices-can-be-dangerous-for-your-family/

21 https://www.emfacts.com/download/children_mobiles.pdf

22 https://emfcommunity.com/warning-dod-announces-emp-drill-november-4-6th/

23 https://phpa.health.maryland.gov/OEHFP/EH/Shared%20Documents/CEHPAC/CEHPAC%20Dec%2013%20Comments%20Part%204.pdf

24 IBID

25 http://www.emrpolicy.org/news/press/pr_iaff_vote.pdf

26 https://www.cbsnews.com/news/rise-in-suicide-and-social-media-is-there-a-link/

27 IBID

28 https://www.dosomething.org/us/facts/11-facts-about-cyber-bullying

29 https://www.mitchellrepublic.com/lifestyle/health/4586263-6-ways-parents-and-schools-can-tackle-spike-teen-suicide

30 https://www.bmj.com/content/349/bmj.g5954

31 https://www.npr.org/sections/health-shots/2018/04/21/604073315/when-teens-cyberbully-themselves

32 https://www.bbc.com/news/education-26357962

[33] https://thewest.com.au/news/7-news-perth/too-much-tech-slows-childrens-reading-rates-ng-b881066427z)

[34] https://www.cbsnews.com/news/groundbreaking-study-examines-effects-of-screen-time-on-kids-60-minutes/

[35] IBID

[36] IBID

[37] IBID

[38] IBID

[39] https://www.theatlantic.com/technology/archive/2018/05/when-did-tv-watching-peak/561464/

[40] https://variety.com/2018/gaming/news/how-many-people-play-games-in-the-u-s-1202936332/

[41] https://www.marketwatch.com/story/people-are-spending-most-of-their-waking-hours-staring-at-screens-2018-08-01

Intuitive

> Come from the heart, the true heart, not the head. When in doubt, choose the heart. This does not mean to deny your own experiences and that which you have empirically learned through the years. It means to trust yourself to integrate intuition and experience. There is a balance, a harmony to be nurtured, between the head and the heart. When the intuition rings clear and true, loving impulses are favored.
>
> Dr. Brian Weiss
> *Messages from the Masters: Tapping into the Power of Love*

One of the most powerful inner guides of our Divine Child is intuition, also known as the sixth sense. It has been described as an insight that arises spontaneously without conscious reasoning.[1] Sylvia Clare, author of *Trusting Your Intuition*, wrote, "Intuition is the highest form of intelligence, transcending all individual abilities and skills."

A number of studies reveal that infants can organize sensory information, supply what is missing, determine cause and effect, and use the information to develop theories about how the world operates. Neurologists suggest that the ability to sense connections with others can be a hallmark of creativity and even scientific discovery.

Small children and babies are naturally intuitive. Have you watched how little children scream in terror or giggle the moment they are picked up by a stranger? It seems that they intuitively know who is not good for them and who is. Their sense of intuition is running on all cylinders, guiding them in each moment to what will bring them more joy. Little children are naturally connected to their feelings and what is happening around them, never allowing pretense, anxiety for the future, or fear of what others might think to dictate what they will do next. Our tiny teachers are simply in the present moment, delighting in what they can create right now.

Researchers from the University of Missouri-Columbia discovered that while infants appear to be helpless, their brains are equipped with a knowledge of "intuitive physics." Kristy van Marle, an assistant professor in the Department of Psychological Sciences in the College of Arts and Science at the university says, "We believe that infants are born with expectations about the objects around them, even though that knowledge is a skill that's never been taught. As the child develops, this knowledge is refined and eventually leads to the abilities we use as adults."[2]

The evidence for intuitive physics occurs as early as two months in babies, when they demonstrate an understanding that hidden objects do not cease to exist, and that unsupported objects will fail. By five months, infants already know that non-cohesive substances like water or sand are not solid. "The majority of an adult's everyday interactions with the world are automatic, and we believe infants have the same ability to form expectations, predicting the behavior of objects and substances with which they interact," says van Marle. She believes that while intuitive physics knowledge is present at birth, parents can assist in developing this skill through normal interaction, such as talking and playing with the child and encouraging the child to interact with objects.

> The intuitive mind is a sacred gift, and the rational mind is a faithful servant.
>
> Albert Einstein

Dr. Stephen Camarata, author of his book *The Intuitive Parents: Why the Best Thing for Your Child is You*, provides the following advice for parents to tap into their intuition for better child rearing. He says, "Tune in to your baby, toddler or young child and tune out fads, marketing schemes, and peer pressure. Trust your own common sense and inner parenting voice to be the absolute finest mom or dad you can be. When you use your parenting intuition, Mother Nature — and the latest brain science — will directly support you."[3]

Other studies demonstrate that babies and small children are intuitive eaters. Consider how a baby will cry until fed, and then turn its head away when full. A number of organizations, such as the American Academy of Pediatrics and the World Health Organization, provide child-feeding guidelines to help parents recognize and respect a child's signals of hunger and satiety — a core principle of "intuitive eating."[4] Following physical hunger and satisfaction cues that guide what, when, and how much to eat[5] has been associated with positive physical and psychological outcomes.[6]

For example, in a 2003 study that followed girls from ages 5 to 9, those girls whose mothers exercised high levels of food restriction were more likely to eat when not hungry than girls who were raised with low levels of restriction. This was true regardless of whether the girls were overweight or not.[7]

Promoting intuitive eating at the dinner table has many benefits. Brandi Olden, RDN, CSP, CD, owner of Creating Peace with Food in Bellevue, Washington, says, "Allowing kids to eat intuitively gives children a greater sense of self-esteem, understanding of boundaries, [and] connection to family and caregivers during meals, and typically they will enjoy a wider variety of foods."[8]

Can Intuition Serve Us Better Than Data-Based Decisions?

Decision-making is part of the human experience, but sometimes we don't have time to gather data to make an intellectual decision based on data, as in the case of a surgeon in the operating room or a seasoned investor considering whether or not to pump money into a start-up venture. There are many times in our lives we need to take action quickly without having much data readily available for proper evaluation.

The left brain and right brain are wired to assist us in this mysterious process of making good decisions by taking both instinct and intellect into account. New research reveals that the old adage, "look before you leap," may not be so true as we previously believed.

> When you reach the end of what you should know, you will be at the beginning of what you should sense.
>
> Kahlil Gibran
> *Sand and Foam*

In a series of behavioral experiments published in the *Proceedings of the National Academy of Sciences* (PNAS) in 2012, Professor Marius Usher of Tel Aviv University's School of Psychological Sciences and his fellow researchers found that intuition was a surprisingly accurate and powerful tool. When subjects were exposed to a series of numbers in quick succession without the ability to memorize them or conduct proper mathematical calculations, Usher and his team found that when participants were forced to choose between two options based on instinct alone, they made the right call up to 90 percent of the time.[9]

In fact, the more they used their intuition, the better the rate of accuracy. For example, when shown six pairs of numbers every second, subjects chose the highest average of a group 65 percent of the time. But when shown 24 pairs of numbers, the accuracy rate soared to about 90 percent. Other research shows that practicing intuition refines our sixth sense, transforming it into a valuable tool that allows us to take action. This could potentially infer that we are more connected to the collective unconscious than previously known.

The study also learned that brain has the capacity to large amounts of information and decide on a specific value. Professor Usher says that gut reactions can be trusted to make quality decisions — a conclusion supported by his early work with Dr. Zohar Rusou and Professor Dan Zakay published in *Frontiers in Cognitive Science* in March 2011.

Are our tiny teachers revealing the power of not only trusting our intuition, but also developing it? In August 1999, UC Berkeley researchers found that a three-year-old's brain is twice is active than an adult's,[10] with about 15,000 brain connections or synapses per neuron in the toddler — far more than the adult brain. In fact, the researchers concluded that the brain of a baby in a crib "has the greatest mind in the universe in the process of solving major philosophical questions with a brain that is smarter, faster and busier than any adult's."

Where Intuition Resides in the Body

The epicenter of intuition has long been associated with the Ajna, the "Third Eye" located in the center of the head that is connected to the energies of insight, wisdom, and inspiration. Associated with the sixth Chakra, our sixth sense provides us with the ability to understand something immediately without the need for conscious reasoning rooted in the five senses. Think of the dot on the forehead worn by Hindus, who make up one in six people on the planet. This identifying mark located on the center of the forehead between the two eyes is a sign for the third eye of intuition, often referred by Hindus as the "bindi," "tilaka," or "bottu."

In other words, this valuable sense transcends the mental body that relies on known facts and the limited ability of the five senses, moving us into the magnificence of Universal consciousness described by Carl Jung. Connecting our consciousness to that of everything and everyone around us brings an infinite number of co-creative possibilities for a more powerful and positive future. The Law of Resonance can supercharge our lives, where we create through a reverberating connection with similar people, ideas, or shared values.

This important energy center is represented by the acorn shape at the top of the caduceus, which originated in ancient Egypt. On this iconic staff, two snakes represent the Masculine and Feminine energies in the body that arise from the Root chakra toward the Crown. The intersection of the two paths of these energies marks each chakra before stopping at the Sixth chakra, the seat of intuition associated with the pineal gland. Responsible for producing melatonin, regulating sleep patterns, and balancing other hormones in the body, the pineal gland has also been traditionally thought of as the center for higher consciousness and spirituality.

The gift of this chakra is the ability to see and understand our inner and outer worlds more fully. In her book *A Wind in the Door*, Madeleine L'Engle wrote, "Don't try to comprehend with your mind. Your minds are very limited. Use your intuition." This energy center becomes opened and engaged to a greater degree when a person enters the state of self-actualization, where the desire for self-fulfillment and to explore one's potential is born. When Abraham Maslow described this level of development, he was exploring growth at our highest level of needs, namely the meaning of life in an extraordinarily creative and robust state of existence.

Intuitive power is an innate gift and natural process, as best-selling author Cyndi Dale shares in her 2021 release of *Advanced Chakra Healing*:

> Intuition isn't an eerie, occult, or paranormal concept; it's a fact. Being intuitive is nothing more or less than interpreting the information contained in energy that moves too slowly or quickly to be easily recognized through your five every-day senses. Any time you sense another's pain, feel a storm coming the day before it arrives, or guess who is on the phone before you answer, you are acting intuitively. You are being the intuitive that you are.

Inspiration in the mind's eye leads to creative expression in the outer world. As humans, we are well-equipped to generate new ideas and manifest them in the material world. It is what makes us a rather unique species on our planet, giving rise to progression and self-realization. It is the Divine Child at work and at play.

The Power of the Third Eye

In the Judeo-Christian tradition, the scripture found in Matthew 6:22 says, "The light of the body is the eye: If therefore thine eye be single, thy whole body shall be full of light." The esoteric meaning of this passage refers to the Third Eye, the spiritual center of intuition and higher consciousness that becomes illuminated during meditation. Kriya Yoga, which was introduced around 1920 to the United States by Paramahansa Yogananda, teaches how to activate the Third Eye to cultivate intuition, inspiration, and higher wisdom by directing both eyes toward the Sixth Chakra, the energy center of spiritual awakening — where this practice has been said to flood the body with higher frequencies of energy.

For thousands of years, it was believed that Nadi Shodhana Pranayama, or "alternate nostril breathing," helps direct energy toward the Third Eye. In fact, scientific research shows that alternate nostril breathing lower heart rate and respiratory rate, lower blood pressure, relieve tension and stress, and revitalize a tired mind and body.[11] In a 2017 study with competitive swimmers, the pranayama practice in concert with two other yogic breathing practices for 30 minutes, five days a week for one month resulted in a significant improvement in lung capacity and number of strokes per breath, suggesting that Yogic Breathing Practices (YBP) can enhance respiratory endurance and athletic performance.[12]

In the field of neuro-linguistic programming (NLP), a number of modern-day researchers[13] have found that when the eyes are directed upward towards this center of intuition and inspiration, creativity is accessed and activated, either recalling or constructing new images.[14] From a subtle energy perspective, looking upward drives energy up in the body, while looking downward moves energy down the chakras and physical body. This could explain why depressed people have a tendency to look downward, as a prolonged downward gaze can access emotional energy to excess that may keep one swimming in his or her emotions.

The profound connection between eye movement and shifting the energy in the body has been found in other important studies. By moving the eyes back and forth horizontally, researchers found that communication between the brain hemispheres was dramatically boosted, which also increases creativity. Published in the November 2009 edition of *Brain and Cognition*, the surprising results of the study also revealed that creativity soared dramatically when participants simply moved their eyes from left to right for 30 seconds.[15] The bilateral eye moment was enough to make a significant difference, similar to how using both sides of the body such as walking or balancing helps connect and harmonize the brain hemispheres.[16]

How Our Natural Intuition Shuts Down

What causes us to suppress or even shut down our inner sense of intuition? What trauma causes us to shrink away from our internal instincts that can powerfully guide us? When we are limited to information rooted in the past that is based on our five physical senses, it is worth exploring what causes this sixth sense to take a back seat and become suppressed.

Sometimes parents, teachers, or other important role models tell us to "stop living in a dream world" or "snap out of it," leaving us confused as to do with our inner world that fuels us. Self-doubt is a potent extinguisher that not only kills our powerful, innate sense of intuition, but also casts a dark shadow on the ability to see our true potential. If we find ourselves stuck in the habit of doubting ourselves and our gut instincts, these patterns can last decades, raining down on our inner parade of joy, passion, and sense of aliveness.

Perhaps the biggest reason we move away from our powerful intuitive guidance is that we are trained to believe that our outer, visible world is far more real than our inner world. Our natural sense of intuition becomes hijacked with formal education that develops our reliance on the five senses of sight, hearing, smell, taste, and touch, while often ignoring our natural instincts. The work environment — the world of grownups — cements that tendency to frame our three-dimensional world based on facts and analysis, leaving intuition behind.

As we become older, we learn about atoms, molecules, dimensions, mathematics, and data. Certainly, the world of logic is extremely valuable and critical to the analytical and reasoning part of our brains. But the reliance on the material world to make our decisions causes our intuitive brain to atrophy.

> Practice listening to your intuition, your inner voice; ask questions; be curious; see what you see; hear what you hear; and then act upon what you know to be true. These intuitive powers were given to your soul at birth.
>
> Clarissa Pinkola Estés

When we largely abandon our inner world that is largely connected to our right brains, an important part of us begins to shut down. At that point, we begin to believe that our reality is based on the five senses. Living in a three-dimensional world that is dependent on what we can see, hear, smell, taste, and touch can cause us to lose sight of a rich, multi-dimensional world that touches our spirit and soul.

Evidence is more than a fact-based reality rooted in our five senses that measures things, because the spiritual qualities and gifts of the Divine Child cannot be easily measured. Research shows that a balanced approach between our left and right brains — "logos" and "emos" — can be invaluable for important decision-making when there is not enough time to gather and evaluate the facts. This does not mean that creating alternate realities based on ungrounded belief or blind faith is helpful, as the contrary is true. Instead, it suggests that in times when we must make decisions quickly without evidence, we can rely on our inner knowingness, where a cultivated gut instinct can be quite valuable.

The Negative Expressions of Intuition

The negative expressions of intuition include mistrust and an overly activated left brain imbalance that can result in rigidity and over-intellectualizing the world. The more our intuitive abilities are shut down, the greater the chance other parts of our non-verbal right brain are also suppressed, such as creativity and emotional intelligence. If we learn as little children that emotions are not safe, a tendency to rely on the rational mind and left brain may develop.

> Intuition is a sense of knowing how to act spontaneously, without needing to know why.
>
> Sylvia Clare
> *Trusting Your Intuition*

A stress-filled life lacking play and balance also wounds our natural intuition. A team of European researchers found that stress and anxiety caused intuition to plummet.[17] Carina Remmers, study co-author and research assistant at Freie Universität Berlin, said, "If this capacity is impaired in psychopathology such as anxiety disorders and depression, then it seems plausible that people suffer from indecisiveness, regret, ambiguity, [and] decision-making problems."[18]

We also give up our intuition when we relinquish our intuitive gifts and other powers by projecting them onto external sources. Projection may well be the cornerstone of most religions, where deities and demons allegedly have authority and control over our lives — a concept assigned by our primordial ancestors who didn't know much of anything. Without the tools of modern-day science, they wrongly assumed that disease was caused by devil dust or devil-wishing, and that tornadoes, tsunamis, floods, and volcanic eruptions were punishment from one or more of the 3,000 gods that they had invented.

Now we know the truth.

The Group Effect

The power of groups can be helpful in our lives when dealing with something difficult, for example, but the group dynamic can also be rather hypnotic and sometimes disabling if the group reinforces false belief systems. Most Bronze Age religions denigrate and subjugate women, resulting in the global epidemic of deep misogyny that still unfortunately plagues the world.

The programming of beliefs is often conducted through group chanting, singing, mantras, or repeatedly reading primary written texts that the group is forced to embrace, while ignoring the original spiritual trauma of fabrication. Repetition can engage and deeply entrench the addiction, especially when the repetitive activities are infused with deep emotion.

One of the primary ways to recover from any addiction — whether it be alcohol or another drugs, sex, shopping, gambling, eating disorders, prescription drugs, or theft — is to examine what is the *causal source* of the addiction, not the addiction itself. Some critics of Alcoholics Anonymous suggest that alcohol is usually not the problem, just as smoking, risky sexual behavior, or gambling are not the root causes of those negative behaviors. It is what we are *numbing ourselves from* that needs to be healed, not the Band-Aids that serve to temporarily mask the pain and injury. Engaging on a profound healing journey involves learning about the painful traumas that usually occurred before age ten.

By defusing painful experiences, we can help people with addictive personalities find their personal power and self-efficacy. A helpful focus would include using the Divine Child's energy to become more curious about our situation, accepting responsibility for what we have done, and to repeatedly empower our consciousness with the truth of our being: We are powerful beyond words, and we are destined to do greater things.

The intuitive, curious, and observant nature of our Divine Child never scapegoats or projects. Instead, our precious inner child inside says, "I am present, vulnerable, and authentic. I accept the issue that is part of me. I own it, rather than to escape what is inescapable. I am curious about my healing journey and will keep exploring to discover the truth of who I am and what I can do to bring more joy to myself and others."

By simply *knowing* the truth of our past trauma and the truth of our strength, abilities, and potential, the healing we need often occurs spontaneously. "Knowing yourself is the beginning of all wisdom," said Aristotle. Truth is the beginning of healing.

How to Reengage Intuition

Do you find that you have difficulty trusting your gut instincts? Is your tendency to keep looking for data that will justify a decision that you want to make, but may be afraid to step out and take action?

In a data-driven world that trains us to think in more analytical, left-brain ways, using tools that cultivate our sixth sense can be invaluable. If you are working for an organization that emphasizes data, analysis, and quantitative tools over intuition and creativity, these tips can help you reactivate your Divine Child's natural instinct:

- <u>Learn what your intuitive voice sounds like</u>. In order to use your gift of intuition, recognizing your inner voice is essential. It is subtle and communicates differently for everyone. For some, intuitive flashes are more like visual insights, while for other people, they can come as goosebumps on the arms, a feeling in the gut region, or an expansive feeling in the chest. Other people may hear thoughts or words that come to them. Learn the language of how your intuitive voice speaks to you, whether it be through visual, organic feelings, or certain words. Legendary actress Ingrid Bergman said, "You must train your intuition…you must trust the small voice inside you which tells you exactly what to say, what to decide."
- <u>Practice meditation</u>. The stillness of your inner voice can be heard through silence. Practicing daily meditation can help you hone your

sensing ability to a razor-sharp degree. "Be still and know that you are divine…and intuitive."

- Ask questions. Lots of them. When you exercise the innate curiosity of your Divine Child, you will expand your natural intuition. Posing questions to your inner self, your Higher Self, or the Collective Unconsciousness — or whatever helpful energy you perceive to be intimately connected to — will bring answers from new sources in this Universal pool of energy and information. Practice answering "what" and "how" questions, while avoiding "why" questions that often don't offer solutions but can instead lead to inaccurate assumptions.

- Journal your intuition. Writing down the intuitive messages you receive can enhance the communication link to it source. It's also a great way to capture the quiet wisdom that arrives just when you need it. Neuroscience research suggests that intuitive insights not captured within 37 seconds will likely never be recalled again,[19] so make intuition a top priority!

- Cultivate trust. For many who have been wounded, trusting others can be problematic. If you have difficulty trusting others, it is likely that you may have issues with trusting yourself and your gut instinct. The key is to heal the original trauma that created a mistrust of others. Then you will have an easier time trusting yourself and your own intuitive instincts.

- Clench your left hand repeatedly. A 2013 study published by colleagues from Montclair State University found that clenching the hand increases neuronal activity in the frontal lobe of the opposite hemisphere.[20] In a world where 90 percent of us are right-handed,[21] we default towards the left brain, which rules logic. The researchers discovered that by simply squeezing a ball in the left hand stimulates the right brain, increasing crystallized intelligence (i.e., the accumulation of knowledge, facts, and skills that are acquired throughout life), creativity, and intuition.

Intuition is absolutely critical for any kind of success, even for survival. Not only is our gut instinct important for managing our interpersonal relationships with others, our sixth sense can help us save our own lives in dangerous situations. Intuition, for example, helps us to detect tiny signals of joy, sadness, anger, anxiety, or fear that allow us to make split-second decisions when necessary. Surgeons or stock traders often rely on intuition when necessary.

Learning to trust our internal instincts brings presence and a deeper observation of yourself and the world. Intuition cultivates curiosity and bubbling joy. When the proverbial pipes are open and clear, energy flows freely. Another gift of our Divine Child then emerges, fueling our mind, body, and spirit, electrifying the world around us with this magic: our passion.

[1] https://www.scientificamerican.com/article/can-we-rely-on-our-intuition/

[2] https://www.sciencedaily.com/releases/2012/01/120124113051.htm

[3] https://www.psychologytoday.com/us/blog/the-intuitive-parent/201508/the-intuitive-parent

[4] Tribole E, Resch E. *Intuitive Eating: A Revolutionary Program That Works*. 3rd edition. New York: St. Martin's Griffin; 2012.; Tylka TL, Lumeng JC, Eneli IU.

[5] Maternal intuitive eating as a moderator of the association between concern about child weight and restrictive child feeding. *Appetite*. 2015; 95:158-165.)

[6] Dockendorff SA, Petrie TA, Greenleaf CA, Martin S. Intuitive eating scale: an examination among early adolescents. *J Couns Psychol*. 2012; 59(4):604-611.

[7] Birch LL, Fisher JO, Davison KK. Learning to overeat: maternal use of restrictive feeding practices promotes girls' eating in the absence of hunger. *Am J Clin Nutr*. 2003;78(2):215-220.)

[8] https://www.todaysdietitian.com/newarchives/0318p14.shtml

[9] https://www.sciencedaily.com/releases/2012/11/121108131724.htm

[10] https://www.berkeley.edu/news/media/releases/99legacy/8-10-1999.html

[11] https://www.healthline.com/health/alternate-nostril-breathing

[12] https://www.sciencedirect.com/science/article/pii/S0975947616300675?via%3Dihub

[13] Dilts, 1976, 1977; Grinder, DeLozier and Bandler, 1977; Bandler and Grinder, 1979; Dilts, Grinder, Bandler and DeLozier, 1980

[14] http://www.nlpu.com/Articles/artic14.htm

15 https://www.scientificamerican.com/podcast/episode/boost-your-creativity-with-eye-move-09-11-10/; accessed January 20, 2020

16 https://www.huffpost.com/entry/balance_b_4260748

[17] https://www.inc.com/jessica-stillman/science-stress-silences-your-gut-instincts.html; accessed January 10, 2020

[18] https://www.psychologicalscience.org/publications/observer/obsonline/anxiety-may-quash-gut-feelings.html

[19] https://www.inc.com/marla-tabaka/tim-ferriss-jeff-bezos-other-entrepreneurial-icons-swear-by-this-secret-weapon-you-have-it-too.html

[20] https://www.psychologytoday.com/us/blog/the-athletes-way/201304/squeeze-ball-your-left-hand-increase-creativity

[21] https://www.apa.org/monitor/2009/01/brain

Passionate

Every great dream begins with a dreamer. Always
remember, you have within you the strength, the patience,
and the passion to reach for the stars to change the world.

Harriet Tubman

Passion is the rocket fuel that propels us to our greatest dreams and
ambitions. This spiritual quality within us is vital for any kind of success, whether
it be in our intimate relationships, or achieving the jobs and career that ignites
our soul. Passion is the essential ingredient to true wealth, whether it be inner
treasures or outer abundance, vibrant health, strong relationships with our loved
ones, and true happiness.

Little children are naturally passionate. With their playful energy, children
act without hesitation and simply go for what they want. They do not care what
others think about them while pursuing their dreams. Their fearlessness is
spiritual gold and wisdom for us adults, as many of us may have lost our
connection to what brings us true joy.

For our small spiritual teachers, the fire of enthusiasm and passion within
seems to be innate and normal. Small kids do not need dynamic motivational
speakers like Tony Robbins or Og Mandino, nor a manual to help them find
their zeal. Children are already connected to their endless well of enthusiasm and
vibrancy that, if unbridled, will propel them forward to act without reservation.

What is Passion?

Passion is the amount of resonance with something that ignites one or more
of the 21 energies of your Divine Child. For example, if you are passionate about
your job, then your work will be play, not tedious struggle. The same holds true
with activities that feed your soul.

For example, I'm a sailor, and I love taking a sailboat where I can feel the
sun and breeze on my skin. Sailing is a spiritual anchor that connects me to my
Divine Child that seeks nature, inner joy, groundedness, playfulness,
vulnerability, curiosity, freedom, and passion. When I sail, these inner spiritual
qualities get activated and come alive. Sailing draws me into the present moment,

completely absorbed by the calming energy of the water and the sense of an expansive Universe.

Our passion gets naturally triggered by an activity, object, or person that brings us more joy. Our inner barometer will instantly tell us if we are attracted to something or not: we do not have to force positive feelings. If there isn't a lot of resonance in the energy of the soul with an experience, it is time to go find another sandbox. In his book *The Light in the Heart,* Roy T. Bennett wrote, "Believe in your heart that you're meant to live a life full of passion, purpose, magic and miracles."

> The saddest people I've ever met in life are the ones who don't care deeply about anything at all. Passion and satisfaction go hand in hand, and without them, any happiness is only temporary, because there's nothing to make it last.
>
> Nicholas Sparks
> *Dear John*

One key to successful living is to keep finding things that ignite your joy, and to keep doing those things consistently that resonate with your internal joy. Do not mistake joy for pleasure, which results from commodities that are bought and sold. For that reason, joy and pleasure are two very different energies, as joy is already inside of you, waiting to be engaged at no price. "The best things in life are simple, abundant, and free," Debasish Mridha wrote. The real bonus is that the energy is not only free and readily available to you because it is within you, but also far-reaching, expansive, and magical.

Where Passion and its Negative Expressions Are Located

Passion is the fire that drives our actions. This energy is primarily connected to the Heart Chakra, the seat of love, compassion, information, and truth, as well as our Third Chakra — the center that rules motivation, physical power, and action. When we are present, our vibrancy and vitality come alive. A.R. Rahman said, "Success comes to those who dedicate everything to their passion in life."

When the fires of passion begin to fade and dwindle, the energy in our soul, mind, and body diminish, a sure sign that we have lost touch with our inner joy. When this happens, boredom, restlessness, and a sense of feeling lost and unmotivated may overwhelm us. Parents, experts, and other role models may try to sell us their dreams for us of what they think we should be, even though those dreams may be better suited for someone else.

Small children guide their curiosity and sense of adventure toward the things that naturally feeds their joy. For them, the infinite vastness of the Universe is their unlimited playground to explore, whereas adults begin limiting their experiences to a much smaller playground that feels safe.

Passion is born from the center of your "body-truth." If we stop listening to our joy and passion that guides our soul's desires, then boredom and feeling tired may show up as unwelcome friends. Our motivation begins to shut down, as we move toward something that we believe will bring us joy, usually as a result of what someone told us, rather than what we discovered for ourselves. Motivation is the physical expression of passion that moves your body to get things done, while passion is the fire that can be expressed not just physically, but mentally, inspirationally, emotionally, spiritually, and even vocally.

Lethargy, boredom, and laziness take over when passion is largely absent. This happens when people lose their sense of what makes them come alive. But if purpose is motivated by our Divine Child, it can create a compelling vision that lights up the world.

How We Lose Touch with Our Inner Passion

The fire energy of passion and motivation gets doused by the wet blankets of dream killers. And yes, there are some in our lives who live in envy due to their own insecurities, when they see themselves as failures. If someone around you has lost sight of his or her heartfelt dreams and passion, he or she may engage in the comparison game with you, based on envy and resentment.

Dream killers come in various packages and sizes. The first varietal comes from parents — the first saviors who towered over us when we were small children. Often, our early role models may attempt to influence us to "get a good, well-paying job" that unfortunately doesn't enliven our joy.

When we lose sight of what feeds our soul, we surrender the precious keys that keep many doors locked to an amazing future. This may be the top way we disconnect from our passion and lose sight of our dreams, which then become buried and lost deep within our souls. It could be many years until our heartfelt dreams come chasing us again. Sometimes, it takes a clearing for us to wake up and pay attention to the little but powerful voice of our Divine Child within.

I call this "spiritual prostitution," where we give up something important to someone in exchange for little to nothing of value in return. With this type of dream killer, we feed them our energy, leaving us deflated and de-energized with unrealized dreams. This common type of energy vampire steals vital life energy, feeding from it because he or she has become too afraid to accomplish his or her own true potential.

The second type of passion killer includes adults that habitually tell children to sit down and be quiet. The English adage dating from the 15th century says, "Children should be seen and not heard," but following this advice is a sure-fire way to extinguish a child's sense of aliveness. The repeated command to be silent without reasoning is a quick and sure way to teach a child that he or she does not matter, and what they say is also unimportant or irrelevant. Silence is only golden when we are not forced into it.

The key is to teach children that they indeed matter, and what they have to say is important and valued. If children learn, either verbally or nonverbally, that what they say is not important, they will begin to shut down. There is a time and place where listening and silence is necessary, when there is tremendous value in learning what someone else has to say, for instance. But more often than not, it seems parents and adults in general tell kids to be quiet out of irritation. "You are a bother" is the silent message.

Another passion killer is the person who tells us our dreams are too big, or that we should be "reasonable." But if someone had repeatedly told Thomas Edison to be reasonable and give up on his passionate, crazy-sounding idea that light can be sustained in a clear glass ball, we may still be living in dimly lit rooms filled with smoky candles and dripping hot wax. "Be reasonable" is often another way of silently saying "you will never be able to achieve that." It often arises from the insecurities, doubts, or negative experiences that the passion killer is projecting onto others.

The anonymous writer Freequill wrote, "In a world of distractions we begin to 'live' on the outside." For some, distractions might be due to the influence of family traditions, where parents want their kids to attend the same colleges or universities that they or perhaps a grandparent attended. Or to follow the same career path as a parent. With family businesses, parents or grandparents may impose undue pressure to keep the business in the family. Pride drives the coercion to conform, which can overwhelm the child's own passionate hopes and dreams. Unwanted tradition thrust upon the shoulders of a child can quickly supplant his or her own natural enthusiasm while bypassing his own dreams.

As kids, we can find that we have put our dreams on hold, not realizing we made the disconnection. While my parents never pressured me to follow any specific career path against my heart's desires, many parents do. Instead, my parents thankfully encouraged me and supported me with whatever I had chosen at the time. And for those young adults who choose careers that don't resonate with their souls, there is always time to rekindle your dreams within, just as I did.

The great work of your life can start much later. Laura Ingalls Wilder was 65 when *Little House in the Big Woods* was published. She continued writing her "Little House" books in her nine-book series, with her last one published when she was 76 years old. In 1974, her popular book series became a hit TV series on NBC, running nine seasons until May 10, 1982.[1]

When Scottish singer Susan Boyle was urged by her mother to audition for *Britain's Got Talent*, she was 47 years old. The youngest of nine children, Boyle was born deprived of oxygen, leaving her with mild brain damage. Diagnosed with learning disabilities in school, kids frequently teased and bullied her.[2] Despite being diagnosed with Asperger syndrome, she bravely stepped upon the stage for her audition in 2009 on *Britain's Got Talent*, launching her rendition of "I Dreamed a Dream" from the hit musical *Les Misérables*. Her critics fell quiet as she boldly and beautifully sang from her heart. She was a hit sensation, as an estimated 100 million people worldwide watched her spellbinding performance online.

In November 2009, Susan Boyle's first studio album, *I Dreamed a Dream*, debuted at the top of the Billboard charts, becoming the second best-selling album of 2009. In 2012, the stage musical *I Dreamed a Dream* was based upon her life's story toured the United Kingdom, with Boyle making cameo appearances. Her biography *The Woman I Was Born to Be* was published in 2010,[3] as Susan Boyle continued to follow her passion that has ignited the world's heart strings.

How Abuse Destroys Passion

Abuse cuts at the core of passion. While physical abuse often comes to mind, the more subtle forms of abuse can be even deadlier. Emotional abuse is rampant in many relationships, where someone projects sadness, anger, or negative emotions onto another. Mental abuse is also widespread, not only in relationships, but in false belief systems, including the seemingly popular negative belief that "I am not worthy of _____." It could be love, success, or happiness that you deserve in life.

In my opinion, "spiritual abuse" is where nearly all forms of abuse begin. Spiritual abuse has been rarely discussed, but it is widespread and lethal to the human spirit. Maltreatment includes force-feeding small children unfounded principles and beliefs, rather than for the child to discover the unfolding truth within herself. Passion is severely diminished through any form of indoctrination — a violation of the Divine Child's spiritual nature and unfettered path.

When children are cattle-prodded into a particular doctrine that restricts open-minded thinking, then curiosity turns into boredom, creativity becomes monotonous routine, and playfulness hardens into rigid behavior. For every spiritual quality, there is its negative counterpart that becomes expressed when aspects of the Divine Child are crushed through these subtle but deadly forms of spiritual trauma.

The Destructive Plague of Child Abuse

A significant blocker to our passion is when we have been abused as children. A 2013 study published in the JAMA Psychiatry journal that followed 7,771 British children from the age of 7 to 50 found that if they were bullied as kids, they experienced increased depression, higher anxiety, lower earnings, lower education achievement, and worse relationships as an adult. The researchers at Duke University also discovered that male bullies who were victims were at increased risk for suicide, while female bullies and victims were at a higher risk for agoraphobia.[4]

In 2011, a King's College London study of 26,000 people found that if you experienced various forms of abuse during childhood, you are more than twice as likely to have recurring depression as an adult. The research revealed the following forms of maltreatment that can lead to substantial depression:[5]

- Rejected interaction from a mother.
- Unstable primary caregiver arrangements throughout childhood
- Reports of physical or sexual abuse
- Harsh discipline from a parent

Previous research has shown that children who are treated badly experience biological changes due to stress placed on their bodies, including negative shifts in the brain, hormone system, and immune systems. Numerous research papers also show that abused children develop brain abnormalities in the pre-frontal cortex region that may negatively impact neuropsychological function, especially executive function such as regulating emotions and sustained attention.

In another study from Harvard that was published in the journal *Proceedings of the National Academy of Sciences* in February 2012, researchers discovered that people who experienced childhood abuse have worse memories and less control over their emotions. Being emotionally, physically, or sexually abused as a child can stunt the development of three key areas of the hippocampus in the brain that regulate emotion and control memory.

When innate passion becomes squelched, then fury and violence emerge. A cycle of anger unintentionally aimed at someone, however, will come back to us like a thrown boomerang. The Buddha said, "Holding on to anger is like grasping a hot coal with the intent of throwing it at someone else; you are the one who gets burned."

Why Spanking is Child Abuse

The question of whether or not to spank children has been evaluated more recently than 50 or 100 years ago, when physical forms of punishment were delivered without raising an eyebrow. Having been raised in the strict teachings of the Bible, I discovered it is loaded with commandments involving Bronze Age barbarism, including the preachment to spank children found in scriptures such as Proverbs 13:25 (KJV): "He that spareth his rod hateth his son: but he that loveth him chasteneth him betimes." King Solomon, whom Christianity hails as the "wisest man who ever lived," instructed in Proverbs 23:13-14 (KJV), "Withhold not correction from the child: for if thou beatest him with the rod, he shall not die.[14] Thou shalt beat him with the rod, and shalt deliver his soul from hell." Again, this sets up the grisly, barbaric idea that punishment is somehow a glorious requirement for redemption and successful living.

This particular verse has been weaponized by religious circles for thousands of years, advocating parents to spank their children with a rod or belt — without a shred of evidence that it actually helps. In fact, the aforementioned research and a multitude of studies indicate the direct opposite is true.

In 1985, the American Medical Association declared, "Infliction of pain or discomfort, however minor, is not a desirable method of communicating with children," when it called for the abolishment of corporal punishment in schools.[6] The report of its 370-member House of Delegates added, "The official sanction of corporal punishment imparts approval to actions that have the potential for serious injury."

Spanking is child abuse, in the opinion of scientific research. A 2004 study by the University of Michigan analyzing data of more than 1800 children confirmed that spanking is detrimental to children. Study author Andrew Grogan-Kaylor, professor of social work and expert in theology and ethics at the university, said "Even minimal amounts of spanking can lead to an increased likelihood in antisocial behavior by children."[7]

Alvin Poussaint, M.D., Professor of Psychiatry, Harvard Medical School, said, "Researchers have also found that children who are spanked show higher rates of aggression and delinquency in childhood than those who were not spanked. As adults, they are more prone to depression, feelings of alienation, use of violence toward a spouse, and lower economic and professional achievement. None of this is what we want for our children."[8]

It is difficult to understand how parents today who strike their children think that is acceptable or helpful. It is ironic, however, how many of those same parents are against beating other adults, including at times when "they need to learn a lesson." That is blatant hypocrisy arising from ancient, barbaric teachings centered largely around punishment, when our ancestors knew little about science, the psychological impact from behavior, and causal factors, for instance.

Instead, our predecessors made up fables and culturalized instruction for corporal punishment without study because they had few tools to study cause and effect, and more importantly, they lacked the willingness, capability, and open-mindedness to look for real answers. Consequently, their myths and badly conceived ideas labeled as truth and justice were passed down through generations via blind inheritance. In his 1931 novel *Brave New World*, English philosopher Aldous Huxley wrote, "One believes things because one has been conditioned to believe them."

Regardless of the time period in which one lives, it is far better to say, "I don't know the answer to this issue, so we will keep studying to find out what is true" — just as our Divine Child explores and learns what is real rather than conjure fiction. It is arrogance and pride that suppresses and subdues truth, open-mindedness and authenticity. Socrates said, "The only true wisdom is in knowing you know nothing." Speaking false statements in the media or through gossip leads to mass forms of spiritual abuse, which have both now become widespread plagues, particularly in American culture.

The saying "spare the rod, spoil the child" is a popular example, originating from a 17th century poem entitled "Hudibras" by Samuel Butler, where he forms a parallel between a love affair and a child. In this poem, Butler mocks spanking as a recommendation to make the love grow stronger. He directed his work at the militant Puritanical fanaticism, pretentiousness, and hypocrisy,[9] using poetry to reveal these offenses by the religious orders in general:[10]

> What medicine else can cure the fits
> Of lovers, when they lose their wits?
> Love is a boy, by poets styled,
> Then spare the rod, and spoil the child.

Without knowledge and understanding the intention and context of Samuel Butler's words, the last line of this poem, along with the biblical book of Proverbs, has been used as a bad supporting argument for parents to beat their children. Regardless of their ill-informed justifications, forms of punishment that include spanking, hitting, and striking a child or adult are still abuse. As someone once said, "Spanking does for a child's development what wife-beating does for a marriage."

The parent who strikes his children is unconsciously teaching them a few things. First, the parent who thinks it is acceptable to strike helpless children unable to protect themselves is acting as a bully and coward, unwittingly passing violence and bullying cowardice to the child. Secondly, it teaches children to embrace hypocrisy, suggesting it is permissible for the adult in charge to hit helpless children to "teach" them positive behavior. Yet, the authority figure himself who delivers the beatings is unwilling to undergo the same physical abuse for things he himself needs to learn.

Striking children also teaches them to blindly accept ideas that were handed down in tradition, however untrue and toxic. Hitting children teaches them to ignore discovery and science, which has repeatedly demonstrated that hitting a child causes long-term damage. Frederick Douglass said, "It is easier to build strong children than to repair broken men."

Finally, spanking children defies the Golden Rule, a direct commandment of Jesus. In his book *Thy Rod and Thy Staff They Comfort Me: Christians and the Spanking Controversy*, Samuel Martin wrote, "When parents sin, they ask God to forgive them, repent and know they are forgiven. When children sin, they are judged, tried, condemned and punished." It is the vulnerable and innocent that often becomes the easy prey.

Smacking children to deliver pain passes a spiritually dark tradition to them, giving the child unspoken permission to continue this abusive domino effect with their children that plagues future generations. A tree's roots spread out as its branches expand and tower. When pain grows unhealed and then normalized through social structures, toxicity becomes cemented within a culture.

Many parents strike their kids because the parents are projecting their own rage, transferring it unto the children using deceitful religious teachings that were established to control others using the threat of punishment. Dr. Asa Don Brown says, "Spanking a child is about the parent, not the child. The child will learn more from positive correction than physical manipulation." Studies confirm that abused children grow up to be aggressive and depressed adults.[11]

In his June 2007 article entitled "The Dangers Associated with Hitting Children," Dr. Ralph S. Walsh wrote, "During my long career evaluating juvenile delinquents (now numbering in the thousands, and still climbing as a Court-Based Assessment Psychologist), I have yet to see the first violent male juvenile delinquent who wasn't raised on a belt, board, extension cord, fist or the equivalent. I have carefully excluded all forms of discipline that were incapable of causing lasting physical marks or damage including hand slaps, hands to the rear, and even a switch to the legs. I am still amazed at the consistency of the 'belt' and its equivalents in producing angry and violent behavior."[12]

Physical abuse usually does not stand alone. It is typically accompanied by emotional, mental, and spiritual abuse as well. Rape is a prime example, where the victim has been traumatized physically, emotionally, and spiritually. In the case of rape, overpowering someone using sexual energy is a spiritual violation of self-control, equality, freedom of choice, and playfulness.

Those who say, "I was beat with a belt or spanked as a child, and I turned out ok" are blinded by ignorance, refusing see the greater picture of life. Inflicted pain doesn't magically disappear. It *always* has negative repercussions, even if we do not see readily them. Striking a child is not only highly damaging to one's own family, but also a dark legacy of misery, pain, aggression, violence, and depression that inevitably spreads like a spiritual cancer.

All forms of abuse to children lead to death on many levels. Laura Davis, communicator and author of a number of books about healing that include *Allies in Healing: When the Person You Love Is a Survivor of Child Sexual Abuse*, wrote, "Abuse manipulates and twists a child's natural sense of trust and love. Her innocent feelings are belittled or mocked, and she learns to ignore her feelings. She can't afford to feel the full range of feelings in her body while she's being abused — pain, outrage, hate, vengeance, confusion, arousal. So she short-circuits them and goes numb. For many children, any expression of feelings, even a single tear, is cause for more severe abuse. Again, the only recourse is to shut down. Feelings go underground."

Children are incapable of protecting themselves. The ancient idea that punishment teaches long-term positive behavior is not only erroneous, but highly toxic, defying substantial scientific evidence. Myth swallowed as truth is foolhardy and dangerous, but learning and discovery teaches us what is actually true. It is the place of freedom, the playground of your Divine Child.

How Institutions Can Spread Abuse Culturally

This form of child abuse in the family unit and religious tribe has now become cultural and widespread, giving permission for many other forms of violent behavior, including sex trafficking, bullying, violence towards women, mass genocide, gun violence, and terrorism, which have now proliferated throughout our schools, companies, movie theatres, churches, and other institutions. If the child is not safe and protected, who else can be?

Uprooting this catastrophe on a personal and institutional level is required to experience peace, safety, and true protection. In his 1919 lecture on the abuse of the fear instinct published in the *Journal of Abnormal Psychology*, Ukrainian-American psychiatrist Boris Sidis said, "As long as the child will be trained not by love, but by fear, so long will humanity live not by justice, but by force. As long as the child will be ruled by the educator's threat and by the father's rod, so long will mankind be dominated by the policeman's club, by fear of jail, and by panic of invasion by armies and navies."[13]

Control and manipulation are aggressively spread by limiting and manipulating someone's freedom. As children and adults, we are told what not to do, rather than what to do. "No" is one of the first words and concepts that most children often learn. The reinforcement of negative behavior originating from ancient barbaric teachings, religious or otherwise, is often based on punishment and potential heavenly reward, rather than to promote positive behavior as the central focus. The Ten Commandments, a tenet of Judeo-Christian ideology, affirm this.

But the Divine Child knows nothing about religious teachings, because the purity and innocence of a Divine Child uses its curiosity, open-mindedness, observation, and exploration to discover what is true, rather than blindly swallowing packaged rhetoric handed to it. Our inner child operates from its own innate awareness and wisdom, based on what brings more joy. As Jesus said, your inner child is the key to your wisdom and success.

Other Silent Killers of Passion

Destruction of passion also occurs when parents don't allow children to make their own decisions. Mental health counselor Laura Dessauer, a board-certified art therapist with a doctoral degree in counseling psychology, says that co-dependency can occur when "a helicopter parent didn't allow you to dress yourself or choose your own playmates and food."[14] Dessaur suggests that when parents do not let their children make their own decisions, they may later seek out relationships in which the partner has the power and control.[15]

Restricting playtime is another destroyer of passion. In a 2011 article published in the *American Journal of Play*, author Peter Gray, Ph.D., emeritus professor of psychology at Boston College, said, "Since about 1955…children's free play has been continually declining, at least partly because adults have exerted ever-increasing control over children's activities." Gray defines free play as an activity that a child undertakes herself or himself that is self-directed and for the sole purpose of play, rather than part of an organized activity managed by others.[16]

His definition liberates the Divine Child to exercise the spiritual qualities of playfulness, curiosity, learning, self-control, freedom, and being present. Gray suggests that parents who "hover over and intrude on their children's play" are a big part of the problem. "It is hard to find groups of children outdoors at all, and, if you do find them, they are likely to be wearing uniforms and following the directions of coaches while their parents dutifully watch and cheer," he says.[17]

In a study that assessed how children ages six to eight spent their time in 1981 and 1997, researchers discovered children played less and had less free time overall. In 1997, the children spent 18 percent more time at school, 145 percent more time doing homework, and 168 percent more time shopping with parents.[18] Gray says that less playtime translates to increased anxiety and depression in children.

> The greater a child's terror, and the earlier it is experienced, the harder it becomes to develop a strong and healthy sense of self.
>
> Nathaniel Branden
> *Six Pillars of Self-Esteem*

Since 1960, playtime for kids has dropped significantly, while mental disorders among children have skyrocketed. Some estimates say that *five to eight times* as many high school and college students today suffer major depression and/or anxiety disorder, versus the number of students just fifty years ago.[19] One study based upon the National Survey of Children's Health that was reported in the *Journal of Developmental and Behavioral Pediatrics* says that about 2.6 million (5.3 percent) American children and adolescents were diagnosed with anxiety and/or depression in 2011 and 2012, with the number of kids with anxiety increasing 17 percent from 2007 to 2011.[20]

Today, one in five American children and young adults suffer from a mental illness or learning disorder, and two-thirds of them are either untreated or undiagnosed.[21] In another study looking at more than 170,000 teens, the number of adolescents suffering from major depressive episodes jumped 30 percent from 2005 to 2014, according to Dr. Ramin Mojtabai of Johns Hopkins University and his colleagues whose report was published in the journal *Pediatrics*. "Each year almost one in 11 adolescents and young adults has a major depressive episode," they wrote.[22]

Are We Ignoring Our Children?

The Information Age beginning in the 1940s gave birth to dazzling electronic toys that are quickly replacing the television as the new electronic distractor. It is disheartening to watch thousands of parents at restaurants plop a screen in front of their children rather than interacting with them. Is this laziness, or have parents become too pressured by stress? By reaching out for the quick and easy fix, the message is loud and clear: "This toy is more important than human interaction." It is no wonder why young adults today spend an average of nine hours each day on social media. With our entrained addictions to electronic gadgetry and social media, we adults have implanted the idea into our children that the source of attention, information, connection, and nurturing is handheld, not heart-held.

When parents pay more attention to their children, they will likely have greater social skills and academic competence, according to a 2014 study of 243 children born into poverty. "Sensitive caregiving" during the first three years resulted in better academic tests in childhood, greater academic attainment in the thirties, and healthier relationships.[23] It is essential for parents to "respond to their child's signals promptly and appropriately" and provide a secure base for their kids to explore the world. Coauthor and University of Minnesota psychologist Lee Raby says, "This suggests that investments in early parent-child relationships may result in long-term returns that accumulate across individuals' lives."[24]

Success in adulthood becomes more probable when mothers take maternity leave to care for their children, according to recent research from the Institute for the Study of Labor (IZA) in Bonn. The mothers' increased time with their newborns led to a decline in the high school dropout rate and a five percent increase in wages at age 30. For mothers with lower education, the impact was even higher for their children, with a 5.2 percent decline in the dropout rate and 8 percent increase in wages at age 30.[25] The researchers cited this as a reason for U.S. policymakers to discuss and implement paid maternity leave programs that can reduce the existing gap in education and income in the United States. The energetic portal of a major experience, such as birth, getting married, or starting a new job, is often the most important moment for investment that leads to big dividends later on.

A study by the University of North Carolina found that paid-leave programs can substantially lower mortality rates of infants and young children and improve their overall health. The study examined data from 16 European countries over the period from 1969 through 1994.[26] A more recent study examining the effects of parental leave on child health in 18 countries, including the United States, found that when job-protected paid leave was available, infant mortality rates declined an average of 2.5 percent.[27]

> The homemaker has the ultimate career. All other careers exist for one purpose only — and that is to support the ultimate career.
>
> C.S. Lewis

While the United States is one of only eight countries that fails to offer paid leave to new moms and dads,[28] some states have made tremendous progress. In 2004, California became the first state to implement a paid family-leave policy that provides eligible employees at least 55 percent of their wages up to six weeks. In 2018, that law expanded the payment up to 70 percent for low-wage earners and up to 60 percent for nearly all other employees.

Other states instituting paid family leave policies include New Jersey, which implemented its law in 2009, Rhode Island in 2014, New York in 2018 (with a phased increase by 2021), the District of Columbia (to take effect in 2020), Washington (taking effect in 2019 and 2020), and Massachusetts, where its legislature passed a paid family and medical leave law that takes effect in 2019 and be fully phased in by 2021.[29]

The father's role is also essential for the child to live life passionately as an adult. Israeli researchers found that the more time fathers take to care for children when they are young, the more the father's brain changes to make them better suited to parent. The scientists noted that the increased activity in the father's amygdala and other emotional-processing centers of the brain causes them to experience parental emotions similar to the mother's emotions,[30] where the father become more emotional and sensitive. "In fathers, their parenting is guided much more by understanding and empathizing in a cognitive way," said study senior author Ruth Feldman, a researcher in the department of psychology and the Gonda Brain Sciences Center at Bar-Ilan University in Israel. The study also included 48 gay fathers who raised infants in a committed relationship.

Another study by Columbia University professors discovered that fathers who take at least two weeks off to care for a child after it is born are more involved in the child's care nine months later. Dr. Lenna Nepomnyaschy and Dr. Jane Waldfogel at the Columbia University School of Social Work used data involving more than 4,500 two-parent families that suggested better father-child relationships can happen as a result of paid paternity leave.[31]

> The greatest thing a father can do for his children is to respect the woman that gave birth to his children. It is because of her that you have the greatest treasures in your life. You may have moved on, but your children have not. If you can't be her soulmate, then at least be thoughtful. Whom your children love should always be someone that you acknowledge with kindness. Your children notice everything and will follow your example.
>
> Shannon L. Alder

The healthy bond between a father and his child is essential for better relationships as an adult. When children have a healthy emotional connection with their fathers, the likelihood of the child entering a healthy, physically intimate relationship with a partner later in life increases, according to a study from the University of Haifa. Lead researcher Dr. Nurit Nahmani said, "The research found a definitive connection between the quality of the father-child relationship and interpersonal relationships later in life."[32]

Eight Ways to Reactivate Your Passion

Getting reconnected to your inner passion will fuel your heart-felt dreams and help make them a reality. To discover, reignite, or expand your passion, here are some tips to engage that magical power:

1. <u>Do what you love.</u> The late great comedian and actor George Burns, who lived to be 100 years old, said, "I'd rather be a failure at something I love than a success at something I hate." Don't cave in to do work just for a paycheck. You'll age faster, be unhappier, and suffer in your relationships.

2. <u>Live your own dreams, not the dreams that others wish for you</u>. Have you found that you are doing what someone else wants you to do? Instead, follow what your inner pulse so quietly yet powerfully urges.

3. <u>Dream BIG</u>. Nelson Mandela said, "There is no passion to be found in playing small…in settling for a life that is less than what you are capable of living." Dreams from your inner child are BIG, allowing you to see what you thought were the outer bounds of your capabilities. When you advance toward those outer boundaries, you will discover that those imaginary limitations you or someone else created for you are fiction.

4. <u>Every day, fan the flames of your dreams</u>. Take a small step each day that leads you even an inch closer to your envisioned outcome. Your fire will never be extinguished, regardless of feeling down, depressed, and empty. There is always a burning flame of passion inside of you, however small, even if it has been dampened by past events or people.

5. <u>Know that only you can fulfill your own destiny</u>. There is only one of you that can fill your shoes and achieve your powerful destiny. If you truly believe in the philosophy that you are destined to do "greater

things," begin celebrating your own birth, your life, and your dreams more than anyone's, including any spiritual master, regardless of religious dogma that may try to convince you that you are smaller than any spiritual teacher. Make your special moments your own holidays — bigger than the Fourth of July, Christmas, or Easter. By reinforcing the power within yourself, you can light up the world with the fuel of passion that can never be extinguished.

6. <u>Let your joy be your guide to your passion</u>. Joy is the barometer of your soul. When you feel badly, it is time for a correction to your path. Remain curious and ask for help. All of your answers ultimately lie within yourself, as the great masters have taught.

7. <u>Serve others</u>. Despite a world filled with self-absorption with the focus on selfies and instant fulfillment of pleasure at the expense of others, you can find ways to live your passion that serves a greater cause beyond just you. The collective you — the tribe made up of you, your friends and family, and everything and everyone else in the Universe — will rise in rich blessing when you discover ways to be of service to the greater good of all. This is the real meaning of love, empathy, and compassion in motion.

8. <u>Recognize that you are a spiritual being, not just a human doing</u>. Your spiritual qualities of your Divine Child are the secret to all lasting success. Spend time cultivating this fertile garden that is subtle and seemingly mystical, but is real and quite powerful. The finer aspects of you are spiritually golden — the heavenly experience that Jesus and other philosophers often referred to that will lead to true wealth and rich abundance in your life.

Most successful leaders have one thing in common: They agree that passion is one of the essential ingredients for success in not only work, but also in finances, relationships, health, and overall happiness. Small children don't need to learn that fact, because this spiritual energy is already vibrant and expressed in them. Many of us adults, however, have lost our innate enthusiasm through some sort of external trauma we experienced, usually in early childhood.

When we have passion, it is difficult to suppress it. These positive spiritual energies radiate outward spontaneously, spreading their goodness and gifts to everyone. Enthusiasm and passion are highly contagious. When passion is shared, this wondrous energy expands exponentially.

When passion is alive within our Divine Child, its energetic sibling is present as well: expressiveness.

---

[1] https://www.biography.com/writer/laura-ingalls-wilder

[2] https://www.britannica.com/biography/Susan-Boyle

[3] https://www.britannica.com/biography/Susan-Boyle

[4] https://jamanetwork.com/journals/jamapsychiatry/fullarticle/1654916?resultClick=3#RESULTS

[5] https://www.theguardian.com/society/2011/aug/15/depression-childhood-abuse-maltreatment?CMP=aff_1432&awc=5795_1546910120_2641b605fa5f063fab102ebf9cb0c05c

[6] https://apnews.com/4b40c16f85596ed1abbb6e2c4f5a9db7

[7] https://news.umich.edu/u-m-study-spanking-can-lead-to-more-bad-behavior-by-children/

[8] Kimberley Blaine. 2010. Jossey-Bass, San Francisco. *The Go-To Mom's Parents' Guide to Emotion Coaching Young Children.* p. 85.

[9] https://www.britannica.com/topic/Hudibras-poem-by-Butler

[10] *Hudibras* by Samuel Butler. Pt. 1-3, ed. by A. Milnes, Parts 2-3, p. 25.

[11] https://www.webmd.com/parenting/news/20010212/early-abuse-leads-to-later-aggression#1

[12] https://www.nospank.net/welsh12.htm

[13] https://psycnet.apa.org/record/1926-01068-001

[14] https://www.independent.co.uk/news/science/25-scientific-ways-your-childhood-influences-your-success-as-an-adult-a6865296.html

[15] https://www.psychologytoday.com/us/blog/business-success-therapists/201108/are-you-raising-codependent-child

[16] https://www.theatlantic.com/health/archive/2011/10/all-work-and-no-play-why-your-kids-are-more-anxious-depressed/246422/

[17] IBID

[18] IBID

[19] https://www.psychologytoday.com/us/blog/freedom-learn/201001/the-decline-play-and-rise-in-childrens-mental-disorder

[20] https://www.sciencedaily.com/releases/2018/04/180424184119.htm

[21] https://www.nbcnews.com/health/kids-health/generation-risk-america-s-youngest-facing-mental-health-crisis-n827836

[22] https://www.nbcnews.com/health/mental-health/depression-worsening-teens-especially-girls-n683716

[23] https://onlinelibrary.wiley.com/doi/abs/10.1111/cdev.12325

[24] https://www.spring.org.uk/2015/01/this-early-parental-behaviour-predicts-a-childs-academic-and-social-skills-3-decades-later.php)

[25] http://ftp.iza.org/dp5793.pdf

[26] https://www.sciencedirect.com/science/article/abs/pii/S0167629600000473

[27] http://massbudget.org/report_window.php?loc=Time_to_Care-The_Health_Effects_of_PFML.html

[28] https://www.bustle.com/p/which-states-have-paid-family-leave-new-york-rang-in-2018-with-big-changes-7744450

[29] http://www.nationalpartnership.org/our-work/resources/workplace/paid-leave/paid-leave-works-in-california-new-jersey-and-rhode-island.pdf

[30] https://consumer.healthday.com/caregiving-information-6/infant-and-child-care-health-news-410/dad-s-brain-becomes-more-maternal-when-he-s-primary-caregiver-study-688176.html

[31] http://www.columbia.edu/cu/news/07/06/paternity.html

[32] https://www.eurekalert.org/pub_releases/2007-02/uoh-tqo021907.php

Expressive

Our heritage and ideals, our code and standards — the things we live by and teach our children — are preserved or diminished by how freely we exchange ideas and feelings.

Walt Disney

The level of our natural enthusiasm determines how readily we express ourselves. It reveals how alive we are inside. The moment you express what is inside of you — whether it be passion, empathy, or joy — it becomes alive and real. If we "love" someone, it is imperative that we share those Divine Child traits that in common with every human being. Those energies are only powerful when we put them into action and shared with others.

Children are naturally expressive. They create giant castles in their imaginations that are even bigger than their creations, assembling forts and houses with blankets and boxes in majesty and grandeur. Instantly, kings and queens arrive on the scene, with scepters made of tree branches in hand. Sandcastles become kingdoms, full of limitless expansion for the dreamer. Even if the waves wash away the kingdom, the child knows that she or he can quickly build an even larger kingdom, perhaps incorporating a protective moat. Our creativity is a way the soul expresses itself.

Communication became ignited on a cultural level in the latter part of the twentieth century, when online social media was born during the Age of Self-Expression. This was the Throat Chakra stage, the fifth stage of development on a global level. Facebook, YouTube, Instagram, Twitter, and other online apps emerged during this time period, attracting billions of users globally. With the smartphone and social media giving the world new ways to express themselves, it seems everyone has become a philosopher, news originator, and distributor, giving their spin on the world to their virtual communities.

The downside of this new medium, however, is the temptation to live there, spending many hours each day where the Divine Child often gets lost in the fray and chatter. Authenticity and joy can easily get crushed when negativity steps in. In the online world, people often assume they will feel safer, but that illusion sometimes encourages behaviors that would not be expressed in person otherwise. Negativity has soared in the digital world, even in communication between strangers.

> Let children read whatever they want and then
> talk about it with them. If parents and kids can
> talk together, we won't have as much censorship
> because we won't have as much fear.
>
> Judy Blume

In her book *Sometimes I Lie*, Alice Feeney wrote, "I can't pretend to understand social media, either. I mean, I get it, I just don't understand why so many people spend so much time engaging with it. It's not real. It's just noise." Is it our Wounded Child or Divine Child doing the talking on social media? If we step away from the conversations for a moment and simply sit in silence, our Divine Child reveals through its Heart center who is speaking. To the extent that you feel expanded or contracted, you can determine the source. Usually, negative emotional responses are from our Wounded Child.

The Importance of Expression

Expression is the natural course of the soul's energy. It brings life and animation that feeds our dreams. As we inhale, we take in vitality into our bodies, and when we exhale, we send our energy to the world. Truly, expression is how the soul creates in the physical world.

Expressing ourselves is not only a key part of the creative process and foundation of our personal power, self-expression can help curb fears. In a 2012 study published in the journal *Psychological Science*, UCLA scientists demonstrated that "affect-labeling" — putting your feelings into words — lowered fears, improved the physiological measurements of the fear arousal, and increased the willingness to face the fear.[1]

The power of speaking authentically about fears and worries was also affirmed in the research by Dr. Sian Beilock and her colleague Dr. Gerardo Ramirez. In their study, Beilock and Ramirez found that when high school students spent ten minutes writing down their worries on paper before taking a high-stress exam, the students boosted their test performance with a five percent improvement in grades. So, journal away your worries and fears! Be your authentic self.

Novelist Pearl S. Buck said, "Self-expression must pass into communication for its fulfillment.[2] Emotional intelligence executive coach Svetlana Whitener emphasized the importance of expressing your feelings congruently, where your tone of your voice, words, and body languages match. Authenticity is another characteristic of our Divine Child in order for the power and fulfillment our communication to be asserted.[3]

In her 2018 article in *Forbes*, Whitener reports that full expression and communication is comprised of three different components: Body language makes up 55 percent, tone of voice makes up 38 percent, and words only 7 percent of our communication. She is referring to the "7 percent rule" that Dr. Albert Mehrabian, psychologist and Professor Emeritus of Psychology at UCLA, discussed in his 1971 book *Silent Messages*. Mehrabian's research concluded that only seven percent of communication of salespeople were their words, while the predominant components of communication were non-verbal, such as body language and tone of voice.[4]

While some have dismissed his research, the studies conducted by Allan and Barbara Pease analyzing thousands of recorded sales interviews and negotiations during the 1970s and 1980s found that body language accounts for 60 to 80 percent of impact in business encounters, such as negotiations. The Peases, who published this finding in their 1978 book *Body Language*, also determined that people form 60 to 80 percent of their initial opinions about a new person in under four minutes.[5]

Nonverbal language is powerful, because it forms recognizable images that can get distributed more quickly and therefore have a greater impact. Regardless of the exact numbers and mix of factors, keep in mind that expressing yourself is much more than speaking your thoughts and feelings. Your non-verbal communication is important in how you connect with others, which says a lot more than words can do.

The Danger of Holding Back

Austrian neurologist Sigmund Freud, who founded psychoanalysis, said, "Unexpressed emotions will never die. They are buried alive and will come forth later in uglier ways." Is it possible that the external violence we witness today comes from suppressed or unresolved anger?

Michelle Farris, a psychotherapist and anger management specialist, believes that health and relationship problems can occur when we suppress our anger. Anger has a tremendous value by telling us that something isn't right and that we need to make a change, she explains.

By suppressing our anger, however, long-term stress creates a damaging cycle. "The body stores the emotions that cannot be expressed until they can be released," says Farris, who has a private practice in San Jose, California. She points to serious problems, including an increased risk for heart attack, stroke, anxiety, and a weakened immune system to those who suppress their anger and other negative emotions.[6] Farris says that holding anger inside leads to "a tendency to overreact, because stuffed emotions are harder to control." To help people express their emotions, she offers a free email course on anger called *Catching Your Anger Before It Hurts* and works with clients to improve relationships, manage anger more effectively, and deal with codependency issues.

Other researchers have pointed to long-term physical and psychological damage from bottling up emotions. After all, many of us have learned "not to cry." Men are taught to suppress their feelings, with the false premise that women are more emotional and therefore the weaker of the two sexes. Psychotherapist Rose Lawrence advises that men run the risk of exploding due to their suppression of emotions,[7] which leads to serious consequences for failing to manage their stress in healthy ways.

Unresolved emotions lead to chronic stress, triggering the fight-or-flight response of the nervous system. This can lead to abdominal pain, since the "brain-gut axis" is part of the central nervous system, as Harvard Medical School researchers discovered. Their 2010 study found that even less severe kinds of stress, such as driving in traffic, public speaking, or an argument can disrupt or slow the digestive process, resulting in gas, bloating, vomiting, constipation, and even ulcers.[8]

Suppressing emotions can also cause neck and head pain, as Lawrence explains, due to the tightening of the jaw muscles. From an energy standpoint, choking back our expressive energy causes the Throat Chakra to begin to slow down its spin, tighten up, and become sluggish, which in turn prevents the energy in the physical body from flowing freely. When the natural flow of the Divine Child's energy becomes restricted and rigid, a domino effect of cascading problems ensues.

When the corrugator muscles — the small, pyramidal muscles near the eyes that furrow the eyebrows — tighten when we suppress our emotional energy, a frown replaces the natural inclination to smile. Psychologist Daniel Golman said that the corrugator muscles are a good predictor of stress in the entire body, where the tightening of these muscles can reduce blood flow to the brain, potentially causing splitting headaches and migraines.[9]

The heart is also at risk with chronically angry people. A study showed that the risk of heart attack increased 8.5 times and lasted up to two hours after an extreme episode of anger, and nearly ten times higher after extreme anxiety. Other data shows that people prone to anger are nearly three times more likely to suffer heart attacks than people with lower levels of anger.[10] Lao Tzu said, "The best fighter is never angry."

Where is Expressive Energy and its Negative Counterpart?

Self-expression is governed by the Throat Chakra, the Fifth energy center of the body located just above the Heart Chakra. It is said that one's past lives are also connected to the Throat Chakra, which illustrates how talents, knowledge, challenges, and lessons to be learned carried from previous incarnations are expressed in verbal and nonverbal communication. Through this vital energy center, we access our strengths and weaknesses, incorporating them both subconsciously and intentionally into unique ways we express ourselves.

With the Third Eye, the seat of inspiration of the Sixth Chakra, expression is born through desire and action. The inspired idea can then be conveyed in the material world, as the energy descends to the Throat Chakra, where outward expression first begins. Perhaps you will speak or write your inspired idea down in your journal or draw a diagram of the image held in your mind's eye.

Other energy centers can be triggered through this process, such as the Second Chakra of creativity, where you put the idea into motion outwardly. With this chakra, your inner child builds elaborate sandcastles, organizes a fashion show with dolls, and stirs up a banquet of mud pies fit for a queen or king, after passing through the Third Chakra of motivation and personal power.

If expressive energy is shut down, it turns dark into its negative counterparts: unfeeling, aloofness, indifference, and apathy. When our nature to express begins to wither, our aliveness dries up. At this stage, others find us unsympathetic and uncharitable, and spiritual and physical hoarding can result. As we shut down, sharing slows substantially, as selfishness consumes our natural state of giving to others.

Insensitivity is another characteristic of someone whose expressive ability has been stunted. In this state, we lose touch with our own feelings and those who are close to us. If we stop expressing ourselves, we close down the channels of communication. Our spirit, once alive and expanding, stops growing and becomes like a dry, brittle leaf.

At this point, the energy turns inward and self-focused in self-serving ways, rather than radiating our positive spiritual qualities that were once alive and giving. The narcissist largely communicates with the negative expressions of his or her spiritual qualities — such as aloofness or apathy — where the energy becomes self-directed rather than shared. In its suffering and wounded condition, the authentic Divine Child has lost its way.

> We are stronger when we listen, and smarter when we share.
>
> Rania Al-Abdullah

Holocaust survivor, Elie Wiesel, who won the Nobel Peace Prize in 1986, wrote, "The opposite of love is not hate, it's indifference. The opposite of art is not ugliness, it's indifference. The opposite of faith is not heresy, it's indifference. And the opposite of life is not death, it's indifference." Aloofness and apathy shatter the human spirit when they overtake the expressive Divine Child.

The way back is to reactivate these powerful spiritual energies. With healing, the authentic, expressive Divine Child is reborn, where we magnetize success on all levels with greater ease.

Expressing our Divine Child Transforms the World

Our Divine Child is also the expressive champion of social causes, elevating our world to new heights. After a long day of work at the Montgomery Fair department store on the December 1, 1955, the seamstress, Rosa Parks, refused to give up her seat to a white man on the bus.

Immediately following her arrest and conviction for violating segregation laws, community leaders quickly organized the bus boycott that day. Parks lost her department store job, and her husband was also fired. The boycott lasted for more than a year, led by the young Reverend Dr. Martin Luther King Jr., and ended when the Supreme Court ruled on November 13, 1956, that the segregation bus laws in Montgomery, Alabama, were unconstitutional.[11]

Through the mastery of her Divine Child, Parks expressed the spiritual value of equality, becoming a national symbol of strength and dignity in the struggle to end deeply embedded racial segregation. Expressing yourself involves not only sharing your talents and gifts with the world around you, but also the innate spiritual qualities that unite us all. Our aliveness gets replenished when we continually express these transcendent values, as Rosa Parks affirmed in her autobiography. She said, "People always say that I didn't give up my seat because I was tired, but that isn't true. I was not tired physically... No, the only tired I was, was tired of giving in."

Unwilling to surrender, she was bubbling with the energy of equality that unites all of humanity. Using the natural power of her Divine Child, Rosa Parks became a spiritual catalyst, and the world is far better because of her sharing.

The Genius of Expressing

Expressing is sharing. Our words, music, art, clothing, food, and other physical creations we generate are conduits that make our expressions magical. These physical objects are carriers of the energies within us. As I discussed in my previous book *Spiritual Values in the Workplace*, it is to the extent that we share these spiritual values with others that we connect and bring value to ourselves and the world.

Our music and dancing come alive through expressing these energetic qualities. True beauty radiates not from a particular shade of lipstick color or how well our top matches our jeans and shoes, but through our inner beauty and brilliance that we share with others. Our inner beauty is the radiant blessing, transcending any social media posting of clothing or a new hairdo. Our spiritual qualities connect to the heart, while our physical qualities connect to the senses.

The genius within us burns brightly only when we express ourselves. Noman Rockwell, who became one of America's cherished artists after leaving high school to study art, said, "Eisenhower had about the most expressive face I ever painted, I guess. Just like an actor's. Very mobile. When he talked, he used all the facial muscles. And he had a great, wide mouth that I liked. When he smiled, it was just like the sun came out."

You, too, radiate when you express yourself. On the other hand, the Wounded Child is aloof, bored, or listless, forgetting his or her natural way to convey what is inside, or being too afraid to communicate authentically. The writer Andre Dubus said, "Shyness has a strange element of narcissism, a belief that how we look, how we perform, is truly important to other people."

I think he was correct. In our externally focused world, people really don't care about your clothes, hairstyle, or shade of lipstick, just as small children do not. The Divine Child simple enjoys being authentic, expressing, and sharing experiences. The purpose of your life is to create from your unique perspective and desire, and to express that inner pulse through your own distinctive creations that only you can share with the world.

Life is exciting when we express ourselves with others. Guy de Maupassant, the 19th century French writer who became known as the master of the short story form, said, "It is the encounters with people that make life worth living."

All success requires flow and expression. When we stop expressing, we stop the flow and diminish our unlimited potential. Successful relationships unfold as a result of communicating on all levels. Our financial abundance is directly related to our ability to express yourselves, regardless of occupation. Physical health becomes supercharged by moving our body, while being sedentary for long periods of time produces decay. Our emotional energy is balanced and harmonious when we convey our feelings in healthy and productive ways.

You cannot be successful and produce things of value unless you express yourself. It requires action. Best-selling inspirational author Don Miguel Ruiz said, "The real you is still a little child who never grew up. Sometimes that little child comes out when you are having fun or playing, when you feel happy, when you are painting, or writing poetry, or playing the piano, or expressing yourself in some way. These are the happiest moments of your life — when the real you comes out, when you don't care about the past, and you don't worry about the future. You are childlike. But there is something that changes all that: We call them responsibilities."

The Power of Gratitude

Many books have been written about gratitude, another important aspect of expressing ourselves. From popular books such as *The Secret* to Dale Carnegie's *How to Win Friends and Influence People*, numerous authors have discussed the art of appreciation and why it energizes and strengthens us. In his best-selling book *A New Earth: Awakening to Your Life's Purpose*, Eckhart Tolle reveals one of the pillars of success: "Acknowledging the good that you already have in your life is the foundation for all abundance." Expressing what is good in our lives delivers more goodness.

> Gratitude is not only the greatest of virtues but the parent of all others.
>
> Marcus Tullius Cicero

What makes expressing our gratitude so powerful? Whether it is with a gracious note of appreciation or telling someone how much we appreciate her or him, the magic ingredient we call gratitude is the state of expression where we send the message to the Universe: "This brings me joy…and I want more of it!"

Reconnecting with our joy and aliveness generates unlimited success for not only ourselves, but for everyone around us. Expressing joy effortlessly and spontaneously kicks our "success engine" into high gear. The expression of gratitude flows naturally, not in a contrived way or employing a technique for material gain. Demonstrating our gratitude is a vibrant magnifier, where this inner vitality is the natural state of our Divine Child.

How Our Expressive Energy Becomes Spiritually Contaminated

As children, we freely express ourselves and hold little to nothing back. I remember a time when visiting my grandmother that my cousin Jenny, who was probably about five years old then, said, "Grandma, you have yellow teeth!" The adults in the living room gasped and tried to suppress their nervous giggles, while Jenny looked sweetly at my grandmother and her yellow teeth. There was no filter nor intention to cause harm or injure — only truth, authenticity, and expression.

Free expression doesn't give us the right to say or do anything we want. The Golden Rule in action suggests how we communicate with others. Is our intention to hurt or damage someone else, or is our desire to help others? Small children usually do not wish to harm someone else, until they learn that it is possible to injure someone else with words or actions where they think it helps themselves. Often, we may have a conscious intention, but many actions are unconsciously driven by early wounding.

Instead, open and spontaneous communication flows naturally for the Divine Child, until it erroneously learns that it isn't safe. When children are punished for authentic expression, they learn to hold back and shut down. When the turtle sees danger, it retracts its head back into its shell and becomes still. Shyness and reservation can emerge from subtle spiritual trauma, where holding back becomes far more frequent than not. The shy child is the Wounded Child who lives in quiet fear, afraid to express and create.

> It is usually the walls of our own self-perception and internal wounding — not external walls of limitation — that hold us back from achieving great success.

Another way that nearly all of us learn to shut down to some degree is due to the nature of emotional energy. Emotions sometimes feel big and unmanageable, and therefore can be misleading, distracting, or intimidating. Anger can feel big and scary, for example. When someone expresses anger, for example, others near that person may become afraid or pull back from that person.

When emotions feel overpowering, either within us or what we sense in others, it can be disconcerting and even frightening. While seemingly harmless, that trauma experienced at an early age is sufficient for someone to start suppressing his or her own emotions, because we may not have learned yet how to manage big emotional energy effectively. That is the role of the Divine Adult to learn, where it can take care of our wounded Divine Child when it starts feeling fearful, anxious, angry, or tense. If we don't have good tools in our emotional toolbox to manage negative emotions in healthy ways that resolve them, the tendency can be to simply suppress them and disconnect.

As with other spiritual qualities, external trauma is what typically causes expressive energy to collapse. As adults, if we experience big feelings that feel overwhelming, it is usually based on a learned pattern due to something that happened to us at an earlier age.

For example, if you were raised by a parent who screamed frequently at you, that pattern will likely carry into adulthood until it is healed, where that screaming adult can show up in your life as a boss, spouse, or other authority figure that causes you to cower the moment the person in charge walks into your office, for example. To the Wounded Child, the boss looks like the screaming parent from the past, since the imprint was absorbed into the physical, emotional, mental, and spiritual bodies of the child through either a single major trauma, or a series of traumatic incidences that create an energetic pattern.

If you have a tendency to yell at others, you can heal it by addressing the original trauma. In her book *The Bimbo Has Brains: And Other Freaky Facts*, Cathy Burnham Martin writes, "If someone yells at me, they are not expressing love. They may be threatening me. They may be expressing great frustration with me. They may simply be trying to control my behavior. However, they are not communicating love."

Shutting down the enthusiasm and expression of a child produces consequences, where the damaging effects can last even a lifetime until the original trauma is healed. Parents have a responsibility to be the guardian of the child, protecting it not only physically, but also emotionally, mentally, and spiritually. As the child grows and develops, good parenting involves protecting the child from trauma while facilitating and encouraging self-expression. This, in my opinion, is the heart and soul of what parenting is really about. As Jackie Kennedy said, "If you bungle raising your child, I don't think whatever else you do matters very much."

How to Ignite Your Expressive Energy for Greater Success

Few people are able to truly express themselves freely and spontaneously like a small child does naturally. At some point, most of us have learned that it feels safe to pull back and suppress ourselves. True safety is an illusion, and the subconscious fight-or-flight mechanism we learned needs to be unlearned for true healing.

English actor and film producer Jason Statham said, "There's a voice in all of us, and you can only get expressive through words. There's a limit to what you can do without speaking." By igniting your natural ability to express more freely, you will enjoy more harmonious and productive relationships, greater prosperity, and better health. Here are some tips to reactivate your expressive energies that lie within you:

- Draw, sketch, and doodle on a regular basis. Perhaps use your non-dominant hand. This reconnects you to your childhood, where we all probably created our own little original works of art. Start your own "Expression Journal" and explore where it takes you.

- Sing and hum, especially in the shower or bathtub. Singing and humming activates the Throat Chakra, opening up the natural channels of self-expression. We all can sing and hum. You don't need to be Barbara Streisand or Ray Charles, because you aren't here to impress anyone. We can all sing for self-pleasure and inner treasure.

- Dance. It's a natural thing many of us did as small children. Move your body and get your energy flowing. Dance in your living room to some great tunes or go out dancing with friends. Gyrating your hips while you move and groove activates the First and Second Chakras, which help you ground and be creative. The renowned dancer and choreographer Martha Graham said, "Dance is the hidden language of the soul." So speak with your body!

- Start building your cherished dreams. Begin with just one big dream inside of you that feeds your soul. Every day, do one thing — however big or small — to nurture and grow that heartfelt desire. Perhaps you can do some research or read about someone who accomplished something similar. By feeding this like a garden, you will attract new resources to you that inspire yourself and others, while achieving the desires of your heart.

- Find your voice and use it. Thomas Oppong suggests that "true creators of any kind must find their voice and freely express themselves."[12] One of the things that makes us special and unique is that we have our own voice — the style, tone, and personality we use. When you find your unique voice, you can change the world in your unique way.

- Stop comparing yourself to others. Measuring your achievements and capabilities by someone's standards limits your ability to express yourself uniquely and naturally. Refuse to succumb to the competition-driven world that craves winners based on statistics. Instead, spend your time discovering your own capabilities and what you perceive to be the outer limits of your potential — then move beyond them.

- Get comfortable with your own emotions...and those of others. "Don't take things personally" is the sage advice of Don Miguel Ruiz. Your EQ (emotional quotient, or emotional intelligence) of your Divine Child is naturally high, so tap into that and let it feed your passion and creative force within.

- Practice being the silent observer. The Divine Child within us looks outward to discover the world and grow, but this energy first burns internally. By turning to that magic within, we can begin to notice where we are holding back. When we discover the stop signs that we erected along our path, we can then find the underlying cause — the original pain and trauma — that halted our expressive nature, and then heal that part of our past.

- Laugh and smile. It is impossible for the miserable, sad, or disgruntled person to live a happy and successful life. Have you have lost your ability to laugh at the joys of life, rather than at the pain? If so, it is time to rekindle that expressive energy. Engage in those activities that truly feed your joy and expand your energy. Living in real joy propels you to greater success, and the expression of that can be found in spontaneous laughter and a generous smile. Laughter is a healing salve for the soul.

- Start a "Miracles Journal." The Buddha said, "If we could see the miracle of a single flower clearly, our whole life would change." Miracles occur for the Divine Child, who sees the world as magical. When you live in the truth that all things are possible, it will create spontaneous and synchronous events that become increasingly common, but that others may deem miraculous and extraordinary. Journal those moments. Capture the essence of the magical energy, and those moments will appear even more frequently in your life. Success begets success.

- Tell someone each day what you appreciate about them. Especially with strangers. It is easy to forget how connected we are to everyone, including those whom we perceive as our worst enemies, or someone has completely different political viewpoints than others. But love them anyway through sharing the Divine Child traits you have in common. You can love them by finding at least one thing you truly love about that person and express it. You can see that light in them that you see within yourself. By sharing the treasure of acknowledging the joy that someone brings for you, this takes the relationship to an entirely new and wonderful level.

Chef and restaurateur Grant Achatz said, "Food can be expressive, and therefore food can be art." Finding your unique voice and way to express yourself is your great gift to the world. It is through expression that we generate success for others, and ultimately, true achievement for ourselves.

When we express ourselves spontaneously and freely, the world is illuminated by our gifts of enthusiasm and joy. Where expression lives, fear begins to diminish. As we communicate on many levels with curiosity and free play, we can be sure that the close companion of expression is nearby: courage.

[1] https://www.ncbi.nlm.nih.gov/pubmed/22902568

[2] Ingwer, Mark. *Empathetic Marketing: How to Satisfy the 6 Core Emotional Needs of Your Customers.* New York: Palgrave Macmillan, 2012. Print.

[3] https://www.forbes.com/sites/forbescoachescouncil/2018/03/08/the-benefits-of-expressing-your-emotions/#506b2ab84443

[4] https://ubiquity.acm.org/article.cfm?id=2043156

[5] https://www.nytimes.com/2006/09/24/books/chapters/0924-1st-peas.html

[6] https://psychcentral.com/blog/how-to-deal-with-anger-when-youre-all-too-good-at-avoiding-it/

[7] https://www.fatherly.com/health-science/health-risks-holding-back-emotions/

[8] https://www.health.harvard.edu/press_releases/why-stress-may-cause-abdominal-pain

[9] https://www.nytimes.com/1986/09/28/magazine/relieving-stress-mind-over-muscle.html

[10] https://www.cbsnews.com/news/angry-outbursts-could-trigger-heart-attacks/

[11] https://www.history.com/topics/black-history/rosa-parks

[12] https://medium.com/swlh/worry-less-about-being-right-and-more-about-self-expression-8ecdf1b83cd4

Courageous

Above all, be the heroine of your life, not the victim.

Nora Ephron
American writer and filmmaker

Small children are naturally bold. Their inherent state thrives in the words of the great poet Robert Frost, who said, "Freedom lies in being bold." The innate courage of children is what gives them boundless energy to pursue their dreams. With freedom comes unlimited success.

Being courageous and free to make your dreams happen also requires that we listen less to the critics in our lives, never giving them the power they desire. Most critics do not wish for our success, but instead, live to critique, judge, and analyze. Ralph Waldo Emerson cautioned us about critics: "Whatever you do, you need courage. Whatever course you decide upon, there is always someone to tell you that you are wrong. There are always difficulties arising that tempt you to believe your critics are right."

At other times, our biggest battles are within ourselves. Each day, the internal wars we fight start with unconscious dialogue, where we beat up ourselves and silently tell ourselves that we are not worthy. When our Divine Child gets wounded, we lose the radiant flames of fearlessness that allow us to "enter the kingdom" of unlimited success. For every battle we have externally, you can bet there is at least one struggle inside.

For example, many who have been abused by others have likely bought into the false belief that "I am not worthy." When trauma becomes internalized, then self-love, love from others, and other forms of success become increasingly elusive. If we live in a state of perpetual unworthiness, we unconsciously radiate that dark energy, attracting similar circumstances for others to abuse us. This natural mechanism serves a valuable purpose: To get our attention so that we can learn about the origin of the pain and heal those wounds.

The return back to our divine nature comes through healing the Wounded Child within. All healing comes from doing, as our small teachers show us. Self-esteem also rises from doing, and the return to knowing that you are worthy will come from you taking action regardless of feeling any pattern of fear rooted in your past.

Positive affirmations may be helpful, but if we lie to ourselves by repeating something that isn't true, there are parts of our Divine Child that will revolt inside. Children heal naturally by living in their body-truth, not by repeating affirmations. Kids are simply being and living in what is true in each moment.

Where Courage and its Negative Expressions Reside

Courage is deeply connected to the present, which is linked to the Heart Chakra. Being present in this energy center calms our fears and helps keep us centered and focused. The courage to act directs our attention to the present moment, enabling us to focus on our target, rather than glance backwards at the past.

All of our spiritual qualities are deeply connected to our natural boldness. Maya Angelou said, "Courage is the most important of all the virtues because without courage, you can't practice any other virtue consistently." In other words, all of those good energy qualities that reside within us are without much value until we put those qualities into action. Thomas Jefferson said, "Do you want to know who you are? Don't ask. Act! Action will delineate and define you."

By examining your goals, you can ask guiding questions that keep you rooted in the magical now moment. Does this end goal feed my true joy? What else do I need to get this accomplished? What can I learn about this experience? Who can help support me in achieving this dream? Sit with each of these questions quietly, and ask you ask each one to yourself, you will feel your energy either expand or contract. That is your intuitive Divine Child speaking to you.

If we allow our fears to overtake our dreams, however, we stop moving forward. It is okay to feel temporary fear, as long as it does not stop or paralyze you from taking action. For those who are not used to change, that alone can be a little scary. Any present fears are a gift, not something to be shunned. Our fears that reside within us are our teachers, instructing us what we need to heal, or what action we need to take with boldness. Mark Twain reminded us of this when he said, "Courage is resistance to fear, mastery of fear — not absence of fear."

Acting with boldness is also associated with the Third Chakra, the seat of motivation, personal power, and beliefs that are connected to the mental body. Tapping into your courage is the secret to staying in the present. When we are out of touch with our natural euphoria, we lose our motivation and willpower to act. This results in boredom, a clear sign that our Third Chakra has become spiritually tainted.

The negative expressions of courage are cowardice and timidity. When our Divine Child has been wounded, fear gets embedded at an early age. Shrinking away from our heart's desires becomes more of the norm, and the embedded fear becomes a blocker to achieving our dreams.

"You cannot swim for new horizons until you have courage to lose sight of the shore," wrote William Faulkner, the Nobel Prize laureate. Faulkner was speaking about a tendency to become obsessed goals, rather than attuned to the beauty of our journey. But our tiny teachers intuitively focus on what is before them, spontaneously creating in the moment without necessarily achieving anything specific. Goals are not the nature of the Divine Child; rather, they are the nature of the Divine Adult.

Small children do not get bogged down by fears. On the other hand, fear patterns for most adults will pull us away from acting courageously. Anxiety, which is the projection of our past fears into an imagined negative future, casts doubt on whether or not we can reach the shore.

Anxiety clouds your dreams and robs you of precious energy and resources. To the Divine Child, however, anxiety is a foreign concept — one that is learned after it has been traumatized. Your Divine Child keeps you focused on the present moment, giving you access to the power and magic that resides here and now. "Do not dwell in the past, do not dream of the future, concentrate the mind on the present moment," wisely said the Buddha.

How We Lose Our Courage

How did we lose our childlike boldness? It usually comes through early trauma, just as our other precious energies become diminished. Dream killers can rob us of our passion, telling us that we should not think big. But our greatest advances were achieved first through a vision that was pursued, despite not quite knowing how it was going to be done. The Divine Child is always up for learning and adventure, leading us to big creations. The lightbulb, computer, the Internet, and the internal combustion engine were revolutionary leaps that began with imagination, creativity, boldness, and a bold, unbridled pursuit of discovery.

Dream killers unconsciously want us to surrender our heartfelt dreams and intuition. If we become sidetracked, we risk losing the childlike passion of our own visions and may find ourselves living the dreams that others want for us. In his speech at the Stanford commencement in June 2005, Apple founder Steve Jobs said, "Your time is limited, so don't waste it living someone else's life. Don't be trapped by dogma – which is living with the results of other people's thinking.

Don't let the noise of others' opinions drown out your own inner voice. And, most important, have the courage to follow your heart and intuition. They somehow already know what you truly want to become. Everything else is secondary."[1]

Another source of spiritual trauma and abuse is when we are told that we do not matter, either verbally or nonverbally. As youngsters are naturally vulnerable, they can become easily wounded. The guarding eyes and protective hands of parents are vital to not only protect their children, but to empower them by giving them the freedom to express and cultivate these spiritual qualities.

Another source of trauma can easily occur by yelling at a child. In a 2014 study published in the journal, *Child Development*, researchers at the University of Pittsburgh and the University of Michigan in Ann Arbor discovered that not only is severe verbal discipline from parents particularly destructive to teenagers and pre-teens, but it is also as bad as physical punishment.[2]

> Courage is a heart word. The root of the word courage is *cor* — the Latin word for heart. In one of its earliest forms, the word courage meant "To speak one's mind by telling all one's heart."
>
> Brené Brown

In the study, adolescents whose parents used yelling as a method for discipline were more likely to have behavioral problems and act out, including with violence and vandalism. The two-year study compared the effects of frequent insults and verbal discipline with those of physical discipline, such as hitting and spanking.

No adult likes to be yelled at. So why do many parents yell at their kids? It isn't for the kid's sake of positive development. Yelling is usually infused with extreme anger and aggression, and this "violent" energy tears apart at the core of children.

A study published in 2003 in the *Journal of Marriage and Family* revealed that in families where 25 or more yelling incidents occur in a year, children are likely to end up with lower self-esteem, higher aggression towards others, and higher rates of depression. The study found the occurrence is frequent, where nearly 90 percent of the 1,000 parents surveyed said they yelled, shouted, or screamed at their kids in the previous year. Nearly 100 percent of parents with children older than seven confirmed they were yellers.

Energetically speaking, severe trauma can be carried through the airwaves from the voice, transferring emotional, mental, and spiritual violence from the parent to the child. Dr. Joan Durrant, Child-Clinical Psychologist and Associate Professor of Family Social Sciences at the University of Manitoba in Winnipeg, says that parents must step back and decode their children's behavior before erupting in a reactionary way. Durrant adds, "Parents need to understand the real reasons behind children's behavior and not simply interpret it as defiance. As adults we need to work on our own self-regulation so that we can help kids with theirs."[3]

It is tempting to yell, because we are hardwired to yell from our primordial ancestors who lived in the open plains. Our survival instincts to protect ourselves including screaming and hollering, where these activities have evolutionarily become embedded into our physical and spiritual DNA. Understandably, it may be hard to abandon a bad habit of yelling at others, especially with our children nearby who are most vulnerable. It may be even more difficult to shake this patterned behavior if one or both parents yelled at us.

While spanking and hitting children has fortunately diminished significantly in the past 60 years, screaming at children still remains, as it feels like we are doing our parenting job. In the 1960s, 94 percent of parents used physical punishment as forms of discipline. A 2010 poll revealed that number had dropped to 22 percent.[4]

With the influence of childhood development educators, the awareness of the toxic nature of physical abuse, such as spanking and hitting, has increased among parents. Dr. Alan Edward Kazdin, research professor of Psychology and Child Psychiatry at Yale University, says that merely knowing that yelling is bad won't help. Screaming isn't a strategy for teaching and instruction. It's a release by parents that unknowingly harms the child.

"If the goal here is to change something in the child or develop a positive habit in the child, yelling is not the way to do that," says Kazdin. Screaming like a maniac is not one of them. "We want to build habits," explains Kazdin. "The practice actually changes the brain, and in the process of that, the behaviors that you want to get rid of — having all kinds of temper tantrums and all the fights — all that just disappears." He also noted, "As a side effect, when you do these things, the parents' depression and stress in fact go down and family relations pick up."

While punishment does not work, building healthy habits that include praise and being positive role models work well. Flowers grow better in sunshine and gentle rain than in storms.

How to Rekindle Your Courage

Courage is essential for success, and it is the authentic nature of the Divine Child that makes courage come alive. The world is tired of pretense…aren't you? I know that I am. We crave genuine people who are the real deal. Authenticity makes us bold. It is an essential ingredient for big success.

If you are feeling as though you have lost touch with your inner boldness, here are some suggestions for how to reignite your courage and overcome timidity or fear:

- <u>Work on healing the wounded aspects of your Divine Child</u>. Most of us want the instant formula to success without honestly looking at ourselves. It isn't easy taking an honest assessment of who we are, but it is an exciting adventure. Even more challenging is figuring out what our unique healing journey looks like. But the truth is that our success is more about healing ourselves and removing our own internal barriers that stop us from achieving our dreams.

> The greatest barriers to your success are not outside of you, but your internal wounds that are waiting to be healed.

- <u>Practice discovering what is true for you here and now</u>. In our primordial stages of development, our world has been plagued with myths and stories that have little to no foundation in truth. They serve as distractions that keep you from discovering the true power and success story that lies within yourself. Question everything and keep on learning. Search for *how to think*, rather than what to think. Legendary fashion designer Coco Chanel, said, "The most courageous act is still to think for yourself. Aloud."
- <u>Do something completely new and bold each week</u>. Extend the boundaries of your experience and self-created limitations. Start an "Expansion Journal" and track what you did that was different, what you learned, and how it changed you. Capture your inspirations of what you want to do next, and create your "Expansion List." Dump

the idea of a "bucket list," and develop a "Life List" instead that engages your vitality.

- <u>Be kind to yourself and to others</u>. If we find that we beat up others and criticize them, it is likely that we are unconsciously doing it to ourselves, too. Practice self-kindness, and others will be kind to you. If being kind to yourself is one of your big issues that needs healing, then start a Kindness Journal to elevate your awareness. Just writing about it will help activate these energies that are already inside of you.

- <u>Read about courageous people at least once a week</u>. Find books to read and articles online about courageous people who have triumphed. You'll go into resonance with their boldness and bravery, rekindling your own powerful energies.

- <u>Get artwork that promotes the energy of courage</u>. Is it possible to activate the Third and Fourth Chakras, where the seat of courage and boldness exists? You bet. Colorful pictures of vibrant sunflowers will do this, as will the famous yellow happy face. Artwork that shows positive movement, such as a happy woman and dog running along the beach is wonderful. Artwork with speeding racecars or sports figure making a competitive jump shot may trigger courage and boldness, but may also trigger unwanted energies, such as aggression, competitiveness, and ego-driving energies that are about proving you are better than someone else. Most people have too much Masculine energy expressed in their bodies and lives, from my experience and research.

  Remember that courage is a universal value and energy quality that supports everyone, and not just feeds yourself at the expense of lowering someone else at a level below you in some trivial, short-term way. True courage has lasting effects that matter 25 years from now, while artificial courage that is about superheroes, idols, and winning that lasts only for a season.

  One more note on artwork that activates courage: Do not put this artwork in your bedroom, which is the sanctuary of quiet and rest. It's too activating for the bedroom and can cause insomnia, anxiety, nervousness, and restlessness. Artwork about courage and boldness is best suited for your work environment, such as a home office, or hallway — a corridor of movement a productivity. An entrance is also ideal for bold and happy art.

- <u>Write down what you think are your weaknesses</u>. Recruit a couple of honest friends to write down their perception of your weaknesses. It's difficult but rewarding! Then write down how you can channel and redirect expressions of negative energy into potent forces for success. For example, if you find that you are impatient, as I sometimes am, then realize that impatience can be channeled into boldly getting things done. This spiritual practice can transform your weaknesses into strengths that *work for you*, rather than beating yourself up for your weaknesses.

- <u>Stay away from dream killers</u>. These energy vampires unknowingly pull and divert your precious energy that can derail your dreams. These are the people that tell you that your ideas don't matter. And sometimes it isn't what people say, but what they *don't* say that really matters, too. If you surround yourself with people who don't encourage you to be your best and support you in your highest goals and visions, dump them, too. These energy drains are usually narcissists or self-absorbed souls who have lost their way. It's "all about them" when you get together. This form of energy vampire, while subtle, can be a giant boulder in your path that will use up your time and resources with their problems and issues, not your ambitions, hopes, and precious dreams. Disengage from them. Love them at a distance. At the same time, practice being a cheerleader who vocally supports the people you truly cherish.

> Courage is the first of human qualities because it is the quality which guarantees the others.
>
> Aristotle

- <u>Don't sweat the small stuff</u>, as Richard Carlson advises in his best-selling book *Don't Sweat the Small Stuff and It's All Small Stuff*. The minutia of life is for the Divine Adult who learns responsibility and details as it grows and evolves. But for the Divine Child, focusing on little details can pull us into the world of small, rather than the world of tall. Details, planning, and execution are important roles for your Divine Adult within, but your Divine Child sees the big picture and exciting dreams that nurture your soul.

- <u>Compliment everyone with whom you spend more than twenty minutes in a day</u>. It takes about 15 seconds to give a gift of authentic gratitude. And do it from the heart, not making up some fabricated mish-mash just to check the box on this exercise. If there is a spiritual quality that you find wonderful in that person, let them know how much you love it or how they inspire you. You will transform yourself and ignite your boldness and courage by doing this simple yet powerful little technique alone. Make it one of your key habits for success. You will shift strangers in amazing ways, supporting them with your bold and radiant energy.

Our world has become so commercialized that many of us have fallen into a trance, focusing on other people's stories — their struggles and their victories — rather than creating our own powerful story. The myths about heroes and saviors are entertaining at best, but remind us that our own courageous hero, power, and salvation truly lies within ourselves, not through relying on them.

Have we lost sight of our own power and gifts within? Jesus said, "You will do greater things than me." But many of us really don't believe those profound words. It is difficult to focus our precious energy on our own dreams and goals when we are busy externalizing our power, projecting it unto saviors and superheroes. If we give our precious energy to archetypes and invisible external beings, what is left for ourselves and our loved ones who are the saviors and angels around us? By remaining ever curious and learning about the magnificent resources and treasures within ourselves, we engage our inner success that soon becomes manifested externally.

True greatness lies within you, as Jesus and other spiritual masters have said throughout the ages. Design your life boldly…your greatness…your legend in the making. Create a powerful legacy that is about how you conquered challenges and achieved your heart's dreams, turning your scars into stars. Make your journey about supporting and inspiring others, rather than just building a home, raising a family, acquiring money in the bank, and retiring when you are old and crinkled. Transforming your life to be a vessel of inspiration for even one person is far more interesting and lasting than who won the last football or soccer game.

Amit Ray said, "Courage is the hallmark of spirituality. Courage comes when you love yourself for who you are." Living vicariously through other champions is illusory and distracting. You are here to create powerfully, to live your sacred dreams, not the dreams that others wish for you. You cannot win the game of life sitting on the sidelines watching others play. Get on the field, go after what you want, and do it big.

Keep on moving forward, and take time to rest, rebalance, and reflect. Celebrate each success, while realizing that it can be an easy temptation to remain in your newly comfortable status quo. Labeling your missed achievements as failures will drag you a swamp of disappointment and negativity. Winston Churchill said, "Success is not final, failure is not fatal: it is the courage to continue that counts."

When our courageous energy is fully engaged, we can find another spiritual energy present. Its kindred spirit is sure to be found, with its potent energy and magnetic force. The companion of courage quietly and powerfully draws the incredible resources to achieve unparalleled success, creating true magic.

That spiritual energy is the Explorer inside of you.

---

[1] https://www.theguardian.com/technology/2011/oct/09/steve-jobs-stanford-commencement-address

[2] https://www.todaysparent.com/family/discipline/yelling-at-kids/

[3] IBID

[4] https://www.nytimes.com/2018/09/05/well/family/why-you-should-stop-yelling-at-your-kids.html

Exploring

We cannot know the consequences of suppressing a child's spontaneity when he is just beginning to be active. We may even suffocate life itself. That humanity which is revealed in all its intellectual splendor during the sweet and tender age of childhood should be respected with a kind of religious veneration. It is like the sun which appears at dawn or a flower just beginning to bloom. Education cannot be effective unless it helps a child to open up himself to life.

Maria Montessori
Italian physician and educator

Living your life boldly means that you are likely insatiably curious. Small children are natural explorers, spontaneously learning about themselves and the world. A key role of parents, teachers, and adults in general is to facilitate the vital process of growing, where the child is not only free to explore, but encouraged to do so. Dr. Maria Montessori emphasized this: "To stimulate life, leaving it free, however, to unfold itself — that is the first duty of the educator."

The first educator in a child's life is the parent. As a role model for learning and discovery, the parent shows the child, by example, how to explore and learn. If the parent is not curious and eager to learn, the child's ability to learn will likely be dampened. Conversely, if the parent is spiritually alive and intrigued by the world, the child's innate energy to explore will be activated and engaged to much greater degrees.

Much research shows that children are "copycats," mimicking behavior learned from parents, caregivers, and characters on television. Carrie Schrier, an Early Childhood educator with Michigan State University, warns, "Remember that your children are watching and copying everything you do. Choose your words and actions wisely. Be very careful about what you do and say. Set a positive example for your children, even when they are infants and toddlers."[1]

Schrier adds, "Think of your home as your child's first classroom." She points to evidence that "television is teaching your children." Mimicry is largely how children learn, and infants love to copy facial expressions. Even babies only a few hours old can copy an adult who sticks his tongue out.[2] Mimicry is a function of how resonance works in the Universe.

Television is the primary teacher for most children ages two to five years, who watch 32 hours a week in front of a TV, according to research published by

155

University of Michigan's School of Medicine. In 2009, youngsters ages 6 to 11 spent about 28 hours a week watching TV, 97 percent of which was live TV.[3] In 2010, 71 percent of 8- to 18-year-olds had a TV in their bedrooms.[4] Today, the multimedia teacher is in the palms of their precious little hands.

The child's environment is a critical factor for learning and success later in life. Montessori said, "The environment must be rich in motives which lend interest to activity and invite the child to conduct his own experiences." She believed that we do not "make" geniuses, but instead, can provide the opportunity for children to fulfill his or her potential possibilities. By giving children the opportunity to freely explore, the genius is born.

Where Exploration and its Negative Expressions Reside

The thirst to explore and discover is connected to the Crown Chakra, the seat of infinite possibilities. By connecting to this powerful place, the Divine Child naturally sees that all things are possible, where spirituality meets quantum physics.

This energy center connects us to the "infinite field of pure potentially." Through this chakra, we engage with the Universe in its dance of consciousness and energy, presenting us with boundless resources that trigger synchronous experiences. Have you ever had something happen to you that seems to occur at the seemingly perfect time, perfect place, and with the perfect people involved? This happens through the engagement of the Crown Chakra, which generates the magic that we call miracles from the pool of infinite possibilities.

> In wisdom gathered over time, I have found that every experience is a form of exploration.
>
> Ansel Adams

Small children don't know about limitations, until they are taught to look for these mental constructs. When little kids approach a wall, they don't stop, whine, complain, or become dismayed, like many of us adults tend to do. Instead, they continue exploring, knowing deep inside that there are unlimited possibilities to investigate.

Their natural way of exploring seems to be driven by the soul's need to live in a joyful state. While many adults focus on their problems, the Divine Child is fully engaged with finding solutions that will bring even more joy and delight. Open-mindedness is letting go of the need to see what new information fits within your existing belief structures, while exploring to see if they are universally true.

Close-mindedness is a negative expression of the Explorer within. When our interest to learn and discover the world has waned and grown dim, it is a clear sign that our Explorer inside has been largely shut down, and the Crown Chakra has become traumatized at some point. Rigidity usually shows up, as does arrogance. The arrogant person stops learning, because he assumes he already knows the answers, and that no further discovery is needed.

The Divine Child, however, is thirsty and naturally ambitious to discover and learn even more, knowing that there is a bigger and deeper meaning to life, where many answers to any solution already exist. Scientists also usually live in this state of consciousness.

The Divine Child teaches us that our Crown Chakra is where the creative force originates. Inspiration and the creative process is first engaged with this vital energy center, where we connect with the "quantum soup" of consciousness and possibility. Full awareness occurs at this powerful energy center, which helps us discover the answers to our problems.

> Your assumptions are your windows on the world. Scrub them off every once in a while, or the light won't come in.
>
> Isaac Asimov

When we ask ourselves, "what else is possible for this situation that can benefit myself and for everyone else involved," the answers will come. Keep exploring and searching, because your Divine Child is continually asking. Sometimes the wounded aspects of ourselves drown out our Divine Child inside. Knowing who is doing the talking in our internal dialogue is essential to success.

One of the reasons why children have boundless energy is because they are connected to the Source of all that is. Living in possibility thinking is expansive, while energy contracts when we think there few or no possibilities exist. Believing in limitations means we give up hope. Have you ever thought that there was no way out of your problem? There have been times that I have.

But our Divine Child inside knows otherwise.

How Exploring Generates Success

Rather than living in fear, we live in liberation when we explore. Life is reborn in this state, bringing illumination and wisdom to everything. It is in this beautiful energy center that gratitude and appreciation live. When we live in joy and bliss, we naturally express our gratitude, reflecting back to the Universe, "I love this…and I want more if it!"

Located on top of the center of the head, the Crown Chakra also engages the brain's thinking faculties. Because small children are naturally connected to this energy center, it may well explain why babies have twice as many brain neurons as adults.[5] According to a 2012 study published in the journal *Neuropsychology Review*, glucose metabolic rates in the brain are also twice that of adults.[6] The brains of our little ones are indeed running on all 21 cylinders! And this can happen to you, too.

In a stunning body of recent research at the Queensland Brain Institute of the University of Queensland in Australia, neuroscientists led by QBI's founding director Dr. Perry Bartlett discovered that when adults learn, they grow new brain cells. This state of "neuroplasticity" — the ability of the brain and nervous system ability to remodel in response to new information — gets activated when the mind and brain are stimulated.[7] Scientists believe this could be the key to treating conditions like dementia and Alzheimer's disease.

In 2017, QBI researchers were the first to discover that new adult brain cells are also produced in the amygdala, the region of the brain that processes emotional memories and fear.[8] Lead researcher Dr. Dhanisha Jhaveri says, "Fear learning leads to the classic flight-or-fight response — increased heart rate, dry mouth, sweaty palms — but the amygdala also plays a role in producing feelings of dread and despair, in the case of phobias or PTSD, for example." When these connections in the brain are disrupted, depression and anxiety disorders, such as post-traumatic stress disorder (PTSD), can occur.

Aerobic exercise, however, simulates new neuron growth in the brain. A study published on April 1, 2016, in the *Journal of Physiology* suggests that sustained, moderate-intensity aerobic exercise like power walking, jogging, swimming, or similar activity can stimulate an even greater growth response in the brain than with resistance training.[9] Drs. Perry Bartlett and Daniel Blackmore are now conducting a clinical trial with 300 people aged 65 and older to discover the type of exercise, amount, and intensity that leads to cognitive improvement. From an energetic perspective, that feeling of euphoria and joy that comes from a moderate aerobic workout connects to and activates the Crown Chakra.

> The most fatal illusion is the settled point of view. Since life is growth and motion, a fixed point of view kills anybody who has one.
>
> Brooks Atkinson

Frequent sexual experiences also connect us to the natural ecstasy and bliss of the Crown center. A 2013 study found that single and repeated sexual experiences spur new neuron growth in the brain. Not only does sex reduce chronic stress that blocks neurogenesis, or brain growth, it can also be joyful. Dr. Amar Sahay, a neuroscientist with Harvard-affiliated Massachusetts General Hospital, explains, "So any activity you find rewarding and that lowers stress levels can have a similar effect."[10]

Do we lose our neurons because we stop learning and living in our natural state of joy? Science seems to suggest what the Divine Child teaches us.

Over-activating the Crown Chakra tends to pull energy from our lower chakras. When this happens, people become disconnected and impractical. Financial or spiritual poverty often sets in, because the energy pulls away from the Root Chakra — the seat of safety, security, abundance, and practicality — and moves up towards the head, the Masculine region of the body.

Nervousness, anxiety, and excess movement are signs that the Crown chakra has become over-activated and congested with energetic noise. An exacerbated Crown center disconnects from our physical bodies, where we become so spiritually focused that we lose touch with our bodily sensations and emotions where the Divine Child thrives.

The body is indeed the temple for your being. As the ancient Egyptians believed, the body is also the template for the Universe within you. It takes balance with the body-mind connection to work together for optimal achievement and success. Motivational teacher Jim Rohn said, "Treat your body like a temple, not a woodshed. The mind and body work together. Your body needs to be a good support system for the mind and spirit. If you take good care of it, your body can take you wherever you want to go, with the power and strength and energy and vitality you will need to get there."

Your body is not just a vehicle for your spirit and soul. It is a valuable barometer that reflects back to us how we are doing and where we are off course. When we aren't feeling good physically, emotionally, mentally, or spiritually, our physical bodies can guide us toward what our individual healing looks like, when the formula-driven, one-size-fits-all solutions by experts are not working for you.

The Crown Chakra teaches us that all of the answers lie within *you*. The key is to remain curious, open, and engaged in the process of learning about your present dilemma. Knock and the door shall be opened onto you. All healing requires exploration and learning, including at the cellular level of our bodies.

Successful People Are Natural Explorers

Maria Montessori believed that the mark of a truly great teacher was one who explores and learns. She said, "It is not enough for the teacher to love the child. She must first love and understand the universe. She must prepare herself, and truly work at it." How beautiful is that!

This "thinking outside of the box" strategy has not just been attributed to our best teachers, but as a success strategy for all leaders in businesses and organizations. Our Divine Child teaches us how to achieve positive results using our natural explorative abilities. According to a December 2017 article in *Inc.* magazine, exploring is a characteristic of the high achiever. Reading about your industry, keeping a daily journal, listening and learning, and discovering what your customer thinks about your business are among the top traits of the super successful.[11]

Great explorers change the world in positive ways. Leonardo da Vinci, Thomas Edison, the great mountaineer Gertrude Bell, Albert Einstein, and Bessie Coleman, the first black female pilot in the world, were curious explorers who achieved incredible success that inspired beneficial change. Journalist Nellie

Bly raced around the world in 72 days to beat the fictional record in Jules Verne's *Around the World in 80 Days*. Through her pioneering investigative journalism and relentless curiosity, Bly brought about sweeping reforms in orphanages, sweatshops, asylums, and prisons.[12]

Best-selling business author Peter Economy, who served as the associated editor for *Leader to Leader* for more than 12 years, writes that one of the top 12 traits that mark successful leaders is that they strive to grow.[13] This a key identifier for the self-actualizing individual, as Maslow put it. Peter Economy says, "The most successful people aren't searching for perfection and instead have an insatiable curiosity and thirst for learning new things and ways of doing things. They have a deep desire to grow personally and professionally and learn as much as they can along their way to huge success."

> Being different will always threaten the institution of understanding of a closed mind. However, evolution is built on difference, changing and the concept of thinking outside the box. Live to be your own unique brand, without apology.
>
> Shannon L. Alder

The Divine Child's natural inclination to explore yields greater success. Spiritual coach Laurel Bleadon-Maffei, said, "We were meant to explore this earth like children do, unhindered by fear, propelled by curiosity and a sense of discovery. Allow yourself to see the world through new eyes and know there are amazing adventures here for you." Exploring leads to learning, and discovery causes us to grow as a person.

Successful people explore themselves more deeply. Self-actualization, the fulfillment of our talent and higher potential, begins when we learn more about ourselves. Legendary singer and songwriter Ray Charles said, "There are many spokes on the wheel of life. First, we're here to explore new possibilities." Have you explored your real potential, including the expansiveness of your mind? A large body of evidence suggests that the human consciousness is non-local, not confined to specific points of time and space, such as the brain or body, or relegated to the present.[14]

Exploring ourselves is also a Divine Adult trait, where that adult part of us seeks to improve. As the Divine Adult grows and matures, its need to explore itself blossoms and unfolds. This fifth level of evolution was discussed by Abraham Maslow in his Hierarchy of Needs, where he believed that as our physical, emotional, and mental needs are met, the need to explore our inner spirit and energies unfolds. At that point, the urge to reach for our full potential is triggered, where self-realization becomes more of a priority.

The Explorer inside of us pursues its dreams, regardless of how difficult circumstances are. One such adventurer was Amelia Earhart, who received an invitation in 1928 to ride in a plane with two male pilots in a perilous ride across the Atlantic. She became the first woman to cross the Atlantic in an aircraft.[15]

Four years later, Earhart flew solo across the Atlantic, successfully flying from Newfoundland to Ireland in 14 hours, which was six hours faster than her transatlantic flight in 1928. She also become the first person to fly over both the Atlantic and Pacific. For her solo transatlantic crossing in 1932, U.S. Congress awarded her the Distinguished Flying Cross.[16] Breaking the glass ceiling barrier as a female pilot in the early twentieth century, this legendary pioneer has inspired many people around the world, especially women, to achieve their dreams.

> You should be excited to meet new people and try new things—to assume the best about them, in the absence of evidence to the contrary. In the long run, optimism is the best prevention for regret.
>
> Brian Christian
> *Algorithms to Live By: The Computer Science of Human Decisions*

Exploration is divinely human. In his book *Space Chronicles: Facing the Ultimate Frontier*, American astrophysicist Neil deGrasse Tyson wrote, "But nobody's ever given a parade for a robot. Nobody's ever named a high school after a robot. So when I don my public-educator hat, I have to recognize the elements of exploration that excite people. It's not only the discoveries and the beautiful photos that come down from the heavens; it's the vicarious participation in discovery itself."

You can achieve peak performance by unleashing the Explorer inside of you. Maslow defined the characteristics of the self-actualized individual,[17] which essentially are the spiritual characteristics and energy qualities of small children:

- Autonomous
- Accepting of self, others, and nature
- Relying on their own experiences and judgement
- Efficient perceptions of reality
- A task their life is centered around
- Continued freshness of appreciation
- Profound interpersonal relationships
- Comfort with solitude
- Non-hostile sense of humor
- Social compassion
- Peak experiences

Maslow said, "Self-actualizing people enjoy life in general and practically all its aspects, while most other people enjoy only stray moments of triumph." But do most of us live in this state of joy and happiness? A 2017 Harris poll found that only 33 percent of Americans surveyed said they were happy, and over 50 percent of Millennials said they were frustrated with their careers. A 2016 Gallop poll revealed that the U.S. does not rank in the top 10 happiest countries. In that study, the United States ranked 14th among 155 nations in happiness.[18]

Entrepreneur Hank Green explains the connection between exploring yourself and living in your joy: "I follow and cultivate my own curiosity. I think curiosity is one of the top two or three human characteristics. It's something that I really like about myself. [...] I want to understand stuff! I want to understand people! Following my curiosity so frequently leads me to better life decisions and better business decisions but also — just feeling better! You're never going to feel bad about your whole life if you loved people and you were curious. I mean, that's kind of all I want!"[19]

How Our Inner Explorer Becomes Wounded

We start exploring the moment we are born. As small children, we discover how dirt tastes and what a hot stove feels like. Our baby feet and toes find a way into our mouths, as we learn about our flexibility and how our bodies function.

The moment we believe that exploring is not safe, however, that energy begins to shut down. The trauma is usually external, where pain becomes our teacher, such as in the case of touching a hot stove or burning embers. The pain may have come from a slap on the hand. Repeat episodes of feeling pain can cause us to shrink, when exploring becomes associated with pain and danger.

Our self-protective mechanisms engage when that pain is emotional, mental, or spiritual as well. Christian Bale was bullied at age 14 by his male classmates after he appeared in the movie *Empire of the Sun* simply because he was a young film star. Bale says he "took a beating from several boys for years," putting him through hell by punching and kicking him. His mother reported that Christian almost quit acting. The community of Bournemouth, England, bullied Bale as well, taunting him in the newspaper and scrawling mean things about him in public toilets. Bale retreated and didn't shoot another movie for nearly two years.[20]

Bale said, "I was not going to be bullied out of the part. I was going to stand up for myself and fight. So when I look back, problems in childhood can make you into the man you become." He took on the popular Leonardo DiCaprio and landed his starring role in *American Psycho*, which became a blockbuster hit. Bale is now one of the top actors today, having landed his role as Batman in *Batman Begins* and *The Dark Knight*.

His long string of hit movie roles also include *Shaft, The Prestige, Terminator Salvation, American Hustle, The Big Short,* and *Vice,* where he plays the role of former U.S. Vice President Dick Cheney. Bale has won a long string of honors, including Four British Academy Film Awards, three Academy Award nominations and one win, four Golden Globe Award nominations and two wins, twelve Critic's Choice Movie Award nominations and six wins, and seven Screen Actors Guild Award nominations and two wins. Bale continues to explore himself in his movie roles while delighting the world on the big screen.

Another example of bullying, although far more subtle, is calling someone a nerd — a term whose origin is steeped in mostly negative connotations. When we sacrifice a human because it craves to learn and discover, we kill off the very thing that feeds our world.

It is the bully, however, who has lost his own way. He projects his self-loathing onto the Divine Child, impaling it with anger, confusion, and control. In many respects, both the bully and victim must reactivate their inner explorer, which can facilitate healing and growth that benefits not only themselves, but everyone whose lives they touch.

How to Reactivate Your Natural Explorer

Exploring yourself and the world around you is essential for kind of any success. Every sales call can be a learning experience, and everyone we meet is our teacher. Remaining extraordinarily curious about each person in our lives can lead to richer, deeper, and more rewarding relationships. Seeking to learn rather than to prove ourselves opens up more possibilities for growing any relationship, rather than creating a block that separates us from one another.

If you want to engage your inner Explorer more fully, here are some helpful suggestions:

- Read a lot of different subjects. Find literature from good writers who inspire you. After achieving success as a TV producer and director, John Lloyd fell into a string of failures that led to depression. He went on long walks, took time off work, and read voraciously. He read about magnetism and light, Socrates and ancient Athens, and about French impressionists and the Renaissance.[21] With no plan or method, Lloyd followed his inner child wherever it took him. His thirst for reading finally led to his successful launch of the hit British TV comedy quiz show *QI* ("Quite Interesting"), which has thrilled millions of viewers with more than 227 episodes in 18 seasons.

- Be willing to ask "dumb" questions and make mistakes. Albert Einstein said, "The important thing is not to stop questioning. Never lose a holy curiosity." Jack Welch, former CEO of General Electric, attributed his success to hiring leaders who ventured and made more mistakes, rather than not taking risks at all. Asking questions and taking risks allows us to grow and become successful. Welch said, "What I looked for in hiring people who could implement well was, first, integrity and authenticity. A good leader also needs to have curiosity and breadth of knowledge, relishes change and is passionate about his or her work, can make tough decisions, even when the information isn't all in, and can handle stress, even failure, because of heavy-duty resilience."[22]

- Practice listening without judgment. Psychologist and coach Dr. Ben Dean says, "Curious people are often considered good listeners and conversationalists. In the early stages of a relationship, we tend to talk about our interests or hobbies. One reason for this is that people tend to equate 'having many interests' with 'interesting,' and for good reason. Curious people tend to bring fun and novelty into relationships." Heated arguments can be avoided by simply asking questions with the intention of learning, rather than to combat. When each person can more fully understand the other person's perspective, it softens things a lot. Often, we discover we have more in common than what we thought.[23]

> The walls we build around us to keep the noise out only reverberate the same ideas, notions and beliefs we enforce, leaving no room for debate. When we opt out of an argument, we are choosing to ignore opposing views, thereby failing to understand the other.
>
> Aysha Taryam

- Get out of your routine. At least once a week, do something different that breaks you out of your routine. Explore things by looking beneath the surface to open up new worlds and possibilities. Sufi meditation teacher Vilayat Inayat Khan said, "The human spirit lives on creativity and dies in conformity and routine."
- Engage with people who have ideas that are contrary to yours. When we keep listening and reading the same sources, our Explorer inside falls into a mental rut and starts stagnating. Exploring the other side of your opinions is a great way to grow. New York Times bestselling author and former psychotherapist Thom Hartmann is a show host of the top progressive radio show in the United States. What makes his syndicated program so interesting and mind-expanding is that he brings people on his show who have opinions that are opposing his. An exploring consciousness is one that is always open to completely new ideas.
- Go exploring outside. At least once a month, spend a day hiking a mountain, exploring a forest, or wandering a new beach. This engages the little kid inside, increases our curiosity and thirst for discovery and

grows our empathy for animals and our planet. The healing power of nature makes it the perfect place to explore and move your body. Then write about your experience in your "Explorer Journal."

Dare to explore. You have everything to gain and little to lose. The trauma of being afraid to go deeper and higher is far greater than the risk of searching the vast oceans and glorious forests. The riches of life and unlimited success can be yours when you explore, using this powerful energy that is already inside of you. Eleanor Roosevelt said, "The purpose of life, after all, is to live it, to taste experience to the utmost, to reach out eagerly and without fear for newer and richer experience."

Exploring the world around you with a sense of joy and adventure will not only be fun and interesting, but it will connect you with who you really are. Each time we venture out to experience something new, we learn more about ourselves, our potential, and the magic the Universe has to offer us. The award-winning British novelist David Mitchell said, "Travel far enough, you meet yourself."

New York bestselling author H. Jackson Brown, Jr. wrote, "Twenty years from now you will be more disappointed by the things you didn't do than by the ones you did do. So throw off the bowlines. Sail away from the safe harbor. Catch the trade winds in your sails. Explore. Dream. Discover."

In our daily adventures, we learn that taking risks can be especially rewarding when we open ourselves up to receive. Exploring becomes far more powerful when we use another related potent force of our Divine Child within. Despite that this trait has a stereotype of being weak, submissive, and risky, the irony is that being *vulnerable* while you explore will connect you more fully to life and to others around you, magnetizing unparalleled success to you.

---

[1] https://www.canr.msu.edu/news/young_children_learn_by_copying_you

[2] IBID

[3] http://blog.nielsen.com/nielsenwire/media_entertainment/tv-viewing-among-kids-at-an-eight-year-high/. Accessed 23 April 2019.).

[4] Rideout VJ, Foehr UG, Roberts DF. Generation M2: Media in the Lives of 8-18 year-olds. Kaiser Family Foundation. January 2010. Available at: http://www.kff.org/entmedia/upload/8010.pdf, Accessed 23 April 2019.

[5] https://www.ncbi.nlm.nih.gov/books/NBK234146/.

[6] https://www.ncbi.nlm.nih.gov/pmc/articles/PMC3511633/.

[7] https://www.health.harvard.edu/mind-and-mood/can-you-grow-new-brain-cells

[8] https://qbi.uq.edu.au/blog/2017/11/can-you-grow-new-brain-cells

[9] https://www.health.harvard.edu/mind-and-mood/can-you-grow-new-brain-cells

[10] IBID

[11] https://www.inc.com/christina-desmarais/33-things-highly-successful-people-are-doing-every-day-that-you-probably-arent.html

[12] https://www.theguardian.com/travel/2016/mar/08/top-10-inspiring-female-travel-adventurers

[13] https://www.inc.com/peter-economy/12-thoughts-of-today-s-most-highly-successful-people.html

[14] https://psycnet.apa.org/record/2014-04669-001

[15] https://www.history.com/this-day-in-history/earhart-completes-transatlantic-flight

[16] https://www.biography.com/people/amelia-earhart-9283280

[17] https://medium.com/@morty.josh/why-we-struggle-with-self-actualization-and-what-to-do-about-it-64d44fef8d1f

[18] IBID

[19] https://www.goodreads.com/author/quotes/7023543.Hank_Green

[20] https://www.ranker.com/list/successful-people-who-were-bullied/kellen-perry

[21] https://www.psychologytoday.com/us/blog/finding-the-next-einstein/201407/seven-ways-be-more-curious

[22] https://www.investors.com/news/management/leaders-and-success/jack-welch-built-ge-success-on-continuous-learning/

[23] https://www.authentichappiness.sas.upenn.edu/newsletters/authentichappinesscoaching/curiosity

Vulnerable

Owning our story can be hard, but not nearly as difficult as spending our lives running from it. Embracing our vulnerabilities is risky, but not nearly as dangerous as giving up on love and belonging and joy — the experiences that make us the most vulnerable. Only when we are brave enough to explore the darkness will we discover the infinite power of our light.

Brené Brown
Research professor, author

It can feel scary to think about letting our vulnerability show. In that moment we enter this world, we are completely open and defenseless. Relying on the protection and nurturing of our first caregivers, usually our parents, we depend upon them for our survival.

And yet, the Divine Child naturally thrives in its vulnerability and does not shrink from it. Susceptible to risk or potential harm means that we are fully exploring ourselves and the world around us. Vulnerability gives small children and adults alike the power to learn and excel rapidly.

Parents, teachers, and other role models that influence the lives of children have a duty to protect them while providing the environment for the child to freely explore and grow. "We owe our children — the most vulnerable citizens in any society — a life free from violence and fear," said Nelson Mandela.

> Vulnerability is a magnet for honesty, and honesty is the very basis of human connections.
>
> Salma Farook
> *What Your Soul Already Knows*

As adults, we have a tendency to protect ourselves and subsequently erect barriers between ourselves and others. The same barriers that have a protective function, however, can also block positive energy that we need to transform and grow. Through body language, we adults learn to cross our arms and legs to energetically defend ourselves, especially if we feel attacked during an argument, for example.

For small children, however, defending themselves is a pattern learned from their role models, as small children do not naturally adopt defensive postures. To the Divine Child, our vulnerable nature is what connects us more deeply to others.

Ironically, we think avoiding vulnerability helps keep us safe, but this strategy fails repeatedly. As Martin Luther King Jr. said, "The soft-minded man always fears change. He feels security in the status quo, and he has an almost morbid fear of the new. For him, the greatest pain is the pain of a new idea." To gain the kind of positive experiences we desire, we must be receptive to change, which comes through being open and vulnerable.

In her best-selling book *Daring Greatly: How the Courage to Be Vulnerable Transforms the Way We Live, Love, Parent, and Lead*, author Brené Brown describes the essential nature of the Divine Child: "Vulnerability is the birthplace of love, belonging, joy, courage, empathy, and creativity. It is the source of hope, empathy, accountability, and authenticity. If we want greater clarity in our purpose or deeper and more meaningful spiritual lives, vulnerability is the path."

Vulnerability is one of our Divine Child's greatest secrets that allows us to fully express ourselves and invite the most incredible experiences of our lives. When we open ourselves up to new adventures, we release simultaneously release many of our 21 gifts, drawing more of them to us. Indeed, vulnerability is an essential ingredient to engage the Law of Attraction and magnetize success.

Holistic educator Eric Micha'el Leventhal said, "We are at our most powerful the moment we no longer need to be powerful." We find our innate strength through the natural state of our Divine Child, a radiance unfettered by the ego or social constructs. When we experiment, we free ourselves from our self-perceived identities. Dynamic and ever-changing, we have the profound opportunity to expand our being, just as the Universe itself expands in each moment.

Our vulnerability beautifully connects us to relationships that matter. Brené Brown, an expert on social connection, conducted thousands of interviews to discover the heart of our deeper connections with others. The analysis of the data revealed that the key ingredient is vulnerability. Brown explains that rather than meaning submissive or weak, vulnerability implies the courage to be yourself.[1] She says that "vulnerability is basically uncertainty, risk, and emotional exposure." When we have learned to avoid uncertainty and emotional risk, we forget that we can still be okay despite not knowing what lies ahead.

> Fragility is not the antithesis of courage. There is enormous strength and power in the softest parts of your heart. In fact, right at the centre of the most unguarded part of your spirit is where you will discover a sense of courage more resilient and timeless than you thought possible.
>
> Sondra Ann Turnbull

Brown illustrated the power of the Divine Child beautifully when she said, "Vulnerability is the core of shame and fear and our struggle for worthiness, but it appears that it's also the birthplace of joy, of creativity, of belonging, of love." Fear, shame, and the false sense of unworthiness arise when the inner child has been wounded from trauma.

Being present in the now moment allows these essential qualities of true success to emerge. Using the natural energies of your Divine Child, you can weather any storm and transform a challenging experience into one of strength and vitality. Let your vulnerability work for you. Explore it. Play with it. Delight in it. This magic within you will help you achieve your dreams. Your vulnerability will unlock the doors to your kingdom and queendom of success that awaits you.

Where Vulnerability and its Negative Expressions Reside

The vulnerable, excited adventurer primarily sits in the Heart Chakra, the center of being present. Information, truth, love, and compassion arise from presence. On the other hand, suffering in our pain and wounds from past trauma pulls us back into our past. Staying stuck in our pain keeps us trapped in negative patterns that can cause us to shrink. And when our vulnerability shuts down, we stagnate.

Interestingly, our vulnerability is intimately connected to our sense of adventure. Stereotyped as weakness, vulnerability requires a great deal of strength. When we explore the possibilities in our lives rather than focusing on our problems, solutions spontaneously emerge. With whatever you face in your life, keep moving forward in the direction of what brings you more joy.

When we fear vulnerability, it is easy to swing to the opposite extreme of over-protection. When we are afraid to be authentic and open to our present situation, we develop patterns that turn into cynicism that stops the flow of energy. Instead of expressing natural curiosity and receptivity, we become cold and hardened. We lose the sense of joy, adventure, and aliveness that is our true spiritual heritage.

When squashed, vulnerability can take on other dark expressions, including ignorance and gullibility. Naiveté in adults sometimes occurs when our sense of curiosity and learning has atrophied. The great appetite for knowing the truth leads to our true salvation, a willingness to go beyond the knowledge of yesterday. Closing our minds to learning not only halts our brains from growing, but it also decays our spiritual nature.

In our success-minded culture, we celebrate strength and toughness, while viewing vulnerability as meek, mild, and even weak. We push our past failures under the rug, rather than using them as teaching tools to feed our successes.

> As we consciously choose to be open, vulnerable, and receptive — paramount for having intimacy in our lives — we must simultaneously call on greater discernment.
>
> Cyndi Dale
> *Togetherness*

We can best learn from our failures by talking about them. It seems counterintuitive to talk about your shortcomings, but sharing them with your cheerleaders can inspire healing, growth, and more intimate connections. Ironically, discussing your failures is actually another road to your success, because sharing those experiences can take much of the negative emotional charge out of them, making them easier to manage and solve. Failures do not lead to dead ends: Your Divine Child takes paths through temporary roadblocks that allow us to learn lessons about when we need to make changes in our lives.

We live more fully through experimental discovery, forays into the unknown that rely on both science and intuition. When we demonize our past, we not only do a big disservice to ourselves, but also to those around us. There is no value in labeling what you did as good or bad, right or wrong. As William Shakespeare said in *Hamlet*, "Nothing in the world is good nor bad, but thinking makes it so."

Simply put, we live in a world of cause and effect. Often, it is enough to ask, "Was this beneficial for myself and others involved? Did it lead to joy?" Our compass will show us the way by how we can lift others up, as well as ourselves.

If we belittle or minimize ourselves, we create our own barriers and limitations with self-defeating behavior. Patterns of past abuse often turn into self-abuse, where we find ourselves beating ourselves up in a trauma cycle. We pick up where others have left off — those who abused us spiritually, mentally, emotionally, or physically.

Similarly, it is easy to get caught in old patterns of false belief systems that lead to hatred, degradation, and subjugation. We energetically hurt ourselves in ways that we would never harm someone else. And like cutting our own physical skin, self-abuse may spark a short-lived rush that seems exciting but is not helpful long-term.

The candid exploration of ourselves is the birthplace of healing, where we openly accept and embrace both the wounded and positive sides of our Divine Child. When we fully embrace all aspects of who we are, we can then discover what our unique healing journey looks like, which has already begun.

Vulnerability Under Siege

When we feel attacked, our instinct for self-preservation gets triggered. Even more subtle emotional or mental attacks will cause us to erect barriers to try to prevent painful assaults from happening again.

Spiritual abuse is even more subtle and often hidden, where it may be difficult to understand how and when we are being undermined. Messages of fear — such as hellfire and brimstone preaching or negative associations in advertising — can easily destabilize and paralyze our sense of our powerful self. These spiritual assaults on our vulnerability are sure-fire ways to a lack of abundance and joy.

Another widespread myth that traumatizes the Divine Child is that success is about being a strong, fierce warrior and leader, rather than encouraging a state of vigorous experimentation that entails vulnerability, trying new things, and discovering their impact.

The magic of our inner child is that it continually seeks to understand and learn, using the past as inspiration rather than self-inflicted punishment loaded with guilt or shame. Disappointment is foreign to even small children, as they instinctively keep on moving. They know how to pick themselves up, ask for help when necessary, and remain open to all possibilities.

Punishment: The Bronze Age Attack on Vulnerability

Parents and other authority figures can unwittingly cause a small child to feel insignificant, smothering the sense of safety that is needed for the child to express vulnerability. Punishment is often the go-to solution, rather than providing opportunities for positive learning.

The impulse to punish arose from the attempt to establish payment for crimes committed or simple daily grievances, such as neighbors taking more than their fair share of food. Over time, laws, customs, and ritual took over the functions of punishment, so that societies did not have decide anew with each new infraction of the social code. Punishment and superstition intermingle in early legal codes, like the Mosaic covenant or the Code of Hammurabi. The "eye for an eye and a tooth for a tooth" ideology originated from commandments written by men but projected as coming from a deity who allegedly issued the proclamation.

Bronze Age societies needed this aspect of divine commandment to authorize the injunction, however severe and extreme. And, for a time, codes like the Mosaic covenant were able to control tit-for-tat violence, to keep it down to a manageable level. The "eye for an eye" functioned as a kind of restraint, to keep retribution from devouring everything. And yet, this law still contains violence within it. As long as humanity remains at this level of retributive thinking where justice is more important than mercy and support, we cannot progress and thrive.

An element of barbarism persists in all forms of punishment, and every legal code retains a shadow of superstition and vengeance. Our Bronze Age ancestors left behind an obsession with punishment that we still have a hard time shaking from our homes, our schools, and in society. We punish others because we are projecting our anger and irritation on the offender, or in many cases, the helpless victim, such as an innocent child.

Institutionalizing punishment does not mean that the punishment will achieve any productive outcome. Punishment usually does quite the opposite, by reinforcing negative behaviors that we meant to correct. Many systems condemn those who have lost their way in the world, rather than allowing natural goodness to shine.

Fortunately, we are learning that the ancient views of punishment do not work to "fix the offender." The ancient tradition of scapegoating stemming from Levitical times — projecting the sins and offenses of the offender onto an innocent person or animal — does not rehabilitate individuals or society, either. Where there is no positive learning, there is no evolution or spiritual shift. Atonement happens not by symbolically transferring guilt onto another, but by truly understanding the harm that one has caused, then taking a new path after owning one's mistakes.

In the past fifty years, numerous studies have moved us from a punishment-based system toward a mindset that is inclusive, progressive, and positive. Dr. Alan Kazdin, director of the Yale Parenting Center, says that punishment might make the parent feel better, but it won't change the kid's behavior. He argues that punishment is a waste of time when trying to eliminate a problem behavior.[2]

Our brains are hardwired to pick up negative things in our environment, suggests Kazdin. It's part of our survival mechanism. Our brain's negative bias will cause us to remember a single negative experience and tell ten people about it, whereas a positive experience may only be shared with one person.

But positive reinforcement and role modeling has better long-term outcomes. Researchers found that the secret ratio for a satisfying and stable marriage is for the spouses or partners to share five times as many positive feelings and interactions as negative exchanges. Other studies found the same ratio in our personal lives, where the ratio of five positive acts for every negative act produces the best results.[3]

Bullying also wounds the Divine Child's sense of vulnerability. This form of physical, emotional, mental, and spiritual attack amounts to another insidious form of slavery, where the victim is subjugated in conscious or unconscious ways. The more subtle form of bullying is largely unconscious.

Between 25 and 33 percent of U.S. students ages 12 to 18 say they have been bullied at school on a regular basis.[4] Approximately 30 percent of young people admit to bullying others, and the most common type of bullying is mental or verbal abuse, where 77 percent of all students are bullied.[5] This kind of abuse can include spreading rumors, yelling obscenities, or degrading someone because of race, gender, sexual orientation, or religion. Denigrating someone because he or she is overweight, has a different financial status, is smart or a "nerd," or suffers from a physical impairment are also expressions of bullying.

This form of spiritual violence demeans and enslaves the victim through cowardly anger that sets up a state of inequality. This behavior is usually learned through a spiritually corrupted inheritance, where either the parents or teachers subjugated the child through indoctrination, brainwashing, or other forms of coercion. Children rapidly learn through modeling, where the example of the authority figure becomes the unquestioned blueprint for acceptable behavior. We can learn about the roles of the bully and of the victim through examples in our lives.

These influences have long-lasting effects. Studies show that kids who are bullied are more likely to incur mental health issues, such as increased sadness and loneliness, depression, and anxiety. They are more probable to skip, miss, or drop out of school, and their academic achievement falls. Bullied children often experience changes in eating and sleep patterns, while losing interest in activities they once enjoyed. Performing a "bully check" is important to learn if you and your family are victims, perpetrators, or both. One incident of bullying can result in years of devastation in someone's life.

This spiritual, mental, emotional, and physical violence to the vulnerable child can later turn into drastic retaliation and extreme violence by the abused. In 12 of the 15 school shooting cases in the 1990s, for instance, the shooter had a history of being bullied.[6]

If you are a parent or guardian with children in school, you can take a proactive stance by not only carefully watching for signs of any form of bullying, but also discussing these with your child to learn if he or she is being bullied. There are a number of children's books written by educators that can help facilitate discussions on bullying in gentle and safe ways.[7]

Gay Conversion Therapy: Spiritual Abuse Through Bullying

Bullying can take an institutional form, as in gay conversion therapy that is used by a number of churches and religious organizations, where irresponsible "therapists" and "counselors" aim to convince young people and adults to relinquish a non-conforming gender or sexual identity. Sometimes called reparative therapy, conversion therapy is not professional psychotherapy, as gay conversion therapy uses unscientific, subversive, and authoritarian practices to embed deep shame, guilt, ridicule, unacceptance, and blame that undermine the psyche of the individual. These negative tactics are highly toxic and damaging to the Divine Child, who knows only acceptance, equality, and joy in its whole and functional state.

In 2018, Maria M. Sanzone wrote in *The Washington Post*, "Gay, lesbian and bisexual individuals are not mentally ill. In 1973, following decades of research indisputably demonstrating that individuals with LGBT sexual orientations are no more prone to mental illness than heterosexuals, homosexuality was removed from the diagnostic manual of mental illnesses."[8] Author Phyllis Christine Cast wrote, "Gender preference does not define you. *Your spirit defines you.*"

Thankfully, we are beginning to turn the corner, and even former "conversion therapists" are beginning to understand the horrific consequences of these practices. David Matheson, a prominent Mormon "conversion therapist" who has been described as the "intellectual godfather" of ex-gay therapy, is now dating men.

LGBTQ nonprofit Truth Wins Out obtained a Facebook post of conversion therapy advocate Rich Wyler, which said Matheson's "living a single, celibate life just isn't feasible for him." Wyler's post indicated Matheson was seeking a male partner. Later, Matheson corroborated Wyler's assertions to the press: "A year ago I realized I had to make substantial changes in my life. I realized I couldn't stay in my marriage any longer. And I realized that it was time for me to affirm myself as gay," Matheson wrote.[9]

After being married to a woman for 34 years, Matheson is now divorced, confirming in an NBC News interview that he is now dating men. He acknowledged that his conversion "therapy" work has hurt some people, but he would not fully renounce conversion therapy. Instead, he blamed the Mormon church for its "shame-based, homophobic-based system," admitting that he also perpetuated that system.[10]

According to the Williams Institute, a public policy research institute focused on sexual orientation and gender identity law, nearly 700,000 LGBTQ adults in the U.S. have received "conversion therapy" at some point in their lives.[11] Its 2018 "Conversion Therapy and LGBT Youth" report notes that "efforts to change someone's sexual orientation or gender identity are associated with poor mental health, including suicidality."

Fortunately, states are beginning to systemize and protect the positive spiritual energies of equality, compassion, and unconditional love through legislation. On April 5, 2018, Maryland lawmakers passed a bill to join ten other states and Washington D.C., "prohibiting health professionals from practicing 'gay conversion therapy' on minors" after a legislator spoke of the pain she experienced when her parents sought it for her. Just days earlier, the woman's father, a state senator, voted against the bill," as reported by NBC News.[12] The state of Virginia is also moving forward to ban the despicable practice of gay conversion therapy to minors in the state.[13]

A Return to Vulnerability

We live in a world that is saturated with fake news, fake online relationships, and the myriad other ways we humans invent to try to gain something for ourselves using a certain amount of deception. With the onslaught of fakery, many people are craving authenticity and openness. How many times have you seen a dating profile online where someone is dramatically lying about his age? We may gain short-term by hiding who we really are, but we hurt ourselves and others in the long run.

Canadian writer André Berthiaume said, "We all wear masks, and the time comes when we cannot remove them without removing some of our own skin." The real pain sets in when we discover we have been living our lives to please others, rather than living as our authentic, open, and adventurous child who succeeds on her or his own merit and truth.

When we give up the most precious aspects of ourselves in exchange for something far less in value, including money, we undermine not only our own true value, but others around us. Our spiritual integrity relies on maintaining our own preciousness, honesty, and ability to give. By sharing these powerful Divine Child qualities that reside inside of us, others will spontaneously reflect that same energy, treating us with more respect, dignity, and compassion as well.

How to Reactivate the Magic of Vulnerability

If you have the tendency to armor yourself with a defensive, self-protective stance around others, it is understandable, as most people have been attacked or abused by others, especially at an early age. Here are some suggestions that may help you return to the joyful, playful, adventurous, and vulnerable nature of your

Divine Child who knows no defense, but learns rapidly, enjoys life, and attracts success:

- Start treating yourself well. Be kind, loving, and gentle with yourself. When you catch yourself beating yourself up with negative self-talk, such as "how dumb I am" or other statements that promote self-worthlessness, stop yourself and pause. Take a breath. Then say at least five nice things about yourself that are true, including, "I am a genius at _____." Everyone is a genius at something.

- Learn to say "Yes, and…". Growing up in an abusive environment can result in defensive posturing patterns. It's how we learn to say "No!" And saying no is sometimes the healthy response. But if we have a habit of saying no and opposing usually whatever comes our way, that negative pattern stops the flow of energy and the good that comes our way. For example, if your friend Lisa says, "Hey…do you want to go to this restaurant with me?" Rather than say, "No," you can say, "That sounds interesting. What do you think about going out to dinner and then see a movie? That feels good to me." When someone extends an invitation, we can create our own powerful invitation that says "yes" to the energy and the idea of getting together, for instance, which keeps the energy flowing, rather than resisting and opposing it.

- Get comfortable talking about your pain and failures. It doesn't make you weak — as long as you spend more time talking about your strengths, rather than what isn't working in your life. Discussing your weaknesses and errors makes you stronger, more powerful, and far more relatable as a human being, and it releases its negative grip on your life. What made Oprah incredibly successful was her authenticity and willingness to share her pain and negative past. People could relate to her struggle with weight and sexual abuse from her childhood.[14] And through her openness and candor, she lit up the world by encouraging others to live in a vulnerable yet powerful place, where healing and transformation could happen with an open heart.

- Practice showing your true emotions. There is widespread notion that being vulnerable and showing your emotions is weakness, while hiding your emotions is denoted by strength of character. Even worse, vulnerability has been equated with weak females, while males have been portrayed as strong and relatively unemotional, even in movies. People have become tired of these age-old stereotypes that still keep many locked up in an emotional prison. Your emotions can help you live more powerfully and authentically, while opening up the hearts of others around you. Learning how to use express them appropriately and with candor is a primary key to success, especially in relationships. Shine your light.

- <u>Create a Vulnerability Journal.</u> Find one way to reveal yourself authentically each day to yourself and others, then write about your realizations. Observe how others react to you when you open yourself more fully to them, such as discussing how you failed at something, or how you are truly feeling at the moment. If you are feeling terrible, just say so. Nobody will punish you. People are relieved the moment they realize that they are like everyone else. Trying to maintain the illusion of false strength is stressful and a waste of your precious time.

- <u>See constructive criticism as a gift</u>. Remember that every attack is a cry for help and is usually not so much about you. Don't take criticism personally, which is often easier said than done. Go beyond the surface of what you perceive as an attack, and see how the critic is suffering, or what he or she means by it. It is more about discovering what can be learned about you and the critic, and how to transform what was said into something that moves you forward in positive ways.

Being vulnerable allows you to live in freedom. In your naturally curious state, you can learn, grow, and achieve extraordinary things. The adventurer in you seeks to discover new horizons and explore the multitude of resources that are available to you. With this Divine Child inside of you assisting in your exciting adventures, you are bound for greater success.

We all want to succeed to some degree or another. Knowing life does not have to be a struggle makes it more fun and thrilling. With inner curiosity, a thirst for learning, and peaceful approach to life, we create magic with yet another trait that is present the moment we are born. In a world filled with aggression and violence, your gentle Divine Child will shine like the radiant sun.

---

[1] https://www.forbes.com/sites/danschawbel/2013/04/21/brene-brown-how-vulnerability-can-make-our-lives-better/#3c27f7d936c7

[2] https://www.theatlantic.com/health/archive/2016/03/no-spanking-no-time-out-no-problems/475440/

3 https://www.psychologytoday.com/us/articles/200306/our-brains-negative-bias

4 https://www.stopbullying.gov/media/facts/index.html

5 https://americanspcc.org/our-voice/bullying/statistics-and-information/

6 https://www.stopbullying.gov/at-risk/effects/index.html

7 https://www.weareteachers.com/14-must-read-anti-bullying-books-for-kids/

8 https://www.washingtonpost.com/opinions/conversion-therapy-is-a-form-of-bullying-maryland-is-right-to-fight-it/2018/04/20/668583d4-3d03-11e8-8d53-eba0ed2371cc_story.html

9 https://www.nbcnews.com/feature/nbc-out/once-prominent-conversion-therapist-will-now-pursue-life-gay-man-n961766

10 https://www.independent.co.uk/news/world/americas/gay-conversion-therapy-therapist-comes-out-utah-mormon-david-matthews-lgbtq-a8744361.html

11 https://williamsinstitute.law.ucla.edu/wp-content/uploads/Conversion-Therapy-LGBT-Youth-Jan-2018.pdf

12 https://www.nbcnews.com/feature/nbc-out/maryland-set-become-11th-state-ban-gay-conversion-therapy-n862926

13 https://www.wusa9.com/article/news/local/virginia/virginia-board-of-psychology-votes-to-ban-gay-conversion-therapy-for-minors/65-f832cb51-5612-44d9-bb6c-4f241e641d2b

14 https://ewn.co.za/2018/01/15/oprah-winfrey-continues-sexual-abuse-discussions

Gentle

> In the long run, the sharpest weapon of all
> is a kind and gentle spirit.
>
> Anne Frank

I remember when a classmate in school burned ants with a magnifying glass. He thought it was cool and fun, but I had a bad visceral reaction watching the ants writhe in pain and agony.

Small children learn cruelty from adults. It does not happen automatically. Usually, kids have to see someone acting in a barbarous manner, such as from a parent, video game, or TV show, in order to emulate that cruel person. It feels powerful to control someone's destiny, but control over others inhibits their natural growth and damages the Divine Child's state of equality.

Children learn aggressive and violent behavior at home, according to a study published in the journal *Health Education & Behavior*. In surveying nearly 9,000 diverse middle school students, researchers concluded that parents are the foremost role models for aggressive behavior, and what kids see at home is the top factor that will determine how they will behave — even more significant than media.[1]

True monsters are not those lurking under the bed, but the ones sleeping in it.

Silje Akselberg Iversen

The researchers also found that students were less likely to fight when they got along with their parents, and students who lived with both parents had significantly lower aggression. Parental involvement also made a sizable difference, where parents who monitored their kids' activities and friends had kids with less aggression.

William Cobbett, the 18th century farmer and member of English Parliament, said, "To have a dutiful family, the father's principle of rule must be love, not fear. His sway must be gentle, or he will have only an unwilling and short-lived obedience." His wise words about the importance of the male parent's role are reflected in a study from the National Center on Addiction and Substance Abuse at Columbia University, where researchers found that teenagers who do not get along well with their fathers are more likely to drink, smoke, and use drugs. Even teens from single-parent families were less at risk to alcohol, tobacco, and drugs than those teens in two-parent families who suffered poor relationships with their fathers.

Pamela Orpinas, PhD, assistant professor at the Department of Health Promotion and Behavior at the University of Georgia, says whether dealing with aggressive behavior or addiction, the message is clear: "Children need to be talked to and monitored starting at a very young age, and parents have to be careful what they teach their children, because children learn from them the most," Orpinas said. Monitoring also includes watching what children see, according to a study published in November 2000 in the *Journal of Pediatrics*, where researchers found that violence is a learned behavior. The study confirmed the strong association between exposure to violence and the use of violence by young adolescents.[2]

Violence isn't just learned from our parents, teachers, or other caregivers. It is also engrained from media, including texts that have wide distribution, such as biblical scripture. The distributive effect of words we treasure — especially books labeled as "sacred" or "holy" despite being extremely violent and barbaric — have a very powerful effect on how violence becomes culturalized and mainstreamed. In *The Age of Reason*, Thomas Paine wrote, "It is from the Bible that man has learned cruelty, rapine, and murder; for the belief of a cruel God makes a cruel man."

Paine was correct. If we were to strip the "holy" label from the bible and have the stories written with different names of the characters, the punishing preachments and violent stories would be unacceptable and soundly rejected by the masses today. The numerous commandments of mass genocide, suggestions of rape with the order to "keep the young virgins for yourselves," and sacrificial rituals of birds, animals, and humans would be revolting to anyone with a moral compass and compassionate heart.

Morality and ethical behavior begin within us, not in barbaric teachings. Culturally, we need a good scrubbing of violent texts and other media from the daily diet we ingest and promote. It is impossible to expect improvement in violence and negativity until we have purged its origins from our spiritual DNA.

Are Babies and Small Children Hard-Wired for Kindness?

It is an age-old question that has been asked by many. A 2007 study by Yale University's Infant Cognition Center startled the scientific world by showing that six- and ten-month-olds overwhelmingly preferred being "good guys" to "bad guys."

Children are naturally altruistic, as they are concerned for the well-being and happiness of others. Melvin Konner, an Emory University anthropologist, physician, and author of *The Evolution of Childhood*, said, "There's another point that needs to be made to parents: Your baby knows more than you think she knows. That's what's coming out of this kind of research."[3]

A Harvard study also confirmed a child's positive social inclinations. Nicknamed "The Big Mother Study" where the mother was watching the child, the research demonstrated that small children helped others regardless of whether a parent suggested to do so or was even present. "Where morality comes from is a really hard problem," says Alison Gopnik, a developmental psychologist at the University of California at Berkeley. "The elements that underpin morality — altruism, sympathy for others, the understanding of other people's goals — are in place much earlier than we thought, and clearly in place before children turn two."[4]

> Only the weak are cruel. Gentleness can only be expected from the strong.
>
> Leo Buscaglia

Children naturally incline towards kindness. Dr. Karen Wynn, director of the Yale lab, and psychologist Paul Bloom, her husband, were curious if babies were developing attitudes as a result of their experiences, or if they were "built" to identify in the world what was good and what was bad. In a designed experiment with Dr. Kiley Hamlin, assistant professor at the University of British Columbia, Wynn and Bloom tested infants ages six and ten months with plush animal puppets helping and hindering each other. The babies had a chance to reach for the puppet of their choice. "Basically, every single baby chose the nice puppet," said Hamlin.

The team of researchers repeated the experiment with three-month-old infants, tracking their eye movements, as the babies could not reach for the puppets. The experiment yielded the same results, where the infants showed a preference for the "good" puppet, while having an aversion to the hinderer.[5] Other studies reveal that babies and small children are indeed embedded with the energy of kindness, gentleness, and the compassion for others.

Where Gentleness and its Negative Expressions Reside

The energy of peace and kindness are associated with two key chakras, in my experience. The grounding energy that accompanies gentleness and kindness is connected to the Root Chakra, the solidifying core of our groundedness, safety, security, and prosperity. When we tend to our own primary needs and are kind, gentle, and loving with ourselves, we operate from the root of our physical being.

Another energy center associated with gentleness is the Heart Chakra, the seat of love and compassion. As the energy center of altruism, this beautiful space activates our internal desire to be concerned for the happiness and welfare of others. While the Root Chakra is prominent for grounding, peace, and gentleness, the Heart center *activates the sharing of this profound energy* with its arms outstretched.

Gentleness is an expression of peace and tranquility. When we are gentle and kind with ourselves and others, an important sense of safety and security grows. This is the core of our physical nature, as described by psychologist Abraham Maslow and his Hierarchy of Needs theory. When our core needs of safety and security are met, we feel stronger and more rooted, and others benefit from our energy, too.

Aggressiveness, its polar negative expression, can forcibly achieve in the short term, but operating from gentleness is essential for long-term success and happiness. The vulnerable yet adventurous child within us is the part that attracts all good things, including financial security. The 19th century poet and author Charles Fenno Hoffman said, "Kindness is the evidence of greatness. If anyone is glad that you are here, then you have not lived in vain."

Aggression is the negative expression of a gentle spirit. This internal spiritual violence arises when too much Masculine energy pulls the quiet, gentle energy from its grounded state, moving our focus into the upper, more Masculine region of the body. If the Masculine energy becomes even more exacerbated, physical violence erupts.

How Our Gentle Nature Becomes Contaminated

If we made a dollar every time we heard someone say, "Oh…you are too kind," we would all be rich. While this colloquialism is a figure of speech, it may be revealing a covert dance that many of us may be grooving to, where perhaps we don't feel particularly deserving of kindness.

Kindness and gentleness are Feminine traits within both males and females. However, when Feminine energy becomes suppressed, it shows up in the individual, organizational, or cultural body. Aggression, anxiety, violence, and fear are the hallmarks that signal this imbalance. This energetic balance gets thrown off when technology increases speed, as human evolution accelerates. In his book *Of Mystics & Mistakes*, author Jaggi Vasudev writes:

> When conquest became the mode, people burnt the feminine out of the planet. We made it like this that the masculine is the only way to be successful…But to conquer is not the way; to embrace is the way. Trying to conquer the planet has led to all the disasters. If the feminine was the more dominant factor, or at least if the two were evenly balanced, I don't think you would have any ecological disasters, because the feminine and earth worship always went together. Those cultures which looked upon the earth as the mother, they never caused too much damage to the environment around them.

To restore our relationship with the earth, we must once again value the sacred Feminine and turn away from practices of domination over others, opting for equality and sharing resources again.

> Every man who is any kind of artist has a great deal of female in him. I act and give of myself as a man, but I register and receive with the soul of a woman. The only really good artists are feminine. I can't admit the existence of an artist whose dominant personality is masculine.
>
> Orson Welles
> *My Lunches with Orson*

As technology keeps piling up around us, it is easy to become more distracted with gadgets, glamor, and materialism, then subsequently grow more disconnected from each other. Agitation, nervousness, anxiety, and fear predominate, while peace, tranquility, and a gentle spirit are lacking in our world. When excess Masculine energy pulls from our Feminine power that connects and grounds us, loneliness is born.

In 2017, former U.S. Surgeon General Vivek Murthy declared that "the world is suffering from an epidemic of loneliness."[6] Cigna's alarming report issued in May 2018 confirms that most American adults are considered to be lonely. In Cigna's survey of more than 20,000 adults, the results were frightening and deeply disturbing:[7]

- About half of Americans reported sometimes or always feeling alone or left out.
- Around 27 percent of Americans rarely or never feel as though there are people who really understand them.
- Over 40 percent of Americans sometimes or always feel that their relationships aren't meaningful and that they are isolated from others.
- About 20 percent of Americans say they rarely or never feel close to people or feel as though there are people they can talk to.
- Generation Z adults (ages 18 to 22) are the loneliest generation and claim to be in worse health than adults who are older.

The survey also revealed some bright spots. People who engage in frequent meaningful interactions in person enjoy better health and much lower incidence of loneliness than those who rarely interact with others face-to-face. It requires putting down our cell phones and returning back to the analog world of reality.

The survey also showed that people who sleep the ideal amount and get the right amount of exercise have lower levels of loneliness. And those who say they work the right amount are also less likely to experience loneliness. Working less than desired showed a six-point increase in loneliness, versus the three-point increase by those who work more than desired.

Social media often produces an artificial sense of connection with others. However, research shows that as people spend more time on social media to "be connected to others," the more isolated they feel. The balance between friends and family, work, play, sleep, and "you time" is critical for feeling closer to others, being happier, and enjoying better health.

With our human-made technology that has erupted on our planet during the past 150 years, we are exposed to far too much Masculine energy that is riddled with excessive motion. While Feminine energy in each of us is characterized by quiet, grounded, peaceful, and calming frequencies, Masculine energy has attributes of motion, movement, and directing energy. A balance of both energies is needed for vitality and good health, but the problem is that Masculine energy has exploded to excess levels since the Industrial Age was globally activated in the mid-19th century.

Technology usually disturbs the peaceful and gentle spirit, pulling energy from the lower chakras to the upper chakras, which moves us further away from the grounding power of our Root Chakra. The physical and psychological symptoms of this include nervousness, anxiety, insomnia, aggression, and the inability to sit still. When the Masculine energy becomes even more agitated and ruffled, aggression can quickly grow into physical violence.

Our true strength, whether we are male or female, lies in living as peaceful pilgrims. Saint Francis de Sales, the 16th century French Bishop of Geneva known for his gentle and patient approach, said, "Nothing is so strong as gentleness, nothing so gentle as real strength." With his deep love for nature and animals, he noted, "Never be in a hurry; do everything quietly and in a calm spirit. Do not lose your inner peace for anything whatsoever, even if your whole world seems upset."

When we turn away from our Divine Child nature that is gentle, kind, and compassionate towards others, the tendency for violence and aggression can emerge, especially in men who are prone to excess Masculine energy. Canadian evolutionary psychologists Martin Daly and Margo Wilson analyzed 35 homicide data sets from 14 countries, including some from primitive societies and some from different eras. Their findings revealed that men committed homicide 26 times more frequently than women. Murders of family members are committed mostly by men, in more than 90 percent of the cases, according to the data.[8]

Interestingly, men are also victims of homicides in 70 percent of cases, with this percentage jumping to more than 90 percent in some cultures. In Russia in 1996, over 86 percent of all serious crimes were committed by men, and in 2006, 85 percent of serious crimes in the United States were committed by males. These statistics are valid for most countries, despite their size or geographical location. The significant differences in the male-to-female ratio also holds true with cruelty and abuse towards animals: 38 to 1 for beatings, 20 to 1 for torture, 17 to 1 for burning, and 16 to 1 for the shooting of animals.

American social psychologist Leonard Berkowitz proposed that men and women are taught that fighting is more suitable for men. He suggested that these roles are constantly reinforced through media and folk literature, resulting in parents buying toy guns for boys and dolls for girls, for example. And therefore, Berkowitz believed that parents were more willing to approve of and even encourage aggressive behavior in boys, and not girls.[9] For decades, even cartoon series on television reflected this bias. As Oscar Wilde suggested, we become our art.

From an energetic perspective, when the tools of violence, such as swords, guns, and knives, are linked to men, it can cause aggression and violence to soar in males. Even carrying tools associated with violence increases that heavily-charged negative energy, as studies reveal. In a 2018 study by the University of Cambridge, the mere presence of Taser weapons and electroshock devices led to overall hostility in interactions between the police and public, which researchers call the "weapons effect." I call this the "energy effect." London police officers who were visibly armed with the electroshock weapons were 50 percent more likely to be assaulted by the public, and also used force 48 percent more often on the public than those on unarmed shifts, according to lead researcher Dr. Barak Ariel from Cambridge's Institute of Criminology.[10] Being associated with the energies of hostility, aggression, violence, and death will negatively affect anyone who is near them.

This is resonance at work. It is a double-edged sword, magnifying both beneficial and toxic energies. Resonance is also what makes the Divine Child so powerful when we share our 21 gifts with others.

Kindness and gentleness can be effective and active, not weak or passive. The bully expresses himself through cowardice, where fear overrides altruism and turns into spiritually or physically violent behavior. The strength of true character, however, is shown through inner fortitude and quiet strength. Keiko Fukuda, the Japanese American martial artist born in 1913 who was the highest-ranked female judoka in history and the last surviving student of Kanō Jigorō who founded Judo, said, "Be gentle, kind and beautiful, yet firm and strong, both mentally and physically."

Another negative expression of kindness and gentleness is narcissism. Stuck at the First Chakra to learn about core needs, the self-absorbed person or narcissist is a Wounded Child who is overly concerned with physiological needs, safety, and security — often exhibiting a heightened fascination to achieve financial success. When someone has not gotten his or her core needs met early in childhood, the energy turns inward, where self-identification consumes him or her. With little energy left to radiate outwards to others, the black hole of the self-absorbed individual pulls others into him or her like a subtle energy vampire.

> Be kind, for everyone you meet is fighting a battle you know nothing about.
>
> Wendy Mass

When the wounded, self-preoccupied child shows up, projection is frequently the behavioral mode. For example, pent-up anger towards the parents for not fulfilling the unmet needs of the child may later be displaced to others. The self-focused person or narcissist generally lacks self-awareness because he has become disconnected from his own true nature, looking outward for quick-fix solutions to alleviate internal pain.

The person overly concerned for his own welfare turns that anger towards others, blaming them for his own mistakes, misfortunes, and shortcomings. Overcompensation takes the form of competitiveness. Grandiosity and exaggeration of achievements stem from insecurity. Envious of others, narcissists unconsciously seek to destroy the credibility of their victims using belittlement, defamation, and slander. Smear campaigns and character assaults ensue, followed by the playing of being the victim. "You hurt me!" screams the narcissist, rather than seeking to solve problems.

This is a form of spiritual violence, where unconsciously attacking others is the desperate attempt to feel better. The problem with the narcissist is that he or she is usually unaware of his or her condition. If a person is unable or unwilling to see himself for who he truly is, there is little hope for shifting spiritually.

Reactivate Your Gentle Nature

In order to find peace and harmony, we can practice self-compassion and loving kindness towards ourselves and others without expecting it back. One such person who spent her life practicing this was Mildred Lisette Norman. Born in 1908, she was an American non-denominational spiritual teacher and mystic, spending much of her life walking as a gentle activist for peace. Referring to herself only as "Peace Pilgrim," this beautiful silver-haired lady walked more than 25,000 miles crusading for peace, wearing a modest blue tunic and carrying only a comb and toothbrush.[11]

From 1953 to 1981, Peace Pilgrim walked across America, sharing her simple yet profound message to thousands of communities: "When enough of us find inner peace, our institutions will become peaceful, and there will be no more occasion for war." The book *Peace Pilgrim: Her Life and Work in Her Own Words* is a shining tower of hope and inspiration. She sweetly described how our gentle spirit can change the world and then ourselves: "Life is like a mirror. Smile at it, and it smiles back at you."

If you are finding that your gentle inner child has become wounded, anxious, agitated, angry, or even violent on some level, here are some suggestions to quell this exacerbated energy and reengage the natural peaceful and gentle spirit can bring you back into balance:

- Find ways to simplify your life by turning off technology each day. Get away from your cell phone. Your grandparents, great-grandparents, and their ancestors all succeeded without looking at cell phones every five minutes — and so can you. By finding time to leave your cell phone out of your eyesight and pocket for at least an hour or two each day, you will be rewarded with a calmer mind, greater peace, and deeper and richer relationships that are real, not online.

- Eliminate any weapon of war and violence in your home. Unfortunately, many people live in a state of fear, believing they need to gear up for battle. Consider getting rid of swords, spears, knives, and guns in your possession. It is impossible to attract and cultivate peace and gentleness when connecting to and resonating with the energy of death by instruments designed to kill. It is the energetic equivalent of installing an electric chair in your home: you will become the victim of its toxic energy. The Divine Child knows no violence, and carrying a gun defies the Golden Rule and the words of Jesus Christ, who said to turn the other cheek when someone delivers violence.[12]

- Practice saying, "I'm sorry." Dr. Wayne Dyer said, "Let go of your ego's need to be right. When you're in the middle of an argument, ask yourself: Do I want to be right or be happy? When you choose the joyous, loving, spiritual mode, your connection to intention is strengthened." Even if you are right about something, your words can be a healing salve when you say, "I'm sorry if I hurt you. I didn't mean to." It's a wonderful way to bring peace and harmony to any relationship. As someone once said, an apology is a good way to have the last word.

- Practice kindness in every situation. One of the greatest challenges is to return kindness when someone causes us harm in some way. But as the Dalai Lama wisely said, "Be kind whenever possible. It is always possible."

Our gentle nature is one of our keys to true success. Lao-tzu, a teacher from sixth century China and author of the Tao Te Ching, said, "I have three things to teach: simplicity, patience, compassion. These three are your greatest treasures." These three treasures embody the energy of a gentle and kind heart.

Each one of us is wounded in at least one major way, with probably a number of other parts within us that have been traumatized, too. There is no shame in this, as long as we keep on learning about our past trauma with a curious and open mind. By uncovering the roots of early trauma, we can begin to heal the wounded Divine Child, restoring this precious energy that empowers us.

> I place a high moral value on the way people behave. I find it repellent to have a lot, and to behave with anything other than courtesy in the old sense of the word — politeness of the heart, a gentleness of the spirit.
>
> Fran Lebowitz

Every child shows its mommy when it has been wounded or injured because it knows no other way. The irony is that revealing how we have been traumatized is not weakness, rather intimacy and connection while initiating the healing process. By exposing the total self just as we are, we create deeper bonds with others and with ourselves. Being kind to ourselves and to others becomes magical when we operate from the source of unparalleled strength: our authentic self.

1 https://www.webmd.com/parenting/news/19991129/children-learn-violent-behavior-home#1

2 https://www.sciencedaily.com/releases/2000/11/001106061128.htm

3 https://www.smithsonianmag.com/science-nature/are-babies-born-good-165443013/

4 IBID

5 IBID

6 https://hbr.org/cover-story/2017/09/work-and-the-loneliness-epidemic

7 https://www.multivu.com/players/English/8294451-cigna-us-loneliness-survey/

8 https://www.psychologytoday.com/us/blog/homo-aggressivus/201409/male-aggression

9 https://www.psychologytoday.com/us/blog/homo-aggressivus/201409/male-aggression

10 https://www.sciencedaily.com/releases/2018/12/181219191048.htm

11 https://www.peacepilgrim.org

12 *The Bible*, Matthew 5:38-40.

Authentic

It takes courage to grow up and become
who you really are.

e. e. cummings

Our spiritual gifts spring from the endless well of authenticity. When we are real, we cannot help but be expressive, too. When we are expressing our true selves, we reveal our vulnerability that connects us to others more deeply. Authenticity energizes us, as we engage life with great curiosity, presence, and joy.

Little children live in the kingdom of success, drawing from the rich well of inner truth. Living genuinely without pretense is what allow us to live more powerfully. There is no hiding, no pretending. When the playful child channels its energy spontaneously to live its heartfelt dreams, it succeeds.

Award-winning actress Andie MacDowell said, "When you are authentic, you create a certain energy…people want to be around you because you are unique." Authenticity is the secret sauce of what creates our charisma and magnetic attraction. Most people are drawn to us not because we invent toys or create cool art, but because we are alive, engaging, and real.

The Liberating Path of Authenticity

One of my long-time dear friends, Liz, has a childlike ability to be playful and spontaneous. She connects with others readily, living in her authenticity and passion. Her hairstyling business of thirty years allows her to share her gifts of authenticity, connectedness, and aliveness with thousands of people in the Detroit area. Liz isn't just styling and coloring hair, she is coloring people's lives with her beautiful, childlike energy that ignites others with joy. This is success.

When I met Liz nearly thirty years ago, I was locked in a proverbial box, relatively uptight and feeling insecure. Being around Liz was a healing salve for the soul, where I was able to reactivate my ability to simply *be myself*, rather than struggle to live my life pleasing others. I didn't realize how much more life could be enjoyed when I stopped trying to fit in or become what people close to me or society wanted me to be. By simply being around her, I healed what was suppressing my Divine Child energies. When I reactivated my authenticity, I felt alive and powerful again.

The Divine Child is our spiritual heritage, remaining true to itself from the moment we take our first breaths. While food and water feed the body, our authenticity nourishes the spirit and soul. As Dr. Seuss playfully said, "Be who you are and say what you want, for those who mind don't matter, and those who matter don't mind."

Small children live in the kingdom of joy, peace, vulnerability, and connectedness by simply being and spontaneously expressing their true nature. "Children are the hands by which we take hold of heaven," said Henry Ward Beecher, a 19th century slavery abolitionist and social reformer.

When we meet people who exhibit the pure authenticity of a small children, we immediately wish that we were like them, too. Holding back from spontaneously expressing our true feelings and thoughts requires energy that unfortunately gets wasted needlessly. Our yearning to be effortlessly genuine is the big secret to any kind of success, where that powerful energy attracts other beacons of light. It is the wisdom and way of our Divine Child.

While studying at the legendary Improv Olympic in Chicago, I distinct remember when Charna Halpern, the co-founder of the famed improvisational school Improv Olympic who has coached and cultivated some of the best comedic talent in the world, shared with the class the secret of authenticity in performance: "The secret to being funny is not to try to be funny. Life is funny enough. Just show that life is like this."

Living your life in grand style requires genuine expression. This magical, dynamic energy makes you distinctive and special. It causes you to shine. Authenticity magnifies your unique gifts that you are meant to share with the world. Best-selling author and motivational speaker John Mason said, "You were born an original. Don't die a copy." Go ahead. It is time for you to light up the world.

Negative Expressions of Authenticity

The Heart Chakra is the seat of truth and information, as well as love and compassion. When we operate from our childlike compassion and love for others, we live in what is true and real. Remaining heart-centered allows us to more fully connect with others and share our gifts in a more profound and sincere way. "Authenticity starts in the heart," said Brian D'Angelo.

Remaining connected to its own presence and spiritual core, the Divine Child has no need for external saviors or superheroes. External distractions have a tendency to cause us to forget about our own capabilities, our gifts, our power. Jesus reminded us, "You will do greater things than me." Believe in yourself and release the Superhero within you.

When we live each moment authentically, only then can we shine our light. This is the spiritual path of living the Golden Rule, the way of the Divine Child. It attracts similar energies in people who are likewise present and genuine.

Expressing our true nature is the secret for attracting abundance. Real power is unleashed when our Divine Child effortlessly connects with others, which unexpectedly draws fresh and profound resources to us through the natural phenomenon of resonance.

Distractions lure us away from the authentic nature of our Divine Child. Illusion is enticing, to be sure. It is easy to forget about the beauty, reality, and extent of our potential when distracted by external toys. In theatrical magic, the illusionist uses misdirection to divert our attention from the real to the imagined. And on the stage of our lives, distractions can similarly reduce our authenticity through manipulation, posturing, and materialism.

Another dark expression of our genuine nature includes all forms of lying and deception. All of us adults, especially as parents, have witnessed the moment a small child discovers how to manipulate the parent. Fake cries can often be distinguished from real tears of pain, fear, and distress. Like a tiny magician, the child can learn how to skillfully influence others to gain what it wants.

> If you trade your authenticity for safety, you may experience the following: anxiety, depression, eating disorders, addiction, rage, blame, resentment, and inexplicable grief.
>
> Brené Brown

It may be possible that when the Crown Chakra gets corrupted through illusion, the physical body around the crown region becomes traumatized as well, potentially showing up as physical disease in the head area of the body. In my private practice, I've observed people who were not living authentically experience severe problems with their scalps, for example.

This can also occur with the Heart Chakra. When we aren't authentic with ourselves, we cannot be authentic with others. We must first admit to the truth of who we are without fabricating or stretching the truth to establish an image based on pretense. Success is more about unveiling these powerful traits of the Divine Child that each of us have, and less about "becoming" someone. We achieve real growth when we heal and reveal our essential spiritual qualities.

Another negative expression of authenticity is the loss of integrity, the alignment between our values, words, and actions. When we miss our commitments to others, we disrespect others and lose integrity with ourselves, too. On the other hand, seeing others as equals, the Divine Child is courteous, considerate, and respectful of others, regardless of race, age, cultural distinctions, social contrast, or financial differences.

The Wounded Child will unknowingly consume precious energy in projecting its pain by hiding, failing to keep its word, or acting selfishly. Insecurity leads to a compromised sense of integrity, and the insecure Wounded Child will bend to fit the ever-changing flow of public opinion.

What is the point of gaining material possessions if we lose the essence of our soul in the process? Being authentic is core to living a spiritually engaged life. "To become conscious and aware, we must become authentic. Authenticity is the highest form of being," wrote Teal Swan.

Contaminated Authenticity

Fear in its many disguises contaminates our authentic nature. When we become traumatized, especially as small children dependent on others, our sensitivity to pain becomes heightened or numbed. When trauma gets embedded in our being, patterns of fear emerge when triggered, playing like a record over and over again.

Even something benign can trigger worry, where we are afraid of saying something that might hurt someone's feelings. Instead of speaking honestly, we may have the tendency to hold back our own authentic thoughts and emotions, then blurt out a little white lie to cover up what we really wanted to say. People often ask, "How are you doing?" Our typical and automatic response may be "good" or "fine," when in reality we are feeling pissed because the dog just made a mess in the living room, we were late for work, or we feel crummy with the onset of a cold.

Pop spiritual culture instructs us to "remain positive" and keep our chins up. Say a few positive affirmations, and the bad conditions in our life will magically disappear. In themselves, positive affirmations can be highly beneficial, as a number of studies reveal.[1]

However, if we succumb to telling ourselves lies, it ends up in internal revolt. Someone suffering from cancer who tells herself "I am in perfect health" will inevitably have some internal parts rise up in rage that say, "What are you talking about? You have cancer, and it feels terrible!"

Fake news begins internally, then it gets externally projected. In a world exploding in fake news, we must first find out what fake news we are generating about ourselves. When inauthenticity becomes widespread, the disease of deception, lying, and manipulation festers on a cultural scale.

When we believe in fabrications or myths without evidence and facts, fake news is born. It is interesting how many people blindly accept something without first carefully examining those beliefs to find out if they are actually true using relevant facts.

Belief is limiting in its effectiveness and power, despite belief being a popular catchphrase on T-shirts and art. There is a big distinction between believing something and knowing the truth. Placing our trust, confidence, or faith in someone or something has real power when we dig to understand the truth.

Just ask those who thought that the earth was flat with sea monsters lurking around the outer edges of it — an idea that was handed down for centuries. Those who accepted that popular belief for thousands of years were not only victims of suffering but were also vastly limited in their success. Those who dared to remain open, curious, and exploring the truth achieved.

We hide behind the false teachings of groups or cliques to keep from having to examine the truth for ourselves. What masquerades as information or entertainment can really be a form of power play, in which influential people in leadership positions distort and manipulate the news for their own purposes. If we get swallowed up by political propaganda or deceptive advertising, we leave our Divine Child behind. When we operate with fake news and beliefs on a cultural level, our society leaves its Divine Child behind and unknowingly heads down a path of decay and potential doom.

We have invented masks to hide behind rather than openly serving our common good. While smiling is helpful and induces better emotions, suppressing sadness, grief, fear, or pain won't make those unwanted things go away. These unresolved emotions brew and fester, seeking other ways to be released and resolved. Chronic negative emotions can transform into a physical disease, such as stress, high blood pressure, cancer, heart disease, or other issues.

With social media, we hide behind self-made avatars and emojis, which serve as more masks to conceal who we really are and what we are feeling. Happy face, sad face, rolling on the floor laughing face, tears of joys face, hearts, thumbs up, thumbs down, winks, and grins — they are all online masks. If you are wanting to communicate openly and authentically, consider leaving emojis and avatars alone. Talking to that person about how you really feel and what you really think is what small children do, rather than use another online tiny mask that hides the authentic self.

> Some of the most faked things are a signature, love, a smile, happiness, an orgasm, intelligence, and good skin.
>
> Mokokoma Mokhonoana

In Alice Walker's 1983 Pulitzer-winning novel, *The Color Purple*, also one of my all-time favorite films, Celie shows how she rescued her Wounded Child. A victim of an abusive father and husband who was cruel and relentless, Celie was abused, degraded, beaten, raped, and twice impregnated by her father. Both her father and husband treated her like property, objectifying and using her in servitude. But she survived.

Celie rescued herself and found strength in knowing that her life was meaningful and special. As she discovered how truly precious she was, Celie said, "Everything want to be loved. Us sing and dance and holler, just trying to be loved." Our precious child inside is just like Celie and the color purple, waiting to be loved, and ready to love. Becoming authentic with herself, courageous, and expressive were the keys to her salvation.

How Groups Can Suppress Authenticity

Don't trade your authenticity for approval. Just learn how beautiful you really are. Society pushes us to try to fit in a group and belong to it. Certainly, groups can be beneficial by helping to fulfill a sense of belonging, nurturing, and feeling connected and valued. Due to their energetic dynamic of resonance, many groups feel powerful.

If we struggle to fit in, we risk losing precious aspects of ourselves where we give them away — only to receive something much less valuable in return. While joining any group or organization can have benefits, it fundamentally means that you give up something. For example, when you join a company for employment, you are usually not allowed to say what you want on social media that contradicts the group. It is why company personnel often scan a candidate's social media content to see if that person "fits in" or not. The corporation often limits our freedom of speech, which we surrender in exchange for a job and a paycheck.

> When you project your authentic self,
> people will respond to and connect with it.
>
> Michelle Tillis Lederman
> *The 11 Laws of Likability*

Most groups rarely encourage authenticity. When we sacrifice aspects of ourselves to placate others, we suffer, and the organization also suffers. Rather than trying to fit in, be your magnificent you. "Be yourself, everyone else is taken," wrote the Irish poet and playwright Oscar Wilde.

There is some pain that can be associated with living authentically, and perhaps that is why we also learn to shut down. In the struggle to try to be friends with everyone, especially to placate a group's needs and desires, it is impossible to please the masses. So just express the beautiful you.

The Divine Child traits that we all have from birth give us richness in spirit. In the pursuit of money, security, fame, and success, it is easy to forget where our spiritual gold lies. The true Holy Grail is about speaking and acting in authentic ways, aligned to our Divine Child. These magical energies, once expressed but now may be hidden, are the secrets to high achievement, joy, and material success.

When you share these energies within you, you engage with the world more intimately. When you shine your light, you ignite these vital energies within others, where they also begin to illuminate the world, too. "Seek first the kingdom of God…and all of these things will be added to you," is the teaching that emphasizes the connection between inner and outer wealth. It is a promise of spiritual inheritance that leads to true abundance on all levels. When you embrace the world through your Divine Child, the world becomes your oyster.

Henry David Thoreau said, "Wealth is the ability to fully experience life." The key to this rich kingdom of joy, learning, and true play is living from these potent forces that are already within you — the Divine Child who is authentic, curious, passionate, and alive. You can grow up in physical poverty and with a myriad of challenges, but the wealth of these potent energies you possess transcends your past. These 21 gifts can propel you to incredible success on every level as the secret ingredients to a well-rounded, happy, and productive life.

Ironically, it is the person who has gone through tremendous pain and a seemingly insurmountable past who often becomes among the greatest healers and catalysts for transformation. This is spiritual alchemy, where we can connect with others heart-to-heart. A past embedded with shame, deprivation, and any other negativity can always be transformed by the light of our Divine Child. We can turn our scars into stars, and dance in the heavens by simply being authentic and open.

Our vulnerability, one of our real powers, allows us to relate to others more fully. The mystical poet Khalil Gibran said, "But let there be spaces in your togetherness and let the winds of the heavens dance between you. Love one another but make not a bond of love: let it rather be a moving sea between the shores of your souls." Through authenticity, true intimacy brings sweet success that can be shared and expanded.

Novelist, playwright, and social activist Janet Louise Stephenson wrote, "Authenticity requires a certain measure of vulnerability, transparency, and integrity." Our honesty is a conduit of hope for others, not the prospect of risk that we often fear. What unites us as a people are our divine characteristics that our tiny teachers show us every single day. Our wonder at small children serves a powerful purpose: To realize that magic lies within us all.

Reactivate Your Authenticity

We all can use a dose of more authenticity, and less hiding and pretending. Revealing ourselves completely and honestly is the only way we can see ourselves as we truly are. It is not only the sublime path for all healing. Authenticity is also essential for any type of true success that separates itself from mere achievement. The healing journey begins by knowing your story, being truthful about it, then revealing it. By sharing your authentic story, you can foster healing in others by connecting with them in synchronous ways.

To reengage your true authentic self, here are some ways you can practice being more fully honest, open, and genuine with yourself and others:

- Surround yourself with genuine and authentic people. And spend less time with those who are pretentious. Be careful to avoid those who swim endlessly in their pain, never pulling themselves out of that dark and dangerous pool of shame, guilt, and perpetual negativity.
- Spend more time with young children. Our tiny teachers are among the wisest, too. Volunteer. Teach in some capacity, while these tiny precious teachers reveal their magic that can reignite these qualities that lies within you.
- Listen more and talk less. Being genuinely interested in others is part of authenticity. We live in a culture that promotes self-absorption, one that encourages "me-ism" with selfie photos and individualism in a world craving global answers to widespread challenges.

> Want to help others? Be yourself.
> You'll inspire others to muster the
> courage to be themselves as well.
>
> Kamand Kojouri

- Write a list of what you are afraid to reveal to others. Then find ways to reveal yourself more fully. Experience the vulnerability of your Divine Child, even when it feels frightened, nervous, attacked, or sad. If being authentic is difficult for you, then consider starting an "Authenticity

Journal," and write in it every day until you find yourself as alive and as engaged as you were when you were a small child.

The wish to be subservient drives us to hide from ourselves and shrink from others. To break the chains of our self-bondage and liberate us from our own prisons requires the powerful energies within each of us: curiosity, creativity, playfulness, joy, courage, and vulnerability. "To become authentic, to be a true individual, we require a thirst for freedom, freedom from the unwise, from psychological traumas, from self-pity, from self-preserving fearful ideas, from primitive instinctual behavior, and from dogmatic beliefs, ideals and values that have been taught to us throughout our entire lives," wrote Mateo Sol, the psychological-spiritual writer who was born into a family of alcoholism, drug addiction, schizophrenia, and mental illness.

True liberation can be achieved when we express who we are authentically and with integrity. Learning about yourself and others is a key ingredient to healing. It opens the doors to ultimate freedom from any prison in which you may find yourself. As Eckhart Tolle said, "Only the truth of who you are, if realized, will set you free."

---

[1] https://www.psychologytoday.com/us/blog/embodied-wellness/201704/affirm-or-not-affirm

Free

The secret to happiness is freedom…and the secret to freedom is courage.

Thucydides
Greek general and historian, c. 460 BC

The energy of freedom is vibrant and alive within your Divine Child. True freedom can always be yours, regardless of your current circumstances. "No one outside ourselves can rule us inwardly. When we know this, we become free," Gautama Buddha said.

From the moment you were born, living freely and openly is what brought you joy. Small children move without restriction. They see only hope, believing that all things are possible. This energy of freedom makes children truly magical, as they live in a Universe with vast and unlimited potential. When children find themselves facing a temporary wall, they try to figure out a way to get over it, under it, around it…and move on. Our child teachers embrace freedom as a natural core value.

If children feel confused, sad, or distraught with their dilemma, then they will cry for help. Small children do not have a tendency to play the victim with the "poor me" attitude. After falling down and scraping their knees, they get back up and move forward on their journey to reconnect with their inner joy.

The child educator and physician Maria Montessori believed that freedom was an essential ingredient that allows children to explore, learn, and develop. In her book *The Absorbent Mind*, Montessori said, "The emphasis on freedom is for the development of individuality. The emphasis on discipline is for the benefit of the individual and of society."

The Divine Adult within us is tiny and immature at birth, while the Divine Child's characteristics and energies are fully present and evolved. The Divine Adult grows as inner and outer discipline, wisdom, protection, and other adultlike energies are discovered, learned, and cultivated over time.

Albert Max Joosten, one of Montessori's earliest students who played a major role in popularizing the Montessori method of education, said in his book *On Discipline*, "Freedom is a conquest and not a gift. No one can give freedom to anyone. It has to be conquered and this conquest is based on discipline. But this discipline, in its turn, requires freedom for its further development. We have to cultivate freedom in order that discipline may develop."[1]

The power of the vulnerable Divine Child is that it learns to adapt. We become smarter, more open, and more successful by discovering how to adjust to challenges and new situations. It is perhaps why small children grow, heal, and evolve so rapidly, because the adventurer inside is hungry to expand and reshape itself. "The measure of intelligence is the ability to change," said Albert Einstein.

Where Freedom and its Negative Expressions Reside

The energy of freedom is associated with the chakra connected to expansiveness and unbounded potential — the Crown Chakra. This energy center connects us to the field of pure potentiality, the quantum field where all things are possible. As a radiant and limitless energy, freedom is to be expressed throughout our lives. American attorney and political commentator Angela Rye said, "Whether it's freedom to express, freedom to live, freedom to earn, freedom to thrive, freedom to learn, whatever it is, I want to make sure that I'm a part of these spaces and opening doors."

> The butterfly's transformation includes the ability to freely move its wings, to freely move on — grateful for the gifts of the past but entirely unencumbered by them.
>
> Cyndi Dale
> *Togetherness*

Freedom and liberty are essential qualities embedded into our spiritual DNA from birth. Freedom should not be something for which we must fight, but unfortunately, with so many people who wish to control our freedoms at many levels, we do need to fight for it. Sociologist Anna Julia Cooper, one of the most prominent African-American scholars in U.S. history who lived to the ripe age of 105, said, "The cause of freedom is not the cause of a race or a sect, a party or a class. It is the cause of humankind, the very birthright of humanity."

The negative expressions of freedom are oppression and slavery. When the Crown Chakra, the highest spiritual center in the body, becomes corrupted, then its polar opposite — the Root (First) Chakra — is also negatively impacted. The Root Chakra is the center of safety, security, and the other physical and basic necessities of life, such as food, water, and shelter. Also, psychological factors associated with mental health are also connected to the Root Chakra, such as comfort, trust, and acceptance.

The Crown Chakra connects to the spirit, where enlivening energy is said to enter into the top of the head, while the Root Chakra is about the connection to earth and the material world. The destructive energy of fear attacks the Root Chakra that takes people off balance, making them far more susceptible to manipulation, deception, and other toxic forms of slavery and control. Whenever any form of slavery is invoked by an oppressor, everyone suffers. "You can't hold a man down without staying down with him," Booker T. Washington said.

Historically, fear has been used to undermine women in most cultures throughout the world, subjugating and objectifying females as mere property. For millennia, women have been prevented from holding office in most cultures in history. The patriarchy silenced them in public and private institutions through aggressive shaming, guilt, and unequal treatment. This gross mistreatment was accomplished successfully through the use of political and religious structures, which were often one and the same for thousands of years.

Indian film actor and former politician Amitabh Bachchan said, "Because you are women, people will force their thinking on you, their boundaries on you. They will tell you how to dress, how to behave, who you can meet and where you can go. Don't live in the shadows of people's judgement. Make your own choices in the light of your own wisdom."

Racism and other forms of inequality block the spontaneous expression of freedom. A number of religious teachings have promoted racism and classism through the concept that God has a "chosen people." In 1963, Martin Luther King Jr. said, "It is appalling that the most segregated hour of Christian America is eleven o'clock on Sunday morning."

Karl Giberson, professor of Science & Religion at Stonehill College wrote, "Fifty years later, this remains true, as America's churches lag behind its schools, businesses, military and almost every other institution in escaping old taboos about mixing the races. Compare the diversity in the pages of *Christianity Today* to that of *Sports Illustrated* or *Rolling Stone*."[2]

Founded in 1927, Bob Jones University, the Bible college in Greenville, South Carolina, has a rather long, racist past. The college did not admit black students until the 1970s. And then for another 30 years, interracial dating was prohibited at that school.[3] But it is difficult to depart from underlying racism when the roots of an institution are embedded in scripture that has been tightly held and revered by many for centuries.

In 1845, the Southern Baptists used the "Mark of Cain" reference in Genesis Chapter 4 as justification for owning slaves, causing a split between the Northern and Southern Baptists at that time. As early as the fifth century AD, Cain's curse was interpreted as having black skin, which has used by millions of Christians to justify slavery. Later in Genesis, we see another Biblical justification for slavery with the "Curse of Ham" by Noah, an archetype of the savior, who declared that Ham's offspring serve those of his two brothers.[4]

How is it possible to have freedom and equality throughout the world when even our religious institutions and teachings have promoted slavery and degradation throughout the ages? In his book *Saving the Original Sinner: How Christians Have Used the Bible's First Man to Oppress, Inspire and Make Sense of the World*, Karl Giberson discusses how Abraham, one of the revered patriarchs of the Bible, owned slaves. While the apostle Paul ordered Philemon to treat the slave Onesimus as a brother, Paul does not teach that slavery is evil, nor does he tell Philemon to free Onesimus.[5]

While many may argue that "cultural differences" thousands of years ago gave justification for so-called holy men to subjugate women and people of other races, it makes it even more difficult for Christians to denounce slavery and completely embrace equality with women and races when the Bible clearly teaches that God and Jesus are unchanging, "the same yesterday, today, and forever."[6] Otherwise, it must be admitted that God made gross mistakes with his reasoning and ensuing laws, then he suddenly changed his mind somewhere along the evolutionary timeline — something that no self-proclaimed Christian is likely to admit.

The negative impact of this spiritual bipolarity is prevalent. Two thousand years after Jesus appears, we still witness vast expressions of inequality and slavery, including racism, unequal pay between the sexes, and the sex trafficking of women. It is as though we have not departed from the dark shadows of misogyny, racism, and classism promoted in both the Old and New Testaments of the Bible, as well as other religious texts such as the Quran.

As long as nearly half of the world's population clings to primitive books labeled as "holy" that contain these dark preachments, there is little chance to heal racism on a cultural level. It is why racism is often more prevalent in the Bible Belt, as Robert P. Jones, author of *White Too Long: The Legacy of White Supremacy in American Christianity*, points out.[7] It is subsequently easy to question teachings such as "if the Son sets you free, you will be free indeed" when freedom is out of reach.[8]

Routine Discrimination

Many of my black and Hispanic friends tell me how nervous they get every time they step into their car to drive, for fear that they will be pulled over by the police and harassed. For many minorities, freedom is still being crushed. Even though there are nearly twice as many whites as Hispanics in Arizona, in Maricopa County, federal investigators found in 2011 that the sheriff's department in the greater Phoenix area pulled over Hispanic drivers a staggering *nine times more* often than other motorists.[9] The stops were part of a crackdown on undocumented immigrants ordered by Joe Arpaio, the Maricopa County sheriff from 1993 to 2016.[10]

The statistics revealing embedded racism today are disturbing. In 19 of 24 states, black Americans are more likely to be stopped than white people. After being pulled over, blacks are also more likely to be searched in all but one state (Virginia, in 2015), even though they are no more likely to be carrying illegal substances.

> We are a nation of many nationalities, many races, many religions — bound together by a single unity, the unity of freedom and equality. Whoever seeks to set one nationality against another, seeks to degrade all nationalities.
>
> Franklin D. Roosevelt

Beginning in 2015, the Stanford Open Policing Project, a partnership between the Stanford Computational Journalism Lab and the Stanford School of Engineering, collected and analyzed data from more than 100 million traffic stop records and searches from 31 states. Black drivers and Hispanic drivers are more likely to get a ticket, 20 percent and 30 percent respectively, versus delivering a warning to white drivers.[11] But how can we overcome a culture of racism and inequality that is based on fear when it has been so prevalent through history?

The use of lynching by white people was used for centuries to control and terrorize black people, using claims of sexual aggression or even contact between black men and white women. The symbolic rite of the mob made the black victim a horrific example, warning the rest of the black population to not challenge the supremacy of the white race, wrote historian Howard Smead in his book *Blood Justice: The Lynching of Mack Charles Parker*. Nearly 25 percent of lynching victims were accused of sexual assault, and about 30 percent were accused of murder, according to the Equal Justice Initiative (EJI). The archives at the Tuskegee Institute tabulate that 4,743 people were lynched by U.S. mobs between 1881 and 1968, and nearly 75 percent of those lynched were black Americans.[12]

Martin Luther King, Jr., said, "Freedom is never voluntarily given by the oppressor; it must be demanded by the oppressed." Without teaching our children about these horrors and remembering our dark past, the toxic energy of inequality and slavery is difficult to shake and eradicate.

But progress is being finally made in our remembrance, as well as in legislation. The opening of America's first lynching memorial, The National Memorial for Peace and Justice in Montgomery, Alabama, in April 2018 was dedicated to the victims of white supremacy on a six-acre site overlooking the Alabama State Capitol.[13] It was just in December 2018 when the United States Senate unanimously approved its first anti-lynching law, outlawing the murdering by mob.[14]

Just as slavery and other forms of inequality were historically systemized through legislation and religious example or decree, the evolution and return to freedom on all levels must likewise be expanded using legislation. John Locke, the 17th English philosopher and physician, said, "The end of law is not to abolish or restrain, but to preserve and enlarge freedom. For in all the states of created beings capable of law, where there is no law, there is no freedom."

> America will never be destroyed from the outside. If we falter and lose our freedoms, it will be because we destroyed ourselves.
>
> Abraham Lincoln

Policy drives behavior, and our values of the Divine Child determine the blueprint of our future actions. It is not enough to wish away our dark past through positive thinking and affirmations. The ugly weeds in our garden must be fully recognized, acknowledged, and eradicated. Only then can growth and positive evolution can take place.

How Our Energy of Freedom Becomes Contaminated

The thirst for power and control initiates the numerous systems of slavery and imprisonment. It begins with fear about loss. This fear is rooted in the survival mechanism, with the alarms sounding that we may lose some aspect of ourselves possibly leading to our own demise. The American lecturer and animal rights activist Gary Yourofsky said:

> Men in America were terrified that if women got an equal say in society, the system would collapse, and their lives would be valued less. Whites in America were scared that if blacks obtained their freedom and equality, the system would collapse, and their lives would be devalued. Heterosexuals are terrified that the psychotic institution of marriage will collapse if gays are given their right to marry. And humans are terrified that if animals are liberated and no longer viewed as inferior subordinates, human life will be valued less.

Rights for one group do not come at the expense of rights for another group. Every time an oppressed group gains liberty, the freedom of the whole increases. Every time we end a long-standing injustice, society improves.

But often, abused individuals will stay in subordination because they have forgotten how to take charge of their own destiny. "Most people do not really want freedom, because freedom involves responsibility, and most people are frightened of responsibility," said Sigmund Freud. Being accountable for ourselves, let alone others close to us, is challenging if we have been traumatized. When our Divine Child has been wounded, it is difficult for our Divine Adult part to grow, mature, and be responsible for our own actions, where we can stand up for ourselves and denounce any form of slavery we may be experiencing.

For some who choose to remain in slavery today, could this be unconscious? "It is difficult to free fools from the chains they revere," said Voltaire, the 18th century writer, philosopher, and historian who advocated for freedom of speech, freedom of religion, and separation of church and state. Without knowledge and education, we are vulnerable to become victims, whether it be the woman in the workplace who is unaware she is being paid 28 percent less than her male counterparts, or the Hispanic or black male who gets pulled over by the police in an unprompted stop.

> To be given dominion over another is a hard thing; to wrest dominion over another is a wrong thing; to give dominion of yourself to another is a wicked thing.
>
> Toni Morrison
> *A Mercy*

At the same time, there are unspoken benefits to being a slave. The slave is usually told what to think and how to act, and the next meal or punishment is relatively predictable. But being told what to think, whether through intimidation or more subtle means, leads to a colonization of the mind itself.

American astrophysicist and author Neil deGrasse Tyson said, "Knowing how to think empowers you far beyond those who know only what to think." Dogma is disastrous for the free thinker. Any belief system that proselytizes what you should think, especially coming from a group, is a narrow path with tall boulders on both sides, limiting perspective, imagination, and ability to think like a free child in an unlimited Universe.

The Servitude of Ignorance

The Divine Child is innately curious, continuously wanting to learn. Human-created problems, like the skyrocketing cost of higher education, keep people enslaved in ignorance and poverty. In a world of social media where people speak their minds and spend many hours a day chatting online, very little of this online activity results in true intellectual engagement beyond the complaining widely seen.

American culture teaches that getting a college education is the path for a better life. It eventually pays off, according to a recent report by The College Board. While college graduates with a full-time job earned a median of 67 percent more than high school graduates in 2016, it unfortunately takes an average of 12 years to recover the costs of obtaining a bachelor's degree.[15] The path to a college degree comes with many hardships for people from disadvantaged backgrounds, especially the high cost of attendance. For those who fail to complete a degree, the resulting debt can be even more crippling.

We have developed a system that punishes our young people and limits their future, encumbering them with a college education that they cannot afford. In 1875, the *New York Times* wrote about the perceived high cost at that time: "Gentlemen have to pay for their sons in one year more than they spent themselves in the whole four years of their course." The newspaper described advanced education as an elitist institution, where "a body of rich men might found a college, as a joint stock company, and charge the pupils with the actual cost of their education, with a suitable addition by way of profit to the owners."[16]

Perhaps times have not changed so much over the past 150 years. Rather than view advanced education as a right and necessity of Americans, we have come to view it as a privilege of the wealthy and well-connected.

> Knowledge is power.
> Information is liberating.
> Education is the premise of progress,
>   in every society, in every family.
>
>   Kofi Annan
>   Ghanaian diplomat

Today, the United States spends more on college than nearly any other country, according to the 2018 Glance report released by the Organization for Economic Cooperation and Development (OECD). Americans spend about twice as much as the average developed country on students, or approximately $30,000 per student per year. Andreas Schleicher, the director for education and skills at the OECD, said, "The U.S. is in a class of its own. Spending per student is exorbitant, and it has virtually no relationship to the value that students could possibly get in exchange."[17]

In fact, a third of developed countries offer college free of charge to their citizens, while another third keeps tuition less than $2,400 per year. And the U.S. ranks number one for spending on student ancillary services, such as housing, meals, transportation, and health care, totaling $3,370 on these student welfare services that is more than three times the average for the developed world.[18]

Despite America falling behind in education globally, some political groups label the system of education and other related necessities provided by other countries as "socialization," demonizing it as some sort of free handout, even though taxes provide education at a lower cost without the duress of profit-taking by private institutions. Yet, many services that Americans enjoy are socialized, including roads and highways, clean water, sewage, libraries, public schools, police and department services, military protection, food safety, public parks, beaches, and numerous other services that the local, state, and the federal governments provide.

Imagine a world without those things. Like the present state of advanced education and healthcare in the United States, unaffordability is driven by private enterprise and corporate profit-taking. No institution should profit from clean water, education, healthcare, and other vital public services vital to the human experience, in my opinion.

> Our greatest happiness does not depend on the condition of life in which chance has placed us, but is always the result of a good conscience, good health, occupation, and freedom in all just pursuits.
>
> Thomas Jefferson

Punishment is not just a way of life for many under the slavery of education and debt; it is the preferred method of our primordial ancestors. The idea of punishing someone for wrong-doing as a way to correct behavior is an ancient concept — and an erroneous one. Punishing someone usually restricts one's freedom and doesn't work so well, as we now know from numerous studies. Zhuang Zhou, an influential Chinese philosopher commonly known as Zhuangzi from the 4th century BC — the height of the philosophies and schools during a period known as the Hundred Schools of Thought — echoed this. He said, "Rewards and punishment are the lowest form of education."

Dr. Benjamin Spock used guilt to invoke the punishing disciplinarian in his groundbreaking book on parenting, *The Common Sense Book of Baby and Child Care*, which sold 500,000 copies in the first month after its initial publication in 1946, and over 50 million copies by 1998. He wrote that a working mother is inclined to shower [her child] with presents and treats, bow to all his wishes, regardless of her own, and generally let him get away with murder."[19]

The departure from a punishment-based system to "teach" children has been replaced with better models developed from scientific study. "Many parents think of discipline as a way to correct their child's bad behavior, often by using punishment," says psychiatrist Alvin Rosenfeld, MD, coauthor of *The Over-Scheduled Child*. "The debate becomes 'What sort of punishment works best?' Instead, parents should ask themselves, 'How do I raise a child who'll become an adult I'll admire and respect?' That's the goal of discipline."[20] This more contemporary approach encourages independence and resilience to promote good behavior. We learn best by example from positive role models.

The punishing disciplinary approach is also widespread in the U.S. prison system, where it is known for harsh penitentiary conditions and overcrowded prisons. In September 2013, the United States had the highest incarceration rate in the world, at 716 prisoners per 100,000 of the national population. The Department of Justice reported that number rose to 860 inmates per 100,000 adults in 2016.[21] Current and former prisoners accounted for 5.8 percent of adult US men in 2010, up from 1.8 percent in 1980.[22]

> It is said that no one truly knows a nation until one has been inside its jails. A nation should not be judged by how it treats its highest citizens, but its lowest ones.
>
> Nelson Mandela

The rehabilitation rates in America are even more tragic. More than 70 percent of freed U.S. inmates are rearrested within five years, while Norway enjoys the lowest recidivism rate in the world at around 20 percent.[23] Norway's model is based on compassion, dignity, respect, and equality — vibrant traits of the Divine Child — rather than degradation, humiliation, and inequality. The Halden prison in Norway, for example, is known as the most humane prisons in the world, writes Christopher Zoukis, author of *Federal Prison Handbook* (2014) and *College for Convicts* (2016).

Cheerful, quiet, peaceful, and modern, the primary goal of Halden is rehabilitation, reflected by bright and airy cells with enclosed suites, bar-free windows, and artwork to inspire a beautiful atmosphere. Designed to hold Norway's worst offenders, the Halden facility features excellent workout facilities, robust vocational training, and a peaceful yard of trees with benches. Guards are trained to motivate, not intimidate, and onsite medical facilities help keep the minds and bodies of prisoners in tip-top shape.

The economy of Norway also reflects the value of rehabilitating prisoners. In 2017, Norway's Gross Domestic Product (GDP) per capita was a staggering 26 percent higher than that of the United States, or $75,314 and $59,792 per person, respectively.[24] Norway's debt per capita in 2016 was 58 percent less than the debt of the United States, at $25,874 per person in Norway vs. $61,769 in America. There are no life sentences in Norway, where the longest prison sentence a person can receive is 21 years, which can be extended in five-year increments if the prisoner needs more rehabilitation.[25]

Norway spends about $90,000 a year to house each prisoner,[26] while the state of California spends about $75,000 per year per inmate.[27] New York City spent $168,000 to guard, feed, and house each inmate in 2012, while the Vera Institute of Justice's 2012 study found that the average taxpayer cost in 40 states was $31,286 per prisoner.[28]

However, a new report in 2017 released by the Prison Policy Initiative found that mass incarceration costs are actually $182 billion each year in the United States, versus the figure of $81 billion that the Bureau of Justice Statistics reported that excludes policing, court costs, and costs paid by families to support incarcerated loved ones, such as phone calls, commissary vendors, and $1.4 billion in nonrefundable fees from defendants and their families.[29] In other words, because of the high rate at which released inmates end up back in prison, the incarceration costs are about that of Norway's or higher, which excludes the billions in dollars in economic costs the United States incurs from lost wages and overall costs to the national economy. This could explain the dramatic differences in GDP between Norway and the United States.

Punishment sets up a system of inequality, which is more about power, profiteering, and control over the child or the adult, as reflected in the U.S. prison system. The Golden Rule may be needed here, as it is difficult to expect good results from someone after we just treated them differently, usually involving some sort of proverbial clobbering over the head.

Reactive Your Freedom

Slavery shows up in many forms. The abused child. A beaten woman. A struggling student buried in debt. Ignorance and dogma. The black man who was stopped at a traffic light. An underpaid female teacher. The family struggling to pay bills. The 25 million children, women, and mean who are victims of human trafficking around the world.[30] The 13 percent of the world who goes hungry every day.[31]

Freedom is about accepting yourself, giving yourself and others permission to be free. Jim Morrison, the late American poet and lead singer of the rock band, The Doors, said, "Friends can help each other. A true friend is someone who lets you have total freedom to be yourself — and especially to feel. Or not feel. Whatever you happen to be feeling at the moment is fine with them. That's what real love amounts to — letting a person be what he really is."

> Refugees come to us seeking asylum, seeking freedom, justice and dignity — seeking a chance just to breathe. And people in our country are saying close the doors and don't let them in?
>
> Mandy Patinkin

If you are wanting to break through any chains, physical or spiritual, that may be blocking your path to success and expand your freedom, here are some practical tips:

- Take time to pay attention to limitations in your life. Sometimes we do not know what freedom looks like until we have a broader perspective. Make a list of any type of limitation, perceived or real, that may be possibly hindering you. Sometimes it requires letting go of a bad habit or changing how you do things. Occasionally, it could require letting go of a relationship that restricts who you are or how you express yourself.
- Practice using your voice. Speaking up is one of the top fears, especially in front of people. Take small steps by speaking what you want and need in your personal life to those close to you. Get feedback from a trusted,

credible source, such as a friend or business confidant. Find your unique voice. Express your feelings and grow your confidence. Live in the power of your vulnerability rather than shrinking from it, even though you may be afraid of what may happen.

- <u>Live more simply</u>. Our world is growing more complex by the day, but you don't need to succumb to that. The truth is that everything that is complex can be broken down to something simple. Get rid of things that create complexity in your life and give you stress, which reduces your freedom.

- <u>Exercise your creative energy</u>. "Art, freedom and creativity will change society faster than politics," said Victor Pinchuk. This philosophy can apply to your life as well. Push beyond your adult boundaries, letting your inner child take over the reins for a while. Sign up for a new art class. Write poetry. Learn how to dance. Build sandcastles at the beach. Practice a new language. Explore a foreign land. Make friends from different nationalities.

Being authentic with yourself is the path of freedom. Jim Morrison wrote, "Expose yourself to your deepest fear; after that, fear has no power, and the fear of freedom shrinks and vanishes. You are free." As you learn about yourselves and others, your deepest fears will evaporate, and courage and playfulness from your Divine Child will shine again.

When you exercise your freedom and speak out with the power of your voice, you will be kinder and more loving to yourself and to others, and that energy will be reflected back to you. Compassion is born from treating people, as well as yourself, with one of the most powerful spiritual qualities we seem to be born with — the necessity to be equal.

---

1 https://amiusa.org/wp-content/uploads/2013/01/Quotes-for-reflection.pdf

2 https://www.huffingtonpost.com/karl-giberson-phd/the-biblical-roots-of-racism_b_7649390.html

3 http://www.jbhe.com/news_views/62_bobjones.html

4 https://www.huffingtonpost.com/karl-giberson-phd/the-biblical-roots-of-racism_b_7649390.html

5 *The Bible*, Philem. 16, Col 4:1, Eph. 6:9.

6 *The Bible*, Hebrews 13:8, Malachi 3:6, James 1:17, Numbers 23:19.

[7] https://www.nbcnews.com/think/opinion/racism-among-white-christians-higher-among-nonreligious-s-no-coincidence-ncna1235045; retrieved 4-11-21

[8] *The Bible*, John 8:36 NIV.

[9] https://statisticalatlas.com/county/Arizona/Maricopa-County/Race-and-Ethnicity

[10] https://www.nationalgeographic.com/magazine/2018/04/the-stop-race-police-traffic/

[11] https://openpolicing.stanford.edu/findings/

[12] https://www.theguardian.com/us-news/2018/apr/26/lynchings-memorial-us-south-montgomery-alabama

[13] https://www.nytimes.com/2018/04/25/us/lynching-memorial-alabama.html

[14] https://www.washingtonpost.com/outlook/2018/12/28/why-it-took-century-pass-an-anti-lynching-law/?utm_term=.d96b5a30fed7

[15] https://money.cnn.com/2017/01/09/pf/college/college-degree-payoff/index.html

[16] https://www.nytimes.com/1875/06/01/archives/the-expense-of-college-education.html

[17] https://www.theatlantic.com/education/archive/2018/09/why-is-college-so-expensive-in-america/569884/

[18] IBID

[19] https://www.parents.com/parenting/better-parenting/advice/temptation-to-spoil-kids/

[20] https://www.workingmother.com/content/discipline-solution

[21] http://www.pewresearch.org/fact-tank/2018/05/02/americas-incarceration-rate-is-at-a-two-decade-low/

[22] https://www.businessinsider.com/america-incarceration-rates-2017-11

[23] https://www.huffingtonpost.com/entry/not-the-worst-but-not-norway-us-prisons-vs-other_us_59b0772ae4b0c50640cd646d

[24] https://countryeconomy.com/countries/compare/norway/usa?sector=GDP+per+capita+%28Dollars%29&sc=XE34#tbl

[25] https://thinkprogress.org/the-u-s-has-a-lot-to-learn-from-norways-prisons-681fd194b6e1/

[26] IBID

[27] https://www.politifact.com/california/statements/2017/aug/09/kamala-harris/does-it-cost-75k-year-lock-inmate-california/

[28] https://www.nytimes.com/2013/08/24/nyregion/citys-annual-cost-per-inmate-is-nearly-168000-study-says.html

[29] https://eji.org/news/mass-incarceration-costs-182-billion-annually

[30] https://www.bustle.com/p/13-sex-trafficking-statistics-that-put-the-worldwide-problem-into-perspective-9930150

[31] https://www.foodaidfoundation.org/world-hunger-statistics.html

Equal

Equality is the soul of liberty; there is, in fact, no liberty without it.

Francis (Fanny) Wright
19th century writer, abolitionist

About a year ago, I had my DNA test done with 23 and Me, the online company that decodes ancestral heritage and genetic traits. I was curious about how much native American blood I had, since some of my great-grandparents were supposedly of that heritage.

After getting the results, I became intrigued by the numerous ancestral DNA reports that revealed my true heritage. While I was told that my background was primarily Germanic and Irish, with some Native American tossed in, the truth was that I am even more of a mutt and less "pure" in terms of any dominant Anglo-Saxon bloodline. According to the DNA reports, the largest share of my ancestors come from a region in Italy, which interestingly is my favorite place to visit.

The report also divulged something more fascinating. I could see how the bloodline shifted over time, and where my true roots were. And to my surprise and delight, my ancestors were 100 percent African as late as 1720. When I read that on the DNA report, it reminded me how much I loved playing piano and organ in a black gospel thumping style in a Pentecostal church for years. I now had a greater sense of connection to that music that made it feel closer to home. More importantly, I embraced a sense of fluidity in my identity which acknowledged that our racial identities are socially constructed through surface appearances, rather than biological in origin that tell the true story of interconnectedness and unity.

> My country is the world, and my religion is to do good.
>
> Thomas Paine

That revelation was followed by another stunning epiphany, after carefully examining the migratory maps that accompanied the DNA and health reports. Researchers from the University of Uppsala in Sweden have found evidence by examining the genetic material in our chromosomes that we are all descended from the same ancestral group in Africa about 170,000 years ago.[1] While some researchers have developed other theories and questioned the evidence from this analysis and other studies, the general consensus by the scientific community is that we all have descended from our African predecessors.

Without knowing our true heritage, along with a good sprinkling of racist propaganda, we adults forget what small children reveal to us: We are all related, and we are all equal. Children do not need a DNA test to remind them how they are connected to each other physically, emotionally, mentally, and spiritually. Their purity rests in their inner knowing and outward showing of equality and belonging, rather than making up stories of being pedigreed that gives them a false sense of superiority as an adult. While examining and constructing our own small family trees is interesting, living the universal family tree each day is far more vast, exciting, energizing, and joyful.

Our Divine Child within doesn't need to learn about equality. That inner powerful part of us intuitively realizes that we are equal as individual threads exquisitely woven together in the glorious tapestry of humankind. Equality strengthens the entire cloth, imbuing it with uniqueness that expands humanity while supporting each individual thread even more. The irony is that when we treat one another as equals, everyone wins and becomes stronger.

> Whenever you find yourself on the side of the majority, it is time to pause and reflect.
>
> Mark Twain

The joy of life naturally bubbles out of this powerful aspect of our inner presence. Children readily play together without judgement, welcoming all into their virtual sandboxes to romp, create, and enjoy life. Seeing others as equals is healing and connecting, without the need to label or control. This is what makes small children spontaneously powerful, while we adults swim in our prejudices, longing to be like them again.

Dignity and respect flow in abundance from the well of equality. Awareness is focused on doing, rather than judging and evaluating. When we honor others as we honor ourselves, our attention and energies synchronize. The Law of Resonance is one of the great secrets to success, and our tiny teachers remind us how we can attract good things naturally.

Treating others equally also emerges from self-esteem and a solid, healthy ego. Devaluing another is only possible if one sees himself as being weak or afraid of loss. When we see others as equals, we value ourselves and others at the same level, as the Golden Rule advocates.

Equality directs our energy in synchronicity, where we can achieve more by working together in common purpose. The 19th century Scottish philosopher and mathematician Thomas Carlyle said, "Nothing builds self-esteem and self-confidence like accomplishment." This world is where our Divine Child thrives.

Locating Equality and Inequality in the Body

The Heart Chakra, the energetic center of the body, is the embodiment of love, compassion, truth, and information. Through the Divine Child's deep knowing of its love impulse and natural concern for all that is, the soul seeks to return to this center when it wanders away from time to time. It is through our center that we rediscover the secret to the true wealth — our inner spiritual gold, which is the ultimate measure of real and satisfying success on any level.

Operating from our powerful Heart center will always guide us to truth. Children intrinsically know what adults may have forgotten is the spiritual law of the universe: That we are all one in unity, and, therefore, are equal. Because small children naturally live from their Heart space, they see only through the lens of equality, the spiritual energy that connects everyone together with empathy and compassion.

Small children create powerful invitations for everyone to join in the festivities. They do not judge others by the color of their skin, compare how rich their parents are, or keep score by assessing differences in physical ability. These types of adult comparisons that divide are foreign to the Divine Child, as they push us further from the path of equality, learning, joy, being present, and compassion. Children are naturally wise, as their inner knowing realizes those judgments would only interfere with their natural joy and ease of living.

Equality is a cornerstone of all true success. Racism, its negative counterpart, arises when we depart from the truth of our nature. The dark energy of racism is a heavy cloud that prevents the radiant light of equality from shining through. When any form of inequality shows up, the Heart center turns ugly and overwhelmed with deep pain and negativity.

Racism is a type of spiritual heart disease. When our spiritual energies become contaminated, disease occurs first on the ethereal level, then works its way down to the physical level to become visible through our words, behaviors, and eventually the physical body. Any form of inequality becomes material and physical.

> All forms of inequality are spiritual abuse.

This happens when parts of the Divine Child have been wounded through trauma, usually imposed by external sources that live in fear and negativity. Trauma starts with a contaminated spiritual heritage that is unconsciously transferred to the child from another source, such as a parent, teacher, or institution.

When we do not treat ourselves as equals, this shows up as feelings of unworthiness and inferiority. A lack of self-esteem means that we have lost touch with part of our Divine Child, which yearns to be restored and revitalized. If our Divine Child has been traumatized, the Wounded Child learns to abuse itself spiritually, subconsciously beating itself up to prove that it is inferior and not equal, while appearing as an adult.

When the Wounded Child believes the lie that he or she is not worthy of love, joy, or the other powerful gifts, the Heart center becomes disturbed. We are then at risk for becoming withdrawn, shy, and unable to fully share our unique gifts to the world. This spiritual paralysis occurs while resonating with the energy of chaos, disorder, disease, and death.

Unable to see that we are beating ourselves up in numerous ways, we unconsciously attract others to join in the parade of abuse. If we lose the insight and ability to see ourselves for who we really are, the alarms ring even louder to get our attention. How other people treat us is often how we have been treating ourselves.

This is our wake-up call. Shrinking from our greatness arises from the slumber of deception and the lies of inequality thrust upon us as little children. This trauma is a sort of spiritual death, smothering precious aspects of us that were once thriving. Our Divine Child yearns to emerge again, as our spiritual destiny is to create magic and joy which can only exist with true equality.

How Equality Becomes Corrupted

I was raised in the United Pentecostal Church until I left for college at age 18. As Pentecostals, we felt superior, but with a good dose of feigned humility because we truly believed that we were "God's chosen people," an idea perpetuated in numerous biblical texts and still preached in churches, mosques, and synagogues today.

Children and adults alike were taught to never question the "irrefutable Word of God," as the preacher on the pulpit issued threats of everlasting punishment with hellfire and brimstone by breaking the rules and religious codes. It was a cycle of pay, pray, and obey that kept one off the sinner list.

> Racism is still with us. But it is up to us to prepare our children for what they have to meet, and, hopefully, we shall overcome.
>
> Rosa Parks

For most of us, the religious beliefs we embraced are usually handed to us through inheritance, because our parents believed in them, and their parents did as well, and so forth. The lack of questioning led to blind faith — a pseudonym for the suspension of our critical faculties of reasoning and analysis, which some might ironically argue are God-given abilities — to accept something as irrefutable truth based on mysterious glory. The Danish theologian Søren Kierkegaard said, "There are two ways to be fooled. One is to believe what isn't true; the other is to refuse to believe what is true."

Rather than to readily gobble ideas without questioning the contents for evidence and facts, it is far better to maintain a philosophy and approach that "we don't know, but we are going to continue exploring until we discover what is true." This is the position that most scientists take, who largely operate more from humility than the arrogance of proverbial know-it-alls that some may perceive them to be. However, scientists realize that the more they know, the more that remains to be discovered.

Ironically, despite the religious rhetoric that "God loves everyone the same" — except for women, homosexuals, and other "sinners" — the corruption of the Divine Child was well underway, where freedom, openness, and equality were attacked. Control, close-mindedness, and mass inequality on multiple levels reigned.

But we churchgoers thought it was normal, gleefully singing songs about how we were going to "fly away to heaven someday" with Jesus as our personal Lord and Savior to ensure our redemption. It was a vicious, troubling pattern of attending church four times a week, but being shamed for committing various sins the previous few days. This was an unending cycle of spiritual abuse.

The feature of the horror show was to be scared out of our britches, then asking for forgiveness while paying the church the required ten percent of our income to please God…and obviously, the pastor and church staff. After Sunday morning and Sunday night service, each about two to three hours long, we would go back into the world and "be tempted by Satan." The miserable, endless cycle would repeat all over again.

> I promise to question everything my leaders tell me. I promise to use my critical faculties. I promise to develop my independence of thought. I promise to educate myself so I can make my own judgments.
>
> Carl Sagan

I witnessed one Pentecostal pastor say while riding in her car, "I think it is going to rain today," which was rather confusing with the sun shining in the clear blue sky. The pastor continued, "I just saw some black clouds we just passed," pointing towards the African-American family that was walking on the sidewalk next to the street.

I didn't think much about it at the time, because it had been part of my cultural experience in a nearly all-white school and a church where the congregants were 99 percent white and where superiority was regularly taught.

In retrospect, however, it is apparent that pastor was a racist with other telling signs. But as a child, I thought it was normal and even appropriate. After all, role models provide us not just food, clothing, and shelter, but also hand to us a steady diet of we should believe and accept to be true about our world.

A role model's behavior, whether beneficial or detrimental, becomes the way a child learns. This is fundamentally how toxic behavior becomes normalized in cultures, especially when it is unquestioned. In *Poor Richard's Almanack* published on December 19, 1732, Benjamin Franklin wrote, "The way to see by faith is to shut the eye of reason." The normalizing is even more profound and detrimental when it occurs by someone who outwardly claims to love everyone under religious order by an invisible deity, but inwardly and more privately, does not. Under these conditions, both vulnerable children and adults who are easily manipulated become unwitting victims.

Globally, inequality and racism have become deeply embedded in our spiritual DNA, which was contaminated through the institutionalization of "superior races" by powerful rulers, many of whom used religion as their weapon of projection. Political and religious leaders alike have long relied on coercion and control to make it a requirement, not an option, to accept without question the superiority of the few and the inferiority of the many.

How the Savior Complex Nearly Destroys Equality

When the patriarchy firmly established the concept of the male savior in numerous cultures around the world, the ruling males created a superior class of mostly male deities that were invisible, mysterious, all-powerful, and unable to be questioned. These male-designed belief systems in nearly every civilization were the key to institutionalizing patriarchal control over the masses, destroying the precious energy of true equality derived from Feminine power.

For the patriarchy, the rules of the game involved the creation of over 3,000 gods and saviors who were mostly male and held peculiar, unfathomable powers, where qualified humans, usually the males, had inexplicably aligned and connected to those gods to be fortunate enough to receive special gifts and a touch of those powers — all self-proclaimed, of course. The privileged and superior class were portrayed as relevant and necessary intermediaries, like healers, priests, religious elders, and preachers who are allegedly "ordained by God." In other words, the ruling class who invented the gods said that the gods had silently ordained the controlling class to rule without question.

This "Savior Complex" creates a spiritually contaminated foundation of inequality, subjugation, and manipulation, where the masses are coerced to accept the disparity under threat of punishment. In this corrupt system, the victims give up their most powerful qualities, such as freedom, equality, learning, exploration, support, and joy — traits and energies of the Divine Child. In return, the followers receive a restricted way of life, characterized by a controlled routine punctuated by gross ignorance, subjugation, and mass fear. Believers are commanded to love, but with many restrictions placed on this dimly understood notion of love to the point of being meaningless.

> I think women are foolish to pretend they are equal to men. They are far superior and always have been.
>
> William Golding
> *Lord of the Flies*

In this form of spiritual slavery, the Divine Child within begins to rapidly wither and die. The con artistry continues under the guise of goodness, mercy, and continued punishment, energetically keeping the slaves on the hamster wheels that goes nowhere. Without learning and discovery, the weakened Divine Child suffocates under the banner of blind faith, readily accepting what is fed to it. When the freedom of choice is absent, radiant joy and passion turn into boredom, anxiety, and fear.

There is a financial cost to the Savior Complex as well, when wealth and abundance rapidly shift toward the few in power, ultimately giving rise to autocratic regimes, even in religious institutions. This great shift in wealth due to inequality has been seen in nearly every civilization and culture across the globe, usually resulting in the destruction of that culture when the slaves began to die.

This phenomenon can be seen in American culture with the decline of the middle class since the 1950s. Today, 78 percent of Americans live paycheck to paycheck,[2] while the top one percent owns 40 percent of the country's wealth.[3] In fact, that same richest one percent owns more wealth than the bottom 90 percent combined.

We see the same imbalance of wealth and subsequent power in many religious institutions. For example, the Vatican's wealth was estimated in 1965 at

$10 to $15 billion, with Italian stockholdings alone at $1.6 billion.[4] The personal net worth of Pope Francis has been estimated at $25 to $28 million, with some estimates higher and lower than those figures[5] — a far cry from being "Christ-like." The Vatican Bank, which held $8 billion in assets in 2015, has been the center of scandal and corruption.[6] When the Vatican, a separate entity, released its 2014 financial statements, it reported having more than $1.2 billion in assets that weren't previously on its balance sheet.

In Evangelical circles, being a religious leader today can pay very well, while Jesus, their chief role model, was not so fortunate. At the time of his death in 2018, Billy Graham was reported to be worth $25 million. According to the Charlotte Observer, his son Franklin Graham received a whopping $1.2 million in 2008 and $880,000 in 2014 for running the two non-profits associated with Billy Graham. According to the *Charlotte Observer*, the Billy Graham Evangelistic Association reported $101 million in revenues in 2010, while U.S. Samaritan's Purse had revenues of $635 million in 2016.[7] According to data provided by GuideStar, the world's largest source of information on non-profit organizations, Franklin Graham's compensation in 2013 from Samaritan's Purse alone made him the highest-paid CEO of any international relief agency in the United States.[8]

> When it is a question of money, everyone is of the same religion.
>
> Voltaire

Rick Warren, the senior pastor of the megachurch — the sixth largest in the United States — in a rather wealthy city of Lake Forest, California, has a reported net worth of $25 million. Bishop TD Jakes, who has been called America's best preacher, is worth $150 million. David Oyedepo, who also with a net worth of $150 million, enjoys the reputation as the richest pastor in Nigeria, where 60 million Nigerians do not have a bank account, 98 million do not have insurance,[9] 8 percent receive no income, and the average worker makes less than $2.75 per day.[10] Religion also pays well for Pat Robertson, who runs the Christian Broadcasting Network in 180 countries and is worth $100 million. Kenneth Copeland, whose ministry is spread over a 1,500-acre campus near Fort Worth,

Texas, is worth a whopping $760 million. If you want to be wealthy and avoid paying some taxes, just start a church.

Joel Osteen, the celebrated minister of positive thinking who has a cash-generating megachurch in Houston, Texas, has a reported net worth of $40 to $70 million. Osteen received enormous criticism for not opening its doors to Hurricane Harvey victims, even though his staff was caught on video meeting at the church immediately following the hurricane's passing. After being shamed on mass media and Twitter, the church finally opened its doors to the victims, but Osteen and his Lakewood Church officials thought it was a good idea to pass the offering collection plates during the services, despite hurricane victims in the audience who had just lost their homes and belongings.[11]

The high net worth of evangelical preachers has come with not only hypocrisy, but legal consequences. In 1988, televangelist Jim Bakker was indicted on federal charges of mail and wire fraud, as well as conspiracy charges to defraud the public. The case against Bakker, the founder of Praise The Lord (PTL) Ministries, exploded in the press when it was revealed he had sex with Jessica Hahn, the church secretary. When the scandal broke, Jim and his wife Tammy Faye Bakker were enjoying success with the highest-rated religious show in America, while their 2,200-acre resort, Heritage USA, built with money made from television programming brought in six million visitors in 1986. I was there.

Jim Bakker was convicted in 1989 and sentenced to 45 years in prison.[12] Released from prison after serving eight years, 81-year-old Bakker is now back on TV with a much darker message: "The Apocalypse is coming, and you better get ready." He appears to be selling doomsday guidebooks, fuel-less generators, and freeze-dried food with a shelf life of 30 years.[13]

There are things about organized religion that I resent. Christ is revered as the Prince of Peace, but more blood has been shed in His name than any other figure in history. You show me one step forward in the name of religion, and I'll show you a hundred retrogressions.

Frank Sinatra

Another cause of fraud and grave hypocrisy involves Houston megachurch pastor Kirbyjon Caldwell, who was indicted for wire fraud and money laundering in 2018. A spiritual advisor to former president George W. Bush, Kirbyjon Caldwell and his business partner, Gregory Smith, were accused by federal prosecutors of defrauding elderly and vulnerable investors by selling them millions of dollars in worthless Chinese bonds. A second civil lawsuit against the pair was filed by the Securities and Exchange Commission.

Both men face 20 years in prison on the wire fraud counts and 10 years for the money laundering counts.[14] In July 2019, while co-defendant Gregory Smith pleaded guilty to wire fraud, Caldwell maintained his innocence.[15] But in January 2021, Caldwell was found guilty and sentenced to six years in federal prison and another year on supervised release for conspiracy to commit wire fraud.[16]

Taking money from the poor and filling the coffers of the few propagates gross inequality, an age-old tactic of those who crave money and power. But control of the masses does not seem to be reserved for the politically powerful or for companies driving by profit at the expense of its worker bees. It holds true for those religious institutions who also employ the use of control, manipulation, and deception for their followers.

Thoughts and prayers have never been shown to be an effective wealth-building strategy, but as Joel Osteen and other religious leaders well know, selling books and jewelry, showcasing entertainment, and gathering offerings from the masses is highly profitable.

With these huge earnings, it is fair to question why Christian followers wear T-shirts and smack bumper stickers on their cars with the simple message "WWJD," meaning "What Would Jesus Do," especially with the apparent forgetting of how Jesus whipped those buying and selling in the temple. The wealth of a number of top religious leaders is contradictory and grossly hypocritical to the simple way of life exemplified by Jesus, who never once took an offering, never built a church, and never told anyone to attend church.

The challenge for those in power is to keep the slave barely functioning, with enough energy to bend and do the work of the master, but not enough energy and knowledge to break free. The subtle forms of slavery today are largely not with physical shackles and chains, but with the mighty constraints of limited consciousness through false belief systems, deception, and hypocrisy, where the craving for what is offered causes someone to give up something far more valuable in return. As long as the slaves pay the slave owners offerings and other forms of self-sacrifice such as time, attendance, and work, the system of servitude is kept intact.

Imagine if your close friend created a new god that joined the parade of roughly 3,000 deities that exist today. Believers of Islam, Christianity, Catholicism, or any other religion that promotes any number of deities may ridicule your friend, perhaps even labeling him as being blasphemous. But your friend has as much credibility and right to create a new god, just as our ancestors did. What makes any god better or legitimate than the others?

In the infancy of their primordial ignorance, our ancestors did not know what caused volcanoes to erupt, lightning to zip across the sky, or disease that arrests the body. They assumed that some mysterious, unknown force must be responsible for both goodness and calamity, as they did not have the method of scientific hypothesis, evidence, and reasoning to discover the causes. Their severely limited comprehension of what caused these catastrophic events that threaten human survival is understandable, given their lack of scientific tools.

> Those who will not reason, are bigots, those who cannot, are fools, and those who dare not, are slaves.
>
> George Gordon Byron

And so began their invention and naming of new gods, such as the Nordic people creating Thor as the warrior god who ruled thunder, or the Egyptians believing that Osiris, their god of the underworld, judged the dead.[17] This spiritual heritage of metaphorical scapegoating became profoundly passed down as the gospel of truth in their respective cultures for thousands of years, but with many ensuing dilemmas and dangerous risks.

The creation of more than 3,000 gods and saviors by humankind established an early precedent of inequality. Lacking understanding, humans proclaimed that a mysterious or supernatural force greater than ourselves must be responsible. To project ignorance onto invisible deities is not only spiritual laziness, but also an arrogant and dangerous control tactic. We would be far better served to admit the truth, which is that we still do not know some of these answers to our questions about the cosmos, and that we will continue our trek of discovery until we learn about the unsolved mysteries.

If Jesus were still walking the earth, I would imagine that he would say, "What have you done by creating religions in my name or in the name of other deities? Did I not tell you that *you* would do greater things than me?"

When we project our strengths, weaknesses, personal power, and wrongdoings onto someone else, we minimize the greatness within ourselves and limit our future by idolizing someone else instead. These self-imposed distractions pull our precious energy away from high achievement, where it becomes tempting to resort to thoughts and prayers, rather than taking necessary action that brings real progress.

It must also be said that the teachings of Jesus maintain a contrarian approach to the majority of the Bible. Teaching love as his only commandment, Jesus emphasized in Matthew 22:40 that "all the Law and the Prophets hang on the two commandments," including loving God with all your heart, and love your neighbor as yourself. This is the essence of the Golden Rule, which is to treat others as you would want them to treat you. Isn't that enough to live your life in peace, harmony, and equality without having to swim through the muck and mire of Bronze Age superstition?

How Equality Becomes Diminished

When the various forms and manifestations of inequality are born, its dark energy soon seeks to replicate itself. Institutionalizing inequality, especially through religion, is a potent way of injecting this form of slavery into a culture, where it embeds itself like a virus into our spiritual DNA, then quickly spreads.

Joseph Campbell, the quintessential teacher of mythology across the perennial philosophies around the world, said, "Every religion is true one way or another. It is true when understood metaphorically. But when it gets stuck in its own metaphors, interpreting them as facts, then you are in trouble." Campbell suggested that nearly all religious have myths that demonized the Divine Child, a function of the Feminine energy that is generative and the birth of all true power. By undermining the Feminine, the Wounded Child takes the helm in the form of distorted Masculine energy that seeks to take control.

Classism, an early form of inequality, emerged from sexism. For most of the world's religions, it originated with the myth that Adam, the proverbial first man, was created by a deity before the woman was formed, which gives men the advantage of being more important and therefore privileged than women from the outset.[18]

In the Judeo-Christian tradition, the credit for how the world and human civilization began goes to Moses, the Israelite leader who allegedly authored the first five books of the Bible. Mosaic authorship of the first book called Genesis, however, has been disproven by documentary evidence.[19] Regardless, a woman unlikely would have never fabricated the mythical farce described in Genesis, which has been embraced as literal fact by billions of people for more than 2,000 years. In keeping with the tradition of extreme patriarchy, the authors for all 66 books of the modern Bible are reputedly male, just as they described their god.

The fable of the creation myth continues, as the god described in Genesis secondarily produced the woman as an "inferior" creation from a mere rib bone from a man, calling her a "helper" and thus setting the tone throughout the entire Bible for women to be eternally subservient to men.[20] With the grave subjugation of the female throughout scripture, it was no wonder that women have been historically treated as property and were prevented from voting.

For centuries, women could not hold office in many countries. Even in the New Testament which allegedly contains the "good news," the denigration of women continues, where they are ordered to be "silent in the church and not allowed to speak"[21] and "subject to their husbands in everything."[22]

According to scripture, even Jesus chose twelve male disciples — a sexist act in and of itself — despite his willingness and repeated actions to counter popular opinion and culture, including that of religious institutions.[23] The impact of these widespread teachings has been devastating long-lasting, taking thousands of years to break through the bondage of these unholy teachings. Despite long-lasting persecution, women are now able to vote in America, giving them voice.

Evangelical Christianity, Roman Catholicism, Islam, and other similar religions have cultivated and spread the disease of inequality under the guise that gods inspired males to write their preachments as truth. By commanding the demeaning and subjugation of women, popular religions may have caused the greatest destruction on our planet, resulting in the spread of wars, violence, poverty, and ignorance in nearly every culture. Feminine energy is the antidote of most of these calamities.

Whether or not elevating males over females was customary, it is spiritual abuse to proclaim that these words were channeled to "inspired" men from an invisible deity to save the world from disaster. No true spiritual, positive energy or force would ever write or speak such degrading, heartless, and sexist words that have resulted in the severe degradation of women and mass destruction of equality in general. Only envious, misogynistic men could be capable of fabricating and propagating these immoral, sexist teachings on a global scale.

The Sexism in Religion Continues

Pope Francis, who is revered as the current vicar of Christ in the Roman Catholic Church, reaffirmed sexism in February 2017 when asked if the Church would ever allow women in the priesthood. He declared that "Saint Pope John Paul II had the last clear word on this, and it stands, this stands." Pope Francis was referring to the 1994 document issued by the previous pope who firmly stated that women could never join the priesthood.[24]

Pope Francis' confirmation of their sexist policies have ignited many activists to take up the issue of women's inequality in the Catholic Church. Kate McElwee, the co-executive director of the Women's Ordination Conference, said: "In this space, we wrestled with the damaging effects of oppressive structures, knowing that patriarchy and hierarchy hurt us all."[25] With an estimated 1.2 billion Roman Catholics in the world,[26] the pope's decree also continues to be a primary source of sexism by promoting the Masculine while degrading the Feminine. But the Feminine energy we all possess is the magic and power of the Divine Child that knows equality, freedom, and truth.

While some may label these stories as "archetypes" or "analogies" as a way of excusing their profound spiritual abuse of women, humankind is far better served by positive role models without demonizing women or other classes of people. Analogy or not, these disparaging and intrinsically evil Bronze Age ideas must be denounced by all as never have been good, humane, moral, or ethical — today, 100 years ago, 2,000 years ago, or even 10,000 years ago.

Cultural analogies or not, these teachings are sexist triumphs by the patriarchy, which is why the Roman Catholic Church, the Southern Baptist Convention, and other religious institutions have not stood up and denounced the damned scriptures that continue to enslave women globally. While progress is being made, the percentage of female clergy remains low. Religious institutions promote misogyny from within: In 2018, only 11 percent of seminary presidents and fewer than 25 percent of faculty and deans at seminaries were women.[27]

Moreover, the cultural excuse for establishing that these misogynistic preachments in the alleged "word of God" contradicts the numerous biblical teachings that God and Jesus do not change.[28] In other words, the Bible promotes two conflicting teachings, both of which are unreasonable: 1) God is unchanging, and 2) that God somewhere along the human timeline decided to change *his* mind and began to promote slightly more equality, which Christianity largely still does not maintain.

Ironically, Bronze Age religious texts subjugating women create slavery conditions for one half of the world, which in turn paralyzes humanity. In fact, many might argue that males are more powerful than females, in terms of physical strength and other attributes.

In the spiritual sciences, however, the opposite is true. The Feminine energy that is connected to the Divine Child is the source of creation and is therefore more powerful. It appears that men figured out this energy secret thousands of years ago and developed ways through religious and political structures to debase and control women. This has led to a global deconstruction of powerful Feminine energy not just culturally, but within the physical bodies and consciousness of both women and men alike.

What, then, is our salvation, if religion does not offer a remedy for inequality? Thomas Jefferson, in his book *Notes on the State of Virginia*, offers a solution based on freedom:

> Millions of innocent men, women, and children, since the introduction of Christianity, have been burnt, tortured, fined, imprisoned; yet we have not advanced one inch towards uniformity. What has been the effect of coercion? To make one half the world fools, and the other half hypocrites. To support roguery and error all over the earth. Let us reflect that it is inhabited by a thousand millions of people. That these profess probably a thousand different systems of religion. That ours is but one of that thousand. ...Reason and persuasion are the only practicable instruments. To make way for these, free enquiry must be indulged; and how can we wish others to indulge it while we refuse it ourselves.

The Benefits of Empowering Women in the Workplace

One of the early, bold voices for women was Moderata Fonte, the 16th century Venetian writer and poet who authored *The Worth of Women* under the pseudonym of Modesta di Pozzo di Forzi. Describing the vital role of the

Feminine energy and the foundation of the Divine Child, she wrote, "Men were created before women. ... But that doesn't prove their superiority — rather, it proves ours, for they were born out of the lifeless earth in order that we could be born out of living flesh."[29]

Companies are learning that women make superior leaders in terms of the bottom line. Statistically, companies with women in leadership roles perform better. Even though only 10.9 percent of senior executives in the world's largest 500 companies are women, another survey of 21,980 companies from 91 countries found that women at the C-suite level (e.g., CEO, CFO, COO, CIO) added a 15 percent boost to profitability.[30]

A new study found that women-led companies perform three times better than the S&P 500. When the Boston-based trading platform Quantopian analyzed Fortune 1000 companies with female CEOs and compared it with the S&P 500's performance between 2002 and 2014, the research showed that the 80 companies with female CEOs produced equity returns 226 percent better than the S&P 500.[31]

In March 2018, Kevin O'Leary from *Shark Tank* stated that while his male-to-female CEO ratio of his investments are about 50-50, two-thirds of his returns come from his female-led businesses.[32] In other words, his female-led companies make *twice* as much money as his companies run by men. He cites the success of women due to better time management and task-balancing skills, their ability to set and achieve more realistic goals, and their excelling at listening to feedback, taking advice, and pivoting. "One thing's for sure: We should be elevating women to the CEO position because we're getting better returns," O'Leary said. "You don't need another reason in business. In my case, the numbers speak for themselves."[33]

For the 37 percent of the largest companies who have all-male leadership teams, it is their loss. At the same time, it is a far greater loss for humanity, as we have a long way to go to experience full gender equality at all levels.

Companies gain by promoting women and equality in general. Joe Carella, the assistant dean at the University of Arizona, Eller College of Management, led a team to conduct its own analysis of Fortune 500 companies, discovering that diverse companies become more creative, innovative, and respected. In fact, their research found that companies with women in top management roles produce 20 percent more patents than companies with male leadership teams.[34]

Why do women bring such benefits? These statistics were no surprise, as Feminine energy is associated with the First and Second Chakras in the body, which are connected with prosperity and creativity, respectively. By infusing the powerful, generative energy of the Feminine, the companies connect with even more creativity, prosperity, and grounding on energetic and physical levels.

Fortunately, progress in gender equality is picking up speed. The empowerment of women will result in the greatest spiritual revolution in our world, giving rise to freedom, education, peace, nurturing, equality, and prosperity.

Equality is the spiritual value that abolishes all forms of slavery, including misogyny, classism, racism, financial inequity, and other types of servitude. All democracies are based on this powerful energy of equality, expressed and upheld by law that protects this important value. Equality is the basis for the Golden Rule, a universal guide for ethical and moral conduct.

However, it seems that relatively few people actually treat others like they want to be treated, especially in business, where cutthroat competition exists. For thousands of years, inequality has become repeatedly embedded into our spiritual DNA, twisting the sacred strands of equality into a dark distortion. When people get a taste of their own medicine, they find out how bitter it really is.

> Women will only have true equality when men share with them the responsibility of bringing up the next generation.
>
> Ruth Bader Ginsburg

However, the "loyalty leaders" — those companies who apply the Golden Rule and treat their customers and employees right — are rewarded. Their compound annual growth rate is more than twice that of their competitors, as research by Bain & Company shows.[35] "Each time you live up to the Golden Rule, your reputation is enhanced; each time you fail, it is diminished," writes author and speaker Fred Reichheld in *Harvard Business Review*. Henry Ford also recognized the veracity of this simple concept that expresses the value of equality, as he was quoted as saying, "If there is any one secret of success, it lies in the ability to get the other person's point of view and see things from that person's angle as well as from your own."[36]

How to Energize the Power of Equality Within You

Most of us are victims of inequality. The ancient fables of sexism and misogyny, racism, and classism have contaminated the world's population, and continue to decimate equality through resonance. Toting around these denigrating words in Bronze Age texts not only spiritually pollutes our innate energy of equality, but it also reinforces and distributes forms of inequality, just as reading the news has the strong likelihood of increasing depression and creating acute stress, mood swings, aggressive behavior, sleeping problems, or even PTSD.[37] On both personal and cultural levels, we become the art we hold close, including the words we repeatedly absorb.

It doesn't matter much if we label the news as being valuable, important, or even correct. It's negativity still has its brutal and toxic effect on our consciousness and lives. The more we are around negativity, the worse our lives become. This isn't necessarily a product of morality or ethics. Rather, it is simply a result of how energy flows and how we resonate with that energy by being in its presence.

To reactivate equality in your life, here are some suggestions that may be helpful:

- Eliminate books, magazines, TV shows, and other forms of media that promote inequality. Being around energies of racism, classism, sexism, and misogyny is as toxic as being around a depressed person. You will absorb the dark energies that radiate from these negative sources.

- Denounce sources of inequality. Stand up, speak up, march, and vote for equality. Donate to organizations that expand equality and stop supporting those that don't. When someone speaks words of inequality around you, let them know how they affect you. Remaining silent makes you part of this spiritual disease.

- Make amends to those whom you have treated as less than you. Making amends is taking responsibility for our actions when we have harmed others, whether it was intentional or not.

- Volunteer for organizations that promote equality, especially when it relates to classes of people whom you have subjugated. For example, if you have repeatedly victimized women either through disparaging words or actions, a good way to make amends is to crusade for women's rights. In every system, energy must always be balanced. Saying "I'm sorry" is a good start, but not nearly adequate for restitution. Equality in action is the healing salve.

- <u>Read about powerful people who have fought for equality</u>. When we read about our heroes of equality, we begin resonating with their energies more fully. Thomas Jefferson, Thomas Paine, Francis Wright, Frederick Douglass, Abraham Lincoln, Benazir Bhutto, Elizabeth Cady Stanton, Nelson Mandela, Susan B. Anthony, Rosa Parks, Desmond Tutu, Malala Yousafzai, Sojourner Truth, Martin Luther King Jr., Shirin Ebadi, Helen Keller, Elizabeth Fry, and Ruth Bader Ginsburg are among important leaders who have revolutionized the world by promoting equality. Find out what they accomplished and how they endured the fight for liberty. Go into resonance with their powerful energy that made the world a better place.

Of the 21 traits of our Divine Child, equality may be the one that has been most damaged. The wounding of equality on a cultural and global scale reflects the energies of inequality still in our literature, media, and other art forms. Creating a world of equality means eliminating these sources of toxicity, just as you wash your hands with soap and water to remove bacteria and other invisible sources that harm you. We must leave these promotions of inequality within museums where they can be observed to remind us of a dark heritage denounced and left behind.

Healing and restoring the energy of equality begins with eradicating the weeds of discrimination, which often arise when someone believes that superiority is necessary for survival. Chris Kluwe, who played eight seasons with the Minnesota Vikings and has become an outspoken advocate for same-sex marriage and gay rights, said, "Every single human civilization has failed over time, and my belief is that it's due to a lack of rational empathy, of understanding that if you don't have equality in your society, the conflicts you breed, whether internally or externally, will eventually cause its collapse."[38]

When we treat others as equals and demand that we are treated that way as well, greater levels of understanding, compassion, and adventure will emerge. New horizons open up when we share our treasured gifts of freedom and opportunity. Iyanla Vanzant said, "The way to achieve your own success is to be willing to help somebody else get it first."

As we fully engage with your energy of equality and share this precious gift, the collective becomes much more whole and solid. With the flames of equality burning bright, its close companion is surely to be found — empathy.

1 https://www.nature.com/news/1998/001207/full/news001207-8.html

2 https://www.cnbc.com/2017/08/24/most-americans-live-paycheck-to-paycheck.html

3 https://www.washingtonpost.com/news/wonk/wp/2017/12/06/the-richest-1-percent-now-owns-more-of-the-countrys-wealth-than-at-any-time-in-the-past-50-years/?noredirect=on

4 http://content.time.com/time/magazine/article/0,9171,833509,00.html

5 https://allthingsfinance.net/the-vatican-and-pope-francis-net-worth/

6 https://money.cnn.com/2015/09/24/news/pope-francis-visit-vatican-catholic-church/index.html

7 http://time.com/money/5168865/billy-graham-net-worth-quotes-money-greed/

8 https://www.charlotteobserver.com/living/religion/article30505932.html#storylink=cpy

9 https://www.thisdaylive.com/index.php/2019/01/09/nigerias-financial-inclusion-journey/

10 https://www.today.ng/news/nigeria/nlc-tells-governors-prepare-implement-n30000-minimum-wage-185587

11 https://www.yahoo.com/news/joel-osteen-church-passes-around-032939829.html

12 https://www.history.com/this-day-in-history/jim-bakker-is-indicted-on-federal-charges

13 https://www.charlotteobserver.com/living/religion/article200297074.html

14 https://www.ebony.com/news/pastor-kirbyjon-caldwell-indicted-3-5m-fraud/

15 https://www.houstonchronicle.com/news/houston-texas/houston/article/Co-defendant-in-Kirbyjon-Caldwell-fraud-case-14118222.php

16 https://www.houstonchronicle.com/news/houston-texas/crime/article/Pastor-Kirbyjon-Caldwell-gets-six-years-for-fraud-15868693.php; retrieved April 10, 2021

17 https://www.thoughtco.com/list-of-gods-and-goddesses-by-culture-118503

18 *The Bible*, Genesis 2:7, King James Version

19 http://www.religioustolerance.org/chr_tora1.htm

20 *The Bible*, Genesis 2:21-22, King James Version

21 *The Bible*, 1 Corinthians 14:34, King James Version

22 Source: *The Bible*, Ephesians 5:21-32, King James Version

23 *The Bible*, Luke 6:12-16, King James Version

24 https://www.theguardian.com/world/2016/nov/01/pope-francis-women-never-roman-catholic-priests-church

25 IBID

26 http://www.bbc.com/news/world-21443313

27 https://www.christiancentury.org/article/news/report-details-trends-us-women-clergy

28 *The Bible*, Numbers 23:19, Hebrews 13:8, James 1:17.

29 https://www.goodreads.com/quotes/409524-men-were-created-before-women-but-that-doesn-t-prove; retrieved May 20, 2021.

30 http://fortune.com/2015/03/03/women-led-companies-perform-three-times-better-than-the-sp-500/

31 https://www.catalyst.org/knowledge/womens-earnings-wage-gap

32 https://www.cnbc.com/2018/03/22/shark-tanks-kevin-oleary-women-make-me-the-most-money.html

33 https://www.businessinsider.com/kevin-olearys-female-ceos-make-all-the-money-2015-5

---

[34] http://fortune.com/2015/03/03/women-led-companies-perform-three-times-better-than-the-sp-500/

[35] http://www.netpromotersystem.com/about/how-is-nps-related-to-growth.aspx

[36] https://www.entrepreneur.com/article/281387

[37] http://time.com/5125894/is-reading-news-bad-for-you/.

[38] https://www.bloomberg.com/news/articles/2013-06-24/chatting-with-chris-kluwe-punter-gay-marriage-advocate-web-geek; Retrieved May 20, 2021.

Empathetic

> Resolve to be tender with the young, compassionate with the aged, sympathetic with the striving, and tolerant with the weak and wrong. Sometime in your life, you will have been all of these.
>
> Gautama Buddha

"Learning to stand in somebody else's shoes, to see through their eyes, that's how peace begins. And it's up to you to make that happen. Empathy is a quality of character that can change the world," said former U.S. president Barack Obama. This sweet yet profound essence is the foundation of the Golden Rule, where we treat others based on how we want to be treated. This is the nature of our inner child.

The English word "empathy" was coined in the early 1900s by two psychologists, Edward Titchener in the United States and Theodor Lipps from Germany, as a derivation of the German word "Einfühlung," meaning "feeling into" or literally "in contact with."[1] Lipps described that feeling from engaging emotively with the world in literature, art, music, people, and animals, for example.

Lipps then applied it to the human experience to explain how one person reflects the feelings of another person. Titchener then took the German word and developed an English word that matches the meaning, anglicizing the Greek word *empatheia* that means "in passion" or "in suffering." When the Heart Chakra became globally activated around the 1940s, other psychologists, such as Carl Rogers and Heinz Kohut, began using the term empathy in their therapeutic practices to describe how their clients were truly feeling.

> Never look down on anybody unless you're helping him up.
>
> Jesse Jackson

There is a difference between sympathy and empathy: Sympathy is a feeling of concern for another person that may not include sharing what that person feels, while empathy implies that we are connecting with others because we feel and share that experience ourselves. Empathy involves the Law of Resonance, where we are resonating and experiencing those energies of another, rather than simply relating to them on a cognitive level.

Empathy is the ability to understand, feel, and share the feelings of someone around you. To be engaged, truly connecting with others requires other Divine Child energies to be alive and active, such as being present, learning, and sharing with others. In the midst of these three spiritual qualities, empathy will inevitably emerge. "Empathy is seeing with the eyes of another, listening with the ears of another, and feeling with the heart of another," said Alfred Adler, Austrian medical doctor and founder of the school of individual psychology.

The late film critic Roger Ebert said, "I believe empathy is the most essential quality of civilization." For a culture to have value, empathy must be expressed towards one another. It requires action — not mere words, thoughts, or prayers. It is the sharing that brings empathy to life.

Empathy is a Natural Characteristic of Babies

Meryl Streep said, "The greatest gift of human beings is that we have the power of empathy." This magical energy ignites when we see ourselves in another person. It comes from our personal narrative that we share with others, and from the story of others that we see inside ourselves. "Stories teach us empathy. They reveal to us ourselves in the skins of others," said the award-winning filmmaker, author, and actor Justin Simien, who was named to Variety's 2013 list of the "10 Directors to Watch."[2]

The phenomenon of resonance allows our natural empathy to be actively shared. Early experiments with newborn babies show they will cry when hearing the cries of other babies, and even more loudly when hearing the actual sound of infants crying than they did when listening to a computer simulation of a baby's cry or other loud, startling sounds. In other words, the natural sense of empathy is already active in babies. "Virtually from the day they are born, there is something particularly disturbing to infants about the sound of another infant's cry," said Martin Hoffman, a psychologist at New York University and author of *Empathy and Moral Development*. "The innate predisposition to cry to that sound seems to be the earliest precursor of empathy."[3]

Several decades ago, contradictory points of view were submitted by the Swiss developmental psychologist Jean Piaget, who believed that children could not feel empathy until achieving cognitive abilities that were developed around age 7 or 8. However, additional experiments by other researchers found that empathy in infants exists long before they acquire the knowledge that they exist separate from other people, which happens usually in the latter part of the first year. Studies have shown that babies react to the pain of others as if it were happening to themselves. If another child gets hurt and starts to cry, a baby will begin to cry, especially if the hurt child cries for one or two minutes.[4]

Around one year of age, babies begin to understand the difference between distress felt by someone else and themselves. "They realize it's the other kid's problem, but they're often confused over what to do about it," Dr. Hoffman said. During this phase, toddlers often use "motor mimicry" to physically imitate the distress of another young child. Marion Radke-Yarrow, chief of the Laboratory of Developmental Psychology at the National Institute of Mental Health, said, "From around 14 months to 2 or 2 1/2 years, you see children feel their own fingers to see if they hurt when someone else hurts their fingers. By 2-1/2, though, toddlers clearly realize that someone else's pain is different from their own and know how to comfort them appropriately."[5]

The next developmental milestone in empathy occurs around age eight, according to Dr. Hoffman. He said, "At that age you can empathize with a person's overall life situation, not just their immediate circumstances. For instance, you could be sad for someone with a life-threatening disease, even if she seemed happy at the moment."

Resonance: The Mechanism of Empathy

Our natural empathy may be deeply embedded into our physical and cultural DNA. Peter Bazalgette, author of *The Empathy Instinct: How to Create a More Civil Society*, discusses how mirror neurons in our brains, similar to those that were discovered in monkeys in the 1990s, allow us humans to feel what a character in a play, novel, or movie is experiencing. He describes how an art historian and neuroscientist tested people who were viewing Goya's series of prints in his *Disasters of War* collection and Michelangelo's *Prisoners*, an unfinished sculpture at the Accademia Gallery in Florence. "They discovered that in their brain activity, they were simulating the emotional expressions and the movement implied in the paintings. There's research which shows similar neurological patterns among dance audiences too," Bazalgette said.[6]

Does the instinct to protect our fellow human come from our need for survival? Our empathy translates to not only our physical survival, but also emotional, mental, and spiritual altruism. When we truly feel the plight of our fellow humans, animals, and plants, we take action.

Yara Shahidi, the American-Iranian actress and producer, said, "The more you learn about someone, how could you not want to protect them and their rights? The more you learn about a culture or a certain identity, it's hard to not feel empathy." Empathy and curiosity are interrelated: As we care for others, we naturally want to know more about them and connect with them.

> Great things can be achieved by leading through wisdom, empathy, and integrity — with no other agenda than humanity.
>
> Richard Branson

Empathy, more than an idle feeling, results in legislation that can change material circumstances. Equal rights protection for have largely been enacted only since the last century, including protections for race, color, creed, age, sex, sexual orientation, disabilities, religion, gender identity, veteran status, national origin, and other classes. Most of these equal opportunity laws, corporate and organizational policies have occurred after the heart chakra activation occurred in the 1940s and 1950s.

For example, the sexual revolution took us from the "Donna Reed" era of the obedient, stay-at-home doting mother wearing the flowery apron and a pasted smile in the 1950s to the liberation of women in the 1960s and 1970s. The imagery of that earlier era is reminiscent of the subservient wife in the New Testament: "Now as the church submits to Christ, so also wives should submit to their husbands in everything."[7] This biblical scripture is perhaps the most revolting biblical commandment to denigrate and belittle women. The irony is that religion's widespread subjugation of women continues to severely damage the source that gives birth to all of humanity.

Our liberation from these archaic, oppressive teachings of sexism, racism, classism, and homophobia will occur when we pass legislation promoting and protecting this vital energy. We are finally beginning to transcend the narrow limitations of our Bronze Age ancestors, who remained stuck in tribal belief systems that were false. Only until recently are we are witnessing major shifts with enacted legal protections for sex, race, sexual orientation, disabilities, and other classes, such as when Congress passed the Civil Rights Act of 1964.

Empathy is global and encompassing, as we cannot act with true empathy on a limited or local basis. For example, the Environmental Protection Agency (EPA) was established on December 2, 1970, by former president Richard M. Nixon to provide federal research, setting environmental standards, monitoring, and enforcement to ensure the protection of not only the environment, but of human, animal, and plant health.[8] In short, the EPA helps ensure that pollution emitted by industries, products, or other manmade sources does not negatively affect our health.

Laws that promote equality expand the energy of empathy, shifting us from the focus on the self to the group at large as we progress toward unity consciousness. John Hickenlooper, the former governor of Colorado, said, "Democracy is based upon empathy and the recognition that some decisions are solely for the community's benefit without regard to one's own narrow self-interest." When legislation is passed that promotes empathy, such as for protecting our environment or preventing cruelty to animals, we move humanity forward and upward. The systematization of empathy creates a distribution channel for this important energy, where it expands care and concern for our fellow humans, animals, environment, and ourselves.

Where Empathy and its Negative Expressions Reside

The seat of empathy is in the Heart Chakra and is intimately connected to the Second Chakra, the seat of emotions in action. This Feminine quality of energy is a natural expression of the Divine Child, which gets expressed in mothers when they have children. Florence Henderson, a favorite mom on the TV hit series *The Brady Bunch* said, "Being a mom makes you far more compassionate. You have more empathy for people, more love. I was always taught to say thank you, and I'm very grateful. And my kids have that quality, too."

Feminine energy is the vanguard and protector of empathy. When we allow this precious energy to become diminished, whether through religious rhetoric or corrupted spiritual inheritance, our humanity and softness turn into aggression, the exacerbation of the Masculine energy within us all. We become imbalanced, stressed, and spiritually ill, and this disease of desecrating our Feminine nature grows like a cancer.

> If you list the qualities that we consider feminine, they are patience, understanding, empathy, supportiveness, a desire to nurture. Our culture tells us those are feminine traits, but they're really just human.
>
> Sydney Pollack

The negative expression of empathy is indifference, where we first lose touch with ourselves. How we treat others is a projection of how we treat ourselves. When we stop treasuring and valuing the beautiful, precious Divine Child that we are, we then project that inner wounded behavior toward others. Our intimate relationships suffer, including our partners, our families, and cherished friends. Even our work relationships suffocate when the Wounded Child expresses itself with rage, bitterness, or resentment.

Advanced stages of the spiritual disease of indifference rooted in self-absorption can manifest into cruelty, which is not only toxic to others, but also hurts ourselves. Malcolm Turnbull, the prime minister of Australia from 2015 to 2018, said, "Let us be honest with each other. The threat to marriage is not the gays. It is a lack of loving commitment — whether it is found in the form of neglect, indifference, cruelty or adultery, to name just a few manifestations of the loveless desert in which too many marriages come to grief."

Plato, in his dialogue between Socrates and Phaedrus, wrote, "Gentleness is the antidote for cruelty." When we unleash this loving, gentle, empathetic nature of our inner child who is ever-present but sometimes suppressed from early trauma, we can bring peace in our world.

It is a tough choice to leave people behind who treat us badly. We may have the urge to change them in order to heal the relationship, thinking that will make things better. But that person must first want to change. Our duty is to let those people know when they have wounded us, because in most cases, their inflicted trauma was delivered unconsciously, not through conscious intention.

But make no mistake about it. Allowing someone to continually inflict their trauma keeps us in a wounded state. Remaining in an abusive relationship is the worst form of toxicity. When the pain from abuse is greater than the joy someone brings to us, it is time to walk away. We can heal only when we are not in a state of being continually re-traumatized by someone. In quiet reflection, perhaps then we can realize that we may have been beating ourselves up all along, and then attracting others to take over the self-abuse.

> Science may have found a cure for most evils; but it has found no remedy for the worst of them all — the apathy of human beings.
>
> Helen Keller

We cannot take responsibility for someone's healing, perhaps thinking that in doing so, that we will also be healed or our relationship with that person will be transformed. We can only take responsibility for our own healing. And it is nearly impossible for us to heal when we are continually subjected to abuse or the more silent form of it — indifference.

Indifference is especially toxic, because it is subtle. When someone sits by us and does not act in care, it isn't particularly obvious how detrimental their inaction is. But it leaves us wanting and craving their love, affection, and care. This can easily become a vicious circle: We beat ourselves up, others join in the ugly circus of beating us up, and then we beg for more attention from the abuser. Our projection of our desire for love can be a reminder that we may have first abandoned ourselves without realizing it, buying into the false belief that we do not matter. Our rescue must begin first with ourselves.

This is a form of sadism, where someone gains pleasure by inflicting pain or humiliating others. Perverted negative attention is the final straw of this expression of toxicity, where we crave any form of attention, even if it means getting emotionally or physically abused. At least we got noticed, the first step towards love. But heartless awareness is dark, empty, and ruthless, engulfing the human spirit.

All forms of slavery are born out of the destruction of the natural empathy of our Divine Child. If enough people are persuaded to energetically prostitute themselves, critical mass is achieved. Humans are turned into virtual slaves, caving to those in charge whose indifference takes over to use, subjugate, and denigrate others for their own benefit.

As an expression of indifference and cruelty, slavery then becomes institutionalized on a cultural level, even in cloaked forms. Sexism and racism are obvious, but more hidden forms of social inequality or economic slavery are subtle but quite damaging. The slave is kept barely alive, functioning enough to work for the slave owner, but diseased and spiritually deformed to the point of believing they are being taken care of in some way.

Breaking free of these bonds requires waking up, realizing that we have been under a dark spell that seeks to control our behaviors and freedoms. Pain is a good signal, because our inner alarm bells begin sounding. When our joy is limited in any way, our suffering is a valuable indicator, beckoning a closer look. Through our curiosity, we can discover the sources of that pain and discomfort, and then change course.

> Desire is half of life; indifference is half of death.
>
> Kahlil Gibran
> *Sand and Foam*

Empathy begins within, where we first nurture, care, and protect ourselves. It is the rare person who can devote a life of sacrifice to the service of others without depleting his or her own energy reservoirs. For most of us, we must first be aware of our own feelings, desires, and needs before attending to those around us. Otherwise, we risk burn-out, where our precious reservoirs of energy become depleted because we have abandoned aspects of ourselves to please people.

When we lose empathy and compassion for ourselves, another dark expression of empathy emerges: loneliness. Grief is the emotional expression of deep loss, which seems to settle in the Heart center. When we lose ourselves, it is easy to remain in the grief of losing things in our lives, including our money, our friends, our family, our loves ones.

How Our Empathetic Nature Becomes Contaminated

Why is it that so many people lose their lack of empathy and compassion for their fellow human beings? At what point does our innate sensitivity become damaged or crushed? That moment seems to come from early trauma, especially when we are little children. When we have become a wounded victim in pain, we learn it isn't safe to express ourselves fully and thus begin to suppress our authenticity. This is the point we start to become numb.

New York Times best-selling author John Bradshaw said, "I know from my own clinical work that when people are beaten and hurt, they numb out so that they can't feel anymore." In his book *Homecoming: Reclaiming and Championing Your Inner Child*, Bradshaw defines the inner child as "the part of you that got repressed." He said, "When you laughed too loud, Mama said, 'That isn't ladylike,' Or you had anger and they said, 'That's not permitted here.' You had to repress those parts of yourself and adapt with a smiling face or a ha-ha-ha or whatever. The part that didn't get expressed is the inner child."[9]

After studying to become a Roman Catholic priest for nearly a decade at a Basilian seminary in Canada, Bradshaw describes it as his first real crisis, where he was required to be celibate.[10] Just days before his ordination as a priest, he promptly left the Catholic church and subsequently married, raising a child with his wife. Bradshaw said, "Prejudice is about polarization. When two groups are polarized, there's no place to meet in the middle. Unhealthy shame tends to gravitate toward unhealthy religions. Because a person will feel less than worthy, they will move toward an organizational sense of absolute power, coming from an absolute God."

> The death of human empathy is one of the earliest and most telling signs of a culture about to fall into barbarism.
>
> Hannah Arendt

In his early books, including *Healing the Shame that Binds You* and *Family Secrets: The Path to Self-Acceptance and Reunion*, Bradshaw describes terms such as "toxic shame," the "dysfunctional family," and the "inner child," which he helped popularize as psychological concepts. He admitted that he grew up in dire poverty with an alcoholic father and a mother who was the victim of incest, who once nailed her husband's dirty underwear to the wall to shame him for his drinking. Bradshaw said, "The most profound spiritual moment of my life came when I was wearing size forty-eight pants, drying out at a state mental hospital, babbling in front of ten psychiatrists and their stenographer. Suddenly, I knew what I didn't want to be any more." After checking himself into a treatment center in 1965, he was sober ever since.[11]

Reawakening From Our Numb Condition

Authentically speaking about our past can be freeing, while repressing past memories leaves us trapped. Both survival and success are based on our physical, mental, emotional, and spiritual well-being. It is likely that all of us have been hurt and damaged to some degree, and admitting it is not so easy. Being numb to emotions contributes to the illusion that somehow not truly feeling past trauma will keep us safe, or that with time, the wounds will heal. But it doesn't work that way.

Whenever something triggers those past experiences of trauma, it can cause a cascading rush of emotions and thoughts, much like picking off a scab from the wound that hasn't yet healed. The broken record plays again, where we relive the trauma in similar ways but with different characters showing up. This spiritual form of PTSD is yet another call for healing.

> I learned to be with myself rather than avoiding myself with limiting habits; I started to be aware of my feelings more, rather than numb them.
>
> Judith Wright
> Australian poet, activist,
> environmentalist

One of my clients, "Charlie," grew up with a bullying, "rage-aholic" father who screamed at him and beat him until he had graduated from high school and left for college. He relived the vivid experiences of his childhood through his work at companies after graduating. Smart and ambitious, he was a rising star who rapidly climbed the corporate ladder. Charlie described his early career: "I thought I was finally in my safe space."

Charlie appeared successful, but deep inside, something quite different was happening. He was numb to what was really occurring. He said that nearly every time his male bosses at various companies would walk into his office, he panicked, involuntarily reacting as though he was about to get into big trouble. His heart would race, and palms would begin sweating, awaiting the news of his punishment from his new father figures who now had control over his life. Charlie had become trapped by his traumatic past.

Charlie's reactions to these benign events were completely unconscious. He was unaware how his traumatized inner child had taken control over his Adult part that could otherwise take care of him. This went on for years, until he finally realized through numerous therapy sessions how his reactions to his managers at work were directly linked to unhealed abuse from his father endured in childhood. The early pain that was thrust upon him had become projected into his work environment. The trauma cycle was ready for healing.

Once he recognized this and began revealing his authentic self to close friends, therapists, and various healers, he began the profound journey to reclaim his Divine Child. He shared with me, "I was determined to heal these wounded aspects of myself, regardless of how much inner work and money was needed. It was the best investment I could make. Once I began healing, the floodgates of success opened up for me in not only my career, but also in my relationships, my health, and my mood."

In my experience, many people may be stuck at the Root Chakra level of wounding, which can be seen in the widespread self-serving attitudes and abnormal focus of "me." It is difficult to be in service to others when we are unaware of what needs to be healed within ourselves. Today, we project that woundedness on our Facebook pages, Instagram posts, and Snapchats, covering up our ears, heads, noses, and other precious parts of ourselves with bunny or cat ears, whiskers, and floating hearts and other emojis. We outwardly make ourselves cuter and more lovable, while the pain remains inside.

Telling our own story authentically is the birthplace of healing. "The truth will set you free," as the expression goes. A compassionate and nurturing friend will take the time to listen and hold our stories in confidence. Sessions with therapeutic professionals can be profound, where simply sharing what happened releases some of the deeply held pain. In revealing the dark secrets of embarrassment, sadness, grief, and deep pain to ourselves, the critical step of clarity is achieved that initiates our healing journey.

> By default, most of us have taken the dare to simply survive. Exist. Get through. For the most part, we live numb to life — we've grown weary and apathetic and jaded... and wounded.
>
> Ann Voskamp

If we do not gain unconditional love and acceptance from those who raised us, we will act out in unhealthy ways to seek that love from other sources. Numbing patterns we take on can include gaining weight to armor ourselves. Alcohol and other drugs provide the illusion of pleasure, distracting us long enough from the pain inside. Sex, where the addiction of "hooking up" is now commonly referred to as "having fun." And when all of that commoditized pleasure has faded, we are left facing our pain and unhealed trauma cycles that still remain.

Then two more characters arrive on the scene: guilt, the feeling that we did something wrong, and shame, its close cousin, where we feel we are inherently bad or broken. Those gnawing feelings cause us to reach for more distractions. We spiritually prostitute ourselves, giving up those precious aspects of who we are, including our physical bodies, emotions, thoughts, and spiritual treasures for others to use.

Addiction to a substance or habit — such as overeating, alcohol, drugs, sex, meditation, religion, shopping, or any other form of escape — is usually not the root cause of the problem. I know this from personal experience, because I had many of these addictions. For example, alcoholism is usually not the problem, but the *origin of trauma* is why we usually engage in numbing. That sense of emptiness likely came from a wounding early in childhood, as research suggests. Author and activist Jean Kilbourne, who is internationally recognized for her work in on women's images in alcohol and tobacco advertising, said, "Addiction begins with the hope that something 'out there' can instantly fill up the emptiness inside."

The pain-pleasure principle becomes engaged through constant craving. Clinical psychologist Frank Tallis wrote, "At first, addiction is maintained by pleasure, but the intensity of this pleasure gradually diminishes, and the addiction is then maintained by the avoidance of pain." Recovering from addiction requires hard work and a proper attitude, along with a vibrant sense of curiosity to discover what is really going on.

The healing journey begins with expressing empathy and compassion for ourselves. Anthon St. Maarten wrote:

> Never surrender your hopes and dreams to the fateful limitations others have placed on their own lives. The vision of your true destiny does not reside within the blinkered outlook of the naysayers and the doom prophets. Judge not by their words, but accept advice based on the evidence of actual results. Do not be surprised should you find a complete absence of anything mystical or miraculous in the manifested reality of those who are so eager to advise you. Friends and family who suffer the lack of abundance, joy, love, fulfillment and prosperity in their own lives really have no business imposing their self-limiting beliefs on your reality experience.

The Deep Pain of Non-Acceptance

Another example of spiritual abuse is when we don't accept others as equals. One of my clients shared with me that he chose to become a police officer for thirty years because his father didn't fully accept him as being gay, so he wanted to prove to his father that he was "masculine." Instead of healing the pain that his father projected onto him, he chose a life-long career he despised in order to try to gain love from his father.

It failed, because love for others begins with self-love. When parents reject their children because they are different — such as for being gay, bi, transgender, or for any other reason — it severely traumatizes the child. Accepting others as they are is an expression of the pure, childlike traits of equality and empathy. Otherwise, early rejection can turn into self-loathing.

A cloaked but highly toxic version of non-acceptance is found in widespread religious teachings, such as "God loves the sinner, but hates the sin." This vile yet popular ideology is a projection of guilt and shame employing the threat of fear and punishment. But the angry god throughout the Bible didn't "love" the sinners. He repeatedly destroyed them rather than saving them.

This spiritual bipolarity reaches a climax in the final scene in the Book of Revelation, where God cruelly rejects the far majority of his own creations and sends them to an eternal hell of burning fire and brimstone — a fate far worse than death. This set-up may be why many Evangelical parents soundly reject their LGBTQ children, often sending them out of their own homes.

My plea to all parents is to please accept your children as they are without trying to mold them into your own image. It is spiritual abuse to reject your child as someone less than who he or she authentically is. The trauma that is inflicted, even unknowingly, is one where the toxicity of unworthiness becomes deeply embedded into the child.

> The greatest gift that you can give to others is the gift of unconditional love and acceptance.
>
> Brian Tracy

In a report released by Reuters in February 2019, 24 percent of the suicide deaths in youth ages 12 to 14 from 2013 to 2015 were among members of the LGBT community. Lack of empathy and acceptance were found to be contributing factors. Study author Geoffrey Ream of Adelphi University said, "We already knew, or at least suspected, that younger people are especially vulnerable to the stress of coming out. This is because they don't have the psychological resources or personal independence to handle things themselves that they will have when they are older."

Interestingly, another study found that teen suicides decreased following the legalization of gay marriage, especially among LGBT teenagers. Published by the American Medical Association, the study examined attempted suicide rates among teenagers from 1999 to 2015, when the Supreme Court legalized gay marriage nationally.

Before the 2015 ruling, the 32 states that had enacted marriage equality saw a sharp decline in suicide rates of seven percent among all students and 14 percent among LGBT students. No change was seen in states without marriage equality. Researchers believe that a decrease in bullying and a more optimistic outlook for LGBT teens might have contributed to the positive change.[12] Legislation is what led to big improvements, as the energies of equality and empathy were distributed by institutionalizing them.

How to Reactivate Your Empathetic Nature

Our woundedness can cause us to shut down, especially when things feel or seem overwhelming. Prominent author and professor of animal behavioral science Temple Grandin, an activist on autism following her personal experience with the condition, revealed what happens when our natural inclination to relate becomes traumatized: "Normal people have an incredible lack of empathy. They have good emotional empathy, but they don't have much empathy for the autistic kid who is screaming at the baseball game because he can't stand the sensory overload. Or the autistic kid having a meltdown in the school cafeteria because there's too much stimulation."

Reactivating empathy on a cultural level requires two big shifts: instituting policy changes on a mass level, and instituting changes in habit on a personal level. You can take part in the political and legislative process by getting involved locally. To reengage empathy within yourself, here are some suggested things you can do:

- Get involved with the arts. Attend plays. Watch musicals. Draw. Color. Paint. Build sandcastles, just as you did as a child. Julie Andrews said, "The arts bridge cultures; they're good for the economy, and they're good for fostering empathy and decency."

- Get in touch with your feelings. This can be difficult, especially for many guys, because being in touch with our feelings can seem uncontrollable or often viewed as a sign of weakness. When you notice your emotions, name them. Write about them. Practice talking about what you are feeling with your friends, family members, and coworkers. As you get comfortable with your own emotions, even those feeling big and out of control, you will become more engaged and connected to others.

- Study your addictions. Probably every one of us is addicted to at least one thing and likely multiple things. Common devices that are potentially addictive that we use to distract us from our problems include food, alcohol and other drugs, shopping, sex, gambling, religion, the Internet, video games, television and other forms of entertainment, plastic surgery, and even risky behaviors, such as skydiving or rock climbing. Be honest and authentic with yourself and write down any numbing devices that you use as crutches. When you name them, they begin to lose part of their negative hold and power. Study them and carefully examine yourself to understand the underlying pain and original trauma that needs to be healed, and how these numbing devices are triggered, distracting you from your healing journey that moves you forward.

> When a good man is hurt, all who would be called good must suffer with him.
>
> Euripides

- Reduce the outer noise you experience. Distractions are mounting in our culture, dramatically increasing the amount of energetic noise in our lives. These increasing distractions numb our senses, hampering our ability to feel. Excess noise may include looking at your cell phone every five minutes or spending hours on it each day, watching the news, listening to music many hours each day, or sitting in a restaurant with ten TVs blaring ten different programs. Take steps to dramatically reduce these stress-inducing distractions, and you may realize how addicted you have become to various kinds of visual, auditory, emotional, mental, and kinesthetic stimulation that can disturb the natural balance of the body and mind. This practice really helped me.
- Slow down. It is easy to get caught up with life's pressures that we sometimes forget to stop and smell the roses. Take time to slow down the pace. Put away your cell phone and Internet for hours at a time. Walk out in nature every day, beholding the beauty of its golden silence and healing force. Appreciating nature will trigger empathy within you.
- Ask people questions. Remain curious. This is the power of your Divine Child, and it requires listening. "We have two ears and one mouth so that we can listen twice as much as we speak," wrote Epictetus, the Greek Stoic philosopher. Your closest relationships are

the best mirrors for discovering yourself, because they will reflect who you are and what you must do to grow and evolve. See everyone around you as your spiritual teacher, even those people who may rub you the wrong way. Sometimes, the teaching is to stay away from those who are toxic, including the naysayers, dream stealers, or anti-cheerleaders who do not support your dreams, but instead unconsciously spread rocks in your path. Your body will be your spiritual barometer to help you discern. Your little child inside will simply know.

- <u>Validate the feelings and thoughts of others</u>. It doesn't mean that you agree with them. It simply means that you say, "I hear you. I understand where you are coming from. I get what you are saying." One of the biggest diseases on our planet is that we have stopped listening to what other people say. Many hurt inside, because they have never felt safe enough to share their innermost stories that hold pain and trauma from their pasts. Be that "safe place" for people who are close to you, and perhaps even a stranger now and then, so they can confidentially tell their stories to you. Healing begins the moment we are able to tell our stories, authentically and openly, where someone listens to them without assessment. The writer John Steinbeck said, "You can only understand people if you feel them in yourself."

- <u>Share your painful stories</u>. This is the path of strength, not weakness, when we choose to be vulnerable, adventurous, and curious about our own lives. Be cautious of one thing, however. You may need your friends to be your "story checker," where they can tell you if you repeat the same painful stories over and over again. Being caught in a pain cycle means you haven't healed the original pain. Do whatever you need to do to heal that original trauma, and your story will become a new one of joy, freedom, and discovery.

Empathy for ourselves, let alone others, is not easy when we have been hurt in the past. The wounding is often done by those who suffered from the same issue but have not healed their original trauma. This is how a negative spiritual legacy is passed from one generation to the next. The domino effect can spread culturally, such as racism and other expressions of inequality.

But you can heal your own world, beginning with yourself. When you heal yourself, you become a spiritual catalyst for others who can see the beauty and aliveness of your Divine Child at play. Your inner child qualities expand you as you become curious, playful, joyful, vulnerable, observant, courageous, gentle, empathetic, and free. You lead by the example of healing yourself first. When you become authentic and vulnerable, others can truly see themselves within you — the magical inner child who is ever present. When you heal, you become a spiritual catalyst for friends, families, and work associates to heal, too.

Max Carver said, "Empathy is the starting point for creating a community and taking action. It's the impetus for creating change." Planting the seeds for big change in our lives begin with the spiritual power of empathy, and it can change the world.

> Empathy is the gateway;
> compassion is the way.
>
> Scott Perry

Empathy first begins within, where we give ourselves the tender care and self-love we need. It is the rare person who can devote a life of sacrifice in the service of others without depleting his or her own energy reservoirs. For most of us, we need to first become aware of our own feelings and tend to our own needs before attending to the needs of others. Otherwise, we risk burnout, where loneliness, exhaustion and lethargy may overtake the passionate and playful nature of our Divine Child.

It is impossible to have full empathy realized within ourselves and others unless we truly honor and respect our natural environment around us. I remember how much joy I had by playing outside with my brothers in the corn fields. As children, we delighted in the biggest playground in the world — the great outdoors — reveling in the healing salve that nature brings.

Our affinity for nature comes from our roots as children. When we rest and play in the revitalizing power of Nature, she teaches us how we, too, can create, grow, and evolve.

[1] Elizabeth A. Segal. *Social Empathy: The Art of Understanding Others.*

[2] https://variety.com/2013/film/news/variety-announces-this-years-10-directors-to-watch-1200910433/

[3] https://www.nytimes.com/1989/03/28/science/researchers-trace-empathy-s-roots-to-infancy.html

[4] IBID

[5] IBID

[6] https://www.theguardian.com/commentisfree/2017/jan/22/peter-bazalgette-what-i-learned-as-head-of-arts-council-england

[7] *The Bible*, Ephesians 5:24, New International Version.

[8] https://www.epa.gov/history

[9] https://www.washingtonpost.com/lifestyle/wellness/john-bradshaw-self-help-guru-who-led-search-for-inner-child-dies-at-82/2016/05/11/c5f49e52-1782-11e6-9e16-2e5a123aac62_story.html?noredirect=on&utm_term=.9459a1d78050

[10] http://menstuff.org/columns/overboard/bradshawj.html

[11] https://www.washingtonpost.com/lifestyle/wellness/john-bradshaw-self-help-guru-who-led-search-for-inner-child-dies-at-82/2016/05/11/c5f49e52-1782-11e6-9e16-2e5a123aac62_story.html

[12] https://www.thedailybeast.com/study-teen-suicide-rates-down-after-gay-marriage-legalization

Nature Lovers

> If the sight of the blue skies fills you with joy, if a blade of grass springing up in the fields has power to move you, if the simple things of nature have a message that you understand, rejoice, for your soul is alive.
>
> Eleonora Duse
> Italian actress

Empathy and compassion for ourselves and others leads to cherishing nature with similar respect. Albert Einstein said, "Our task must be to free ourselves by widening our circle of compassion to embrace all living creatures and the whole of nature and its beauty." Mahatma Gandhi expressed it similarly when he said, "The good man is the friend of all living things."

As the child grows, the Divine Adult within us likewise matures and takes action. The love for nature and empathy for all transforms that love into environmental activism. Love is not expressed from an armchair. Rather, love must be expressed by sharing our passion through our deeds. If one definition of love is to nurture, care for, protect, and provide us with sustenance, then it can be said that our planet, sunshine, trees bearing fruit, the many vegetable plants, and other living things do indeed love us.

And yet, Nature herself does not need us. Harrison Ford said, "Nature doesn't need people — people need nature; nature would survive the extinction of the human being and go on just fine, but human culture, human beings, cannot survive without nature." For 165 million years, dinosaurs roamed the land, sky, and sea, and around 65 million years ago, the world's climate suddenly changed, becoming darker and colder. Food became scare, many plants died, and 75 percent of the animals living on earth became extinct. While scientists debate what caused this quick and drastic change, two leading theories include giant volcanic eruptions and an asteroid striking the planet.[1]

Mama Nature is indeed powerful, with the profound ability to regenerate herself over time. The evolution and development of modern humans during the last 300,000 years has resulted in incredible technology, where we now resemble the 3,000 gods and saviors that our ancient ancestors invented. Aided by the incredible ability to create energy or destroy civilizations through nuclear power, for example, we humans *feel* powerful. And yet, nature can wipe us all out in blink of an eye with tornadoes, hurricanes, volcanic eruptions, storms, and tsunamis.

> Just living is not enough…one most have sunshine, freedom, and a little flower.
>
> Hans Christian Andersen

We are in awe of the magnificence and grandeur of Nature, with her self-creating and evolving abilities. While nature is efficient with its resources, we humans are not. In 2014, the United States spent $9,237 on health care per person — far more than Japan, the UK, and Greece ($2,100 to $3,000), whose citizens enjoy a higher life expectancy that that of Americans.[2] In 2016, that figure for Americans surpassed the $10,000 mark.[3]

While nature does not waste energy with its incredible organizing abilities, a staggering eight percent of America's Gross Domestic Product (GDP) is spent on health administration costs.[4] Does much of our unnecessary expense come from profiting the few? Clearly, plants and other animal species on the planet have not figured out how to create mass economic suffering for themselves at the expense of others, but we humans have.

The Playground of the Curious Child Within

Learning from nature can teach us important lessons. Mesmerized by the grand universe, the great mathematician and physicist Albert Einstein said, "We still do not know one thousandth of one percent of what nature has revealed to us." The seeming effortlessness of nature is breathtaking and awesome. "The sun, with all those planets revolving around it and dependent on it, can still ripen a bunch of grapes as if it had nothing else in the universe to do," said Galileo Galilei, the Italian astronomer who advanced the theory that the Earth was not the center point of creation. Despite the evidence that Galileo provided, he did so at the expense of his freedom after the Roman Catholic Church proclaimed in their Inquisition he was a heretic and sentenced him to indefinite imprisonment, where he spent the remainder of his life under house arrest.[5]

When we dishonor our scientists, we sacrifice the real saviors who can keep us safe and healthy. Science is not only about the discovery of the wonders and secrets that Nature holds. Practicing the scientific method diligently can lead to admitting the gaps in our knowledge, a healthy kind of humility that keeps the process of discovery and innovation moving forward. This approach, developed more recently in the timeline of humanity, improves vastly upon the superstitious stories and fabrications that handed down ignorant blather from generation to generation.

We must remain vigilant. Otherwise, we risk crucifying the scientist who can save us from polio, COVID, or the next disease. We risk never finding solutions to damage from floods, storms, and hurricanes increasing in intensity due to human-caused climate change. Science, however, offers an active path to discovery that vastly improves upon the idle prayers that characterized the approach of earlier generations toward the unknown. It explains why Christians ignore biblical scriptures promising automatic healing when they have cancer or even a cavity in their teeth, rushing to their doctors and dentists instead of the gods for salvation.[6] If they didn't and opted for the thoughts-and-prayers approach of our ancestors, the sick would perish. Perhaps science and knowledge gained through the study of nature is what gives humans the ability to do greater things, as Jesus said.

> My soul can find no staircase to Heaven unless it be through Earth's loveliness.
>
> Michelangelo

Bathing in the life-giving and sustaining energy of Nature is restorative and healing. Numerous studies, such as the research at the University of Exeter Medical School, confirm this energetic phenomenon, where scientists analyzed health data from 10,000 people who had lived for more than 18 years. The researchers discovered that people living near more green space reported less mental stress, regardless of income, education, and employment.[7]

A 2009 study by Dutch researchers discovered that people who lived within a half mile of green space had a lower incidence of 15 diseases, including anxiety, depression, diabetes, heart disease, asthma, and migraines. In 2015, an international team that examined more than 31,000 Toronto residents found that those who lived on blocks with more trees had a boost in heart and metabolic rate that one would experience with a $20,000 increase in income. Fewer stress hormones and lower mortality rates have also been attributed to living close to nature.[8]

Mother Nature is not just leading us to our own salvation. She is a wonderful spiritual teacher. The actress Diane Lane said, "All the lessons are in nature. You look at the way rocks are formed — the wind and the water hitting them, shaping them, making them what they are. Things take time, you know?" Through her quiet revelation, Nature sits and unveils the secrets of creation, as well as the hidden knowledge within us when we remain curious and open.

Where the Love for Nature and its Negative Expressions Reside

Love for others and for the environment emanates from the Heart Chakra, the seat of love, empathy, compassion, and truth. The first three chakras below the heart center are about identification with the self (First Chakra), identification with you and another person (Second Chakra), and the identification with the collective group, tribe, or community at large (Third Chakra). These lower three chakras are about understanding the needs of each of these, learning their importance, and how those needs relate to everyone involved.

When our Heart centers are open and functioning in healthy ways, we can move beyond intentions and beliefs rooted in the Third Chakra. By seeing how our actions can affect others both positively and negatively, we learn to make better choices through our actions. Being present and aware are functions of the Fourth Chakra, which puts empathy and service to others into action.

It is easy to throw a piece of trash out the car window or toss our gum on the sidewalk. But imagine what our world would look like if everyone did this. We and our natural environment would suffer greatly. Being connected with our Heart centers brings awareness of the karma, or consequences, of our actions and how they affect others and our environment. The Shambhala Buddhist monk Sakyong Mipham said, "Karma moves in two directions. If we act virtuously, the seed we plant will result in happiness. If we act non-virtuously, suffering results."

The other center within us that is deeply connected to nature is the Root Chakra, the seat of grounded energy and material creation. The earth is about safety, stability, and security. Clairvoyants through the ages have observed that the earth's energy is connected to the Root Chakra, the gateway to abundance and security. When we are connected to the greatest source of material energy, we experience prosperity and abundance.

The negative expressions of our love for nature and the environment are self-centeredness, narcissism, greed, and apathy. The "unwealthy" individual, regardless of the bank account's size, is one who seemingly cannot obtain enough. When our core needs have not been fulfilled early in life, the lower three chakras become damaged. Woundedness can show up as self-centeredness, as our traumatized child seeks to fill those holes through other means can lead to addiction.

Self-centered people can be empathetic at times and have clear moral values, but narcissism is a more severe condition. The narcissist feels special and entitled, where rules don't apply to them. Cutting in line or cheating on a partner then blaming others for their own actions to deflect or avoid criticism are examples of how the narcissist operates. The self-centered individual wants people to notice him or her, while the narcissist will crave the same while ridiculing or insulting others in order to artificially feel better.[9]

The person wounded in the Heart Chakra at an early age is often selfish or stingy. Disconnected from true inner joy, this person may be sad, depressed, or stuck in grief. This person has lost touch with his or her own feelings and likely has difficulty connecting with others. Misery loves company, and the black hole left by a wounded heart will unconsciously try to pull others into a negative story.

Do you have people in your life who spend far more time telling you what is going wrong, who is sick, and who just died? This type of person is dangerous to be around for any length of time, because the spiritual abuse is subtle, often appearing as an attempt to be helpful or appear empathetic. In reality, it is just being stuck in a broken record and letting their whole world know about it. This wounded individual has little desire to heal, having learned early in life how to garner attention through negative behavior.

Self-pity, a display of the "poor me" attitude, is a role that many self-centered people play quite well. Using guilt to unconsciously draw others into their dark web, they repeat their stories of negativity, pain, and despair, pulling others into their perpetual state of sadness. Overly consumed by being stuck in the pit of neediness, it is difficult for this type of wounded person to see himself or herself, as well as the consequences of their actions. This is victimhood, the unwillingness or refusal to heal, usually stemming from being unaware.

Steeped in self-involvement, self-pity gradually leads to apathy and despair. In this calloused state, the apathetic soul has lost touch with how his or her words, emotions, and actions affect others. This type of wounded person may frequently say "Whatever!" when he or she feels threatened or unimportant. It is easy for this person to find other similarly wounded people who are also stuck in their negative sob stories. You'll overhear them compete for the crown of victimhood, repeating woeful tales of how others have wronged them, but doing nothing about it to leave the abuse or to heal a negative cycle.

It is a lonely place to sit and stew in self-pity, narcissism, or apathy — even if one is among friends. The appearances of not being alone do not heal our Wounded Child who is crying inside for help. But when we heal by getting those core needs satisfied, we can become alive again.

> We won't have a society if we destroy the environment.
>
> Margaret Mead
> American cultural anthropologist

Another hallmark of the person who has been wounded in the Heart Chakra is disorder and chaos. Self-created noise shows up in many distracting forms, including over-stimulation, literal noise, and creating negative drama in order to continue the state of victimhood. A popular example of this is posting your sad story on Facebook before hundreds of so-called friends and strangers, then checking your posting to see how many "friends" liked your post and what they had to say. Expressing negativity may temporarily help you feel better, but in the end, it usually does not heal deep pain. Most people really don't care enough to help, outside of a cheap, quick comment or "like" on social media.

There is real delight in giving to others and being of service to our fellow human and natural environment. Sharing and giving is how we add value to the world and merit to our own lives. Spontaneous joy is the antidote for lackluster and boredom. Grief from loss can be transformed when we learn to be of service to others, putting our precious talents to work in positive ways.

It is impossible to respect ourselves if we do not honor and respect the environment. The way we treat others, including the environment, usually is a reflection of not only how we see and treat ourselves. If we engage in risky behaviors that endanger ourselves, for example, it is likely that we will put our environment and world at risk. When we truly love and accept ourselves, we will cherish the environment and take action to nurture and protect it.

How to Reactivate Your Love for Nature

Caring for the environment means that you care about the lives of not only our fellow humans, but our animals and their homes. Engaging your empathetic and compassionate energy inside of you is a daily practice. After all, love is a verb.

Here are some suggestions to help reconnect with your sense of empathy for the environment:

- Reconnect with nature every day. Famed architect Frank Lloyd Wright beautifully said, "Study nature, love nature, stay close to nature. It will never fail you." Leave your cell phone behind and take a walk in nature each day. Hug a tree. Walk on the beach barefoot. Take off your shoes and dance in the grass. Smell the flowers. Sit in silence under a tree, feeling its presence and healing force. Let Nature feed and nurture you, revealing its power and the beauty of its silence.

- Play in nature. This is another opportunity to let your inner child play and create in your natural surroundings. Build sandcastles on the beach, where its crystalline energy removes stress and excess energy that may have built up in your body. When you feel relaxed or even "tired" after spending a day at the beach, it is because you are probably used to be over-stressed and wired. Go swimming in the ocean, if possible, where the salt water can help balance your energy. Jacques Yves Cousteau said, "The sea, once it casts its spell, holds one in its net of wonder forever." Splash. Swim. Wiggle. The healing waters are where you first lived.

> For in the true nature of things, if we rightly consider, every green tree is far more glorious than if it were made of gold and silver.
>
> Martin Luther

- Practice being present with whatever you are doing. Be present with those around you. Do not waste away the importance of human interaction on a digital façade. Put away your cell phones. "Multi-tasking" is not a real thing. It's an illusion. The truth is that your brain can only work on one thing at a time, and so can you efficiently. Engineering professor and STEM education researcher Barbara Oakley said, "Multitasking is like constantly pulling up a plant. This kind of constant shifting of your attention means that new ideas and concepts have no chance to take root and flourish."

- <u>Enjoy the profound silence of nature</u>. We live in a culture of noise. Rabindranath Tagore said, "Mother Nature is always speaking. She speaks in a language understood within the peaceful mind of the sincere observer. Leopards, cobras, monkeys, rivers and trees; they all served as my teachers when I lived as a wanderer in the Himalayan foothills." For those who are addicted to a noise cycle, it may be uneasy at first to practice silence. You may well feel the urge to talk...to check your phone...to create some sort of noise around you or entertain more chatter in your head. In my experience, however, the more you practice silence, the easier it will be for your mind to settle and quiet, and the more that external noise will annoy your inner spirit, body, and mind. In the calming silence that Nature offers, a healing sanctuary awaits you.

Blaise Pascal said, "Nature is an infinite sphere of which the center is everywhere and the circumference nowhere." The profound beauty of nature reveals how interconnected life is, and how we are intertwined with it. Nature shows us how precious everything is, reminding us of our specialness, too. "One could not pluck a flower without troubling a star," said anthropologist and philosopher Loren Eiseley.

> The goal of life is to make your heartbeat match the beat of the universe, to match your nature with Nature.
>
> Joseph Campbell

Nature Lovers

The great masters of art and architecture knew that your environment profoundly influences your quality of life, then creates it. When your surroundings are joyful, you will be too. If you live in a prison of any sort, your consciousness and your life will reflect a life of restraint and limitation as well.

Take care of your environment, and your environment will take care of you. Mother Nature is powerful beyond what we can comprehend. Ask the dinosaurs and the citizens of Pompeii in ancient Italy. We are at the mercy of nature, so let us honor its gifts and mysterious energy that sweetly call to us. "Look deep into nature, and then you will understand everything better," said Albert Einstein.

In a world of concrete and steel we have built that is largely artificial, nature brings life and healing. "Nature is full of genius, full of the divinity; so that not a snowflake escapes its fashioning hand," Henry David Thoreau said. Nature is our biggest playground, our greatest teacher. In her quiet but steady voice, we hear her beckoning call with one of the greatest life lessons that Mother Nature can offer: That to be grounded in her vast energy is to be truly powerful.

---

[1] https://www.popsci.com/how-did-dinosaurs-go-extinct#page-2

[2] https://www.npr.org/sections/goatsandsoda/2017/04/20/524774195/what-country-spends-the-most-and-least-on-health-care-per-person

[3] https://www.chcf.org/blog/national-health-spending-passes-10000-and-we-should-be-concerned/

[4] https://www.reuters.com/article/us-health-spending/u-s-health-spending-twice-other-countries-with-worse-results-idUSKCN1GP2YN

[5] http://newsroom.ucla.edu/releases/the-truth-about-galileo-and-his-conflict-with-the-catholic-church

[6] *The Bible*, James 5:14-16.

[7] https://www.nationalgeographic.com/magazine/2016/01/call-to-wild/

[8] IBID

[9] https://www.psychologytoday.com/us/blog/fixing-families/201509/narcissist-or-just-self-centered-4-ways-tell

Grounded

> The love of wilderness is more than a hunger for what is always beyond reach; it is also an expression of loyalty to the Earth, the Earth which bore us and sustains us, the only paradise we shall ever know, the only paradise we ever need, if only we had the eyes to see.
>
> Edward Paul Abbey
> Author, essayist, environmentalist

Small children connect to Mother Earth from their moment of birth. Rolling on the floor, babies are naturally rooted in this nurturing, calming, and healing energy. Soon after, they begin crawling around on the floor, continuing their curious adventures on the Earth. And even sitting upward, they connect with rooting energy with their seats firmly planted on the ground.

Being grounded means that you feel safe and secure in your life. By developing a stable foundation, you can roll with the punches when life brings its ups and downs. Steve Goodier wrote, "Get yourself grounded and you can navigate even the stormiest roads in peace." The roots of the tree are its primary source of nourishment and strength. Similarly, the earth as our rooting source feeds, shelters, and clothes us. Earth energy is the seat of prosperity and abundance.

Being rooted is one of the secrets to being truly happy, and that inner joy is contagious. This joy spreads to others quickly, then returns back to you. It is a key to great success. The happier you are, the better your life will be. A buoyant attitude that is grounded makes it easier to navigate rough waters and pass through those times.

Being grounded and happy is easier to attain with good health and vitality. The Roman poet Virgil said, "The greatest wealth is health." When we are healthy in body, we can have a healthy mind and be more joyful. It is challenging to be happy without honoring our body and properly taking care of it. Without good health, life can be difficult to experience fully. Eat well, because you are precious. Exercise daily, because you and your body are deserving of happiness and abundance. Reduce your stress and distractions so that your mind and body will be clear and focused.

We realize health benefits when we literally "ground" or "earth," which refers to direct skin contact with the Earth with our bare feet or hands or with various grounding systems. Many reports from indigenous cultures around the world indicate that walking barefoot on the Earth provide feelings of well-being.

Despite many people being reluctant to walking outside for various reasons, unless at the beach on holiday, for example, studies show that physically grounding to the Earth has sustained health benefits. This includes grounding either by frequently walking on the Earth or using simple conductive systems which can be used at the home or office that connects you to the Earth. A wide variety of conductive methods that utilize a cord or wire includes mats, sheets, wires, wrist or ankle pads, or adhesive patches.

In a multi-disciplinary research study published in 2015 in the *Journal of Inflammation Research*, Gaétan Chevalier, director at the Developmental and Cell Biology Department at the University of California at Irvine, and Richard Brown from the Human Physiology Department at the University of Oregon examined the effects of human body contact with the surface of the Earth. Their research confirmed that electrically conductive contact by "grounding" or "Earthing" has positive effects on "inflammation, immune responses, wound healing, and prevention and treatment of chronic inflammatory and autoimmune diseases." Brown and Chevalier wrote, "Specifically, grounding an organism produces measurable differences in the concentrations of white blood cells, cytokines, and other molecules involved in the inflammatory response."[1]

> It turns out that people who are grounded and secure don't change much under stress. That's what being grounded means.
>
> Michael Gruber

The research found that physically grounding reduces or prevents inflammation following injury, including redness, swelling, pain, heat, and loss of function. This was confirmed in numerous cases with medical infrared imaging. By connecting the body to the Earth, free electrons from the Earth's surface spread over and into the body, where they have antioxidant effect. Researchers hypothesized that these free electrons moving into the body from the Earth can "prevent or resolve so-called 'silent' or 'smoldering' inflammation." Brown and Chevalier noted that "grounding appears to improve sleep, normalize the day–night cortisol rhythm, reduce pain, reduce stress, shift the autonomic nervous system from sympathetic toward parasympathetic activation, increase heart rate variability, speed wound healing, and reduce blood viscosity."[2] Indeed, Mama Nature heals!

Breathe Like a Baby Again

The Divine Child is *energetically* grounded at its core — the seat of Feminine energy that is calming, nurturing, and generative. As technology produces more chaos on our planet, this energetic noise is alluring and exciting, but destabilizing. Being able to return to our center is critical for a healthy mind, body, and spirit. Our center is what nourishes us and brings balance to our daily lives.

Our tiny teachers are naturally skilled at proper breathing that helps center and ground them. Babies breathe using their diaphragms where the chest barely moves, but the belly moves in and out with each breath they take. Deep, natural breathing is one way we energetically root and ground ourselves.

As we get older, however, we learn to hold the belly in, tightening up these important muscles. Doctors call this "paradoxical breathing," which occurs when the pattern of breathing using the diaphragm, the primary muscle that controls breathing, becomes reversed.

As we age, we learn to hold our breath and tighten our bellies when we feel afraid, for example. Retracting the gut muscles can disconnect us from our emotions, which is probably the primary reason why we forget how to breathe properly. You may catch yourself holding your breath during moments of anxiety or other forms of fear, for instance. This pulls the energy toward the upper chakras, which creates more stress, rather than allowing the deep, natural belly breath to relieve tension, stress, and fear.

Another primary cause for learning bad breathing habits may be due to societal pressure to have a big chest and small waist. Many personal trainers and fitness magazines instruct us to contract our abdominal muscles, which can become an unconscious habit outside of the gym, too. The expectation that you will be more loved if you have a small waist and big chest — the stereotypical "36-28-36" for women — can create undue pressure on people to look good at the expense of their physical, emotional, mental, and spiritual health.

The medical community warns that paradoxical breathing can be dangerous, with symptoms including dizziness, weakness, difficulty catching the breath, a rapid heart rate, and being unable to take a deep breath. This type of "reverse" breathing can also bring pain, weakness, or tension in the chest or stomach.[3] In addition to bad breathing habits, chest injuries, neurological problems, electrolyte imbalances, hormonal shifts, or sleep apnea are among the causes for this.

On the other hand, diaphragmatic breathing, which is sometimes referred to as "belly breathing," reduces stress, boosts the immune system, and helps lower blood pressure. Belly breathing is the cornerstone of most relaxation and meditation techniques. It can also help manage depression, lower anxiety, improve irritable bowel syndrome, and alleviate sleeplessness. Many people who suffer from post-traumatic stress syndrome (PTSD) have benefited from belly breathing. It also lowers chances of injury and improves the body's ability to tolerate intense exercise.[4] Thich Nhat Hanh suggests that proper breathing can help manage emotions: "Anger is like a storm rising up from the bottom of your consciousness. When you feel it coming, turn your focus to your breath."

The breath creates flow and, therefore, gives us life. Our breath is also what teaches us to let go and release the things that no longer serve us in our lives. In his book *Letting Go of the Person You Used to Be*, Lama Surya Das reminded us that each new moment, each new breath holds an opportunity to be reborn that is not confined to major transitions, such as graduating from college, getting married, or retiring from work as chances to begin anew:

With every breath, the old moment is lost; a new moment arrives. We exhale and we let go of the old moment. It is lost to us. In doing so, we let go of the person we used to be. We inhale and breathe in the moment that is becoming. In doing so, we welcome the person we are becoming. We repeat the process. This is meditation. This is renewal. This is life.

You can learn how to breathe like a baby again. Lie on the floor or sit upright in a chair with your eyes closed, and place one hand over your navel with the other hand on your chest. Breathe naturally, allowing your belly to expand and contract on its own. If you feel any movement in your chest, simply become aware of it, and allow your stomach to expand with the breath. This simple exercise may be the most important one you could ever practice on a daily basis. Your breath is at the physical core of liberation, centeredness, harmony, and true power.

Bad habits can be broken, but it may take some practice to get back into the groove of proper breathing that will empower you. As you develop an awareness of your breath, you will engage with your inner power more fully. In his book *Om Chanting and Meditation*, author and teacher Amit Ray wrote, "If you want to conquer the anxiety of life, live in the moment, live in the breath."

This is the true nature of your Divine Child.

Where Groundedness and its Negative Expressions Reside

Being centered and grounded occurs at the Root Chakra, the core of our physical being. Located around the perineum, our first energy center is the polar opposite of the seventh chakra, the Crown, which connects us to all possibilities the Universe has to offer. Conversely, the Root Chakra is about focusing that energy to express itself in the material world. The Crown Chakra is "Father Heaven above," the proverbial Garden of Eden and realm of all possibilities, while the Root Chakra is "Mother Earth below" and the world of creating and materializing a specific goal.

This energy is calming, centering, and focused — qualities that small children naturally embody. In their eagerness and adventures of learning and discovery, children are focused, not multi-tasking. Nor are they struggling to accomplish a long list of goals.

This is also where loving yourself begins. Self-esteem comes from doing, not from wishing it to be so. Believing in yourself does not come from positive affirmations or tricking yourself into believing something that is not true. It comes from *knowing* who you are and what your strengths and weaknesses are. Norman Vincent Peale said, "Believe in yourself! Have faith in your abilities! Without a humble but reasonable confidence in your own powers you cannot be successful or happy." As you act on this self-knowledge in your daily life, you gain confidence in what you do.

> I feel no need for any other faith than my faith in the kindness of human beings. I am so absorbed in the wonder of earth and the life upon it that I cannot think of heaven and angels.
>
> Pearl S. Buck

Loving yourself fully is one of the most important things you can ever learn to do. Hemal Radia, the author of *Find You & You Find Everything: The Secrets to the Law of Attraction*, wrote, "There is only one true love affair...the one with yourself. All others are expressions of it." If you aren't able to fully love yourself — including your strengths, weaknesses, your beauty, and your shadows — you will be unable to love others authentically.

Entrepreneur Mastin Kipp, who founded the inspirational website TheDailyLove.com, wrote, "Love is an action, a choice. Love is not really an emotion." I agree wholeheartedly. Love is a verb. It can only be expressed by putting our 21 gifts into action and sharing them with ourselves and others.

Our small teachers remind us that loving ourselves is about looking at ourselves in the present, not at what happened to us in the past. It is easy to identify with our past, and even to live in a past time where you experienced strong emotional ties. If you find yourself being pulled into a negative past, there is a way out. Know that your past stories do not define who you are; rather, they are simply what happened to you along your journey of revealing yourself to yourself.

If our own needs are not met early on, our focus turns inward. This shows up as self-absorption, where we become overly self-involved. Charity for others diminishes, where if a self-absorbed person gives, it is often out of getting recognized or self-promotion, where the spotlight is again turned upon the selfish "giver."

A darker version of the self-absorbed person is the narcissist, who becomes abusive on multiple levels. Psychologist Lindsay Henderson said, "The term narcissist is used often to describe a wide variety of people that we find difficult or offensive." The narcissist's mood depends on others. "They require regulation from others to maintain their framework of 'the self,'" said neuropsychologist Dr. Rhonda Freeman.[5]

Contentment with what you have leads to true abundance. If you are focused on what is missing in your life, you will likely be unhappy and ungrateful. This can be a problem with becoming too goal-oriented, because it potentially buys into the idea that what you are missing will make you happier. It runs the risk of looking at the empty side of a glass half-full, rather than appreciating what you have in the present.

How Our Grounding Energy Becomes Contaminated

The negative expression of groundedness is chaos, a result of our Masculine energies becoming over-exacerbated. Clearly, we are becoming increasingly addicted to excess motion, movement, and action. We are inventing more distractions to pull our attention away from existing distractions.

Technology is producing more distractions via electronic apps and games, for example. While these inventions can be creative and sometimes helpful, they also supplant our ability to let our minds wander and play freely. We lose our connection with the real world as digital worlds seduce our minds.

When the average adult spent nearly six hours a day online and 3.3 hours each day accessing media on their smart phones in 2017,[6] the alarm bells began sounding. According to Pew Research in August 2018, even teens believe they have a problem with attachment to their phones, where 60 percent of teens between the ages of 13 and 17 said spending too much time online is a "major" problem facing their age group.[7]

The addiction to the virtual world is increasing. Common Sense Media recently reported that teens spend an average *of nine hours a day* online, while kids ages eight to twelve spend about six hours online. Robert Lustig, a professor of pediatrics specializing in endocrinology at the University of Southern California and author of *The Hacking of the American Mind*, said at a conference in February 2018 that kids are definitely addicted. "It's not a drug, but it might as well be. It works the same way... it has the same results," he noted.[8]

> The cell phone has become the adult's transitional object, replacing the toddler's teddy bear for comfort and a sense of belonging.
>
> Margaret Heffernan

In her article entitled "How Your Smartphone is Ruining Your Relationship," Mandy Oakland discussed the research that reveals the dark side of cell phones. While smartphones have been marketed as devices that keep us in touch with our schedules, loved ones, and even our physical health, the opposite may be true.[9]

In a study published in the journal *Psychology of Popular Media Culture*, college lovebirds were asked to report on their own smartphone use. The study found that people who were more dependent on their smartphones were less certain about their intimate relationships, while their partners said they were less satisfied in their relationship.[10] Are we becoming slaves to our technology we create and use, believing that it will make our relationships stronger and more intimate? Matthew Lapierre, assistant professor in the department of communication at the University of Arizona, who authored the study, says, "Smartphones are fundamentally different from previous technologies, so their effect is much more powerful. I don't want to say it's uniformly negative, but it definitely hints in that direction."[11]

A simple and orderly environment is important for creating a supportive environment. "A chaotic household can intensify ADHD symptoms," said Aniesa Hanson, a licensed mental health counselor at Hanson Complete Wellness in Tampa, Florida. "In a chaotic home, a child has limited expectations of structure, which leaves them to develop an askew understanding of boundaries." She explains how this can create the potential to impede school or other activities. "A chaotic household can have such an impact that children even without ADHD can experience symptoms of inattention, impulsivity and even anxiety."[12]

Her statements echo the findings of a study conducted by a German research team from five universities. Published in 2017 in the *Journal of Attention Disorders*, the study found that "a highly chaotic and unstructured household, to which the children's ADHD symptoms are a contributing factor, makes it difficult for their parents to be authoritative in their upbringing. At the same time, it can be assumed that the parents — despite the prevailing chaos — are fond of their children, speak positively about them and enjoy spending time with them." Andrea Wirth, research associate at the Department of Educational Psychology of Goethe University Frankfurt, added, "Household chaos seems to be some kind of mechanism through which the symptoms of children with ADHD have a negative impact on their parents' behaviour towards them."[13]

In my work with numerous clients who suffer from stress, anxiety, restlessness, nervousness, insomnia, ADD, ADHD, and autism, their energy fields consistently reflect chaos and increased exposure to energetic noise. In every case I've seen, their upper chakras, namely the Crown (7th) and Brow (6th), are over-functioning. Generally speaking, this happens when the person has been exposed to far too much motion and excess movement.

Examples of causes for disturbances to these important energy centers involve absorbing too much information with the news, watching television or movies, or playing video games in excess, while not spending enough time grounding in nature or in quiet settings. Consequently, symptoms of this condition may show up, such as stress in the upper body, such as upper back, shoulders, neck, and head tension, chronic headaches, eye stress, or being consistently tired.

The solution to many of these conditions is two-fold. First, reduce the amount of "Masculine energy" sources if you or a loved one is experiencing these problems. Most people, in my experience, have far too much Masculine energy and not enough Feminine energy in their lives — a result of technology, excess movement, motion, and noise.

The second recommendation is to increase the Feminine energy, which is connected to your inner child. Taking time to nurture yourself is critical, as is spending plenty of time in quiet. Put away your cell phone and turn it off for long periods of time, even for a weekend. You will survive…and even thrive.

Ground yourself in the healing power of nature. Read more, as this gives you time for reflection and contemplation. Watch TV shows and movies less frequently, as this will make you less reactive and connect you to your calm and grounded state with presence. Spend time each day in meditation. Twenty minutes or more each day will significantly improve your physical health and boost your mental and emotional states. Create a special place in your home that is reserved for only meditation, so this meditation spot becomes a physical anchor and spiritual portal that transports you instantly into the sanctuary of quiet. In pure silence, the infinite field of pure potentiality in our vast Universe opens up to you.

Turn off the television and radio. After I graduated from college, I found myself in a habit of immediately turning on music or the television set after getting home from work, then I would walk out of the room. I had become addicted to noise. When I began practicing silence, it was difficult and uneasy at first to sit in the silence of my home and car. But the realization was clear at how addicted I had become to noise in my life, including being busy. And it was also clear how I would numb myself to counter the effects of the racket and clamor. It was a vicious cycle of exposing myself to noise, then numbing, then increasing the volume of noise, then numbing again.

After practicing peace and quiet, I began to crave more silence in my life. I started cultivating a rich relationship with my centering force, learning more about my inner thoughts. It was an oasis to move away from noise, chaos, and being excessively busy to the point of stress and mental, physical, and emotional exhaustion. Restlessness melted into more peaceful moments, quiet, and stability. I became less stressed and more vibrant yet relaxed.

Today, I enjoy driving in my car usually in complete silence — without the desire to hear the noise of the music, news, or talk shows. The level of peace that inner and outer stillness brings is healing, calming, and nurturing.

Since the 1950s, many studies on the effects of noise have been conducted, primarily with adults. These studies (e.g., Hellbrück and Liebl, 2007; Szalma and Hancock, 2011) largely show that noise with low to moderate intensity, depending on the characteristics of sounds and tasks, may in fact evoke substantial impairments in performance.

For children, a number of experimental studies show the negative effects of acute exposure of noise on speech perception and listening comprehension. Noise also disrupts non-auditory tasks, such as reading or being able to recall visual lists, negatively impacting children more than adults. Children suffer lower performance in verbal tasks when exposed to indoor noise and reverberation in the classroom.[14]

Another study found that exposure to airport noise impaired the reading ability and long-term memory in children.[15] Adults working in noisy office environments were found to be less motivated and more stressed — even with low levels of noise, according to a Cornell University study conducted by environmental psychologists. Interestingly, the workers themselves did not report higher levels of stress in noisy offices. Gary Evans, professor of design and environmental analysis and a leading expert on environmental stress such as noise and crowding, said, "But just because people fail to report that environmental conditions are negative, we can't assume that there are no adverse impacts," pointing to a limitation of internal corporate surveys.[16]

Noise pollution is ungrounding, because it disturbs many of the chakras, pulling energy from the Root Chakra that grounds us and moving it up toward the higher chakras in the body that are associated with finer vibrations of energy. Consequently, sound pollution can trigger the body's stress response, as the physical body becomes more ungrounded. Noise has been linked to health problems such as high blood pressure, heart disease, stroke, and musculoskeletal problems.[17] Other studies show that noise pollution disrupts sleep cycles and sleep quality, while lowering immunity to all diseases.[18]

The Destructive Energy of Noise

While white noise machines have been widely promoted as beneficial for babies, young children, and adults alike, a study published in the journal *Pediatrics* reveals that use of white noise machines "raises concerns for increasing an infant's risk of noise-induced hearing loss." The study concluded that infant "sleep machines" (ISMs) are "capable of producing output sound pressure levels that may be damaging to infant hearing and auditory development. We outline recommendations for safer operation of these machines." The study found that three ISMs produced output levels exceeding 85 A-weighted decibels, which "exceeds current occupational limits for accumulated noise exposure in adults and risks noise-induced hearing loss" if played at these levels for more than eight hours.[19]

Multiple studies also have found that ongoing white noise can induce the release of the stress hormone cortisol, the body's built-in alarm system. Excess cortisol impairs the prefrontal cortex function in the brain — the emotional learning center that helps regulate planning, impulse control, and reasoning functions.[20] Recent studies from 2018 found that short-term memory relies most heavily on this area of the brain as well.[21]

> Soon silence will have passed into legend. Man has turned his back on silence. Day after day he invents machines and devices that increase noise and distract humanity from the essence of life, contemplation, meditation.
>
> Jean Arp

Stress and the ongoing "noise in life" could be an underlying cause for dementia and Alzheimer's disease. Studies at Harvard Medical School suggest a link between these memory diseases and lack of quality sleep. Another study published in 2014 in *Alzheimer's & Dementia* involving more than 1,000 men who reported on sleep experiences over a span of 40 years discovered that those who cited regular sleep disturbances had a 150 percent increased risk of developing Alzheimer's later in life compared to those who did not report any sleep problems. The risk increased if sleep issues occurred later in life.[22]

Because older adults spend less time in deep sleep and are therefore more easily awakened by noises, a quiet bedroom environment is especially important for older adults. Researchers from Harvard Medical School recommend installing double-paned windows to help block external noise and decorating the bedroom with rugs and heavy drapery that absorb sound. Avoiding watching television or using a computer after 9 p.m. is highly suggested, as bright light at night can suppress the body's production of melatonin, making it more difficult to sleep. Reading at night from a backlit electronic device, such as a laptop, Kindle, or iPad, is also discouraged.

Babies and small children are also highly susceptible to noise. According to an article published by John Hopkins Medicine, loud sounds can damage the delicate hair cells in the inner ear and hearing nerve, resulting in sensorineural hearing loss or nerve deafness. Deafness can happen immediately or slowly over a period of years, and either temporarily or permanently.

Researchers from John Hopkins say that sources that can cause hearing loss due to their loud noises include hair dryers, blenders, food processors, traffic, and tools and equipment, such as lawn mowers and leaf blowers. Children are also susceptible to recreational activities that generate excess noise, such as snowmobiles, go-carts, radio-controlled airplanes, or loud concerts. Another popular source of hearing loss found in kids is listening to music on an MP3 player or personal device, especially with the volume turned up too high.[23]

Symptoms of noise-induced hearing loss in a child include trouble hearing soft or faint sounds, or if normal conversation seems unclear or muffled. A child can also experience tinnitus, which is buzzing or ringing in the ears. Your child's healthcare provider can examine your child if you suspect problems with damage from excess noise, or an ENT (ear-nose-throat specialist) or audiologist can conduct hearing tests to determine if your child has been affected.

How to Reactive Your Grounding Energy

Connecting to Earth energy is perhaps one of the most important things you can do to help you navigate a stress-filled world increasing in noise. This can be accomplished by activating your Root Chakra, the core of your physical being, connecting to Mother Nature, or bringing this nurturing and calming energy into your environment.

Here are some suggestions on how to increase grounding energy that will benefit you in many ways:

- <u>Become aware of your thoughts</u>. Self-awareness is the first step of empowerment in anything we choose to do. Our consciousness reveals how we are responding to the external environment, and how rooted we truly are within ourselves. "Start observing your own mind. Do not try to escape; do not be afraid of your thinking," said Swami Rama. Being the quiet observer is a fantastic way to being truly successful, abundant, and happy in life. Daily meditation for 20 minutes or more is one of the best ways to watch our own thoughts and get grounded in the process. "Be the witness of your thoughts," said the Buddha.

- Breathe like a baby again. From your belly, as described earlier. Practice it each day, becoming aware of your breath. Noticing your breath will guide you. Heal the *fear of feeling vulnerable* — a learned pattern from past trauma. Know instead that your vulnerability is your power.

- Get plenty of good sleep. Good rest each night is essential for excellent health, vitality, and longevity. It is also important for grounding. From an energetic perspective, laying horizontally on the floor, ground, or bed "deactivates" the energy of the body, allow it to come to rest and receive balancing and harmonizing energy. Conversely, being upright activates the energy in the body, where a vertical body position serves as a beacon, radiating energy upward and outward.

- Reduce inflammation in the body. Inflammation is a widespread health problem, indicative of a cultural energetic issue, a result of too much Masculine energy in the body. The excessive "heating up" of the body can lead to symptoms of high blood pressure, heart problems, gout, rheumatoid arthritis, obesity, asthma, joint pain, stiffness, rashes, chest pain, cancer, tumors, autoimmune disorders, chronic infections, excess mucus (i.e., needing to clear your throat or blow your nose frequently), fevers, chronic mouth sores, fatigue, low energy, abdominal pain, poor digestion (including bloating, constipation, loose stool), heart disease, diabetes, and neurogenerative diseases such as Alzheimer's.[24] Energetically and emotionally, too much Masculine energy shows up as anger, nervousness, excess tension, insomnia, recklessness, anxiety, or agitation. *In my experience, inflammation is largely caused by unresolved emotional and mental trauma from the past,* but can be exacerbated by sugar, dairy, caffeine, excess simple carbohydrates, gluten, and other foods that cause sensitivities. Daily moderate exercise can help. Supplements, such as probiotics, resveratrol, fish oil, and turmeric can also reduce inflammation. Green leafy vegetables, nuts, sees, and some herbs and spices are very helpful.[25] It is unlikely that anyone who has unresolved mental and emotional past trauma will see long-term resolution of inflammation problems. In my experience, internal pain that inflames from unhealed trauma usually leads to physical inflammation.

- Simplify your life. Get rid of those things that create chaos in your life or don't feel good. They are destabilizing and ungrounding. There is a difference between things that positively challenge you and those activities or people that exhaust you. Know the difference and separate yourself from those people and circumstances that pull your energy without giving back in supportive ways. They are the worst of energy vampires in your life, but usually are completely unaware of their toxicity.

- <u>Express gratitude every day</u>. Gratitude is the soul's way of saying, "I love this…and I want more of it." There is a vast difference between pleasure, which is often a result of a purchased commodity, and true joy, which is internal and beyond monetary measure. Alcohol or other drugs, for example, can be purchased and bring momentary pleasure to the senses, which can lead to crashing down to a new low — financially, energetically, physically, emotionally, mentally, or spiritually. Things that activate or increase your internal joy, however, are free and abundant. These are the true riches of heaven and earth. Expressing gratitude for these riches will magnetically attract more of that into your life. It is also the secret of true happiness.

- <u>Practice silence each day</u>. Most people feel as though they could never survive without their cell phones for even one day. This is likely a result of being addicted to noise and chatter that comes from the device, which can also be about being disconnected from yourself. When you live in a "self-referral" state, you naturally enjoy being in your own company, even sitting in silence for longer periods of time. Living in an "object-referral" state, however, keeps you in a place of victimhood, where your happiness is dependent on what happens to you, rather than the living in the knowing and power of who you truly are. A number of people have attended meditation retreats where they were in silence for a week without speaking.

The astrophysicist Neil deGrasse Tyson wrote about the energetic balance between us and the Earth when he said, "I would request that my body in death be buried not cremated, so that the energy content contained within it gets returned to the earth, so that flora and fauna can dine upon it, just as I have dined upon flora and fauna during my lifetime." When we recognize and honor the Earth, we honor ourselves in greater ways.

Connecting with the Earth is essential to being truly grounded in your true nature. This activates the Earth energy within yourself, the foundation of who you are. Being calm and at peace begins with being rooted. It is about knowing who you are that transcends what you have. Stedman Graham said, "Most people are defined by their titles, their cars, their house, where they came from, their color, their race, their religion. And so, it is up to you to take control of your own life and define you. As long as you understand who you are and you have a solid foundation of understanding what your talents are, what your skills are."

When we are grounded, we accept ourselves fully. Self-acceptance is one of the traits of the Divine Child, as our tiny teachers reveal to us. Small children fully accept themselves, as well as others. The child does not even consider it as a choice. This is one of the truly beautiful traits of small children. By accepting others as they are and not judging them, they treat others as equals. To them, life is not a competition, as they never experience the urge to get ahead of others. This energy within us all — acceptance and non-judgment — is the path to our inner power.

As adults, it is our journey to return to that sacred space of complete acceptance, which is an endless fountain of joy, fulfillment, presence, and true abundance.

[1] https://www.ncbi.nlm.nih.gov/pmc/articles/PMC4378297/

[2] Chevalier G, Sinatra ST, Oschman JL, Sokal K, Sokal P. Review article: Earthing: health implications of reconnecting the human body to the Earth's surface electrons. J Environ Public Health. 2012; 2012:291541.

[3] https://www.medicalnewstoday.com/articles/319924.php

[4] https://www.healthline.com/health/diaphragmatic-breathing

[5] https://www.bustle.com/p/9-subtle-differences-between-being-a-narcissist-vs-just-being-self-centered-8968106

[6] https://www.pcmag.com/article/361587/tech-addiction-by-the-numbers-how-much-time-we-spend-online

[7] https://qz.com/1367506/pew-research-teens-worried-they-spend-too-much-time-on-phones/

[8] IBID

[9] https://time.com/4311202/smartphone-relationship-cell-phone/

[10] https://psycnet.apa.org/record/2016-19944-001

[11] http://time.com/4311202/smartphone-relationship-cell-phone/

[12] https://health.usnews.com/health-care/patient-advice/articles/2017-06-02/is-a-chaotic-household-linked-to-risk-of-children-having-adhd

[13] https://www.sciencedaily.com/releases/2017/03/170308131334.htm

[14] https://www.ncbi.nlm.nih.gov/pmc/articles/PMC3757288/

[15] https://www.verywellmind.com/stress-and-noise-pollution-how-you-may-be-at-risk-3145041

[16] http://news.cornell.edu/stories/2001/01/even-low-level-office-noise-can-increase-health-risks

[17] https://www.verywellmind.com/stress-and-noise-pollution-how-you-may-be-at-risk-3145041

[18] https://www.verywellmind.com/getting-quality-sleep-when-stressed-3145263

[19] https://pediatrics.aappublications.org/content/133/4/677

[20] https://www.scientificamerican.com/article/ask-the-brains-background-noise/

[21] https://qbi.uq.edu.au/brain-basics/memory/where-are-memories-stored

[22] https://www.health.harvard.edu/staying-healthy/alzheimers-wake-up-call

[23] https://www.hopkinsmedicine.org/healthlibrary/conditions/otolaryngology/noise-induced_hearing_loss_85,P00458

[24] https://www.healthline.com/health/chronic-inflammation#effects-on-the-body

[25] https://www.parsleyhealth.com/blog/5-signs-chronic-inflammation/

Accepting

Happiness can exist only in acceptance.

George Orwell

In the last century, acceptance has become a popular term used by numerous spiritual thought leaders, psychologists, and therapists. It's an intriguing concept, one that we adults have difficulty embracing, because many of us have forgotten what came naturally to us as little kids.

Most suffering comes from not accepting what is. This may account for why our ancestors made up the idea of a savior and superhero who can rescue us from our dire situation, rather than to accept responsibility for ourselves. When we refuse to accept difficult realities, we get trapped in suffering while waiting for someone else to solve our problems.

Acceptance also does not mean that you necessarily agree with how someone treated you or approve of what happened, as author and senior clinician Karyn D. Hall, PhD writes. Rather than to say that something "should not have happened," we acknowledge the event happened. The language we use is important. For example, if your partner cheated on you, suffering is created when you say that he or she should not have cheated on you. The fact remains that your partner cheated on you. Accepting that reality makes it easier to move forward in a positive direction for yourself and others involved.

> The greatest gift that you can give to others is the gift of unconditional love and acceptance.
>
> Brian Tracy

Another myth of "radical acceptance" that Hall dispels is that anger or withdrawal are necessary for protecting yourself when someone hurts you. It is easy to stew in anger or resentment as a way to armor yourself from getting hurt, or perhaps even to "forgive" someone who repeatedly hurts you in the same way, leaving yourself vulnerable for getting hurt again. Moving forward with wisdom, Hall says, is acknowledging what happened and what is true about our emotions, however painful they feel. Rather than run away from our emotions or numb from them, we gain freedom from suffering when we accept what is, learn from it, and move forward in productive ways — just like our tiny teachers seem to do.

Eckhart Tolle said, "Acceptance looks like a passive state, but in reality, it brings something entirely new into this world. That peace, a subtle energy vibration, is consciousness." When we decide to be fully aware of what is, acceptance is about taking action, rather than choosing the status quo.

Acceptance moves us forward. When we accept the conditions of what happened, we take that wisdom from our discovery and live more powerfully on our next adventure. With deeper awareness, we can choose better paths.

All healing begins with our awareness. The more awareness we have, the more powerful we become, and the greater the levels of acceptance and joy we will experience. Nathaniel Branden said, "The first step toward change is awareness. The second step is acceptance."

> As I get older, the more I stay focused on the acceptance of myself and others and choose compassion over judgment and curiosity over fear.
>
> Tracee Ellis Ross

Without deeper levels of consciousness and awareness, we will remain stuck in our issues, often repeating them like a broken record. The pain of our suffering grows louder and louder to get our attention, so that we can learn the steps of our own healing process.

The key is to remain curious and adventurous despite feeling the pain, and dive into the pool of ourselves. By keeping the vulnerable heart of our Divine Child open and curious, we can discover the truth and learn more about our situations of crisis, however great or small. Acceptance is the birthplace of healing and progress.

Creating Powerful Invitations

Acceptance allows us to create powerful invitations and to move forward. Creating clear and concrete invitations is a way for our Divine Child within to engage with other Divine Children around us. A compelling invitation is one that paints the vision of what you desire, seeks out resonance within others around you, and creates a clear invitation.

Invitations create openness, communication, curiosity, and playfulness. "Come play in my sandbox," you say. Or "I would like to play with you in your sandbox, so we can build castles, forts, and parks together." Acceptance also means remaining detached to the outcome of whether or not someone else will accept your invitation. How many times have you extended an invitation to someone you really like for a first, second, or third date, but secretly worried so much that he was going to reject you?

> A real conversation always contains an invitation. You are inviting another person to reveal herself or himself to you, to tell you who they are or what they want.
>
> David Whyte

It's better to know if someone doesn't want to play in your proverbial sandbox or his or her sandbox. You can go find someone else who wants to play with you. Or you can create other invitations with that same person, if you have resonance with that person on multiple levels. Rather than be fixated on someone specific to accept your compelling invitation, acceptance means that you remain hopeful and open that *the right person* instead will show up — or that maybe you can be open to creating an even more wonderful invitation that leads you to greater success.

As adults, we still play in our virtual sandboxes, even though they are disguised as homes, workplaces, outdoor activities, hobbies, or vacation spots. They are all sandboxes, ready for our Divine Child to play with others. Everything is sand, and we are always creating. Sometimes we create sandcastles, and other times, we inadvertently create sad castles. We may find ourselves getting stuck doing the same thing over and over again, even when it doesn't bring us joy. And other times, we build the same castles over and over again, because each one brings us more joy.

Little kids do this spontaneously and successfully. They find others to join them to create and play together. The more joy they get, they more they keep playing together. When they stop playing, they find new playmates to play in their sandboxes or find something else to do.

If we don't create and accept powerful invitations on a daily basis that propel us closer to your hopes, dreams, and wishes, then we end up inadvertently accepting the invitations and visions of others, living the life that others want for us. Our own dreams become manifested when we take action that is aligned with others, where the Law of Resonance and the power of synchronicity go to work for everyone involved.

Acceptance is also about remaining opening to accepting wonderful invitations from others. How many times have you said, "but you shouldn't have done that" when someone hands you a lovely gift? Rather than to stop the flow of energy and tell the Universe that you are undeserving of wonderful things, you can instead say "Thank you! I love this!" This type of self-acceptance that values yourself more fully will create greater joy, and it will open up the floodgates of synchronicity and more intimate connections with your sandbox friends. *By sharing these 21 gifts with others, everyone wins, and the Universe expands in positive ways.*

Our goals, hopes, dreams, and wishes are all sand, ready for us to take action and form beautiful, amazing sculptures. Turning dreams into reality by co-creating with others is far more powerful than building our castles alone. Keep creating and accepting fun, playful invitations with others, whether it be at home, work, school, or at play. Because it is all can be play.

Unclear Agreements Result in Assumptions

Have you found yourself getting upset with someone because you assumed he or she should know what you are thinking or anticipate your needs and wants? I have. It's easy to assume with a spouse, significant other, or friend we have known for a long time. And if we don't get our needs fulfilled, especially after not clearly asking for what we want, then we may find ourselves stewing over it.

Frequently, it is a result of not having clear invitations and agreements with others close to us. Musical artist Sonya Teclai said, "Rarely have I witnessed assumptions turn into facts." When we communicate clearly with others, we turn on the light switch to success. And if we don't know what is true about ourselves, others, or a situation in our lives, it is easy to travel down the road of assumption that ultimately may get us into trouble or reach a dead end.

> After an argument, silence may mean acceptance or the continuation of resistance by other means.
>
> Mason Cooley

Assumptions, which are essentially unspoken ideas that may not be agreements, are poisonous for relationships. When we believe something without knowing it is valid, it has the ability to destroy a relationship. "You should know this already about me" is a common assumption in an intimate relationship. Or we may think that it is unnecessary to nurture and feed our relationships with those close to us. When we stop nurturing a relationship, it will surely wither and die, much like a plant will shrivel when it does not receive daily water, sunshine, and food.

Maintaining that sense of discovery, the vibrant curiosity, and the presence to ask questions is how our Divine Child inside can not only save us but leads us to greater success. Integrity is about aligning our actions with our spiritual qualities. As Bob Marley said, "The greatness of a man is not in how much wealth he acquires, but in his integrity and his ability to affect those around him positively."

Where Acceptance and its Negative Expressions Reside

The term "acceptance" has been especially popular in recent articles, books, and other literature especially within the last 75 years. This dramatic surge in public interest is not surprising, given that the energy of acceptance is connected to the Heart Chakra, the fourth energy center in the body that became globally activated on the planet around the 1940s. The energies of love, compassion, and acceptance ballooned globally with this activation, pulling humanity's attention towards these spiritual qualities when the Information Age was born.

These matters of the heart are associated with being in the present moment, which is how our Divine Child helps us to thrive in the state of acceptance. This is the place of courage, where our inner child plays fearlessly in the present. Living in the past is a waste of time, because projecting into the future from a place of fear leads to anxiety — a rampant disease that plagues many adults and teenagers alike.

Living in a natural state of acceptance is what keeps us present and centered. It is also what alleviates stress and banishes fear. When we accept our present conditions, we learn and grow, taking that wisdom to create something even more powerful that takes us closer to our dreams and heartfelt goals.

Another dark expression that opposes acceptance is denial, where we refuse to look at and accept what is true — especially when it is about ourselves. If we deny and avoid looking at what is true, we cannot heal from our past wounds. Instead, we will distract ourselves in every way imaginable, whether it be through chatter on social media, virtual or real sexual encounters, using alcohol or other drugs, or addiction to shopping. Religion or other strong ideologies can also be a form of escape, in which we flee from the real world into an imagined utopia.

Denial shuts down the curious, adventurous, joyful energy of the Divine Child that seeks to discover what is always true. When you meet someone who is in denial, just know that that person is suffering from past trauma that was likely inflicted upon him or her.

> Marriage equality is about more than just marriage. It's about something greater. It's about acceptance.
>
> Charlize Theron

The Heart Chakra is usually the first place that closes when we have been traumatized, because closing our hearts is an unconscious way of protecting ourselves from pain. But being closed also means that receiving the good things in life, including the love, compassion, and nurturing from another, is far more difficult and unlikely to achieve.

Gratitude brings us the good things in life by attracting joy, prosperity, and happiness. Best-selling author Melody Beattie, who wrote *Codependent No More*, *The Language of Letting Go*, *Playing It by Heart*, and *Denial*, said, "Gratitude unlocks the fullness of life. It turns what we have into enough, and more. It turns denial into acceptance, chaos to order, confusion to clarity. It can turn a meal into a feast, a house into a home, a stranger into a friend."

To be clear, accepting what is present does not necessarily mean we want to spend time with everyone simply because we accept them. Especially in the case of those who are continually abusive — either physically, emotionally, mentally, or spiritually — it is critical we leave those people until they largely heal their trauma and refrain from projecting their trauma and abuse onto others. Even when someone causes harm subconsciously, we still feel those harms. Always remember how unique, precious, and special you truly are. Preserve your energy as sacred, for it is your destiny to bless the world with your unique talents and amazing gifts.

> You learned to run from what you feel, and that's why you have nightmares. To deny is to invite madness. To accept is to control.
>
> Megan Chance
> *The Spiritualist*

"Unconditional love and acceptance" is a popular catch phrase heralded by many spiritual thought leaders, religious enthusiasts, and pop psychologists alike. On the surface, the concept sounds nice, and we see this Hallmark greeting card phrase in books, too. But what is love and acceptance? What does this look like in action? American psychologist Albert Ellis said, "Acceptance is not love. You love a person because he or she has lovable traits, but you accept everybody just because they're alive and human."

This is the difference between love and acceptance, both of which are born out of truth. Not everyone has loveable traits, and some are downright toxic for you. So "loving everyone" is a simplistic and unlikely proposition. It just doesn't happen. Instead, agreements you make with people and keeping an open heart not only creates the space for resonance to occur, but it is the seat of truth and acceptance, which is the expression of love.

Another dark counter expression of acceptance is war. This destructive energy is contrary to our inner child, who knows instinctively how to create. Synthesis is the creative force in the world, bringing people together in commonality and purpose, while fighting separates people. As Sun Tzu, the Chinese military general, writer, and philosopher from the 6th century B.C., said, "The supreme art of war is to subdue the enemy without fighting."

Fighting for worthy causes is really about marching for spiritual values. The wars to defeat negativity never have worked, nor will they ever be effective in the long run. Negative breeds negativity, while moving forward with the vision of what we want takes us to higher ground.

The war on poverty, for example, has never solved anything. In their report "Changing Poverty, Changing Policies" published in 2009 by the Russell Sage Foundation, Maria Cancian and Sheldon Danziger wrote, "The official poverty rate in 1968 was 12.8 percent. The official measure roughly follows the business cycle and seems to never get solved: Poverty rose with the recession of the early 1980s, then declined during the improved economic times of the late 1980s. Poverty rose again in the downturn of the 1990s but declined during the economic boom. Poverty rates increased again in the recession of 2001."[1]

The war on hunger also has not improved the situation. A 2014 study revealed that one in five children in Chicago go hungry every day,[2] while one in six people in America faces hunger. In 2011, households with children reported a significantly higher lack of food rate than households without children: 20.6 percent vs. 12.2 percent.[3] According to the U.S. Department of Agriculture's Food and Nutrition Service data from 2010, "over 20 million children receive free or reduced-price lunch each school day. Less than half of them get breakfast, and only 10 percent have access to summer meal sites."[4] This is shameful for a nation with a military budget of $716 billion in 2019, making up 17 percent of the total $4 trillion budget.[5] The United States can project military power anywhere in the world, but it ignores hungry children on its own soil. If just a fraction of resources were more wisely spent, 49 million Americans would not be going hungry.

The war on drugs hasn't worked, either. The National Institute of Drug Abuse reports an explosion in national drug overdose deaths, soaring from 16,849 deaths in 1999 to 70,237 deaths in 2017. In the same time period, overdose deaths due to any opioid nearly 600 percent, and more than doubled to 47,600 deaths over the past four years alone.[6] On January 18, 2019, *The Washington Post* reported on the prescription drug epidemic, where overdose deaths by benzodiazepines soared ten-fold with 1,135 deaths in 1999 to 11,537 deaths in 2017.[7] Alcohol, the worst drug of all, kills more people than all other drugs combined, including pharmaceuticals. Approximately 27 percent of all U.S. adults reported engaging in binge drinking in the past 30 days, while 7 percent admitted to heavy drinking during the past month.[8] The social acceptability of alcohol abuse makes it even more difficult to combat, especially when drinking alcohol is glamorized in media.

> We think that fear must be played out in fight, with military intervention, or in flight, via isolationism — but we are not hunted game, and those are not the only options. There is also the possibility of acceptance, with its corollary of understanding and its ultimate manifestation in embracing.
>
> Andrew Solomon

The war on crime has made progress in certain areas, but not in others. The consecutive activation of the upper chakras during the past century — namely the Fourth Chakra in the 1940s, and the Fifth Chakra in the 1990s — accurately predicts that crime will move from the physical levels to the more ethereal levels, such as white-collar crimes. According to the Coalition Against Insurance Fraud (CAIF), insurance fraud is now the second largest criminal activity in the United States, costing Americans more than $80 billion each year[9] — which costs each family more than $1,000 each year in increased premiums, according to the FBI.[10]

Wire fraud and crimes related to computer viruses have both soared in the past 40 years. The FBI also reported that mortgage fraud is skyrocketing in the United States, with schemes including foreclosure rescue, loan modification, illegal property flipping, equity skimming, air loans, builder bailout in condo conversions, and other types of mortgage fraud. The agency reported dollar losses soared from $813 million in 2007 to more than $3 billion in 2011.[11]

Fighting to end something we don't want is loaded with negativity that is not in resonance with the Divine Child. Your inner child does not know about fighting, competition, or combat. It knows no war, but only peace and true connection. If we are not resonating with our authentic selves — the energy that lies deep inside each of us — solutions will surely evade us. As Carl Jung said, "Your vision will become clear only when you can look into your own heart. Who looks outside, dreams; who looks inside, awakens."

During my kung fu training in Detroit, I learned that "winning" is accomplished by using the partner's energy in the direction of his motion, not by resisting or combatting the opponent, such as in karate. The Bronze Age mentality of war and combat does not ultimately bring peace. The energy of war is intended to fight and kill, not bring resolution. British historian, mathematician, and philosopher Bertrand Russell said, "War does not determine who is right — only who is left."

This is what makes some martial arts so wonderful as a spiritual lesson, because the spiritual leader knows that fighting solves little to nothing but ends up taking everyone down. Acceptance means we have nothing to prove by winning over someone else, but to simply accept the truth of what is.

The moment trauma occurs, the "fight-flight-freeze" response usually is engaged usually with the instinct to pull back. This is natural evolution at work, where we instinctively fight the attacker, take flight, or freeze the moment we experience some sort of attack or harm, even if that trauma is on the invisible level that is not so easily seen.

The first two natural reactions — "fight or flight" — are more commonly discussed by trauma specialists and therapists. We became afraid, running from the source of trauma. Taking flight allows us to escape from what is causing us pain. It is like the child pulling its hand away from the stove the second it feels the painful burn.

Running away from abusive sources is often what many animal species do when they are under attack. In his book *Waking the Tiger: Healing Trauma* that discusses "somatic experiencing," author Peter Levine describes how many animals flee the moment they experience a life-threatening situation. Levine says that the final response to trauma in the chain of events is to "energetically release the trauma" by closing down for a while or shaking it off. After releasing the absorbed energy of attack and ensuing pain, the animal is able to move on.[12] When attacked by lions, for example, antelopes will instinctively flee and then literally shake for a while, which releases the negative energy that has accumulated as a result of the trauma.[13]

Another response to trauma is to fight, which comes also out of fear of some sort of pain. When our survival on some level is threatened, it can be our natural instinct to fight, especially if we become angry or enraged from the trauma. This is our survival instinct at play, which our ancestors learned over the course of millions of years of evolution. The tendency to fight may be embedded and then expressed in our DNA, as many studies suggest.

> Acceptance doesn't mean resignation; it means understanding that something is what it is and that there's got to be a way through it.
>
> Michael J. Fox

In a study published in April 2018 in the journal PLoS Genetics, a team of Korean and American researchers revealed distinct differences in "battle-ready" human and chimpanzees, compared to our more peaceful primate relatives, the bonobos and Rhesus macaques.[14] The research revealed that the tendency to fight seen in humans and chimpanzees is exhibited in a lower expression of the gene called ADRA2C, which helps inhibit the fight-or-flight response. Subsequently, the sympathetic nervous system in humans shifts resources to attacking or running away, including increasing the breathing rate, elevating the pulse, and creating a tunnel vision effect that focuses on seeing what is directly in front of you.[15] In short, humans and chimps are physiologically prepared to launch into battle, versus the calmer macaques and bonobos primates.

Walter Bradford Cannon, M.D., a physiologist at Harvard Medical School, first coined the phrase "fight or flight" in 1915 to describe an animal's response to threats.[16] The third reaction called "freeze," which has more recently emerged among psychologists, is similar to the proverbial "deer in the headlights" phenomenon, which is quite literal and real.

Why do many of us stay in abusive situations, where we are victims of attacks by our so-called "loved ones"? When we become repeatedly traumatized in intimate relationships, even in a close friendship, family relationships, or work relationships, most of us end up freezing, as we become too attached to abuse that has become normalized.

Freezing is the reaction that most people seem to spontaneously experience after trauma. Frozen inside, the Wounded Child takes over, where it is difficult for our Adult part to take responsibility to get us out of an unhealthy condition. Consequently, we become unable to move and take positive action, remaining in a state of numbness, unable to feel, see, and experience our lives as they truly are. Acceptance is not possible in this frozen state, where truth and reality escape us with our blurred vision. When abuse has been going on for a while, it becomes cyclical, then frequently normalized.

We often make excuses on behalf of abusers for their toxic behaviors, where we end up living in codependent relationships marked by woundedness projected onto others. In this frozen state, we may try hard to change the other person, blaming them for our "bad" relationship. We may say, "If only he or she would change, then everything would be great in our relationship." But in truth, we have not accepted that we, too, are wounded. Our own Divine Child has been damaged and is now crying for help and healing.

Because we have not arrived at a place of acceptance and truth, we remain blind to what is happening, afraid of admitting to ourselves the truth of what is or what happened to us. Taking necessary action, including walking away from the abuser so that we can finally heal, feels scary, too. In our frozen state, we remain stuck.

Reactivate Acceptance

Our Wounded Child may have difficulty accepting reality due to being numbed. Regardless of our past, however painful and deep, we can heal trauma that was inflicted upon us and rise above our negative past. Best-selling author Sarah Ban Breathnach wrote, "Pain is part of the past. There isn't one of us who doesn't still carry childhood wounds. Some are more horrific than others, but no matter how painful your young memories are, there were also glorious moments that kept you alive, or you would not be here today."

As long as we remain open to learning and discovering what is true, we can move forward. Opening our hearts means we are becoming aware of what is true. Remembering who we are as a Divine Child means that we remove the roadblocks that prevent us from seeing our reality. Maria Erving said, "The awakening process is not about 'finding who you are' but more about finding out about the ego, about who you are not." Learning about our wounded nature is an important part of our healing journey.

To rediscover the power of acceptance, the following suggestions may be helpful:

- Practice focusing on solutions instead of the problem. Complaining does not help. Brainstorming solutions and taking action moves us forward in positive directions. When we define the problem and accept the challenges we currently face, it opens up a world of immense possibilities. Acceptance is the gateway to the Universe of answers.

- Practice letting go…differently. Let's face it. It isn't always easy "letting go" of something that is difficult. Part of the answer is to stop thinking about the problem, and begin to ask your Higher Self, your spiritual helpers, your Higher Power, or whoever or whatever you find that helps you along your journey to answer this question: "What possibilities are out there that can solve this challenge in the best possible ways for all involved?" Keep asking that, letting go of initially judging what ideas may come to you. Sometimes asking this question just before you fall asleep can be effective. Allow the answers to come during the night, upon awakening, and throughout the following day, writing down what comes to you. Keep asking and inquire from those close to you who may be able to help.

> If you want to forget something or someone, never hate it, or never hate him or her. Everything and everyone that you hate is engraved upon your heart; if you want to let go of something, if you want to forget, you cannot hate.
>
> C. Joybell C.

- Embrace the beauty around you and within you. Our survival mode can easily take our focus from what is working to what isn't working. A negative mindset triggers the alarm bells inside, bringing our awareness to the problems and difficulties we may be experiencing in the moment. Take the precious time to walk outside in nature. Turn off your cell phone. This is your valuable time to commune with yourself and with the healing power of nature. Practice silence. Close your eyes and look toward the sun, smiling at it. Feel the wind flowing across your face and listen to the sounds that nature sends your way. See the inner beauty and power of who you are. The best time to acknowledge your gifts is when you can anchor them in during positive emotional experiences, such as walking in nature. It is a wonderful time to think about your past successes and what gifts you bring to everyone around you. Know that you are deeply connected to the magic and power of the Universe that can bring you an infinite number of possibilities to every challenge you may face. Create the daily habit of connecting to the rich well of these vast resources that are available to you now.

- Engage your curiosity. As adults, it is easy to think that because we have finished formal schooling, we no longer are learning. Achieving our dreams and goals, however, requires continuous learning in the school of the Universe. When your Divine Child is actively engaged, boredom will be a foreign concept. In every moment, everything and everyone can teach you something valuable and fascinating. Remain curious by asking yourself, "What can I learn in this moment right now?" Stay in this playful, adventurous mindset that brings you more joy. Everyone is your teacher, and everyone is your student. Become insatiably curious about others and yourself.

- Acknowledge what is difficult to accept. Especially what isn't easy to accept about yourself. When we refuse to acknowledge our weaknesses and the dark shadows of ourselves, we stunt our own growth, caught in the confines of our self-created limitations. However, the moment we accept ourselves as we are, embracing ourselves fully, we take away the negative power of anything that is dark and needs to be healed. This is the secret to healing, growing, and achieving. Barriers become much smaller when we define and name them, diminishing the fear of what is unknown.

- Dig deep to heal your past trauma. Begin with the thing that bothers you the most or is the biggest barrier to your success. If you look back on your struggles, you may notice the patterns. Keep learning about what it is that you can do to heal yourself. After studying a number of healing modalities over the past 30 years, I personally find EFT Tapping to be one of the easiest and most effective ways to heal any problem in your life, whether it is a physical issue, emotional problem, mental dilemma, or spiritual difficulty you are experiencing. Tapping properly with an experienced practitioner is a way to open up the doors to awareness and learning, while balancing the energies within yourself. It is the gateway to connecting to the Universe of possibilities, shining the light of hope in the darkness of despair and negativity. "Knock, and the door shall be opened to you."

Acceptance is about keeping an open mind, an expansive heart, and an adventurous attitude of discovery. Learning is the path to acceptance, freedom, and success. In our search to find out what is true about a challenge, we can breathe a sigh of relief and take positive action. The discovery of the world first begins within us. "Knowing yourself is the beginning of all wisdom," Aristotle said.

In our acceptance of what is — our present circumstances, our strengths, weaknesses, shadows, and the light and power of our individuality — we can embrace ourselves fully. Our energy can then be focused on what we can achieve, and how we can share our 21 gifts with others to light up the world.

Discovery and acceptance keep us intimately connected to ourselves and to the hearts of others. In a state of acceptance, we readily see another powerful spiritual characteristic that our precious little teachers show us. The renowned soccer player Julie Foudy may have said it best, "With acceptance comes opportunities. And with opportunities come numbers and, most importantly, hope."

---

[1] https://www.ssc.wisc.edu/~gwallace/Papers/Meyer%20and%20Wallace%20(2009).pdf

[2] https://chicago.cbslocal.com/2014/04/21/1-in-5-children-at-risk-of-hunger-in-cook-county/

[3] Feeding America. "Map the Meal Gap: Child Food Insecurity 2011." Feeding America, 2011. Web Accessed July 22, 2014.

[4] https://www.dosomething.org/us/facts/11-facts-about-hunger-us#fn7

[5] https://www.washingtonpost.com/news/wonk/wp/2018/06/19/u-s-military-budget-inches-closer-to-1-trillion-mark-as-concerns-over-federal-deficit-grow/?noredirect=on&utm_term=.32742502f377

[6] https://www.drugabuse.gov/related-topics/trends-statistics/overdose-death-rates

[7] https://www.washingtonpost.com/business/2019/01/18/prescription-drug-epidemic-no-ones-talking-about/?noredirect=on&utm_term=.ab3648c5e8de

[8] https://www.verywellmind.com/prevalence-of-alcoholism-in-the-united-states-67876

[9] http://www.insurancefraud.org/80-billion.htm

[10] https://www.fbi.gov/stats-services/publications/insurance-fraud

[11] https://www.fbi.gov/stats-services/publications/financial-crimes-report-2010-2011

[12] http://helphealingtrauma.com/2011/03/13/waking-the-tiger-healing-trauma/.

[13] https://www.everydayhealth.com/columns/therese-borchard-sanity-break/10-quick-ways-to-calm-down/

[14] https://journals.plos.org/plosgenetics/article?id=10.1371%2Fjournal.pgen.1007311

[15] https://www.inverse.com/article/43910-chimp-human-fight-war-evolution

[16] https://home.cc.umanitoba.ca/~berczii/hans-selye/walter-cannon-fight-or-flight-response.html

Hopeful

> Infuse your life with action. Don't wait for it to happen. Make it happen. Make your own future. Make your own hope. Make your own love. And whatever your beliefs, honor your creator, not by passively waiting for grace to come down from upon high, but by doing what you can to make grace happen... yourself, right now, right down here on Earth.
>
> Bradley Whitford

Hope recognizes that *you* are the creator of your life. When you have hope, you take action. Like love, hope involves action on our part. You must keep reaching for your heartfelt dream. It usually requires a little more elbow grease, accompanied with the open attitude knowing there are infinite possibilities and solutions. "A little more persistence, a little more effort, and what seemed hopeless failure may turn to glorious success," Elbert Hubbard said.

Whenever a small child walks up to a barrier, the child tries to find a way through it, over it, or around it. Obstacles and walls are not symbols of defeat for our tiny teachers. They become even more curious about the wall, determined to learn more about it. Occasionally, the child may cry or ask for help, gathering support for its adventures in the present moment.

Keep the bright flames of hope alive in your soul and spirit. The Buddhist monk and author Thich Nhat Hanh wrote, "Hope is important because it can make the present moment less difficult to bear. If we believe that tomorrow will be better, we can bear a hardship today." A positive attitude will remind yourself that regardless of your circumstances, the solution may be easier than you might think.

Keep knocking on the doors and asking for what you need, as many of the great masters have taught. Small children are especially good at economically preserving their energy, never seeking more than what they need. An intuitive approach focuses their energies on the present moment — the only true reality that exists. The future is faint, and the past is but a memory. But the present is where hope lies, from which we can draw the rich resources of the Universe that enliven our adventurous journey of discovery.

Like all of our 21 gifts, hope connects us to all of humanity. Nelson Mandela said, "Our human compassion binds us the one to the other — not in pity or patronizingly, but as human beings who have learnt how to turn our common suffering into hope for the future." When we are able to connect to others in synchronicity, it opens up new doorways of opportunity that surpass our greatest expectations.

> We must accept finite disappointment, but never lose infinite hope.
>
> Martin Luther King, Jr.

Being hopeful is not just about trying to achieve your goals and heartfelt dreams. Those are a side show. The true purpose in life is foremost about transforming yourself. This is the path of the self-actualizing leader — the person who looks at his or her life, makes authentic and candid self-assessments, and takes action to improve. "I always hope to be a better person tomorrow than today," Mahershala Ali said.

Small Children Are Naturally Hopeful and Optimistic

Research shows that children have a bias for hope and optimism. Janet Boseovski, Associate Professor of Psychology at the University of North Carolina, says that psychologists aren't exactly certain why kids are so optimistic. While adults may have more of a tendency to judge someone's character, young children are much less cautious about making such character judgments. Small kids tend to focus on positive actions or selectively process information that promotes positive judgments about themselves, others, or animals and objects.[1]

Boseovski cites a key study that confirms even preschoolers can tell the difference between experts and non-experts, and these young children can track the accuracy of people to decide whether they can be trusted as learning sources. She and her colleagues also found that children ages three to six only need one positive behavior to decide that a story character is nice but need to see several negative behaviors to assess that a character is mean.

Their research also found that children ages six and seven trusted a non-expert who gave positive descriptions, but disregarded negative descriptions by an expert, such as a zookeeper who described an unfamiliar animal as being "dangerous." Another study published in August 2017 in the journal Social Development confirmed the same positive outlook by small children, who mistrusted an expert's negative judgment of artwork but instead trusted a group of laypeople who assessed the art as positive.[2]

> Hope is like the sun, which, as we journey toward it, casts the shadow of our burden behind us.
>
> Samuel Smiles

Hope and positivity are engrained in the spiritual DNA of children. Their bias for optimism is present as early as 3 years of age, and research also reveals that it weakens in late childhood. Studies suggest that trauma from harsher realities and negative experiences, such as bullying, dampen a child's optimism. But when youngsters understand that negative feedback is more improvement-focused and intended to be helpful, they are more willing to accept negative evaluations and remain more optimistic.[3]

Research also shows that the bias for positivity in children opens them up to try new things fearlessly. A positive and courageous approach also helps young children to transition more successfully through school and achieve greater social success as well.[4] Carol Dweck, Professor of Psychology at Stanford University and author of *Mindset: The New Psychology of Success*, points out that kids also benefit more when teachers and parents emphasize the process of learning rather than achievement.[5] This research underscores the natural connection between hope and young children, who are drawn more naturally to being in the flow of the present moment, and less to achieving a specific outcome — a learned trait that is associated more with adults.

Where Hope and its Negative Expressions Reside

While we may not know yet exactly why small children have a natural optimism and a hopeful outlook, we can learn from our tiny teachers to filter out the negative and gravitate towards the positive. Examining what supercharges the body may be the key to understanding why children hope, effortlessly and naturally. As the words subscribed to Jesus suggest, small children hold the answers for "entering the kingdom" — the land of true abundance, spiritual wealth, and ultimate success. By knowing that all things are possible, which is the essence of hope, we tap into the vast resources of the Universe that are available to us, whether we see them or not.

Famed architect Frank Lloyd Wright said, "The present is the ever-moving shadow that divides yesterday from tomorrow. In that lies hope." Hope is connected to the Crown Chakra, the source that connects us to the infinite field of pure potentiality. To be effective, hope requires that we live in the present. Deepak Chopra, the medical doctor and best-selling author on alternative medicine and spirituality, wrote that the first spiritual law of yoga — the Law of Pure Potentiality — is the realm of awareness that leads to infinite possibilities.[6] A theist or deist point of view might suggest that the Crown Chakra connects us to the pure essence of God.

> Hope is the thing with feathers that perches in the soul — and sings the tunes without the words — and never stops at all.
>
> Emily Dickinson

The Crown center gives us hope, knowing that all things are possible in every given moment. It is the constant river of optimism, not blind faith, that feeds the Divine Child within us. When we tap into this knowingness seen at the quantum level of science, we connect to the place where miracles can occur. Everything in the Universe has a profound dual quality about its nature, expressed as both a particle and energy wave simultaneously. The character Eleuth in Greg Bear's fantasy duology, *The Infinity Concerto* and *The Serpent Mage*, poetically describes the mystery and magic of quantum physics when she says, "All is waves, with nothing waving, over no distance at all."[7]

Before bringing a beetle from Earth back to the Realm, Eleuth continues, "The Sidhe part of a Breed knows instinctively that any world is just a song of addings and takings away. To do grand magic, you must be completely in tune with the world — adding when the world adds, taking away when the world takes away."[8] Real power spontaneously unfolds when we are in resonance with the magic of the Universe.

By connecting to the Crown, we are transported to the portal of enchantment, the place of hope, optimism, and infectious enthusiasm that ignites our dreams and goals. The infinite resources that are available to you start at the energetic and spiritual levels, not by first seeking the material resources you need. Values are what drive every successful company and every achieving leader. Spiritual gold is the underlying force that launches great kingdoms, after the kingdom inside of you has been discovered and realized.

The other spiritual gateway to this magical experience is the Heart, the energy center that connects us to all of humanity and nature in more physical ways, versus the Crown Chakra that connects us in a spiritual or energetic way. The Heart Chakra bridges the spiritual and physical worlds, as seen in the archetype of the Vitruvian Man that was first created by the ancient Egyptian temple masters, developed by the Roman master architect Marcus Vitruvius Pollio, and later studied and elaborated on by the great master inventor and artist Leonardo da Vinci.

> There was never a night or a problem that could defeat sunrise or hope.
>
> Bernard Williams

Today, scientists at the HeartMath Institute are conducting profound research that examines the powerful ability of the Heart center to connect us to everyone and everything. Their Global Coherence Research project, started in 2008, is carefully studying the human-earth interconnectivity, using a global network of 12 ultrasensitive magnetic field detectors specifically designed to measure the earth's magnetic resonances. The science-based, co-creative initiative to examine heart-focused care involving more than 160,000 people in 154 countries uses devices to measure both planetary magnetic and energetic fields to demonstrate how they affect human and animal health, emotions, and behavior.[9]

Their research during the past decade shows that each individual affects the "global information field," which I believe connects to not only the Heart Chakra, but also the Crown Chakra. This groundbreaking research is confirming that "information is communicated nonlocally between people at a subconscious level, which, in effect, links all living systems and influences collective consciousness."[10]

The Negative Expressions of Hope

When hope has been damaged, it shows up as despair. This occurs after being traumatized as a child, usually by parents, research shows. They did not intend to hurt you, as psychologist Mark Wolynn points out in his award-winning book *It Didn't Start with You: How Inherited Family Trauma Shapes Who We Are and How to End the Cycle*. He describes how inherited family trauma gets passed down through the DNA. Inherited traits and even behaviors are transferred literally and physically, not just in a spiritual or energetic sense.

Not only does early trauma that your parents experienced gets embedded into your genetic code before you were born, but research also demonstrates how this epigenetic phenomenon generationally passes down trauma that occurred with your predecessors, as much as several generations or more before you. Subsequently, we can unconsciously reenact the same kind of trauma experienced by our grandparents, great-grandparents, and so on. This is why knowing what happened in your family history can be helpful to learning about your healing journey, where you can discover why you are subconsciously acting out trauma, even though there may not be any apparent cause.

Research also reveals that those who have harmed us usually aren't aware of it. Inflicting wounds is usually an unconscious act of projection. As long as the origins of our trauma remain unhealed, we continue projecting, where our energy is spent repeating our wounded behaviors in a trauma cycle to many others in our lives. It adversely impacts not only us, but negatively affects our intimate relationships, friendships, finances, and work relationships, creating a domino effect.

Adults unwittingly crush hope in children and dampen their enthusiasm. One of my clients said that she would daydream a lot. Transfixed by something in her environment, she would become lost in it, completely absorbed by staring at it and experiencing it fully. But a number of her family members would make fun of her, telling her to "keep on dreaming" in a mocking tone, or that "you are just a dreamer."

She felt so hurt by that, recalling feeling deflated and saddened whenever they said this. Eventually, she discovered that she had unconsciously *normalized* the subtle spiritual abuse by others over the years, partly due to the cultural mantras of "it's my family" and "blood runs thicker than water." Sometimes on her family vacations to Walt Disney World, for example, she would be caught up in a reverie, entranced by the rollercoasters. When she awakened from her dream state, her family was gone, where they had abandoned her and left her behind. She was not even ten years old, and the trauma cycle had already begun to repeat itself.

In the long run, however, she learned to pick herself up and brush off that dream-killing energy. She also discovered the importance of staying away from those who subconsciously wished rain on her parade, as misery seeks to find company. The phenomenon of resonance is why energy is so contagious.

Children dream big, until the point that someone tells them to stop doing so. "Hope is a waking dream," said Aristotle. Youngsters dream of being astronauts, veterinarians, firemen, and fashion designers. They practice caring for animals and each other, applying band-aids to wounds and their healing touch to a little injury. Small kids make delectable mud pies, serving up creative slices to their guests. When our tiny teachers dream, they dream big. "Where there is no vision, there is no hope," wrote George Washington Carver, the prominent black scientist who taught botany and agriculture to the children of former slaves.

Every person who dreams big has people in their lives who will second guess and naysay their ideas. If we allow our sandboxes to get dirty from human spoilers, it contaminates and clouds our dreams. Our sense of hope and optimism becomes traumatized by energy vampires around us, unwittingly spreading their toxic energy. Their Wounded Child is simply projecting at an unconscious level to others, where unhealed woundedness generates envy, jealousy, and scorn.

To stop patterns of abuse, it is essential to communicate what abusers are doing to you and how you were hurt as a result of their behaviors. The far majority of them are completely unaware of what they are doing, because they likely had their dreams also stomped by their own parents, siblings, friends, and teachers. Giving the gift of awareness to those who have harmed you is vital. Confronting abusers kindly is a way to say "No" to trauma, and "Yes" to connection, healing, and progress. Otherwise, abusers may never know what they did, and the trauma cycle continues for everyone involved.

Maintain a healthy distance between yourself and habitually negative people. Their toxic energy will only leave you feeling badly in the long run, even if their negativity is disguised as fun or a joke. The party pooper who is the first to tell you about who is sick or dying will traumatize hope and optimism within your Divine Child. Negative cycles are spiritual cancer, which will spread to you if you don't protect yourself by loving the energy vampires in your life at a distance.

> Optimism is the faith that leads to achievement. Nothing can be done without hope and confidence.
>
> Helen Keller

These are the ones who often figure out why something won't work, or what is wrong about a situation, instead of saying, "Let's work together to find a way…and we will." The naysayer says "stop" instead of "go," and "no" instead of "yes." They will continually oppose you, exhausting you physically, emotionally, mentally, and spiritually. Say "yes" by getting them out of your sandbox or go find other playmates who will support your hopes, dreams, and wishes.

Surround yourself with the cheerleaders in your life. They are the ones who consistently look for what is beautiful and unique in you, rather than what is wrong and needs to be fixed. Your best cheerleaders will also alert you when you may not see something in your life that you need to shift. *Looking at what isn't working in your life is as important as focusing on what is working well.*

While chronically negative people are spiritual poison, your cheerleaders and supporters see your extraordinary gifts and share opportunities for positive experiences. The cheerleaders in your life simply feel good to your inner child, who will always instinctively know the difference. Practice tuning in and listening to your body, noticing what your gut is telling you. If you tune in properly and keep this intuitive energy alive and fully functioning, the powerful inner voice of your Divine Child will never lead you astray.

The Most Widespread Disease in the World

The biggest disease on the planet is not heart disease, cancer, or diabetes. Those physical diseases are merely symptomatic of a far greater problem that plagues humans on the spiritual level: a sense of unworthiness. When children have experienced early trauma, it deflates hope. When the wounded child becomes an adult, the fear of public speaking can emerge, for example, where the wounded individual mistakenly believes that people will not accept him or her.

The sense of not being worthy of love and acceptance leads to dysfunctional relationships, where a Wounded Child finds himself or herself in a relationship with another Wounded Child. When the Wounded Child is hollering and acting out, it is difficult for the Adults to take action when needed. And when the Wounded Child is in charge, success and happiness become virtually impossible to attain, as trauma cycles tend to pull us back into negativity.

People who suffer from chronic unworthiness will often manifest this in their Heart Chakras as deep grief, sadness, a sense of emptiness, or depression. Having lost touch with their passion, they may suffer from frequent boredom. The sense of adventure, curiosity, and playfulness turns into restlessness and distraction, where this type of Wounded Child is seduced by momentary pleasures that later come crashing down. The cycle of boredom, distraction, pleasure, and emptiness repeats.

When we lose hope in ourselves, believing that we are broken, shame emerges. When people step on our natural optimism, we begin buying into the false idea that we are also limited in some way. Then we start making excuses about why we cannot do something or achieve a dream. "I'll do this after A, B, and C happens," we may say. This is where despair can turn into hopelessness and depression.

I worked with one client, "Rachel," who had a chronic condition of unworthiness. She was overweight most of her adult life, making excuse after excuse about why she couldn't lose the excess fat, or setting up conditions for herself. "When I lose 30 pounds, then I'll buy some new clothes." But her feelings of unworthiness stopped her from buying new clothes for herself, even though she could well afford it. Rachel was financially wealthy, but spiritual poor.

Victims of past abuse will begin abusing themselves. It's a way of reinforcing and proving to themselves that they are not worthy. She abused herself daily, talking on the phone on most days with her negative mother, who "vomited in her ear" by complaining about how miserable her life has always been. This went on for many years. Rachel also abused herself by stuffing down her emotions of pain, sadness, and grief, leaving her chronically depressed and enraged inside. With feelings of helplessness and desperately unworthy, her Wounded Child was in charge.

Essentially, she was punishing herself by establishing small rewards connected to nearly insurmountable tasks, which were never achieved. When she began loving herself more fully and unconditionally treating herself to new clothes, she shifted the internal self-dialogue that continually sent out a new, clear message: "I am worthy of wonderful things, despite my outer circumstances." And the excess pounds began to melt away, especially after she divorced her husband who felt threatened by other men who found her attractive, rather than celebrating her beauty.

Until the victim decides *enough is enough* and breaks away from the chronically negative abusers, it is difficult for her to heal. Subsequently, the victim will unconsciously spread the unhealed inherited family trauma to her children, future generations, and even friends. Abuse on this level closes the Crown and Heart Chakras that keeps the Divine Child healthy, happy, and functioning. To the toxic people in our lives, we can say, "I love you...at a distance."

No therapist will rescue you. No savior can offer you salvation from this trauma. Just as the slaves fled the plantations from their oppressors to freedom, walking out the door is the first step to reclaiming your beautiful, magnificent self when you are faced with a chronic abuser in your life. What are you willing to do to experience your own freedom and live in a place of hope, optimism, and joy? When we experience difficulty in our lives, the choice is ours which path we will take. The Dalai Lama said, "When we meet real tragedy in life, we can react in two ways — either by losing hope and falling into self-destructive habits, or by using the challenge to find our inner strength. Thanks to the teachings of Buddha, I have been able to take this second way."

Protect Your Spiritual Gold

Your cherished dreams and goals are precious. Hold them close to your vest, sharing them only with those who are the cheerleaders in your life — those who truly support you and can help you turn them into reality. With poetic splendor, Charlotte Bronte wrote:

> The human heart has hidden treasures
> In secret kept, in silence sealed;
> The thoughts, the hopes, the dreams, the pleasures,
> Whose charms were broken if revealed.

Sharing your hopes and wishes is a sacred journey, one to be taken your cheerleaders who support you and empower you. Avoid giving away your secret treasures by sharing them on social media or with untrustworthy people who do not support you. The world is full of dream stealers, naysayers, and energy vampires who will attack you at the psychic level, unconsciously projecting their jealousy, envy, or contempt.

Your spiritual gold must be protected from negativity on a daily basis, safeguarding these energetic assets as the foundation for your hopes and dreams. Do you want to give that away to just anyone? Even so-called friends may try to rain on your parade, usually unknowingly. Keep your dreams shielded from fair-weather friends who do not support you along your journey, for true friends are few.

Many families have issues with betrayal, jealousy, or envy, where these get projected onto a child, sibling, or extended family member who then becomes the victim that carries the trauma cycle passed down in the family. Do not share the golden treasures of your dreams with family members just because they are family, for some of them may betray you, too.

Ziad K. Abdelnour, author of *Economic Warfare: Secrets of Wealth Creation in the Age of Welfare Politics*, wrote, "Trust is earned, respect is given, and loyalty is demonstrated. Betrayal of any one of those is to lose all three." Make sure the people who are close to you have earned your trust with their solid track record of truth, authenticity, kindness, creativity, and support. If a family member or casual friend does not respect you, is not loyal to you, or consistently mistreats you, it is far better to keep him or her at arm's length. We must be wise about how we share our energy, especially our heartfelt goals and dreams. Your Divine Child needs the protection and support of your Divine Adult.

For the toxic people in your life, it is advisable to simply stick to discussing the weather, sharing recipes, and laughing at comic strips. But don't let them into your precious sandbox or tell them about your heartfelt dreams. I learned this lesson the hard way after decades of trusting people blindly, only to be repeatedly crushed. Have you experienced times when fake friends and fair-weathered family members unwittingly will show up during the good times, but abandon you when times are challenging?

Just say no. Learn when to walk away, as you say "Yes" to new possibilities. When someone generally delivers more toxic energy than beneficial energy to you, it's a clear signal to keep them at a distance or extract them from your life if the energy is that bad. When you practice intuition, you'll be able to quickly discern when these types of people don't feel good for you.

Listen to your Divine Child who is curious, playful, joyful, ever present, and highly observant. Your intuition will be a powerful guide, because it is part of your Divine Child that connects to the Universe filled with hope and possibility. An optimistic attitude is the joy of knowing that you can access endless possibilities now available to you. It requires the presence of your Divine Child, channeling that energy of curiosity, creativity, playfulness, expressiveness, and adventure into happy experiences. Joy is the barometer of the soul. When you live in this space, the bright, radiant energy of hope will transform yourself and everything around you.

Jonas Salk, the American medical researcher who developed one of the first successful polio vaccines, said, "Hope lies in dreams, in imagination, and in the courage of those who dare to make dreams into reality." The courage of your Divine Child knows no fear. When you live in your Divine Child energy, you will attract other courageous, hopeful, and optimistic Divine Children, where you can co-create magic with them.

Just keep moving forward and ask for what you need. Believing in yourself means that you know that all of this magic and power is inside of you — your abilities, your strengths, and even your wounded parts. Dig deep to discover everything about who you really are and what is true in your world. Heal any wounded aspects of yourself, as they only pull your energy down and distract you from your heartfelt dreams.

How to Supercharge Hope

Most of us struggle with hope. We have suffered from trauma from our parents, family members, so-called friends, coworkers, teachers, and false preachments. Usually, the trauma is passed to us unconsciously with no direct intention to harm us. Studies suggest that inherited family trauma is the most common method of transferring abuse that impact our physical, emotional, mental, and spiritual levels.

If you frequently find yourself suffering from sadness, pain, depression, negativity, lack of optimism, or hopelessness, you are likely a victim of past trauma where your sense of hope and optimism was likely suppressed or crushed at an early age. The moment that you become more aware of the connection to the original pain and trauma, know that the healing process has already begun and that you have access to the support that you need.

The easiest way that I know of to activate the potent energies of success from the Divine Child within yourself is by resonating with people and art that radiate the energies of the Divine Child. Energy is contagious: When you are around positive energies, you become them. Getting rid of the toxic sources from your life is the first step, however, either by removing yourself completely from the source of toxicity or separating yourself considerably from them.

> You may not always have a comfortable life, and you will not always be able to solve all of the world's problems at once. But don't ever underestimate the importance you can have, because history has shown us that courage can be contagious, and hope can take on a life of its own.
>
> Michelle Obama

Engaging these energies and magnifying them will accelerate your ability to attract better health, happier relationships, increased abundance, a greater sense of peace and harmony, and more joy. Here are some suggestions for reactivating the energies of hope, optimism, and healing that are already within you:

- Practice intuition. If you aren't able to trust your gut instincts, chances are your intuition was wounded when you were a small child. You may have learned to shut down and protect yourself, closing yourself off the energy that guides, protects you, and tells you when you are in resonance with someone who is there for you. Opening the gateway of your intuition allows you to tap into this valuable resource that allows you to quickly see who is toxic and who is more beneficial for you. Reactivate your intuition through daily silent meditation. Listen to your inner guidance, as little hunches, images, or feelings. Practice trusting these inner prompts each day.
- Realize that limitations are opportunities to transcend them. Many of our limitations are self-created. But sometimes life brings us challenges that seem insurmountable. Know that when you live with hope and optimism, you can create miracles in your life despite what life delivers you. Gabe Adams is evidence of that. Born with an extremely rare congenital defect called Hanhart syndrome that causes malformed arms and legs, Gabe was abandoned at birth in Brazil. Janelle and Ron Adams, who have 13 biological children of their own, adopted Gabe despite him having no arms or legs.[11] He hops into the shower, gets himself dressed, cooks, walks up and down the stairs without any legs, and even performs with a dance team, wowing audiences.[12] He is an inspiration for hope and optimism. I put a photo of Gabe in front of my office desk to

remind myself each day that I, too, can transcend any perceived limitation. Each day, you can practice visualizing yourself as an unstoppable force, moving through current challenges with greater ease.

- Surround yourself with happy people. I have spent decades trying to change chronically negative people in my life. It doesn't work. When I discovered that I kept *attracting* those people into my life, *I finally realized that I was toxic and negative. I was the problem.* It took getting away from those energy drains before I could heal myself. Being around continual negativity is the worst environment for healing. In fact, it may be nearly impossible to do your inner work and transformation if you are swimming in an energetic swamp. People change best by being around others who positively energize them, and so will you. Go into resonance with happiness by surrounding yourself with those who radiate the 21 gifts, and you will reactivate that happiness and joy within yourself, too.

> Stay positive and happy. Work hard and don't give up hope. Be open to criticism and keep learning. Surround yourself with happy, warm and genuine people.
>
> Tena Desae

- You become the company you maintain. If you are continually around people who are happy, you are likely a happier person. If you find yourself attracting negative people in your life, it is probably that you are negative yourself. Birds of a feather flock together. It is how the Law of Resonance operates. Look at whom you are surrounding yourself with. They are a reflection of you. If you need to do a "friends and family cleanse," do it. Like you remove poisons from your body, remove them from your "friends and family body," too. Remove the weeds in the garden of your life, getting rid of those things that bring you down. What are you hoping to gain from being around them? Maintain a healthy distance from those who drag you to a lower plane.
- Take a news break. News is another killer of hope and optimism, and most of it is mind chatter that distracts you from your life in the present moment. Comedian Tracy Morgan said, "Bad news travels at the speed

of light; good news travels like molasses." A 1997 study of three different segments of 14-minute news bulletins — one made entirely of positive news, the second was emotionally neutral, and the third segment consisted entirely of negative news — revealed that those watching the entire negative news segments were sadder and more anxious than the other two groups. Researchers learned that people who watch negative news begin to worry more and catastrophize,[13] as the watchers of negative news go into resonance with that energy.

A study published in 2015 in Harvard Business Review found that if people watch even three minutes of negative news, 27 percent of participants were more likely to be depressed for the next 6-8 hours of their day.[14] A recent survey from the American Psychological Association found that more than half of Americans say that the news causes them stress, where many report sleep loss, fatigue, or feeling anxious.

Graham Davey, professor emeritus of psychology at Sussex University in the UK and editor-in-chief of the *Journal of Experimental Psychopathology*, said, "The way that news is presented and the way that we access news has changed significantly over the last 15 to 20 years. These changes have often been detrimental to general mental health."[15] Davey says today's news is "increasingly visual and shocking," pointing to smart phone videos and audio clips as newer examples. He notes that these forms of online news media can cause symptoms of acute stress, such as problems sleeping, mood swings, aggressive behavior, and even PTSD.

> The more wonderful the means of communication, the more trivial, tawdry, or depressing its contents seemed to be.
>
> Arthur C. Clarke
> Science writer & futurist

What are you hoping to gain from watching the news? How is it serving you? Your life will go on if you skip it for a day or a week, and you will likely feel far better and more positive. Unless you plan to take action on it, such as join a local political action group or writing your congressperson, consider avoiding it for long periods of time — such as days or even weeks at a time with zero news.

See how you feel. It's like taking a vacation for your soul. Spending your energy and resources on things that take you in the direction of your hopes, dreams, and wishes, rather than the negative news of the past, will pay off.

One of my favorite songs of hope and inspiration is "Look to the Rainbow" sung by the late great Aretha Franklin, the queen of soul music. First released by Russ Case and His Orchestra with Audrey Marsh and the Guild Choristers in December 1946, this beautiful work has been recorded by many artists, including Dinah Washington, Patti LaBelle, The Mormon Tabernacle Choir, and Barry Manilow with Barbara Cook.

As a tribute to her late father, Reverend C.L. Franklin, Aretha shared the moving story about how her father once told her prophetically, "One day, you will sing for kings and queens." And she has ever since. While he influenced her singing style, her father also became her first manager before she turned 14, the stunning age when she released her first album "Songs of Faith," sparking her legendary music career that ignited the world.

This beautiful love poem is a story about hope. It's also a sweet reminder to find the cheerleaders in your life — those special people filled with optimism and hope who will support you on your sacred journey to realize your treasured dreams. May you find that special someone who lifts you up and continually shines the light that reveals how special and treasured you truly are:

> On the day I was born said my father, said he
> I've an elegant legacy waiting for ye
> 'Tis a rhyme for your lips and a song for your heart
> To sing whenever the world falls apart
> Look, look, look to the rainbow
> Follow it over the hill and stream
> Look, look, look to the rainbow
> Follow the fellow who follows a dream
> Follow the fellow, follow the fellow
> Follow the fellow who follows a dream.

---

[1] https://www.weforum.org/agenda/2018/04/children-are-natural-optimists-which-comes-with-psychological-pros-and-cons/

[2] IBID

[3] IBID

[4] https://www.jstor.org/stable/1130613?seq=1#page_scan_tab_contents

[5] https://www.penguinrandomhouse.com/books/44330/mindset-by-carol-s-dweck-phd/,

[6] https://www.yogitimes.com/article/deepak-chopra-law-of-pure-potentiality

[7] https://www.forbes.com/sites/chadorzel/2015/07/08/six-things-everyone-should-know-about-quantum-physics/#6cbb004f7d46

[8] *Songs of Earth and Power: The Complete Series* by Greg Bear. Chapter 22.

[9] https://www.heartmath.org/research/science-of-the-heart/global-coherence-research/

[10] IBID

[11] https://www.today.com/news/brave-teen-no-arms-or-legs-inspires-family-classmates-dance-t70771

[12] https://www.youtube.com/watch?v=Ur8_IUldv-I

[13] https://www.psychologytoday.com/us/blog/why-we-worry/201206/the-psychological-effects-tv-news

[14] https://medium.com/thrive-global/how-to-stay-informed-with-the-news-without-getting-depressed-67f135508a28

[15] https://www.psychologytoday.com/us/blog/why-we-worry/201206/the-psychological-effects-tv-news

Scapegoating: How Projecting Trauma Stops Success

> The search for a scapegoat is the easiest of all
> hunting expeditions.

> Dwight D. Eisenhower

In my experience, the number one reason why people have difficulty creating and attracting success is due to unconsciously projecting past traumas and even strengths onto others. This age-old tactic is an unconscious but popular way we avoid taking responsibility for our own actions, and even shrink away from sharing our 21 gifts and other talents with others.

Scapegoating is the act of shifting blame onto someone or something else, or to suffer in one's stead. In traditional psychology, the ego defense of displacement occurs, where the person projects uncomfortable feelings of anger, guilt, envy, shame, frustration, and insecurity to another person or group who is usually more vulnerable. Unprotected scapegoats, such as outsiders, minorities, or immigrants, are then persecuted, as the scapegoater is distracted from his or her negative feelings. The scapegoater likely displays self-righteous indignation, or feigned anger, as a result of not taking responsibility.[1]

The scapegoat usually will take the fall and be blamed for another's deeds. Both the scapegoater and the victim have Wounded Child aspects: The scapegoater doesn't accept responsibility for his or her actions, while the scapegoat is unable or unwilling to leave the state of victimhood and abuse. Fear often overtakes the scapegoat, who repeatedly carries the burden. Others in that tribe join in the game, allowing this form of spiritual abuse to happen, where some tribes even promote it. Thus, the trauma cycle is born, where the normalization of toxic behavior thrust upon the scapegoat becomes acceptable by everyone involved.

Families and tribes can have one or multiple scapegoats, the vulnerable victims selected to consistently blame for problems in the inherited family trauma structure. For example, if your brother drew on the walls with crayon, you might get blamed because you didn't stop him. Or it was your sister's job to take out the dog, which ended up making a mess in the living room, but you get faulted for not taking out the dog or cleaning up the mess.

The Origins of Scapegoating

The concept of "scapegoating" arose from Judeo-Christian texts, where the tribe ritualistically piled their sins onto a goat by symbolically strapping on sticks, stones, and other objects on the poor goat's back. The tribe would then drive that goat into the desert to suffer and die. Through the tremendous suffering of the goat, tribe members would be alleviated from the egregious actions they committed in attempts to purge themselves from the enormous guilt and shame born from their deeds.

For thousands of years, this barbaric, despicable practice was used in many tribal civilizations throughout the world. Seen in Levitical times, it may have been the earliest forms of mass projection promoted by religious practices: "And Aaron shall cast lots upon the two goats: one lot for the LORD, and the other lot for Azazel," says Leviticus 16:8. Other texts promote letting the goat loose in the wilderness on Yom Kippur.[2]

With fear, guilt, and deep shame embedded in ritualistic custom, many religious traditions have adopted the barbaric ideology of scapegoating, including Christianity, which is based on the central idea that Jesus died for our sins. However, it is interesting to note that there is not a shred of evidence that Jesus said he died for our sins.

The same story of vicarious redemption and profound denigration of women, who have been blamed by religion for original sin, is found in the Quran. According to Islam, blood sacrifice does not replace the necessity of repentance nor add to "Divine grace." However, sacrifice is done to help the poor and in remembrance of Abraham's willingness to sacrifice his son at God's command, where human sacrifice replaces the killing of innocent animals.

The Church of the Latter Day Saints includes this same Islamic and Judeo-Christian story in their religious texts as well, where Abraham's son, Isaac, asked where the lamb was for the sacrifice. Abraham told Isaac not to worry but proceeded to build an altar with wood. The grisly story of manipulation and human sacrifice to appease God continues, where Abraham ties up his son Isaac, places him on the altar, and holds a knife over Isaac to murder him.

This hideous tale of barbarism paves the way for ultimate form of scapegoating and human sacrifice, setting up the grand proclamation that God created his son Jesus to die for everybody's sins, as also described on the website of the Latter Day Saints: "Abraham was ready to sacrifice his son. But an angel spoke to Abraham. He told Abraham not to sacrifice Isaac. Abraham had obeyed God. God loved Abraham."[3]

Myth or reality, these ancient stories merge blind faith, loyalty to the point of extremism, and human sacrifice, culminating into a rather disturbing formula that bird, animal, and human sacrifice is not just permissible, but a direct commandment from an alleged "loving" deity given to its chosen people. Wrapping that into a book filled with other violent stories then labeling it as "holy" and "the unadulterated Word of God" is how dark spiritual legacies are born.

Human Scapegoating: The History of Human Sacrifice

Since the beginning of prehistoric man, the horrific practice of human sacrifice has occurred in at least 25 cultures around the world predominantly as a religious ritual to appease the gods. China has practiced human sacrifice for thousands of years, as archaeologists have found thousands of human sacrifices among the sites in the modern-day city Anyang that occurred during the Shang Dynasty (1600 to 1040 B.C.). The practice became rare or stopped by the time Qin Shi Huang, the first emperor of China, unified the country. His famed terracotta army made of thousands of life-size clay warriors allowed the emperor to take an army with him to the afterlife without sacrificing live warriors.[4]

The ancient city of Ur in modern-day Iraq contains the remains of 68 women and six men, many of whom appear to have been sacrificed around 4,600 years ago. Archeologists discovered that Native Americans sacrificed hundreds of people by malnourishment and clubbing them to death at Cahokia, a city that flourished from 1050 to 1200 A.D. near what is now St. Louis, Missouri.[5]

During the 15th century A.D., the Inca practiced child sacrifice, indicated by child mummies unearthed by archeologists near the remains of the shrine at Mount Llullaillaco, a 22,100-foot-tall active volcano that borders Chile and Argentina. Before being sacrificed, these children were fattened up with a llama meat and maize, then given maize beer and coca leaves before their deaths, likely to numb the victims before being cast to their perilous deaths.

The Maya people practiced human sacrifice in their temples at the ancient city of Chichen Itza. Even members of losing or winning teams from playing Maya ball games are believed to have been sacrificed, as noted on depictions of Mayan art, which is somewhat reminiscent of ancient Roman gladiator games. The Aztec civilization in Mexico also regularly sacrificed humans at temples, where remains of skull racks have been discovered at the Templo Mayor at Tenochtitlán.[6]

Hitobashira, the practice of human sacrifice that occurred for centuries in Japan, included kamikaze pilots who were ordered to crash their planes into Allied ships during World War II. Remains from human sacrifices have also been found within the walls and floors of castles and other important buildings constructed as early as 1576 A.D.

As a way for the elite to maintain control of the Hawaiian population, clubbing people to death on rocks was conducted on the islands as late as the 19th century. Archeologists have also found remains in temples built with altars from as early as 1300 A.D.

> It is ironic that the United States should have been founded by intellectuals, for throughout most of our political history, the intellectual has been for the most part either an outsider, a servant or a scapegoat.
>
> Richard Hofstadter
> American historian

The ancient Romans also are believed to have resorted to human sacrifice, as documented by a number of ancient writers that include Titus Livius, who died around 17 AD. Archeological remains and supporting texts indicate that the ancient Greeks practiced human sacrifice, especially with children, at least 3,000 years ago, including the discovery of skeleton of a male teenager at an altar dedicated to the god Zeus at Mount Lykaion in Greece.

Researchers debate how widely human sacrifice was practiced by rulers in the Western African kingdom of Dahomey between 1600 and 1894 A.D., when the French conquered the empire. Sati, an ancient Hindu ritual where a woman is coerced or chooses to leap into the funeral pyre of her husband after he has died, is outlawed in India today. However, on some occasions, it still occurs. In 2006, for example, BBC News reported that a woman in her forties leapt in the flames of the funeral pyre of her deceased husband.[7]

When the roots of such practices are entrenched in the soils of tainted spiritual practices and religions from early primitive cultures, those unhealed practices find their way into religious texts, only in much more sanitized and glamourized ways. The more recent religious texts from several thousand years ago arrived with fresh stories that link your ultimate redemption to animal and human sacrifice by instilling fear into the masses on a repetitive basis, teaching that you must love, respect, and serve the one who committed or commanded these atrocities.

> A scapegoat remains effective as long as we believe in its guilt.
>
> Rene Girard

Images in religious art compound this outrageous toxicity. Numerous religious paintings, for example, glamourize the suffering of sacrificial humans, birds, and animals with the suffering victims posed in adoration and glory, seeking to get followers to accept this ghastly practice rather than seeing the hateful projection of torture and unthinkable suffering for what it truly is. Why are we holding on to these highly toxic parts of our dark history?

This is not love and compassion. This is barbarous, immoral scapegoating that leads to negative and extreme outcomes.

We are better than this now. We are more evolved than our ancestors when we act out of our better nature. The disease of this cruel practice has spread globally and has become embedded in our books, our collective consciousness, and our lives. We must finally embrace the idea that no compassionate human being, let alone a "loving" deity, would ever allow this type of practice to be acceptable, let alone promote it by commandment. Only evil and barbaric men could fabricate such hideous stories that violate the Golden Rule and basic teachings of Jesus himself.

Vicarious redemption — throwing your sins onto someone else, whether bird, animal, friend, or stranger — is not love. It is an appalling projection and unhealed woundedness born in the Bronze Age era or prior, where the attempt to mitigate one's own responsibility for misbehavior leaves the victim traumatized and suffering in pain. In his book *Letters to a Young Contrarian*, Christopher Hitchens wrote:[8]

> I find something repulsive about the idea of vicarious redemption. I would not throw my numberless sins onto a scapegoat and expect them to pass from me; we rightly sneer at the barbaric societies that practice this unpleasantness in its literal form. There's no moral value in the vicarious gesture anyway. As Thomas Paine pointed out, you may if you wish take on another man's debt, or even to take his place in prison. That would be self-sacrificing. But you may not assume his actual crimes as if they were your own; for one thing you did not commit them and might have died rather than do so; for another this impossible action would rob him of individual responsibility. So the whole apparatus of absolution and forgiveness strikes me as positively immoral, while the concept of revealed truth degrades the concept of free intelligence by purportedly relieving us of the hard task of working out the ethical principles for ourselves.

We would readily dismiss any contemporary author suggesting a new practice that sacrifices birds, animals, or humans for our own absolution of guilt, loss, pain, and trauma that we have caused others. Parents would never allow these stories to be told in children's books, so why are churches still teaching kids and adults today that these ancient barbaric practices were commanded by loving deity?

Ancient practices of animal and human sacrifice, however endorsed and promoted by popular biblical scriptures and many religions, must likewise be treated with the same disdain and immediate, unequivocal rejection. Exploring the roots and extent of this primitive practice is required in order to completely uproot the embedded trauma that leads to more contemporary yet subtle forms of scapegoating, such as the denying a fellow human being safety, shelter, clothing, food, and water — or killing of millions in mass genocide, blaming them for being a different race, sex, sexual orientation, or color.

Scapegoating and projecting our own woundedness onto others have kept us trapped in our trauma cycles, where they have metastasized. It is a grave form of spiritual abuse that cascades to the mental, emotional, and physical levels when religious or political leaders continue to uphold the Bronze Age texts that promote these practices, labeling the texts as "holy." When embedded into the moral fabric of a culture, deep stains are much harder to remove from our cultural and individual DNA after thousands of years of repeated spiritual contamination.

> Not everyone has been a bully or the victim of bullies, but everyone has seen bullying, and seeing it, has responded to it by joining in or objecting, by laughing or keeping silent, by feeling disgusted or feeling interested.
>
> Octavia E. Butler

A reverse course of action must be taken to eradicate anything that resembles animal abuse or human sacrifice of any sort. To purge ourselves, educating our children of the dark, grisly history of animal and human sacrifice is essential. At the same time, we must collectively pronounce these barbaric, hideous practices as not only morally wrong, but agree that it has contributed to the widespread tragedies of mass genocide, barbaric imprisonment, and the unfathomable torture of millions by religious and political leaders.

The tragedy of inequality is perpetuated with even subtler forms of human sacrifice, such as the redistribution of wealth from the wallets of the poor and middle class into the coffers of the few modern political, institutional, and religious ruling empires. Indeed, the negative consequences of promoting animal and human sacrifice are far-reaching.

Forgiveness: Another Popular Form of Scapegoating

When we project our responsibility for our past negative actions onto others, we cannot heal our own trauma, and thus become stuck. To free ourselves, we must do the heavy spiritual lifting ourselves, as no goat murdered in the wilderness or savior allegedly dying on a cross 2,000 years ago for our wrongdoings will erase what harm we have done to others. And one must ask who died for everyone's sins before the alleged crucifixion of Jesus and the first sacrifice of birds and animals? To expect someone else to "forgive" our past and future transgressions is not only a ludicrous proposition, but spiritual laziness. We must do the work to atone for our mistakes and wrongdoings ourselves.

When we are encumbered with scapegoating, it is easy to forget the true teachings of Jesus, which was to treat others as you would like them to treat you. Human and animal sacrifice violates the Golden Rule taught by Jesus and other perennial philosophers, severely traumatizing our innate sense of equality for all. If we ignore personal accountability — a Divine Adult trait — the world becomes a darker place.

Indeed, projection is a process of denial and avoidance of our past pain and trauma. It occurs when we do not want to take responsibility for our own actions. We are afraid of experiencing our own pain and the suffering have we caused others. For the victims, it can also be difficult to face the perpetrators of abuse and hold them accountable. Projection is understandable, but a negative path.

Throughout history, we have blamed the gods and devils for our traumas: "The devil made me do it" or "it was God's will for this to happen," for instance, but who can proclaim to know the mind and will of any invisible deity? Religions, too, blame the victims for the trauma, labeling them as "sinners," such as a child born gay but is already condemned. It is nearly impossible to blame an invisible deity for our problems who is continually watching us and counting the sins we are committing, especially when that deity is responsible for determining if we will spend eternity in bliss — or suffer in everlasting punishment filled with extreme pain and torture. Some have called this ideology the worst type of extortion under fascist rule.

One of the main problems with the traditional "forgive-and-forget" philosophy is that it focuses the attention on the victim — not to the scapegoater who caused the trauma. It also hands the victim additional burdens: to heal from the physical loss and recover from deep emotional, mental, and spiritual trauma. Many perpetuated religious doctrines scapegoat by projecting the burden of healing to the victim — admonishing the victim to "let go and forget" or to "move on."

> Ninety-nine percent of the failures come from people who have the habit of making excuses.
>
> George Washington Carver

But this popular approach doesn't work, because it leaves both the scapegoater and victim trapped in their respective trauma cycles: The scapegoater remains unhealed and free to repeat the same trauma again, while the victim also remains stuck in abusive patterns. It can be argued that the reason why so many relationship issues are never healed is because energetic balance has not been restored.

The "forgive-and-forget" strategy underscored by human and animal sacrifice ideology has ultimately failed us, because behavioral patterns in both the abuser and victim are not corrected. Relying on the victim to do the heavy spiritual lifting of "forgiving" the offender is an energetic cop-out, even spiritual laziness. There is no easy way out, particularly in scapegoating someone or something else like goat or a sheep to "take care of" your offenses.

If it is true that we must truly pay for our own sins and bad behavior, then perhaps there is a better way for healing and evolving. The act of restitution and working hard to heal our issues and spiritually shift may provide a better solution that actually works.

Forgiveness is a Process of Accountability

In a biblical story, a man approached Jesus and asked him, "Lord, how many times shall I forgive my brother who sins against me?" Jesus had a rather unsettling answer: "seven times seventy,"[9] or 490 times. Does this mean that we should roll over and accept pain and the infliction from someone, constantly forgiving that person while we tally up to 490? Or could Jesus have meant that forgiveness involves much more than simple words that lack action?

The process of forgiveness is more than the victim saying, "I forgive you." It requires a sincere and heartfelt apology from the offender. Nor is forgiveness involve counting how many times we say "I forgive you" to the offender. The return to balance is not attained by trying to forget about a hurtful past.

Rather, it seems that forgiveness is a result of a multi-step approach that is simple, but not easy. Like every healing journey, forgiveness is a process, not a quick uttering of "I'm sorry, I forgive you and will try very hard to forget about the pain you caused me."

The Three Steps of True Forgiveness

For true forgiveness to occur, three key steps emerge that are to be taken by both the perpetrator and the victim. When these three steps have been satisfied through a clear and mutual agreement, then forgiveness can finally emerge as a result.

The balancing out of someone's offenses happens much in the same way that all energy moves throughout the physical Universe. Energy achieves homeostasis, or balance, when energy flows back into the system where it was removed or damaged, as science shows. This concept of spiritual harmony and balance is profoundly important when it comes to the three essential steps in the process of forgiveness:

1. Tell your stories: Recognize the offense and apologize sincerely to the person harmed.

2. Make amends for the offenses via mutual agreement.

3. Do the inner work to spiritually shift.

Step One: Tell Your Stories and Make the Apology

In today's world, we seem to have difficulty sitting down long enough to listen to someone's story. Our attention spans have grown incredibly short, as the increasing pressure to absorb more data and information has exponentially grown during the past century, primarily as a result of emerging technologies in media. We are trained to nibble on information packed in little morsels we can easily digest, and if the information becomes too big, then we grow restless or become saturated. We want to see resolution to problems within a half-hour or hour after first seeing them.

But there is no easy way out. The first step involves the abuser and victim having a candid discussion to fully understanding what pain, trauma, and injury occurred. Listening to someone's story requires maturity and patience — a trait of the Divine Adult within us that grows and develops with experience and maturity, as well as openness and curiosity of our Divine Child. Admittedly, telling the story of woundedness or listening to it can be uncomfortable, but knowing exactly what happened is vital to true healing. Fully understanding comes through clarity, where simply being aware of trauma patterns can often initiate the healing process. "There is a surrendering to your story and then a knowing that you don't have to stay in your story," wrote Colette Baron Reid.

Small children readily do this, showing us what hurts. When the child shares her story of injury with the parent, then the trauma be understood and managed. Similarly, when an abuser and victim share their stories with each other around a traumatic event, the healing process begins, and the stories become a nourishing ointment for all parties involved.

As small children naturally reveal, sharing can soothe the spirit and calm the soul. It says, "this is what happened to me when you did A, B, and C. This is what it was like for me." As the offender, simply listening and witnessing the person whom you offended is profound, as it says "I care about you. I honor your path and circumstances that I may have harmed, and I want to hear about what it was like for you." This is equality in action.

Candid sharing often releases much of the pent-up emotional pain and mental anguish, reducing the volume substantially. Telling each other simply what happened from a personal perspective without judgment or analysis is a gift for both the abuser and the victim.

Once the victim has told his or her story, and the offender has fully listened and acknowledged the story, then they trade roles. The offender can tell his or her story of what happened without making excuses — "This is what it was like for me" — while the victim listens. Embellishing what happened or trying to determine *why* it happened at this point can interfere with the healing process by creating more angst and tension.

After both sides of the story are told completely and honestly, then a proper apology can be made. It requires spiritual maturity to give an honest, heartfelt apology that also recognizes the pain caused: "I'm sorry that I did A, B, and C that hurt you in X, Y, and Z ways." A contrite, authentic spirit and open mind are effective Divine Child traits that assist in the true process of forgiveness.

Step Two: Make Amends

After telling our stories and making the apologies, it takes even greater spiritual maturity to make amends for his or her wrongdoings. We have been brainwashed into thinking that we can ask a deity or an intermediary, such as a priest, for forgiveness to make things better. But it is not any invisible deity who has been offended: It was the person to whom you deeply offended, and only that person can help initiate the process of forgiveness if you take the second necessary step of making amends.

Suppose that you gossiped to others about a friend, and that your words were hurtful. Words can instantly destroy a friendship and create horrible pain and misery for your friend. It can also destroy trust that was established and built over the years. It takes many years to build a beautiful city, but in an instant, that city can be destroyed to tatters. Even hurtful gossip can have devastating consequences.

Dale Turner wrote, "It is the highest form of self-respect to admit our errors and mistakes and make amends for them. To make a mistake is only an error in judgment, but to adhere to it when it is discovered shows infirmity of character." Making amends is the fundamental way of balancing out the injury and trauma, involving both an offer and acceptance of that offer. If I have offended you, I can offer you a gift to make up for my "sins" and harm that I inflicted upon you. For example, if I neglected to feed your cat during your trip, and the cat unfortunately died, I might offer to buy you a new cat, or perhaps offer to paint a room or two in your home.

Essentially, the physical gift of making amends is much more than physical restitution. The material gift becomes a *spiritual anchor* for sharing the gifts of the Divine Child, restoring joy, authenticity, passion, freedom, and equality in a broken relationship, for example. This energetic conduit for sharing our powerful gifts is spiritual gold.

Step Three: Do the Inner Work and Shift

"Everyone thinks of changing the world, but no one thinks of changing himself," wrote Leo Tolstoy. The inner work involves asking ourselves how we can learn about responsibility and accountability, and what we need to do to take action. Very few people, from what I have observed, actually get to this step that requires both our Divine Child and Divine Adult working together. For example, if Lisa didn't feed your cat like she promised, and your cat died because of it, the root of the problem is not that Lisa neglected to feed your cat.

The root problem is that Lisa may need to shift spiritually in some way. Perhaps she may need to learn about taking responsibility for her actions or learn to be more fully aware of others and situations around her. When Lisa discovers the underlying cause for the neglect that led to your cat dying, then she can undertake the journey to learn more about responsibility and awareness, for instance.

Patience is required in the self-actualizing process of being present and taking an honest look at ourselves. This spiritual practice of self-examination isn't easy, where we admit to ourselves that we need help and highlight the areas where we are spiritually deficient. We must listen to the constructive criticisms of those around us to be the mirrors to ourselves, so that we can see ourselves more clearly. It requires the authentic, open Divine Child and accountable Divine Adult to speak honestly and examine ourselves. Integrity from our Divine Adult, which is the alignment between our words and deeds, relies on the openness and authenticity of our Divine Child.

When someone has been abused, responsibility for changing must be taken by both the abuser and the victim. The abuser who inflicted trauma must take responsibility for making amends and shifting, and the victim can also take responsibility as well by gathering resources and support in order to leave the abuser and live in a more empowered way going forward. This happens not just through grit and determination, but by finding loving communities and support that can guide the abused through the difficult process of rediscovering freedom.

Forgiveness is "for giving" — a sharing of yourself and your Divine Child qualities. It is for giving your authentic story, and for listening to the authentic stories of others. It is to stop scapegoating others, even if you are the victim, so that you can take resolute action for your own redemption. It is for giving an honest and heartfelt apology to others when you recognize and feel their pain, while giving them the opportunity to receive your heartfelt gifts where everyone involved feels better.

Surrendering our ancestral need to scapegoat our greatness and weaknesses onto ancient saviors and demons — as well as their contemporary versions of superheroes, archenemies, and celebrities — is the first step toward empowering and saving ourselves. The "Savior Complex" that has plagued humanity for thousands of years continues to keep many trapped. The purpose of every story and myth is about *revealing who you are*, not making it about an external savior, superhero, celebrity, or demon.

Stories are about your own healing journey. Removing the internal roadblocks in your life that block you from your success is symbolic of personal "crucifixion," a letting go of negative patterns and trauma cycles. Your own resurrection is about transcending a dark past and your wounded aspects. Otherwise, all stories and myths are only entertaining distractions and projections if they do not serve the purpose of guiding you to look at yourself more authentically and then taking action.

Our experience of the world is a mirror to ourselves, a way for us to see exactly who we are. Our most intimate relationships with our special partner, family members, friends, and closest co-workers reflect our strengths, weaknesses, and the pain and trauma that remains to be healed within us. The urge to blame others for our "bad" relationships is there, for instance. It is easy to say, "if only my husband, my wife, my significant other would be better, then things would be great in our relationship."

But that is projection based on our own stories we created. The truth is that we need to look at ourselves, "the man in the mirror" that Michael Jackson described as being the key to healing the world. All of our relationship problems stem from something within ourselves that remains to be healed, even if we are repeatedly the victim. The beauty of looking at ourselves in the mirror is that we see both our Wounded Child and our Superhero filled with powerful gifts and unique talents that supercharge our world.

Make your own story a powerful one about learning, discovery, healing, and triumph. As fun and entertaining as they are, the Marvel superhero films really are about you. Your blockbuster story is the greatest story yet to be told. "Don't be satisfied with stories, how things have gone with others. Unfold your own myth," said the great poet Rumi.

Confucius said, "They must often change, who would be constant in happiness or wisdom." When we do the inner work that is required of us — either as the abuser or the victim — we not only shift ourselves, but the people close to us begin to heal and shift, too. We can live more fully and happily by sharing our gifts with others and ourselves, which can be defined as "unconditional love."

When we do the deep inner work, we can bless the world in powerful ways with our talents. By making amends to those whom we have harmed, we magnetize success and happiness on every level when we share our 21 gifts.

---

[1] https://www.psychologytoday.com/us/blog/hide-and-seek/201312/the-psychology-scapegoating

[2] *The Bible*, Leviticus 16:10 and 16:26.

[3] https://www.lds.org/manual/old-testament-stories/chapter-9-abraham-and-the-sacrifice-of-isaac?lang=eng

[4] https://www.livescience.com/59514-cultures-that-practiced-human-sacrifice.html

[5] IBID

[6] IBID

[7] IBID

[8] *Letters to a Young Contrarian*, Christopher Hitchens, Basic Books, 2001, p. 58.

[9] *The Bible*, Matthew 18:21.

Healing our Wounded Child: The Return to Our Powerful State

> By developing a relationship with the painful parts of ourselves — parts we have often inherited from our family — we have an opportunity to shift them. Qualities like cruelty can become the source of our kindness; our judgments can forge the foundation of our compassion.
>
> Mark Wolynn
> *It Didn't Start with You: How Inherited Family Trauma Shapes Who We Are and How to End the Cycle*

Becoming aware of our core trauma is not always easy when we are living our busy lives in a pressuring world. Balancing work and play is a challenge. We are surrounded with even more distractions that our parents had, where these new playthings cloud our spiritual perception and awareness.

The journey for healing begins with looking at the identifiers that reveal embedded traumas. These patterns are relatively easy to spot, because they pop up over and over again, where we seem to repeatedly attract similar circumstances or the same type of abusive person. Our belief systems, unresolved emotions, and even physical disorders and diseases provide clues about the cause of our problems. Our clothing and art, for example, reveal not only our strengths and weaknesses, but also the unresolved wounds in our lives. The words we speak and how we phrase them, as well as the times we remain silent and victimized, also point toward our way home.

How to Heal Unworthiness and Other Expressions of Trauma

Our common behaviors and phrases we speak can reveal unhealed wounds. "You shouldn't have done that," we commonly say when we receive a gift from a friend. Underneath, we may feel unworthy at the unconscious level to receive their love, care, and nurturing. Or "stay in touch" is one that we commonly hear, for example. Rather than taking responsibility for contacting you, that person wants you to do the initiating.

Our words give birth to our reality. Even if what we say is a "figure of speech," our expressions reveal our woundedness and fragility, as well as our power and strengths. Abraham Joshua Heschel, a leading American theologian and philosopher born in Poland in 1907, said, "Speech has power. Words do not fade. What starts out as a sound, ends in a deed."

The words we speak create our reality and *reveal* our reality we created in the past. Another common phrase that stops the flow of energy and disconnects is, "We keep missing each other." That isn't really true, is it? It may have happened a few times, but not all of the time. That expression is an invitation to repeated failed meetings, rather than creating a pathway for a successful connection. The Wounded Child sits in the pain of what happened, while the responsible Adult part of us grabs that spontaneous, present Divine Child by the hand and picks up the phone to initiate contact.

Surrendering our power can happen in other ways: "You make me feel angry. You piss me off. Every time you do this to me, you drive me crazy!" The truth is that nobody makes you feel anything. We simply become *triggered* from embedded past patterns, and therefore have a response to what someone does or says. When we think we hate someone, we are despising the harmful actions of that person that caused us pain, not the individual himself.

A potential replacement phrase that is probably more accurate might sound like, "When you did this to me, I felt this way. When this happened, I felt angry and confused." Your truth is your own. Nobody can question how you felt about what your experience was like for you. When you tell your story of what something was like for you, then you accept responsibility for your feelings and healing the wounds, rather than focusing on blaming others. This is the first step to healing.

When you feel pain or discomfort arise within you, it is likely a replay of past trauma, not a new wound. Whether the physical, emotional, mental, or spiritual wounds are fresh or old, begin telling your story. "There is no greater agony than bearing an untold story inside you," Maya Angelou said. When you share your stories of pain for the first time, you remove the grip that a trauma cycle has on you, empowering yourself in your healing journey. Taking responsibility for your own healing will also initiate some level of healing in others. "Sharing our truths can provide the opportunity for great healing," said Kristen Noel.

We can use the power of language to magnify our talents and strengths, rather than to subconsciously express our spiritual wounds. "If you don't toot your own horn, someone else will use it as a spittoon," Kenneth H. Blanchard said. It isn't bragging or showing off, where excessiveness overtakes balance. Revealing your gifts and talents is living in the present reality of who you are.

Your gifts, talents, and strengths aren't just about making money; they are the gifts you bring to the world, which are part of what makes you special. No person achieves greatness without sharing his or her story, including Jesus.

Waiting for someone to make the first move is another sign of a wounded Divine Child. "I haven't heard from you in a long time," says someone who is close to me. The truth is, I haven't heard from her in a long time, either. It is a sign of abandonment that plays the "poor me," expressing pain rather than taking action. It's living as a victim in a repetitious trauma cycle, sitting in the painful shadows of the past, waiting to be loved.

Create the experience you want. If you want to call, hug, kiss, or massage someone, create a powerful invitation. *This is the Golden Rule in action, where you initiate to create something new, putting out the energy first.* Rather than to say, "I really miss you," how about saying, "I really love our connection and conversation. I'm excited to see you again." Do you feel the difference in the ease, harmony, and power of those words? The latter approach creates movement forward, a vision of what you want, rather than repeating what you don't want. Someone will love to play with you in your sandbox, as long as you are sharing one or more of the 21 gifts that connect you together in glorious synchronicity.

Rather than be upset with someone who doesn't want to play with you, create invitations again and again with other people who resonate with you. Someone will accept your invitation. Jeanette Winterson, author of *Why Be Happy When You Could Be Normal?*, said, "What is 'no'? Either you have asked the wrong question, or you have asked the wrong person. Find a way to get the 'yes'."

Proactively sharing our gifts puts the Law of Resonance to positively work for you. What you give out, you will receive. Through sharing our 21 gifts, we engage the Law of Attraction in synchronous ways.

> Nothing annoys people so much as not receiving invitations.
>
> Oscar Wilde
> *The Importance of Being Earnest*

Try practicing invitations saying, "May I propose something? This is what I'd like to do with you...A, B, C. Is that ok?" I love the idea of telling the recipient why: "Because I enjoy sharing time with you and care about you." And then let it rest for a moment. You just created an invitation of a co-creative experience with someone you care about. Let the invitation sink into that person, finding a level of resonance. That person can accept the invitation, turn it down, or create another. All of it is ok. If you have learned at an early age that expressing yourself authentically wasn't safe, it can be difficult to ask for what you need from others. Keep practicing, and you will strike gold.

Leo Burnett, who built a global advertising empire that he started in 1935 in Chicago, said something which also applies to creating powerful invitations that make relationships stronger: "Make it simple. Make it memorable. Make it inviting to look at. Make it fun to read." Let your Divine Child create the joyful, playful invitation, and your Adult part deliver the co-creative experience. Make it fun, inviting, and tantalizing — one that will feed you and your sandbox partner, bringing each invitation from your Heart center.

Part of the healing journey is to find new language for the words we use by changing popular, overly-used expressions into empowering invitations we want, rather than disempowering wounded language that we don't want to experience. Words do matter. Speak what you mean. Express what you want. Build a compelling and authentic "power vocabulary" that works for you. "The best word shakers were the ones who understood the true power of words. They were the ones who could climb the highest," Markus Zusak said.

How Popular Negative Expressions and Labels Can Be a Trap

Our language reveals how we perceive ourselves, including our strengths and weaknesses. The trauma revealed in our words can sometimes be obvious, or far more subtle at other times. Many popular colloquialisms contain wounded expressions that reflect the level of well-being in the culture. "I'm so stupid" or "people are so stupid" are key markers for unworthiness that identifies with failure. Someone likely inflicted these words upon the victim — usually a parent or two who was caught in the web of inherited family trauma such as projected anger, rather than the unconscious abuser actually believing that someone else is stupid.

Have you ever heard someone say, "I'm just an average Joe" or "I'm just a normal guy"? It could be a sign of having lost that sense of feeling special and ability to be extraordinary. But you weren't born to think of yourself as average, as Jesus and other spiritual teachers have taught. You are destined to do great things.

Some nicknames and negative ways people refer to themselves reveal self-deprecation, as was the case with Rick, who frequently introduced himself as "Rotten Rick" to get a laugh. Self-denigration is never beneficial. Labeling oneself with negative terms reaffirms and embeds the sense of unworthiness even deeper, radiating that to the Universe. It is pain cloaked in dark humor.

Early trauma profoundly affects how we see ourselves and our future. Mark Goulston, MD, author of *Post-Traumatic Stress Disorder for Dummies*, wrote, "Unlike simple stress, trauma changes your view of your life and yourself. It shatters your most basic assumptions about yourself and your world — 'Life is good,' 'I'm safe,' 'People are kind,' 'I can trust others,' 'The future is likely to be good' — and replaces them with feelings like 'The world is dangerous,' 'I can't win,' 'I can't trust other people,' or 'There's no hope.'"

"No problem" is a popular one for those who may believe that success is difficult or out of reach due to many difficulties. It seems benign to respond with "No problem" after you say "Thank you." But the Universe doesn't know what "no" means, but it does know what images look like.

In their book *Words Can Change Your Brain*, authors Andrew Newberg, M.D. and Mark Waldman write, "The most dangerous word in the world is 'No.'" Their research discovered that an fMRI scanner shows clear neural changes in your brain when the word "NO" is flashed before you for just one second. Instantly, dozens of stress-producing and neurotransmitters are released, impairing logic and reasoning, interrupting brain function, impeding language processing, and muddling communication.[1]

Could this explain why research shows that those countries whose people attend weekly worship, which implies they are more exposed to the "thou shalt nots," have significantly shorter life spans than those who don't attend church?[2] The Bible is loaded with negative stories and commandments on what NOT to do, probably more than what to do. "NO" and "NOT" stop the flow of energy, and sometimes I find myself caught in the common pattern of using them, likely because as babies and toddlers, "NO" is one of the first words we learn.

In fact, just seeing negative words for a few seconds will make an anxious person feel worse, research shows. The more time we spend ruminating on negative words, the more it damages key functions that regulate memory, emotions, and feelings.[3]

With continual threats to our survival, we are hardwired to worry. The artifacts of ancestral memories are embedded into our DNA.[4] Fear-provoking words like death, illness, and sickness also stimulate the brain negatively. Even if the fearful words or thoughts are conceptual for you and not part of your present reality, the other parts of your brain, such as the amygdala and thalamus, fire away and react to these negative visual concepts as though they are actual threats.[5]

Newberg and Waldman wrote, "After you have identified the negative thought (which often operates just below the level of everyday consciousness), you can reframe it by choosing to focus on positive words and images. The result: anxiety and depression decreases, and the number of unconscious negative thoughts decline."[6]

Communication improves and people regain confidence and self-control when therapists teach clients to transform negative thoughts and worrying into positive affirmations. Newberg and Waldman point out that the problem is that the brain is so hardwired for negativity — the tendency to look out for danger — that it barely responds to our positive thoughts and words.[7] Because positive words aren't a threat to our survival, the brain takes a longer time to respond than it does to negative thoughts and words.

To overcome the adult brain's bias for negativity which isn't usually found in small children, Barbara Fredrickson, professor of psychology at the University of North Carolina at Chapel Hill and co-founder of Positive Psychology, says we must consciously and repetitiously generate more positive thoughts to retrain the brain. She discovered that we "need to generate at least three positive thoughts and feelings for each expression of negativity. If you express fewer than three, personal and business relationships are likely to fail." This research is confirmed by John Gottman's studies with marital couples and Marcial Losada's research on corporate teams.[8]

If you want your personal relationships and your business to flourish, you'll need to generate a minimum of five positive messages for every negative word or phrase you say, as Losada, Gottman, and Fredrickson discovered in their research. Negative expressions like facial frowns or shaking the head count, too.[9] Retraining your brain is the key to increasing your wellbeing, life satisfaction, and sense of happiness.

> If somebody offers you an amazing opportunity, but you are not sure you can do it, say "yes" – then learn how to do it later!
>
> Richard Branson

This is the return to your Divine Child. It is returning to optimistic, hopeful brain functioning, the naturally joyful state of mind that you once had when you were a little kid. Speak your words slowly and choose your words wisely. Studies reveal that this simple yet valuable technique interrupts the brain's tendency for negativity. By repeating positive words like peace, love, and compassion and incorporating those positive words that are part of the vision you want for your life, you will turn on specific genes that lower emotional and physical stress.[10]

Each day, find ways to say "YES." Rather than to say "NO" to someone, how about saying, "Well, that sounds interesting. I'd like to suggest A, B, or C. Is that okay?" Create affirmative invitations in the direction you want to go. Keep on practicing, and you will transform your brain into the power of your optimistic Divine Child that shines bright.

The Spiritual Gateway to Our Past and Future

The Fifth Chakra is connected to the energy center of past lives, which is how inherited family trauma or organizational tribal trauma passes from one era to another. Because it is unlikely that any person, family, organization, or culture will be able to heal its trauma or wounded nature in a single lifetime, significant research from Dr. Brian Weiss, Dr. Ian Stevenson, and others seems to suggest that people choose to reincarnate to have another opportunity to heal past trauma. It is a matter of time before science confirms that past-life trauma gets embedded into the genes, then passed down to future generations, much like behaviors, physical features, and diseases are transferred through the DNA. In my experience, unresolved trauma gets passed through the physical DNA of the body, as well as through spiritual DNA of the energetic body, which is linked to the Throat Chakra.

The Fifth Chakra — the Throat energy center that represents ether, or space — is about expression, which includes expression at the soul level. The Sanskrit term *akasha* means space or ether in both a metaphorical and elemental sense, as the Throat Chakra is said to be the seat of one's "Akashic Records." This applies to the individual's soul, as well as the organization's soul, which is simply the collection of all of its past incarnations, whether in a human or an organization. While the spirit is the energy lifeforce of the present body, the soul is the collective recording of every characteristic, thought, emotion, and action that entity has ever experienced.

This is why people who have been sexually abused often have trouble speaking in general, especially about their past pain and trauma. A number of clients I have worked with who have experienced sexual abuse have difficulty expressing themselves, showing up as scratchy voices, choked words, or frequent hoarseness. Because energy spreads in the body at the subtle and fine level, contamination easily spreads from the lower chakras to the upper, such as the throat, in this case.

> When people don't express themselves, they die one piece at a time.
>
> Laurie Halse Anderson
> *Speak*

The theory is that the Throat Chakra records experiences including trauma, then that energy steps down and expresses itself in the four lower chakras — Heart, Solar Plexus, Sacrum (Sexual/Generative), and the Root — with their qualities and characteristics of both the strengths and the weakness and trauma that remain to be healed. For example, the experiences of unhealed racism are recorded in the Fifth Chakra from the past, then move downward, expressing themselves as inequality in the Fourth Chakra; power, manipulation, control, and false beliefs in the Third Chakra, sexual emotional abuse, pain, grief, and perhaps even depression in the Second Chakra, and finally, physical assault and abuse in the First Chakra.

The interrelationship between trauma in the first five chakras is associated with the archetype of the five elements in ancient philosophy — earth, water, fire, air, and ether. These five elements correspond to the Root (earth), Sacrum (watery emotions and creative force), Solar Plexus (the fiery seat of movement, motivation, and power), the Heart (the airy aspect of information, love, compassion, being present), and Throat (self-expression, the spoken power of the individual or organization). Because energy flows between the chakras, trauma usually affects multiple chakras.

Traumatic cultural events are difficult to heal because the wounding gets distributed and embedded in many people in the tribe. Subsequently, traumatic pattern repeats themselves throughout history until they are healed. Consider the Holocaust in the 1930s and 1940s, an expression of inequality that showed up as unhealed slavery before and after the Civil War, for instance. Unhealed trauma on a social and more global level can be traced back in time, such as deception of the masses, where Adolf Hitler used new media to showcase his rallies, quickly distributing inequality that was portrayed as fun, excitement, and loyalty to his brand. He built a 2,000-mile border wall based on racism — the Atlantic Wall designed to promote and defend the Third Reich.

Today, the expression of this unhealed trauma shows up as the rapid distribution of fake news, televised rallies in mass media, blind loyalty to a negative brand, and the "urgent need" to build a wall on the 2,000-mile-long southern border of the United States to keep out minorities and the disadvantaged. If we do not heal this global trauma crisis this time around, we will have the opportunity the next time — perhaps with the same cast of characters that include the victims and the bullies alike. To heal a collective trauma, it requires that the collective tribe get involved. "The Holocaust is not only a tragedy of the Jewish people, it is a failure of humanity as a whole," Moshe Katsav wrote.

> Thou shalt not be a victim, thou shalt not be a perpetrator, but above all, thou shalt not be a bystander.
>
> Yehuda Bauer

Because of its distributive qualities that move energy, the Masculine nature of media and its shifting imagery moves energy even more quickly. This results in potential chaos to biological function, as well as the risk of diminishing precious Feminine energy that grounds, nurtures, and calms both males and females. Abhijit Naskar, author of *The Bengal Tigress: A Treatise on Gender Equality*, wrote, "The representation of women in the society, especially through mass media has been the most delusional act ever done on the grounds of human existence." The emerging forms of new media — namely, 3D video games, animation, and virtual reality — will likely worsen the current imbalance between Masculine and Feminine energies, calling for the greater need for more Feminine energy to stabilize the world.

This is why media has the tendency to focus on the negative, as it stirs and activates the danger-alert system engrained in our DNA. Media usually does not inform us of our beauty inside. Rather, it shows us what we are missing, what companies tell us that we need to be embraced. The hidden but very clear message is, "If you drink this brand of soda, then you will be loved."

It's a type of spiritual violence to the Divine Child, the bright beam of light that radiates from inside. The function of news, however, primarily plays on the Wounded Child's learned patterns of fear, using images, colors, words, and music that manipulate our attention. Most news, therefore, feeds on our weaknesses, rather than builds upon our strengths and true beauty.

> Whoever controls the media, controls the mind.
>
> Jim Morrison

A number of genetic and epigenetic studies now suggest that our strengths, weaknesses, past victories, and traumas — what I often refer to as our "spiritual DNA" — we have experienced become subsequently stored in our physical DNA. When these spiritual qualities or the wounded version of those qualities becomes triggered, behavioral patterns that have been stored become triggered, resurfacing over and over again. This is why numerous studies reveal that being exposed to negative news on television or Facebook, for example, creates negative emotional states within minutes.

How Past Life Trauma Plays Itself Out...Again

Based on thousands of cases of regressed patients, a number of past life experts believe that the suffering in a past incarnation gets replayed in subsequent lifetimes, if the trauma remains unhealed on some level. An example of this is being thrown from high temples or mountains. This occurred with Elaine, a patient of past life expert Dr. Brian Weiss, a well-known psychotherapist who had a large practice at Mount Sinai Medical Center in Miami. His patient Elaine suffered from a phobia of heights, neck and upper back pains, and fear of floods. During an advanced technique Weiss uses called "Past Life Regression Hypnotherapy," Elaine clearly recalled the details of what created the trauma.

"I see darkness, and I realize that I have been blindfolded. Then, I see myself outdoors. I stand at the top of a Tower, one built with rocks and used as a fort. My hands are bound behind my back. I am about twenty, and a soldier belonging to the side that lost. Then I feel a great pain in my back. I feel that I am biting my teeth tightly, my arms are stiff, my fists clenched. I had been stabbed, I can feel that I am pierced from the back, but I refused to show any emotions. I did not make any sounds. Then I feel that I am falling, and then I feel submerged under water." Sometime after that session, Elaine said, "I was always scared of heights and floods. After I woke up from the hypnosis, I was still shivering, and was in extreme pain for the next few days. I was unable to touch my face because it was extremely painful. But after I woke up the next morning, I found that there were some changes, very major changes."[11]

Elaine had found that her back pain and heights had disappeared. In follow-up treatments, she discovered another lifetime as a poor man in his twenties in the Middle Ages in France. Although he was innocent, he was accused of a crime and sentenced to death by public hanging. After Elaine recalled this lifetime, her neck pain vanished.[12]

> For truly we are all angels temporarily hiding as humans.
>
> Dr. Brian Weiss

Upon being aware and seeing the experience from a new perspective, numerous patients often receive immediate resolution for past trauma. Being fully aware of their story connects the dots for them and seems to release the trauma that has been locked and trapped within the body. The value of experiencing one's full story of the past is that the victim become consciously aware of past trauma, which helps release that locked pain that has plagued the person for years, for decades, and even for many lifetimes. I have experienced this phenomenon on a number of occasions myself, seeing past lives where people I know from this lifetime had killed me in previous incarnations, for example.

Like Elaine, my chronic neck pain disappeared after seeing another lifetime where I had been killed by choking. This is an example of inherited trauma that may have been passed down through the "spiritual genes" via the etheric body in past incarnations, and subsequently becoming part of the physical DNA that later relives itself as the reenacted trauma in the body. The trauma from the past incarnation creates an "energetic scar" in the etheric, or energy layer, of the body that is transferred from lifetime to lifetime until it later resurfaces. When we consciously recognize this negative pattern, we then have the golden opportunity to heal it.

I worked with a client named Connie from Minnesota who had been referred to me by a well-known clairvoyant. The client wanted to learn how to energize her home with creativity to aid her work, but I knew something deeper was ready to be healed. At the end of our phone conference, I asked if she needed any other help. Connie replied, "Yes, there is one thing. I have this recurring hip pain that just won't go away. I used to be a park ranger and did a lot of climbing. But this daily pain has plagued me for 20 years on one side of my hip, and I have been through six hip replacement surgeries. Nothing has worked."

While on the phone, I scanned her body and energy fields, where I found a long object stuck in her hip. Through dowsing, I could measure how long the object was. It appeared to be a long spear, and I shared with her what I had found. Using a past-life technique I developed involving a combination of journeying similar to Dr. Brian Weiss' method, dowsing, Pranic Healing, and shamanism, I took her back to that lifetime, where we learned that she had been killed by a spear, lying wounded on the field where she eventually died of blood loss and anguish. More importantly, the spear also had anchored deep guilt, anger, rage, and other emotional, mental, and spiritual trauma into her etheric (energy) body that she had experienced during that past life death.

> Do you have any idea how many lives we must have gone through before we even got the first idea that there is more to life than eating, or fighting, or power in the Flock? A thousand lives, Jon, ten thousand!... We choose our next world through what we learn in this one..."
>
> Richard Bach
> *Jonathan Livingston Seagull*

As part of the journeying process, I stepped her through a piece of forgiveness, not only for the person who had impaled her with a spear, but even more significantly, forgiveness for herself. In my practice, when people have been killed by others, the victim may often hold tremendous guilt and other self-victimizing feelings. During our session, it was as though I could hear her soul say in that past lifetime her regretful words as a male soldier, dying on the field of battle: "I should not have been there. I left my family behind. They didn't want me to leave them, but I left them anyway out of sense of duty." The intense negative emotion of guilt and self-punishment was what was really creating her pain.

I removed the etheric energy of the spear that had remained lodged in Connie's hip for decades, and perhaps even many lifetimes. Working together on the phone, she finally released her self-abuse that kept her in a state of victimhood and suffering. Twenty years of hip pain was simply a big wake-up for her, calling itself to be noticed, and to be released and healed.

Instantly, her hip pain vanished, and after checking with her years afterward the consultation, Connie has remained pain-free. We were both elated. I subsequently invited Connie, her husband, and their daughter to Chicago for dinner so that I could personally meet them. I filmed her stunning testimonial, which is available for viewing on YouTube.[13]

How Trauma Becomes Normalized

Whenever we experience trauma, whether it be on an individual, tribal, or global level, the characters involved will first absorb the trauma, then become adversely affected by it. Typically, several things will usually happen as a result of this wounding. First, the characters will usually act out the trauma unconsciously, like wounded kids fighting each other but not really knowing exactly why. After experiencing the pain repetitively, the traumatized person may decide to embark on a healing journey, but this second response requires being aware and conscious of the trauma, as well as learning what the healing journey looks like for that person or tribe.

Secondly, avoiding or projecting trauma is a function of survival, which usually happens unconsciously. If we don't realize we are wounded or are abusing ourselves and others, it frequently turns into unconscious scapegoating and blaming others for our problems. Even though trauma usually starts at the spiritual level — which involve the energies and powerful characteristics of the Divine Child — there is a tendency to try to solve the root of the problem using the mental body. The "need to know" why something happened, and attempt to solve a spiritual, emotional, or physical problem is frequently done at the mental body, which may often end up futile.

The third dynamic that usually occurs is the "sanitization" of trauma, where people begin to normalize the behavior so that it doesn't feel or look so bad. The survival mechanism kicks in, based on avoiding the possibility of rejection from those who love us. Normalizing our trauma is a coping mechanism we unconsciously use to mask or numb negative emotions — such as fear, guilt, anger, rage, sadness, depression, or shame — that have been embedded and buried deep as a result of the wounding.

At a cultural level, superiority has been sanitized and projected in various ways. Immigration policies and a border wall are expressions and symbols of inequality sanitized as a means of "protection from outsiders." Have we forgotten the roots of the foundation of America, as denoted by the inscription on the Statue of Liberty? The first section of this poem, "The New Colossus" written by Emma Lazarus on November 2, 1883, whose words on the Lady Liberty emphasize the return to our equal state.[14] My eyes still well up with tears every time I read these powerful words of the Divine Child at work:

> Not like the brazen giant of Greek fame,
> With conquering limbs astride from land to land;
> Here at our sea-washed, sunset gates shall stand
> A mighty woman with a torch, whose flame
> Is the imprisoned lightning, and her name
> Mother of Exiles. From her beacon-hand
> Glows world-wide welcome; her mild eyes command
> The air-bridged harbor that twin cities frame.
> "Keep, ancient lands, your storied pomp!" cries she
> With silent lips. "Give me your tired, your poor,
> Your huddled masses yearning to breathe free,
> The wretched refuse of your teeming shore.
> Send these, the homeless, tempest-tost to me,
> I lift my lamp beside the golden door!"

These profound words are a living expression of the Golden Rule, a basic tenet of human kindness and expression of empathy and compassion for our fellow human that is part of nearly every perennial philosophy on the planet. Jesus said, "What you do to the least of my brethren, you do onto me," while the majority of the Bible is conversely based on an "eye for an eye." As the expression goes that is often attributed to Mahatma Gandhi, "An eye for an eye leaves the whole world blind." How are we to bring about equality on the planet when we are surrounded by the many expressions of inequality that get re-embedded into our physical, spiritual, and cultural DNA? Have we become blind on a mass level?

Holding onto ancient, Bronze Age barbaric texts that have some beneficial teachings — but are largely false, negative, violent, and contrary to the Golden Rule and our Divine Child — is as toxic as having a constitution laced with disparaging precepts that subjugate any race, sex, sexual orientation, creed, or religion. It would never be allowed to have the U.S. Constitution contain numerous references to killing children, commandments for mass genocide, and teachings that women were born second after men, the originators of sin, ordered to be silent, and restricted from speaking.

Words contained in spiritual texts are not necessarily sacred. At a cultural level, the widespread acceptance of these barbaric texts written by our primordial ancestors has now resulted in the normalization of toxicity to the point of even labeling them as "sacred" and "holy," which they are neither.

To be clear, the Bible, the Quran, and nearly every other religious writ contain helpful moral teachings and inspirational ideas that are highly beneficial. And it must be recognized that religions, like other organizations, can potentially serve a valuable purpose through community service, cultivating empathy and other positive traits, and facilitating the healing of the heart.

However, these positive benefits are quickly overshadowed by the large swaths of passages that promote lies and dangerous ideologies, such as the commandment in both biblical Testaments to subjugate and denigrate women, or the numerous orders to commit mass genocide. The common argument of religious adherents and apologists says, "These are merely analogies." But even as mythical stories or cultural analogies, they are highly detrimental to the individual, tribe, and culture at large, which is why we still see misogyny permeated throughout nearly every modern tradition around the world. To believe the words of Moses describing how women are twice as unclean because they have given birth to a little girl is not only laughable and foul, but quite dangerous, as it leads the gullible mind into accepting a wider range of falsehoods and fabrications. In my opinion, this is why we see the wide acceptance of fake news today. The karma of accepting fabrications has become normalized and multiplied.

Denouncing these lies is a rather large moral and spiritual dilemma but is one that must be now undertaken. Just as the Bible and primary texts maintained by other religions were constructed and assembled by the hands of men, these religious writings must be readily disassembled to remove these toxic Bronze

Age horrors, retaining only the goodness they bring that can advance human evolution to a better place.

> Silence is the language of god. All else is poor translation.
>
> Rumi

Unhealed trauma first begins in our words, in our thoughts, in our consciousness. Our woundedness, as well as our strengths, gifts, and true power, become sealed for centuries by the written word. When the vibration of consciousness materializes into the spoken and written word, it becomes energetically institutionalized, where those thought forms, emotions, and spiritual energies, however beneficial or toxic, will spread in a highly distributed fashion. Alan Watts, the chain-smoking British-American philosopher whose work I have deeply admired for many years, said, "We seldom realize, for example that our most private thoughts and emotions are not actually our own. For we think in terms of languages and images which we did not invent, but which were given to us by our society."

Indeed, there is hope, but a spiritual scrubbing is first required. Weeding our collective garden and cleaning our sandboxes will allow us to move beyond a traumatized state of surviving to the kingdom of thriving, insuring a brighter future for all.

The Era That Ignited Inner Healing

The opening of the Heart Chakra on a planetary level occurred in the 1940s, moving global civilization from the Third Chakra that was about power, uniformity, and groups. The "one-size-fits-all" mindset that began in the mid-1800s led to uniform insurance and cars, for example, which said everybody gets the same type of insurance and car color, no matter what. The era of the Third Chakra also led to standardized education. Everyone received reading, writing, and arithmetic, leaving those with special needs behind.

The Fourth Chakra era of the love, compassion, equality, and the present moment, ushered in a completely different new energy that directs the focus to the individual, rather than the group. During this era, organized religion began to significantly decline, as the mass move from religious groups to a personal spiritual experience transpired.[15] Individual access to the Internet, personalized shopping, and even learning revolutionized the planet. Everyone's life and healing journey finally became far more unique, rather than institutionalized and structured.

The soaring cases of ADD, ADHD, and autism that emerged during this Fourth Chakra era of the Heart are teaching us that that "one-size-fits-all" formula no longer works for them, because their healing and learning journeys are unique, too. The escalating opioid deaths, let alone the millions who are suffering from prescription drug addiction, are a signal that we cannot afford to simply throw money at a mass problem, but instead must engage the healing on a more intimate level that addresses one person at a time.

Everyone's healing journey is unique and special. Learning about our own story and path to restoration is where our sacred adventure begins.

Discover Your Story

Telling our buried stories can initiate awareness, learning, and healing. Put on the hat of your curious Divine Child and discover your own history. Write it down. Interview your parents and siblings. Ask your grandparents and great-grandparents about their own lives and experiences, if they are still alive. Learn what issues they struggled with, challenges they experienced, and how they felt about them. In your detective work, you will discover the patterns of the past that have defined your present.

You will begin to connect the dots about how unhealed trauma from the ancient past was passed down in your familial lineage, finally arriving to you. Their emotional experience will likely trigger additional memories that become a richer, more complete story. You may find that by simply listening to stories without judgment, a catalytic healing reaction may spontaneously occur.

When I interviewed my parents, I found myself more compassionate and understanding of my parents, siblings, and grandparents. Before, I had blamed them for whatever I thought was the problem, whether it was true for not. For years, I projected my problems onto them, rather than take responsibility for my own healing. I was stuck in the endless cycle of blaming, but not shifting myself.

I realized that they, too, had suffered similar problems from their parents and influencing role models, and that they were unconsciously passing along their unhealed trauma, just like I had been doing for many years. I finally understood how similar we were. My blaming them had separated us, rather than connecting us in truly intimate and wonderful ways.

The power of authentic storytelling lies in being aware and present. I listened to their stories, and I told them my own. As we recognized we shared life experiences in both pain and triumph, the tension between us relaxed. With that recognition through authentically sharing, healing could begin. It was no longer "me versus them." Sharing our stories without judgment was connecting and therapeutic. What I noticed is that it triggered spontaneous memories that had been buried for decades, which initiated even more healing.

The stories are not just about healing the wounds from our inherited family trauma. It is also about reconnecting with your inherited family strengths that give you real power. Your inherent abilities are your *inherited* abilities, coming from your ancestral lineage and possibly from past incarnations, too. Your creativity, inventiveness, compassion, nurturing, optimism, joy, and other traits and specific talents likely came from your parents, as well as your grandparents — even if they later unconsciously learned to suppress them.

It is all too easy to find fault with our family members or teachers when we focus on their negative traits or behaviors. But by also reconnecting with the strengths, talents, and personal power gained from them, you go into resonance with these strengths, supercharging them and transforming yourself into the virtual Superhero that you are. The magic of connecting with your parents and grandparents is that you not only have the golden opportunity to heal and transform, but to expand and grow your abilities, talents, and inherent strengths.

Stop Blaming and Start Searching

Your Divine Child's nature is curiosity, learning, and adventure, the keys to wisdom, growth, and personal evolution. When we stop projecting our issues onto others by blaming them, we can then progress. Projecting our trauma weakens us and others. It is the negative drama where we give away our power and responsibility to heal ourselves.

Blaming others is a form of self-betrayal, where we project our pain back to those who delivered that pain to us in the first place. Acceptance, on the other hand, allows us to own the pain, embrace it, and use it to heal and transcend.

At the same time, it can be important to tell those who have created pain for us what our experience was, but to say "you did this to me" without healing that past trauma has little to no value. It is simply complaining about a pattern without resolving it. To be clear, it is extremely rare when people intentionally try to hurt you and create trauma in your life. Most often, they pass on unhealed traumatic patterns just like you and I do.

When you discover the original pain behind a chronic issue, you can begin to heal it. Keep searching for how you can heal the emotional pain attached to the event of what happened. Learning about the original trauma diminishes its negative grip on your life. You will likely never forget the painful event itself, even after you have resolved the original trauma. But when you disconnect the emotional or mental pain from the actual experience, the trauma will be dissolved, and its negative power over you will be gone.

> People that have trust issues only need to look in the mirror. There they will meet the one person that will betray them the most.
>
> Shannon L. Alder

At that point, a clearing happens. A grand stillness sets in. When the soul is able to sit free of noise and the bombardment of unwanted energies, then can healing transpire. Energies that were expended in maintaining negative trauma cycles now can be channeled into positive directions, where we share our 21 gifts and spontaneously attract magical experiences that fulfill our greatest hopes and dreams.

Get Real and Authentic

When I heard Elisabeth Kübler-Ross would be appearing to speak in Ann Arbor, Michigan, in the 1990s, I cleared my calendar. She was the proverbial goddess of "Death and Dying," the subject material of my favorite course while studying engineering in college. My professor teaching the course was also the school's registrar, whose radiant humor, playfulness, and natural buoyancy was the perfect salve for a delicate subject.

I was mesmerized by the subject matter, learning how Kübler-Ross had pioneered the five states of death that could be applied to most experiences of loss — denial, anger, bargaining, depression and acceptance. Her energy and wisdom had also entranced me. I was more eager to learn about the subject of death, which probably has been the biggest reason why our ancient predecessors invented their respective religions.

During her talk, Kübler-Ross spoke about the power of authenticity, referring to her work with numerous patients who were experiencing their last days on earth before death. At one point during the talk, she said, "In my many years of working with people, the only truthful people in the world are small children and dying patients. The rest of us are full of phony baloney."

The crowd erupted in laughter, but the painful truth is that most adults are inauthentic. As small children, however, we were genuine, open, and authentic, hiding nothing. Part of our spiritual wounding was that we learned to cover up, put on masks in order to survive, and learned to lie for personal gain at the expense of others. We adults tell people that we are "fine" when we are not so fine. Covering our trauma and our little white lies, and sometimes our big ones, is part of the game we play in our wounded state.

Returning to the nature of our Divine Child brings truth and light. Authenticity is the gateway to freedom and healing.

Be the Safe Space for Yourself and Others

One of the greatest gifts you can give someone is to simply listen to their stories. Many of us have been stopped from expressing ourselves authentically when we were little kids. Muzzling expression of a child leads to wounding in the inherited family trauma cycle, becoming a learned pattern that gets passed down to future generations.

Consequently, most of us never grew up in an environment where we felt safe enough to be our authentic selves. We learned to bottle up our emotions and thoughts, burying them deep within our souls. Our survival instincts took over, where we subconsciously erected barriers to protect ourselves and avoid pain and punishment. Then that buried toxic energy exploded outward, expressing as rage, disease, depression, or cutting. It came out as numbing through alcohol and other drug abuse, or eating ourselves silly, adding more protective layers. As the pain grew, we became increasingly disconnected from ourselves.

Everyone needs a safe space to tell their dark stories. When someone close to you begins divulging a traumatic event that occurred in her life, create the safe space of privacy, trust, and confidence that person needs and craves. With so much verbal violence and attacks happening throughout social media, especially on Facebook pages, it isn't always easy to feel as though anywhere is a safe space, even though they exist.

You can be that safe place of privacy, integrity and trust for yourself, your friends, your family, and others close to you. When pain is deep, it often shows up as a chronic condition, where the same expressions of buried trauma repeat themselves in trauma cycles. Chronic pain usually begins inside of us, as spiritual pain, mental trauma, or emotional pain. If that pain is unresolved, it often shows up in the physical body as chronic pain, inflammation, and other disorders.

A repetitive negative story can be a sign of deep chronic pain. With a heart of compassion, love, and empathy, we can quietly listen to someone's story as she bares her soul to us. It is easy to roll our eyes around when we hear friends telling the same story again and again, but they are merely crying for help. They simply don't know the way out. Sharing their story fully can initiate the healing process.

Listening without judgment or interruption to your friend, parent, or sibling in pain can soften the impact of past trauma and sometimes even heal it, especially if the pain is about healing the energy of self-expression. Most of all, resist the urge to make it about you. It is helpful, however, to empathize with the occasional "I know how you must feel…I felt the same way" without launching into your full-blown story about how you were traumatized, too. By relating to your friend's pain and trauma that is similar to your own, we go into energetic resonance with them for a moment. With a shared experience of pain, he or she will feel safer and part of the collective group, rather than feeling isolated and alone.

Sometimes that person may stop for a moment, especially when reaching a part of the story that is particularly painful or sensitive. If you sense a roadblock, a gentle approach than can keep the flow going can be by asking "What was that like for you?" This can help someone continue to share a painful story in a safe, trusted environment.

Sharing painful trauma from the past is a rather intimate experience. Be sure to let your friend, sibling, or parent know that they can fully trust you to keep their stories private and in strict confidence. Cultivate trust by ensuring that you will keep their stories confidential.

This is the role of your Divine Child. To refrain from judging, evaluating, or analyzing, but to simply listen and keep the sacred walls of the safe space you created for your friend. By simply listening to their painful stories, you will facilitate healing in that person and in your own life, too. "Be here now," said Ram Dass.

Self-Discovery and Healing is a Lifelong Adventure

At the height of the Second World War, England was very much at risk. On October 29, 1941, Winston Churchill inspired the nation with a speech that he gave at Harrow, a London boarding school, where he said, "...never give in, never give in, never, never, never, never-in nothing, great or small, large or petty — never give in except to convictions of honor and good sense. Never yield to force; never yield to the apparently overwhelming might of the enemy."

Use this powerful philosophy in your healing journey. Keep moving forward, determined to heal any remaining trauma in your past that continues to repeat itself in a cycle. This is the signal and call for healing. Find out what works in the long-term. Ask the "experts" and practitioners who have successful track records with real results. Seek out books, workshops, and modalities that have worked for many others, rather than stumbling alone. Follow the paths that speak to you deeply. Sometimes it isn't the modality itself that is helpful, but the people you meet along the journey that can help you to your next steppingstone.

Many modalities are good for alleviating acute trauma, but not healing original wounds. While I enjoy regular massages and occasional acupuncture treatments, these two examples of healing modalities do not necessarily heal the origin of pain and early trauma. In my experience, these modalities and others heal the symptoms of pain, but often do not address the cause. Pain usually begins on the spiritual level, then cascades to the mental and emotional level, which is why physical solutions are typically unable to resolve the origins of trauma patterns.

At the same time, these modalities can provide tremendous benefits and even possibly heal deep original trauma. A therapeutic massage from a licensed, experienced practitioner can reframe what safe touch is about for the person who has been physically abused through rape or even physical punishment, for example. The brain and DNA will begin to re-pattern, replacing the physical and spiritual trauma of pain, subservience, and false beliefs such as "I am unworthy of love" embedded in the physical body. New energies will nurture the body and soul with the positive attributes of the Divine Child, including joy, passion, and self-exploration.

Healing our trauma takes real work beyond what thoughts and prayers can do, which do not inform or enlighten us about original wounds. Most unhealed trauma requires more than one "instant fix" session with a practitioner or workshop. We are complex beings with many layers to ourselves, like spiritual and energetic onions. Peeling each layer reveals more of ourselves, allowing us to see the hidden aspects of ourselves that include our strengths, weaknesses, inherited family trauma, and our inherited talents, too.

Three healing modalities that have been highly effective for clients and me to help resolve past trauma and supercharge the energy are 1) EFT Tapping, 2) Inherited Family Trauma Work, and 3) energy patterns, including energy signatures, symbols, shapes, colors, and other vibrational techniques that da Vinci, the ancient Egyptian temple masters, and others have kept secret for thousands of years. I continue to use these methods in my consulting practice with numerous individuals and corporate clients to shift the energy in their homes and workplaces.

Additionally, many people are developing a growing interest in the vast research that has recently surfaced about past incarnations. The theory of reincarnation and personal evolution over lifetimes is that our unhealed trauma gets embedded into our "spiritual genetic code," where the trauma then resurfaces in another lifetime for the opportunity to be addressed and healed. Doing the past life healing work discussed by Dr. Brian Weiss, Dr. Ian Stevenson, and other serious researchers can be wonderfully illuminating and therapeutic.

The Journey Home: Reclaiming Your Divine Child

From the beginning of humankind several hundred thousand years ago, inner transformation has been hailed in myth and story as spiritual alchemy. The philosopher's stone was the mystical symbol of achieving perfection and heavenly bliss. The Holy Grail was traditionally believed to be the cup that Jesus drank from at the Last Supper, with other legends involving Joseph of Arimathea, the Knights Templar and the Crusades, the mystical literary figure King Arthur, and the tale of the Fisher King.[16]

For more than two thousand years, the desperate searches for the Holy Grail have been futile. The supreme quest of alchemy to transform lead into gold has led to dismay for centuries. The outer pursuit for these sacred mysteries has distracted the masses from the true place where these rich gifts exist.

The Holy Grail is you.

Writing this book has been a cathartic and healing experience for me as a source of discovering spiritual gold that is within. With the penning of each chapter, my own unhealed trauma became far more clarified. The mirror of my words has revealed the truth of my stories, allowing me to carefully contemplate my weaknesses, woundedness, strengths, talents, and real power. I clearly see myself in my parents, my siblings, and my friends. I see myself in everyone, as we all have been wounded.

> I have always quested and still do for the Holy Grail, but I stopped looking in the earthen caves and in the stars. I started questing through the valleys and mountains of my own soul.
>
> David Paul Kirkpatrick

Your story and healing journey is far more important than that of Jesus. Or Arjuna in the Bhagavad Gita. Or Abraham. Or Noah. Or Mohammad. Or the Buddha. Or the Devil. Or any other person, deity, or external demon. These stories are mere archetypes of the greatest story that has yet to be told, which is your own.

Our stories reveal the power of who we are and our weaknesses and trauma that remain to be healed. All myths and stories become purposeful when they become personal. Like you, I'm another Wounded Child who is finding his way home.

Embrace your pain and trauma, rather than run away from it. It is part of you, but it won't remain with you. The beautiful irony of looking at your stories of trauma is that they also reveal your stories of strength, unique talents, and extraordinary abilities that are unique to you. This is the journey of awakening, and your own transformation heal others as well.

My compassion, nurturing, and love for myself and others have soared through this revelation, paving the way for true healing and forgiveness. That journey starts with me. I take complete responsibility for my own healing. I refuse to allow my own dominoes to fall on the next person, including my family, my friends, coworkers, and neighbors. When I do it to myself, I do it to others. When I bless others with evil or goodness, I do it to Mohammad, Buddha, Jesus, or any other spiritual teacher or human being. In a seemingly separate world, this is the mystery of connectedness and unity.

You are the Christ. You are the Anointed One. You are the Chosen One. You are Brahma. You have been invited to save yourself from the biggest things stopping you from achieving success: the traumas that were inflicted upon you. As Jesus beautifully said, you will do greater things than he did. It begins with coming as a little child within. Your rediscovery of your true nature initiates your own journey of awakening.

This is your destiny, whether you choose to delay it or take action now. This future for you is inevitable. Your rich spiritual inheritance promises true wealth and abundance for you. It starts by healing yourself. The choice is when. You only have the present moment, as tomorrow is never promised.

Now take your Wounded Child by the hand and guide it gently. Embrace this traumatized part of you, letting your precious child inside of you know that it is now safe and protected. Ask your inner child its glorious stories of how it became wounded, when it happened, and where the wounding occurred. Learn about the stories of your parents and grandparents. Keeping a journal and asking questions to yourself just before the moment of sleep can be therapeutic, as dreams may unfold that reveal the answers you need and next path forward.

The greatest thing you can ever accomplish is not gaining a promotion. It isn't winning the most likes or followers on Facebook, Instagram, or TikTok. It isn't achieving an Oscar, Emmy, or best-selling book or movie. It isn't creating the hottest fashion trend and getting your face plastered on magazine covers. It isn't leading a Fortune 1000 company or inventing the next version of sliced bread. It isn't even landing the love of your life or giving birth to another child.

The greatest achievement is reclaiming your Divine Child — this magic source of spiritual power, guiding intuition, and boundless energy. Your inner child is what showers you with hope, optimism, and joy. Your Divine Child is the secret to activating the Law of Attraction, where the Law of Resonance and synchronicity ignited through sharing these potent 21 gifts will magnetize your greatest dreams and wishes.

The true love of your life is you. Your love for others is a continued expression of your ability to love, nurture, and care for yourself. Your traumas did not start with you, as they were inflicted upon you. But they can certainly end with you. It is your destiny. This healing journey to reclaim your true power has already begun.

You are the Divine Child.

[1] https://www.psychologytoday.com/us/blog/words-can-change-your-brain/201208/the-most-dangerous-word-in-the-world

[2] https://www.pewforum.org/2018/06/13/why-do-levels-of-religious-observance-vary-by-age-and-country/pf-06-13-18_religiouscommitment-01-01/

[3] Some assessments of the amygdala role in suprahypothalamic neuroendocrine regulation: a minireview. Talarovicova A, Krskova L, Kiss A. Endocr Regul. 2007 Nov;41(4):155-62.

[4] Wright, R. *The Moral Animal: Why We Are, the Way We Are: The New Science of Evolutionary Psychology.* Vintage, 1995.

[5] What is in a word? No versus Yes differentially engage the lateral orbitofrontal cortex. Alia-Klein N, Goldstein RZ, Tomasi D, Zhang L, Fagin-Jones S, Telang F, Wang GJ, Fowler JS, Volkow ND. Emotion. 2007 Aug;7(3):649-59.

[6] https://www.psychologytoday.com/us/blog/words-can-change-your-brain/201208/the-most-dangerous-word-in-the-world

[7] IBID

[8] https://www.researchgate.net/publication/247752186_The_Role_of_Positivity_and_Connectivity_in_the_Performance_of_Business_TeamsA_Nonlinear_Dynamics_Model

[9] https://www.psychologytoday.com/us/blog/words-can-change-your-brain/201208/the-most-dangerous-word-in-the-world

[10] Genomic counter-stress changes induced by the relaxation response. Dusek JA, Otu HH, Wohlhueter AL, Bhasin M, Zerbini LF, Joseph MG, Benson H, Libermann TA. PLoS One. 2008 Jul 2;3(7):e2576.

[11] https://www.pureinsight.org/node/219

[12] IBID

[13] https://www.youtube.com/watch?v=J2lZZTtT7WI

[14] https://www.nps.gov/stli/learn/historyculture/colossus.htm

[15] https://religionnews.com/2014/01/27/great-decline-religion-united-states-one-graph/

[16] https://www.history.com/topics/middle-ages/holy-grail

For more information and to order consultations,

visit CaryWeldy.com.

Made in the USA
Las Vegas, NV
28 December 2021

39742317R00207